Nicola Guy gained her PhD in History from Durham University in 2008. She has tutored on modern European history courses at the Open University, Durham University and the University of York, and has studied Albanian at Indiana University. She has published a number of articles in academic journals and presented papers at international conferences in the UK, USA, Austria and Greece. Guy currently works for the British Civil Service in the Department for Digital, Culture, Media and Sport.

T0348042

'This sophisticated, analytical and impartial study... judiciously integrates the Albanian question into the mainstream... a major step forward.'
Jason Tomes, *Diplomacy and Statecraft*

'The reader will find a treasure of detailed information, critically analysed, on the evolving interests, policies, and actions... By careful and serious use of abundant archival material [Nicola Guy has] set a high standard in the maturing field of Albanian history.'
George W. Gawrych, *American Historical Review*

The Birth of Albania

Ethnic Nationalism,
the Great Powers of World War I and the
Emergence of Albanian Independence

Nicola Guy

BLOOMSBURY ACADEMIC
LONDON • NEW YORK • OXFORD • NEW DELHI • SYDNEY

BLOOMSBURY ACADEMIC
Bloomsbury Publishing Plc
50 Bedford Square, London, WC1B 3DP, UK
1385 Broadway, New York, NY 10018, USA
29 Earlsfort Terrace, Dublin 2, Ireland

BLOOMSBURY, BLOOMSBURY ACADEMIC and the Diana logo
are trademarks of Bloomsbury Publishing Plc

First published in Great Britain 2012
Reprinted by Bloomsbury Academic 2019 (twice)

Copyright © 2012 Nicola Guy

In association with the Centre for Albanian Studies

The right of Nicola Guy to be identified as the author of this work has been asserted by
the author in accordance with the Copyright, Designs and Patents Act 1988.

All rights reserved. No part of this publication may be reproduced or
transmitted in any form or by any means, electronic or mechanical,
including photocopying, recording, or any information storage or retrieval
system, without prior permission in writing from the publishers.

Bloomsbury Publishing Plc does not have any control over, or responsibility for,
any third-party websites referred to or in this book. All internet addresses
given in this book were correct at the time of going to press. The author and
publisher regret any inconvenience caused if addresses have changed or sites
have ceased to exist, but can accept no responsibility for any such changes.

A catalogue record for this book is available from the British Library.

ISBN: 978 1 35013 667 0

A catalog record for this book is available from the Library of Congress.

Design: Westrow Cooper

To find out more about our authors and books visit
www.bloomsbury.com and sign up for our newsletters

Contents

Acknowledgements

The individuals and organisations who have assisted in the research, preparation and writing of this book are numerous and far too many to detail. Here I have selected a few individuals who have been particularly significant. Any errors which remain are of course completely my own. Firstly, and most importantly, my parents Angela and David, have been an especial source of support and help. My Dad particularly has read and re-read more drafts of both my PhD and this book than it would be possible to count. He must by now know much more about the Albanian question than he could ever have wished to. Both went far beyond anything I could have ever expected or hoped for.

My PhD supervisors and examiners, plus other colleagues and academics, have read and commented on various chapters and offered invaluable insights to help improve the text. Particular thanks goes to Professor David Moon who challenged me to think in so many new ways and guided me through the tricky last two years of my PhD and Dr David Sweet who first introduced me to the question of Albanian independence when I was an undergraduate student and has continued to offer immense advice and support.

A number of people have contributed in other ways. Five stand out particularly. Bejtullah Destani and the Centre for Albanian Studies in London have provided me with considerable amounts of useful and illuminating primary material and introduced me to the delights of the Aubrey Herbert papers. Jakup Azemi has translated many documents from Albanian into English and been a valuable friend. Liz Friend-Smith, formerly of I.B.Tauris, was supportive and secured agreement to publish this book, Westrow Cooper for his efforts in putting it together and Sara Magness at I.B.Tauris for this second edition. Finally, many thanks to the staff at the many libraries, depositories and archives I visited that have assisted with my many, varied and often unusual queries and requests, to the Albanian Embassy in London, and to Molly Morse and the Anglo-Albanian Association whose celebration of the 100th anniversary of the independence of Albania has generously included support for this book. Without all of you *The Birth of Albania* would never have become a reality.

NCG February 2018

A Note on Spellings

There are alternative and sometimes historical, national and political differences and other considerations in the spellings of Balkan and Albanian names. I have followed those most generally used by officials in the British Foreign Office at the time of my study (1912-26), except where common usage dictates something else, for example Serbia has been used instead of Servia.

A special exception to this is my use of both 'Kosovo' and 'Kosova' in the text. Kosovo will be used to refer to the former Ottoman *vilayet* of Kosovo, being how the term was understood at the start of the twentieth century, despite having only being created as recently as 1877. Kosova will be used to refer to the present day independent state of Kosova, which from 1945 until 1999 had been the Yugoslav autonomous province of Kosovo and Metohija or Kosmet. As Appendix A illustrates, today's Kosova is only about one quarter of the size of the Kosovo that existed under Ottoman rule.[1]

Introduction

'Right, as the world goes, is only in question between equals in powers, while the strong do what they can the weak suffer what they must.' [2]

On 17 February 2008 Hashim Thaçi, the Prime Minister, finally proclaimed the independence of Kosova, which had been under United Nations control since 1999. It had taken nearly ten years, from when the plight of the fleeing ethnic-Albanian Kosovan refugees had first grabbed international attention, for Kosova to emerge as an independent state. The United Nations mediator, Martti Ahtisaari, had determined in March 2007 that whilst Kosova should be independent, there should be no alteration of boundaries, no return to Serbian control, no partition (between Albania and Serbia) and no union with another state. [3] It took another year for that independence to become a reality, but, in 2012, Kosova still remains unrecognised by many states, including Serbia and Russia, there are a number of internal problems, not least the high levels of unemployment and the statelet's existence remains somewhat precarious.

The issues involved in the complex and protracted decisions about Kosovan independence were remarkably similar to those 1912-26, when Kosovo and other areas with an Albanian-speaking majority population became part of Serbia and Montenegro (later Yugoslavia) or Greece, rather than part of an independent Albanian state. Essentially, these issues are: the bases on which Balkan states should be formed; where their frontiers should be drawn; the respective roles of ethnicity and geopolitical considerations in determining those frontiers; and, not least, the implications of such decisions for the longer-term stability of the region. This book addresses these issues for 'Albania' and 'Albanians' in the formative and central decade from the Balkan wars of 1912-13 to the establishment of the 'new Europe' at the end of the Peace Conference of Paris, after World War One. This study explains the establishment of an independent Albanian state by 1921, and the settlement of its boundaries by 1926. It identifies three phases by which Albania emerged as an independent state. In the first phase (1912-14), the idea of Albanian independence was first mooted and accepted, in the second (1914-19), the experiment was undone, and, in the third (1920-26), Albania's representatives had to campaign for it once more, and were eventually successful.

Tiovo Raun has shown that, since the 1990s and the emergence of new ethnic states in eastern Europe, there has been a resurgence of interest in what determined the creation of new nation states there.[4] Since 1999, there was much debate within the international community on what the future status of the autonomous province of Kosova should be. However, there seems to have been little consideration as to why Kosovo (the Ottoman *vilayet*) and the other majority Albanian-speaking areas (parts of Montenegro, western Macedonia and Chameria, in north-west Greece) did not become either independent or part of an independent Albanian state, despite the legacy of these decisions. Tom Winnifrith observed the need for a scholarly and impartial account of the formation of independent Albania in 2002, whilst Basil Kondis earlier noted that there was no recent, and comprehensive, English study of Albanian independence. Indeed the most accurate, comprehensive and dispassionate studies in English still remain those by Edith Stickney (1926) and Joseph Swire (1929).[5] These works, however, require updating with a wider range of primary sources, and a consideration of the Albanian question in terms of current theories of nationalism and international relations. More recent studies have not developed significantly upon these early accounts. For instance, in 2003 Owen Pearson included extensive factual details on the question of Albanian independence in his three-volume work *Albania in the Twentieth Century*. However, his strictly chronological (day-by-day) approach made his study seem fragmentary and lacking in analytical depth.[6]

In a seminal early work (1906) on the ethnic complexities of Macedonia, the radical English journalist H.N. Brailsford, champion of the rights of small nations and critic of great-power imperialism, observed that Europe had a 'deplorable habit of ignoring the claims of the Mohammedan inhabitants of European Turkey'.[7] This comment, contrary to the pro-Slav tendency of traditional liberal opinion, was of course particularly applicable to the inhabitants of 'Albania', whose cause had yet to attract support in Britain; and it remains largely applicable today. This study aims to meet the need for a thorough and systematic analysis of the processes of Albanian independence, with particular regard to contemporary considerations of ethnicity and national identity. At the same time, it seeks to place the question of Albanian independence within the context of power-political relationships, and the framework of the great-power system, within which it would have to be achieved, if it was to be achieved at all.

Ethnic Nationalism and International Relations

In their work on nationalisms in eastern Europe during and after World War One, Ivo Banac and Katherine Verdery identified three key issues for any elite seeking to deploy a national independence programme: building the newly emergent state; establishing the state's participation in the international community; and defining the 'nation's' identity, which usually took a 'collectivist' vision and therefore placed it in opposition to other national or ethnic groups.[8] In all these three areas, the new state has the potential to have an impact on the international system, and to be affected by the international system within which it operates. Moreover, as Fredrik Barth first showed, nationalism and identity formation is not purely about self-ascription.[9] Of at least equal importance is the acceptance of such an identity by others, which traditionally means the international community at the time. Such acceptance is particularly important in the validation of a nation's sovereignty and boundaries, and also for small states in ethnically mixed regions, where territory is contested and the small state is likely to need great power endorsement and protection to establish and then maintain its frontiers.

Nevertheless, the theoretical literature on small-state nationalism in a great power system, the type of international system that operated at the start of the twentieth century, is underdeveloped in relation to the voluminous literature on both nationalism and international relations. A number of studies from various disciplines have set out to explore these issues for different national questions, but the bulk of their discussion is in discrete chapters. This allows for little direct consideration of the inter-relationship and inter-reaction between nationalism and the international system.[10] A major theme of this study is to explore this interaction, using the question of Albanian independence as a case study.

Although the literature is under-developed, there appears a clear correlation between these two forces, especially in 'national' questions, where two or more ethnicities or 'nationalities' overlap, and are competing for control of the same territory. Notable examples include Israel/Palestine and Kashmir and, specifically in the Balkans, Macedonia and Kosovo/a. This oversight seems particularly surprising in studies of the era of World War One, when issues surrounding the viability and independence of various small states were at the forefront of European diplomacy, and were most cogently articulated by President Wilson as self-determination.

It appears that the interplay of nationalist and international forces may vary from being reinforcing or supportive to contradictory or opposing. In the simplest sense, nationalism has the ability to upset or impact upon the international system, especially when perceived in balance-of-power terms, as it brings about the prospect of new states, and a shifting of the relative strength of those already in existence. In reverse, the international system can influence a national movement in a variety of ways. It may be restrictive or prohibitive, by refusing to recognise a nationality as sufficiently distinct from another, or sufficiently stable to maintain a separate existence. Alternatively, it may be positive, principally through sponsorship or endorsement of a national programme. In Kosova today, all these impacts can be clearly identified. The clash between Serbian and 'Kosovan' nationalism, the exodus of Kosovan-Albanian refugees, and the feared impact on international stability, prompted NATO eventually to become involved in 1999. The delay in settlement of the Kosovan question was primarily caused by the international community's concern of the impact that 'final status' would have on the Balkan balance of power. Hence the refusal to allow Kosovan-Albanians to join their co-ethnics in other parts of the Balkans, and the delay in advocating Kosovan independence, for fear of inducing retaliation and instability within Serbia by such an announcement.

Ethnic Nationalism and Small States in South-eastern Europe

Eric Hobsbawm has maintained that there are problems in applying theories of nationalism to small states, because there is a lower limit of population that is capable of maintaining modern linguistic cultures at all levels, and because of the inability of small states to determine their own fate.[11] By contrast, Miroslav Hroch has developed a theory of nationalism that aims to elucidate the experience of small national and ethnic groups in Europe, although the Albanians are not included within his modelling. Hroch considers that small national groups go through three phrases of national awakening. In phase A, the said nationality attempts to develop its national culture, language and ethnography. In phase B, the nationality attempts to increase the amount of patriotic agitation, or the growth of patriotic agitation, in the population. In the final phase C, these develop into a national movement.[12] However, his model focuses solely on national factors, and provides no role for the international factors that this study intends to consider. Rather than ignoring small nationalities, as Hobsbawm does, or ignoring international factors, as both Hroch and Hobsbawm do, it is necessary to focus on these 'other factors' and to determine the roles they play, and their importance. As more traditional theories of nationalism focus on the 'national' factors, the intention of this book is to focus on the 'international' ones, and also to show how they fit in with the more traditional 'national' influences. In this way, the study hopes to illustrate the benefits of 'internationalising' 'national' questions, similar to the way in which many international historians have been seeking to 'internationalise' 'international' history, by expanding their studies to include the consultation of archives and collections from more than one state.[13]

Since 1945, there has been considerable debate in various disciplines (anthropology, political science, history, sociology, etc.) on the bases of nations and nationalism, especially the upsurge of so-called ethnic or primordial nationalist movements in nineteenth- and early twentieth-century Europe. These focus almost exclusively on the internal and national causes and origins, and therefore, although they are important, they are of only limited use for this study. In these debates, the modernist school has tended to predominate: it has viewed nation-states as modern constructions based on 'invented traditions' or 'imagined communities', to cite two of the more popular dictums, in order to serve present-day political purposes. In this approach, a past regime, such as Ancient Rome for the Italians, was used to legitimate the nationalist goals of the present. Modernists therefore tended to be critical of the arguments that national movements had longer histories. Hobsbawm is particularly critical of the many fissiparous, small-scale, ethno-linguistic nationalisms that proliferated in central and eastern Europe between 1870 and 1914, and of which the Albanians can be considered a late example.[14]

By contrast, perennialists, led by Adrian Hastings, concede that, although the nationalist movements (both large and small) of the period were themselves new, the communities upon which they were based were genuine, older and rooted in ethnic foundations.[15] A third grouping, often referred to as pre-modernists, has meanwhile drawn a distinction between 'old continuous nations' in western Europe, and the 'more recent' and 'imitation' ones in eastern Europe and Asia, including the Serbs, Croats and Romanians.[16] Perennialists and pre-modernists tend to criticise modernist historiography because, amongst other things, they consider it pays too little attention to the importance of myths, traditions and shared memories amongst socio-cultural groups, which hint towards more ancient and 'ethnic' foundations. Modernists, Hobsbawm in particular, reject these because they deem them either a fabrication or irrelevant to the nationalisms of late nineteenth- and early twentieth-century Europe. Indeed, Ernest Gellner's comment that the 'cultural shreds and patches used by nationalism are often arbitrary historical inventions'[17] is perhaps nowhere more true than in the Balkans, especially in multi-coveted regions like Kosovo and Macedonia, where protagonists will use any piece of evidence, however small or tenuous, to support their claim. The other schools maintain that, regardless of their authenticity, and especially in regions such as the Balkans, reference to golden ages, holy lands and past heroes has played an important role in sustaining oral traditions, and developed effective myths and legends that could be utilised for political nationalist purposes.[18]

In the Balkan peninsula, most nineteenth-century nationalisms (for instance, the Serb, Bulgarian and Greek) fit more closely with the perennial school. These nationalisms tended to centre on what Anthony Smith calls an 'ancient ethnic core' that centred on both 'history' and 'landscape'.[19] In the Balkans, this tended to include two main features: a common religion, specifically Christianity (Orthodoxy), and the rebirth or resurrection of a past culture, centred on a glorious age (Ancient Athens for the Greeks), holy land (Kosovo for the Serbs) or past hero (Lazarus for the Serbs; Alexander for the Greeks). In simplistic terms, it has been argued that these respective cultures and 'nations' were sustained through an oral tradition, and then developed by nineteenth-century nationalists, to fit their political objectives. Modernists may argue that these ethnic origins were manufactured, distorted or even invented versions of the past, but, nevertheless, at the time they proved effective vehicles for promoting and sustaining their national movements, in a similar manner to that described by Hroch.[20]

The basis of the late nineteenth-century Albanian national movement was more complicated, yet firmly grounded in ethnicity. It fits none of the traditional theories of state formation, or the experiences of its neighbouring Balkan states. Instead of emphasising a glorious national past and common religion as the two prime (ethnic) markers of their identity, the Albanians determined a very different basis for their ethnic or national identity: a common Albanian spoken language. In using such a limiting definition of Albanian nationality, Albanian nationalism differs from perennial theories, which highlight the importance of a written vernacular.[21] Once this definition was settled, Albanian national efforts focused on having it accepted and supported by the great powers. Histories written under Albanian regimes since independence, especially those under King Zog (1925-39) and Enver Hoxha (1945-85), have however attempted to present Albanian nationalism in terms similar to those used in other Balkan states.[22] They referred to the Illyrian origins of the Albanian people, and to the medieval hero Skanderbeg (Georgi Castrioti), who had defied the Ottoman Turks in the early fifteenth century, and lived in semi-independence. In reality, during the 'national awakening', most Albanian nationalists were realistic enough to recognise that such an ethnic understanding of Albanian identity would not be very successful. Unlike the other Balkan 'nations', no Albanian state had existed before 1912, either in its own right or under a different name. More problematically, such a 'historic nation' clashed with the various other Balkan 'nations', and most obviously with Serbian claims to Kosovo.[23]

The issue of religion would have proven even more divisive and was likewise avoided. The Albanians were divided on the basis of four religions: Sunni Muslims, Bektashi Muslims (a liberal Shiite sect), who together constituted about seventy percent of the population, Orthodox Christians (at this point primarily Greek Orthodox until the separation of the Albanian church in 1923), who made up about twenty percent, and Roman Catholics, who constituted about ten percent.[24] However, these faiths were somewhat inter-changeable. It appears to have been common practice, especially in the Scutari and Monastir *vilayets,* and between Catholics and Muslims, for the inter-marrying of faiths and for two faiths to be practiced regularly within one household (often Islam in public and Christianity in private).[25] Early in the nineteenth century, John Cam Hobhouse, friend of Lord Byron, radical in politics and fellow-Philhellene, travelled with him through Greece and Ottoman Empire; Hobhouse observed, unusually but perhaps presciently, that 'Only the Albanians are conscious of nationality; all the other peoples of the Empire are grouped according to religion.'[26] As indeed, under the *millet* system in the Ottoman Empire, they were; and this has generally been taken to have inhibited the development of a national consciousness among the Albanians, since they were so divided in religion. Both Serbian and Bulgarian nationalisms were assisted by this categorisation, but the *millet* hindered the development of an Albanian national consciousness. For instance, until 1877 and the reorganisation of provincial boundaries, Albanians in Kosovo were divided between several Ottoman districts.[27] By the late nineteenth century, religion was giving way to the German conception of nations in eastern Europe, based on linguistic foundations. However, in the Balkans, religion remained an important marker of identity far longer than elsewhere. Only when the *millet* system broke down did the Albanians emerge, professing a distinct ethnicity or nationality based on the German model.[28]

Hastings contends that Judo-Christianity was the 'constructor' of nineteenth-century nationalism, and Islam its 'restrainer'.[29] It will be shown that his views were only partially accurate for the Albanian question, and that both Muslims and Christians were heavily involved in the Albanian movement.[30] The role of Christianity was also markedly different, both to that described by Hastings and from that experienced in other Balkan nationalisms. Only a small number of prominent bishops (most obviously Bishops Fan Noli and Luigi Bumçi) were involved in the Albanian movement, and this seems to have been for reasons other than confessional issues. The absence of an autonomous Albanian Orthodox church also prevented religion having a role similar to that in other states. Hastings' views, that the nationalism of this period is a purely Christian phenomenon, clearly fits the Albanian case no better than do the modernist predictions.

In addition to the ethnic basis of small-state nationalism, a second common feature of small-state national movements is the centrality of a common danger. Anthony Smith has shown that this 'defensive nationalism' materialised only under threat, often in periods of protracted warfare, when a national sentiment, as distinct from genuine nationalism, emerged for a relatively short period.[31] The smaller and weaker the state, the more susceptible it was likely to be to such encroachments on its sovereignty. Maria Todorova and L.L. Farrar Jr. have shown, of other Balkan nationalisms, that national sentiment tended to have weak roots, was imported and was often 'foisted' on the people, the bulk of whom were illiterate peasants.[32] In this respect, the Albanian experience displays a closer fit to other south-eastern European nationalisms of the period. Albanian nationalism was actively pursued by a very small vanguard of Albanian nationalists, although admittedly from all four faiths, from Albania and from colonies abroad. It was not a mass movement, and it proved popular only in times of crisis, such as protracted warfare, or when other options appeared to have failed. Outside such crisis points, support waned and the promotion of an independent Albania often depended much more on pro-Albanian organisations, such as the Albanian Committee in London (1912-14) and the Anglo-Albanian Society (1918-23), and the policies of great power representatives. This again emphasises the importance of considering these external or international influences.

Small States in the Great Power System

Numerous problems arise when considering the position of small states in any international system and applying international relations (IR) theories to them, not least because most IR theory is overwhelmingly focused on the great powers.[33] The role of small and fledgling states in the international system, and their effect on the policies of the great powers, has been insufficiently articulated in the literature, and needs further study. This is particularly true of the so-called great-power system. This system operated from about 1815 until 1945, in which between four and six great powers, typically the strongest and largest states (economically, politically, geographically and numerically) dominated the international system. The problems of applying IR theories are particularly pronounced in the case of an independence question, in which the 'state' concerned is merely aspiring to statehood, is not recognised for much of the period under consideration and has no formal place within the system.

There are also problems regarding the definition of small states, but typically they are deemed to include a number of common features: small in population, small in geographical area, often located in marginal geographical areas, weak economically and often lacking political stability. Typically, therefore, they hold a weak or uninfluential position in the international system in which they operate. It is argued that there is a strong correlation between a state's 'indicators of vulnerability' and its actual vulnerability, and its ability, therefore, to impact upon the international system or its relations with the great powers.[34] However, even a small state can improve its own chances of survival. As various writers have shown, small states have in practice more power than IR theorists project.[35] As Michael Handel has maintained, although small states are 'vulnerable' they are 'not helpless'.[36] For Handel, the key variable in the interaction of small states and great powers is the small state's ability to mobilise the support of others. Robert Rothstein meanwhile contends that a small state can have a more direct impact, by altering great power expectations about its position and its likely response in different situations.[37] This book will also illustrate how it was possible, at certain points, for a small state, even one operating in the great power system, to make considerable gains in its national aspirations without support from the great powers.

In relations with great-power states, a small state's success in its independence question appears to be heavily dependent on a variety of factors.[38] Starting with size, although small size is usually considered a disadvantage because it may make a state weak, dependent upon other stronger state(s) for support or patronage, and allows only a small margin of error for policy makers in external relations, small size might also be an advantage. It could help foster national spirit and unity, avoid the difficulties of the large bureaucracies needed to run larger states, or the problems associated with gaining too much territory and, in the process, large numbers of ethnic minorities.[39]

A second important factor for small states is their geographic position and perceived strategic value to other states. Many of the weakest states in nineteenth-century Europe were located at its periphery (the Balkans, Scandinavia, Iberia). By contrast, an important geographical position, for instance, located on an important trade route, having access to a coastline that sustained good ports, having good natural resources or being located in a zone where the interests of two or more powers merged, could help make even 'small' states stronger. Patrick Salmon has shown the importance of geography in enabling the Scandinavian states to achieve a 'certain remoteness from international confrontation' in the twentieth century.[40] However, for a newly aspiring state, its location could also be a drawback, as other stronger states might seek to retain or gain such a strategic position for themselves, or their allies. Other states also feared the potential of a new state that might be unstable, or susceptible to outside influence from rival powers.

A third factor was the differing perspectives of a great power and a small state in relation to the national question, as referred to in Sven Holtsmark's 'asymmetry of expectations' thesis. For instance, within the small state, policy will usually be determined by leading politicians (such as the prime minister or foreign minister), whereas within the great power, this responsibility will often be delegated to much more junior-ranking ministers, even officials. This imbalance in the relationship usually means that the small state affords greater priority to the negotiations, whilst the great power enjoys far greater flexibility in its relationship and policy.[41] If a small state can succeed in reducing such disparities and secure a more balanced relationship, the small state usually proves more successful in merging or incorporating its own national interests with that of the great power and, in turn, in harnessing great power support for its national programme.

The fourth crucial component is the particular point in the international relations cycle and the type of international system. The great-power system rested on the balance of power between its leading members. When this balance was relatively stable, small states generally found it difficult to advance their national programme (with notable exceptions such as Belgium (1830-31)). However, during and following periods of crisis and conflict (such as 1853-56, 1875-78, and 1912-18 in the Balkans), small states were able to make considerable advances. As the balance upon which the system rested was disrupted, and a new balance was being sought, the system was in a state of flux from which the new and aspiring small (and great) states could benefit. The small states were themselves often responsible for provoking these crisis points, and deliberately aiming to shift the balance to their benefit.[42]

The Albanian Case

Several international historians have written of the serious limitations of attempting to employ a political-science approach to the study of individual historical events.[43] Such ideas are particularly pertinent when considering a small-state national question that does not readily fit such theories. The historian of international relations, and of small-state nationalism within the great-power system, will prefer to consider the case according to the criteria of ethnicity and international relations prevailing at the time, rather than late twentieth-century theories. It is not the purpose of this study to determine the validity or otherwise of the Albanian national identity as it was defined at the beginning of the twentieth century. Instead, this work aims to illustrate the degree of success the Albanian nationalists had in having such an identity accepted in 'Albania', and by great-power policy makers. Also, in reverse, it intends to explore how great-power policy makers defined 'Albania', and the impact this had on the construction of an Albanian identity and an independent entity. In so doing, the book sets out to produce a more synthetic view of the pivotal years in achieving an independent Albania. The study is intended as a case study that focuses on the question of Albanian independence in the period 1912-21, rather than a comparative study with other states, or with the Albanian experience in other time periods. My approach will be broadly chronological, empirical and narrative, in common with most international history, because of the rapid variability of events, and in spite of the criticisms of this approach by practitioners of other disciplines.

The main focus of the study is on British and, from 1917 onwards, American policy and perceptions, my main areas of research have been in the primary and printed archives of these great powers. My archival sources include principally those of the British Foreign Office, other government departments, and personal papers located in the National Archives, Kew, and the House of Lords' Records Office, both in London. The Foreign Office papers include the official records of the London conferences (1912-13), and of the Albanian boundary commissions (1913-14), which do not appear to have been utilised elsewhere. On American policy, I have used the Department of State records, located in the National Archives College Park, Maryland. In addition, I have explored the collections of the papers of Aubrey Herbert, MP for Somerset South (1911-23) and President of both the Albanian Committee (1912-14) and the Anglo-Albanian Society (1918-23), in the Somerset Record Office. These include a large number of documents written by and to prominent Albanians. This archival research has been supported by the study of some documents available in print in English, Russian, Italian and French, of which there are extensive collections. Relevant documentary collections on Albanian affairs, principally in English and French, were also consulted. A small number of selected Albanian and German language documents were translated and provided pertinent examples at particular points. The secondary literature used is primarily that in English, but with the addition of some literature in French, Italian, Russian, Bosnian-Croatian-Serbian and Albanian, plus Albanian in translation into both English and French.

There is therefore, and intentionally, a clear English language and British focus to the study: no Greek or Turkish language material has been considered, and the study of other language sources, especially Albanian ones, is limited. However, the amount of available 'Albanian' material is less extensive than might be supposed and I am sceptical that a more detailed examination would have been very productive. There was no codified Albanian language until 1908 (with the Monastir Alphabet Congress), and much continued to be written in English, French or Turkish. My preliminary investigations indicated that very little documentation from this period survived in the Albanian archives, whereas the Herbert papers, in particular, include a number of sources written by Albanians, and these have been utilised wherever possible, especially as they have not been used in any study of this type before.

In this study, Chapter One explores the emergence of an Albanian nationalism based on spoken language, diplomatic attempts by Albanian patriots to have such an identity accepted by the great power concert, and military efforts to prevent partition by rival Balkan states. Chapter Two details the great power deliberations in 1913 on what would be meant by 'Albania', their acceptance of language as the basis of ethnicity and statehood, and the persistent sacrifice of this criterion to other, power-political objectives. Chapter Three shows the difficulties of sustaining the independence of a small state in practice, particularly without help or support from the great powers, and when little nascent national sentiment existed. Chapter Four considers the reasons for, and the implications of, the decision of the Entente powers to rescind Albanian independence, and to envisage partition of the state between Italy, Greece and Serbia. Chapter Five illustrates the ascendancy of counter-national forces in Albania, and the subsequent revival of an Albanian ethnic nationalism, during World War One; together with attempts by the great powers to foster and control this for their own geo-political purposes. Chapter Six shows how, at the Paris Peace Conference, the principle of self-determination was initially supposed not to apply to the Albanian question, but how President Wilson then secured the reinstatement of an ethnically-based settlement for Albania, by March 1920. Chapter Seven explores the reasons for the Albanian nationalists abandoning their dependence on the great powers, and the ultimate success of a small-state nationalism, applying both diplomatic and military means against its rivals, whether small states or great powers. Chapter Eight considers how the Albanians used a third tactic (working through international organisations) to realise the emergence of their independence, but had to moderate their ethnic ambitions in order to secure that great-power endorsement which was so essential to their success.

Chapter 1

National Ambitions and Linguistic Nationalism: the emergence of an Albanian identity in 1912

On 28 November 1912, a congress of Albanian notables in Valona proclaimed the independence of what it called 'ethnic' or 'ethnographic' Albania. This encompassed the Ottoman *vilayets* of Scutari and Janina, the *sanjaks* of Prizrend, Novi Bazar, Prishtina and Ipek, the *kaza* of Kalkadelen from the *vilayet* of Kosovo, and the sanjaks of Koritza, Elbasan and Dibra from the *vilayet* of Monastir (Appendix A). In the light of the impending defeat of the Ottoman Empire by the Balkan League (a confederation of the Balkan states of Bulgaria, Serbia, Greece and Montenegro), Albanian nationalists announced their independence, because they no longer viewed Ottoman suzerainty as a sufficient guarantee to protect their rights, customs and interests. This was the opposite of what the League states had intended: one of the League's motivations in the war had been to prevent the successful establishment of an autonomous or independent Albanian state, which would have obstructed the League's opportunities to intervene and claim this territory for its members.[44] As early as 1906, Brailsford had recorded that Albanian nationalists had claimed: 'Our programme is Albania for the Albanians, and we do no intend to submit to any foreign domination, and certainly not to the Slavs'.[45] In reality, this chapter will illustrate that even as late as November 1912, the majority of Albanian nationalists were still demanding, at most, autonomy within the Ottoman Empire. Only the prospect of Ottoman defeat prompted a small band of nationalists to proclaim independence.

The Great Powers and the Foundations of Albanian Nationalist Activities (1878-1912)

At the Congress of Berlin (1878), the great powers agreed to establish an autonomous Bulgaria nominally within the Ottoman Empire, agreed to enlarge and recognise Serbia as independent, envisaged the enlargement of Greece, and afforded international recognition to an enlarged, independent Montenegro. This established the international framework within which the relations and conflicts between the nascent Balkan states would be conducted for the next thirty-five years. The first international problem for any aspiring Albanian national movement was therefore to secure recognition from the great powers, and acceptance by its Balkan neighbours, that there was any separate Albanian identity at all, distinct from that of the surrounding Slav, Greek and Muslim populations. Under the terms of the Treaty of San Stefano (March 1878), which the Congress was summoned by the great powers to renegotiate, the Russians had imposed the establishment of a large Russian-protected Bulgaria on a weakened Ottoman government: its frontiers were established according to ostensibly ethnographic criteria, embracing practically the whole of Ottoman 'Macedonia', and were pushed so far to the west as to incorporate Monastir, and extended even to the west of Lake Ochrida. Thus they included extensive areas with undeniably Albanian-speaking populations. Furthermore, in this treaty, and at the subsequent Congress itself, it was proposed to provide compensating territorial gains, at the expense of the Ottoman Empire, to Serbia, Montenegro and Greece, again incorporating areas with Albanian-speaking populations, including Muslims, Orthodox and Catholics.

The Albanian national movement therefore first became active in the international arena at the time of the Congress of Berlin of 1878, as the Albanian League or 'League of Prizrend' (1878-81). The League resolved to forestall the allocation of areas of the western Balkans with Albanian-speaking populations to one or more of the neighbouring Orthodox Christian states. They referred to themselves as 'Albanians', but they did not seek establishment of an independent 'Albania'. They merely sought the retention of areas of Albanian-speaking people within the Ottoman Empire, because they identified themselves as distinct from the neighbouring Slavs, Greeks and Ottoman Turks. However, the success of this proto-national programme depended on the representatives of the great powers assembled in Congress accepting the Albanian claim to the status of a recognised nation or nationality. Eventually, they ruled that there was no such entity as an Albanian 'nation', rather that the 'Albanians' or Albanian-speaking people were merely the inhabitants of a geographical area loosely known as 'Albania'. Although 'Macedonia' was restored to Ottoman rule, the powers assigned some areas of territory with a majority Albanian-speaking population to other states: specifically, Antivari, Hoti, Gruda, Triopchi, Kichi, Podgoritza, Plava and Gusinje to Montenegro and part of southern Epirus, between the Gulf of Preveza and the Kalamas River, to Greece. The Albanians were isolated and enjoyed little support, except for some Austrian sympathy for the Catholic minority, and some assistance from the Ottoman Turks, which was designed to merely limit Ottoman territorial losses. When the boundary commissions of the Congress arrived to delimit the frontier, the Prizrend League opposed by force the handing over of these territories and managed to retain control of Plava, Gusinje, Hoti and Gruda. Montenegro was given the port of Dulcigne as compensation, whilst the Greek frontier was instead fixed at the Arta River. When the commissions had finished their work, the League of Prizrend was suppressed by the Ottoman authorities.[46]

Thus, on the first occasion that the governments of the great powers had been confronted with the question of a distinct Albanian ethnicity, and after they had actively promoted the claims of Slav-Christian national groups, defined according to current ethnographic criteria, they specifically declined to recognise an equivalent Albanian ethnicity. Furthermore, even contemporary sympathisers with the Albanian cause questioned whether the Albanians were 'ethnologically … really a single stock', given the tribal and religious differences, which made it difficult to establish an accurate definition of the Albanian 'nation'.[47] As well as the diversity of religion, there were marked divergences with some areas, especially in the north, that were isolated and in winter inaccessible, and there were also major cultural and traditional differences, particularly the contrast between the seasonally migratory tribal groups in the north (Ghegs) and the more settled populations in the south (Tosks).

There is indeed evidence that the division between the Ghegs and Tosks did create problems in creating a common identity, despite the criticism of those who have belittled this distinction as over-simplistic.[48] Its experience at the Congress of Berlin showed the Albanian movement suffered from the serious disability that it had no great-power patron or protector. As long as the Ottoman Empire remained a viable suzerain power, Albanian interests might for the time being be adequately protected if a satisfactory autonomous state within it could be secured; but once that viability was compromised, it became essential for the Albanians to secure a great-power patron. For this role the least unpromising (though scarcely disinterested) candidate looked likely to be Austria-Hungary, if only because of its determination to prevent Serbia securing access to the Adriatic through Albanian territory.

Cultural Awakenings and Historical Traditions (1878-1908)

In the light of these major problems, in the thirty years after Berlin the small Albanian national movement, while not giving up the search for great-power support, set about the task of forging a national identity based on establishing and deepening national traditions and common bonds. As Stavro Skendi has shown, this focused on three main fronts: the pseudo-historical in the legend of Skanderbeg, the literary and cultural, and the linguistic.[49] In truth, these three initiatives went hand-in-hand, as literary and cultural works sought to promote the Skanderbeg legend and the use of a distinct Albanian written language. Skanderbeg was indicative of the Albanian resistive tradition. He encompassed many of the 'virtues' that commonly marked the 'heroic origins' model (martial valour, generosity, temperance, self-sacrifice, endurance, loyalty and, above all, patriotism),[50] that had proven so successful in the nationalism of the Orthodox Christian states. It was hoped that Skanderbeg could be used as a 'historical' example of why the Albanian people deserved the right to their own state, and should not become part of others. Gelcu Maksutovici considers that the Skanderbeg legend proved an effective vehicle for the promotion of Albanian nationalism, and emphasised the work *Istori e Skenderbeut* (*The History of Skanderbeg*) by Naim Frashëri, in disseminating this message to educated Albanians.[51] However, he over-emphasises the Skanderbeg legend. Admittedly, when independence was proclaimed, the hero's flag (the black double-headed eagle on a red background) was ceremoniously unfurled after nearly five hundred years, and would become the Albanian national flag. But, Skanderbeg had never lived in or sought an independent or autonomous state, and instead achieved simply an informal linking of Albanian princes, but not of their territories. After Skanderbeg's death, his descendants and followers soon emigrated to Italy, or once more became loyal Ottoman subjects. Moreover, literacy rates amongst Albanians were very low, and the book was read primarily by Albanians living abroad, whilst many initiatives in 1912 started within Albania.[52] As Benedict Anderson has shown of elsewhere in south-eastern Europe, national print vernaculars (including national histories, grammars and dictionaries) aimed at instilling the population with a national consciousness were not very effective vehicles in promoting national consciousness.[53] According to Faik Konitza, the Albanian-American who was influential at the Monastir Alphabet Congress (1908) in getting a unified Albanian script adopted, few Albanians before 1877 imagined that their language could be written. Even after the adoption of the codified written vernacular, when the Latin script was adopted and thirty-six characters created, intellectuals tended to write in Turkish, Greek or French. There were also practical problems in the formation of the common written, and also spoken, language. For instance, Isa Blumi records that, by 1900, there were only two Albanian-language schools, and that, by 1914, in Mirdita, a predominantly Catholic region in north-western 'Albania', only three individuals were able to read in 'Albanian'.[54] When the cabinet of the newly created Albanian state met between March and September 1914, they conducted their meetings in Turkish because the 'Albanians' could not understand one another, and some members did not even speak Albanian.[55] In the thirty-year period after Berlin, there does not seem to have been much advancement of the Albanian national programme, except for a small educated intelligentsia, who tended to live outside Albania. Active colonies included those in Bucharest, Lausanne, Boston (Massachusetts) and Constantinople. Many divisions remained amongst the Albanian people, and a national or autonomous programme was of little interest to the bulk of the Albanian people, who were relatively content with their life within the Ottoman Empire. The majority Muslims did not want to jeopardise the important privileges they received as Muslims. The mountainous terrain in eastern and northern 'Albania', especially, and the distance from Constantinople, meant that the Ottoman regime was very light, especially in comparison to those Balkan regions nearer Constantinople. Even Christian Albanians endured little interference with their local customs, traditions and practices, and they saw no significant reason to upset the established system.[56] Nevertheless, the Albanian spoken language would soon become the defining feature of identity and the national movement.

The Young Turk Revolution and Threats to Albanian Identity (1908-12)

In 1908, Albanian lifestyles and customs were disrupted by the Young Turk revolution, headed by the Committee of Union and Progress in Constantinople, and carried out by the officer corps of the Ottoman army in Macedonia. The Committee, which pursued a nationalising agenda of modernisation and centralisation, was received with much alarm by the Albanians. In 1908, a number of prominent Muslim Albanians (such as Hasan bey Prishtina and Nexhib Draga) from across the four *vilayets,* had been elected as Young Turk deputies. However, these men soon became distanced from the centralising policies of their party because of the impact on Albanian customs and practices. Many would go on to become leading members of the Albanian national movement. From 1909 onwards, there were continual revolts in 'Albania', some led by these 'politicians' for the protection of local rights, especially regarding local conscription and taxation privileges. However, the movements remained small-scale, unorganised and localised, with no central plan or co-ordination, although gradually some of the groups started to work together to promote their claims more effectively, including those representing different faiths. Perhaps most importantly, although no body attempted to co-ordinate the various uprisings, some understanding of what it meant to be 'Albanian' emerged, and played a part in the protests to the Porte in Constantinople. By 1912, it had been confirmed, for instance by the Gerche memorandum (June 1911), the Cepo resolutions (July 1911) and the Valona petition (July 1912), that the idea of a unified Albania, which had been proposed in 1878, and based on territory where Albanian was the majority spoken language and Ottoman provincial boundaries, was generally accepted.

Nevertheless, Albanians were still calling for at most autonomy (and many not even for that), and the majority remained loyal subjects of the Sultan. Albanian divisions and rivalries remained prevalent, and uprisings were as much against other 'Albanians' as they were against the Young Turk policies. In one typical incident in Zadrima, a village located near the town of Scutari, the inhabitants insisted upon receiving from the Porte the same exemption privileges as their neighbours, despite never having had such privileges before. Such demands placed the Ottoman Government in a difficult position. If they denied the demands, the inhabitants of Zadrima would continue to revolt; if they granted them, their neighbours would interpret it as a loss of privilege and seek redress themselves.[57]

By the start of 1912, Stavro Skendi has identified three main groupings of Albanian nationalists. He contended that they were divided geographically, tribally and to a certain extent religiously. Only one of these groupings considered itself in anything resembling 'nationalistic' terms. The first group, the Hamidists, were strong in Kosovo, primarily Muslim, and wanted a return to the pre-1908 constitutional conditions under Sultan Abdul Hamid. The second group, the *itilâfists* (or followers of 'Liberty and Entente') were strong in Kosovo, central and southern Albania, were both Orthodox and Muslim, and sought autonomy within the Ottoman Empire. Their programme was based upon the earlier constitution agreed by the Sultan, and later satisfied by the offer of the Young Turks in July 1912. The third group known as the 'enlightened intellectuals' came mainly from southern Albania and the diaspora, but also Hasan Prishtina. It included Orthodox Christians and Muslims, especially a number of prominent Bektashis and many involved in the earlier cultural and literary endeavours. They were influenced by the enlightenment, western and diasporic liberalism, advocated autonomy within the Ottoman Empire (on the basis of the Gerche memorandum), and were similar in many ways to the intelligentsia in other European states. They appear to have referred to themselves as 'nationalists', and sought things on behalf of *all* 'Albanians'.[58]

The Italo-Turkish war (1911-12) prompted the next development. It brought about significant changes in Albanian ideas and tactics. Albanian patriots correctly appreciated that the neighbouring states were unlikely to remain inactive. Their intentions were clearly illustrated by the activities of the Serbian government, which helped guerrilla bands in Kosovo, especially those led by the patriot Isa bey Boletin, and by Montenegrin links with some of the northern Catholic tribes. The problems arising from having no great-power protector remained as vital as before. As inhabitants of a majority Muslim region, most Europeans considered the Albanians as Turks, and the Ottomans did nothing to dispel these assumptions. Being inhabitants of the Ottoman Empire also made it more difficult to present Albanian claims at the international level. Based on their experiences during the Berlin Congress, a number of prominent and educated Albanians determined that it was necessary to secure international support for their autonomous movement. It was hoped that pressure from the great powers would assist in persuading the Porte to implement the administrative reforms that many Albanians were demanding. Ismail Kemal bey Vlora has often been cited as the main advocate of the pursuit of great-power recognition of Albanian national interests, but British sources seem to imply an equally extensive role for Hasan Prishtina, albeit in close association with Ismail Kemal. Ismail was a prominent Albanian from the coastal town of Valona (Vlora in Albanian) in southern Albania. He served as a deputy in the Ottoman parliament, where in 1910 he had first raised the question of a unified and integral Albania. Both men appear to have been amongst the most far-sighted Albanian patriots at the time. They appreciated the value of 'national' efforts for the preservation of 'Albania', but they realised that these were unlikely to be successful unless they had the support of great-power statements. Therefore they considered that the preservation of 'Albania' would depend as much upon the 'support and rivalry of the great powers' as on Albanian efforts. This was because they recognised that the Albanians had many internal divisions, and were weaker militarily than the neighbouring Balkan states and the Ottoman Empire. Given Austrian interest in the Albanian littoral and eastern Adriatic, it was decided that the Ballhausplatz (the Austrian Foreign Ministry) was likely to be the most receptive to Albanian claims. To the Ballhausplatz, Ismail Kemal stressed the urgency of the recognition of the Albanians as an 'ethnographic entity', and invited it to press the Porte for the 'recognition of the existence of an Albanian nation'.[59]

These two men also sought to 'nationalise' the uprisings in Albania, in order to give greater weight to their negotiations with the great powers, and also to put pressure on the Ottoman authorities to grant the administrative and other concessions that 'Albanians' had demanded in previous revolts. The most significant initiative appears to have begun in December 1911. At a meeting of prominent Albanians, in Constantinople, organised by Ismail and Prishtina, they devised plans to facilitate a general Albanian insurrection the following year. This would start in Kosovo, where Prishtina had considerable influence and supplies, and then spread to the other Albanian-speaking areas. Prishtina was assigned responsibility for organising the preparations in Kosovo, whereas Ismail Kemal resolved to secure funds and 15,000 guns from governments 'friendly' to the Albanian movement, which presumably meant the Austrians. Despite this central plan, when the revolt broke out it was obvious that the problems experienced in the 1911 uprisings still existed: there were no unifying ideas, motives or leadership. Nevertheless, by 23 July 1912, the Ottoman government had signed an armistice with the Albanians, in order to concentrate on the war with Italy. This did not satisfy the Albanians, who, according to Sir Edward Grey, British Foreign Secretary, were finally of 'one mind and they were quite determined to see the thing through'. He highlighted in particular the co-operation of Muslim and Christian Albanians.[60] More significantly, a vision of what constituted an 'ethnic Albania' had definitely emerged. Other aims differed, but the definition of 'Albania' and its boundaries was the same in all the petitions submitted to the Porte (for example from the Albanian Central Committee in Constantinople (28 July 1912), and from the southern Albanian chiefs (29 July 1912). The one concession granted by the Porte satisfied only the *itilâfists*. The rebel groups from central and southern Albanian continued to resist, and to call for full implementation of their demands, above all autonomy for the four *vilayets* of 'Albania'.[61]

In July and August 1912, the majority of 'nationalist leaders' appear to have been persuaded that their claims were likely to prove more successful if they worked together. They would then be able to show a united front and appear stronger, which they considered would both apply greater pressure on the Ottoman authorities, and impress the great-power representatives. The Hamidists, led by Isa Boletin, and the 'enlightened intellectuals', led by Hasan Prishtina and Nexhib Draga, who, like Prishtina, was from an influential Albanian family and had served as a deputy in the Ottoman parliament, developed a compromise arrangement, which is usually referred to as the 'Fourteen Points of Hasan Prishtina' (presented 9 August 1912).[62] This agreement was crucial for the fledgling Albanian nationalist movement. Most significantly, it represented an alliance between the two Albanian 'nationalistic' groupings that were most antagonistic towards one another, and had the greatest ideological differences. It called for the recognition of local customs and the carrying of arms, to satisfy the Hamidists, and for school rights and a national programme, in line with the aspirations of the intellectuals. The memorandum was presented on behalf of *all* Albanians, and it made clear that it was not aiming for the preservation of the rights of a particular locality, village or clan, but of those of all Albanian-speaking people. The majority of the demands were accepted by the Ottoman government, largely because Albanian forces had advanced as far east as Uskub, but they were not implemented in full. The Porte granted some customary laws in the four *vilayets*, but not the demands for regional service or any form of autonomy. It claimed that it was unable to consider the autonomy question because there were problems in defining the geographical limitations of 'Albania'. It therefore made no reference to the 'Albania' defined in the petition or to any of the other versions that had been mooted. The Albanians had not succeeded in securing an acceptance of the definition of 'Albania' that had first been proposed internationally in 1878.[63]

Interestingly, it was the intellectuals who persuaded the Hamidists to accept the Ottoman proposal, although the main intellectual goals had not been agreed to. The intellectuals, especially Prishtina, appear to have been willing to accept this more limited offer because they did not want to lose the valuable other concessions it granted.[64] These goals were at least as important, possibly more important, than the 'national' ambitions. Seeking autonomy within the Ottoman Empire was only one means of achieving them. If they could be achieved and secured through other means, and ones that ordinary Albanians could relate to, then this was acceptable. It would then not even be necessary to secure autonomy. An independent Albanian state was an even more remote possibility. Most individual Albanian nationalists were fairly moderate or conservative. Their protests began as the protection and preservation of existing rights that they perceived to be under threat. In this way, Albanian nationalism fits with the ideas of defensive nationalism. The promotion of an Albanian identity based on their oral ethno-linguistic foundations materialised not for itself, but in an attempt to protect other older and more established privileges and rights. That they all (supposedly) spoke Albanian was the key unifier, although in other areas there were many differences. Language thus provided a basis on which to define the areas that they deemed should be granted autonomy, and it coincided fairly neatly with the reorganisation of Ottoman boundaries in 1877. It was therefore plausible that, in claiming provincial boundaries that were already established, their proposal might be more effective. The Albanians framed their 'Albania' in the language of the day ('ethnographical limits'), that which fitted their case (language as opposed to religion), and gave it a political basis (a definition based on the *vilayets*) in an attempt to appear reasonable and moderate, and to gain support from the Porte and the great powers.[65] Significantly, although they now called for reform on behalf of all Albanians, they still wanted reform within the framework of the Ottoman Empire, because this afforded protection from the ambitions of the neighbouring small states. However, in response to the activities of those states in the Balkan League, Albanian claims would become radicalised, and favour independence.

Balkan Wars (1912-13): the accelerator for independence

The Balkan League was formed by a series of treaties and agreements between March and October 1912. In accordance with those treaties, on 8 October 1912, Montenegro declared war on the Ottoman Empire, and the other three states followed suit ten days later. In line with their national aspirations, and usually defined as part of their 'historic nations', the leaders of the other Balkan states had different and contradictory understandings of the disputed territory, but they agreed that none of them considered it 'Albania'. One clerk in the British Foreign Office summed up these problems by asking 'who can say where "Albania" ends and "Macedonia" begins? And in Macedonia itself, what are the boundaries between Serbs, Bulgars and Kutso-Vlachs?'[66] None of the treaties made any specific reference to 'Albania', although the Serbo-Bulgarian Treaty (13 March 1912) allowed for the possibility of Serbia gaining territory in Albania as a means of acquiring an outlet on the Adriatic; and the secret annex to that treaty envisaged that 'Albania' was to be divided between Serbia, Montenegro and Greece.[67] This meant that, to fulfil the Balkan League's ambitions, the great powers would have to agree to a division of 'Albania', and to the division of the 'Albanians' between the various Orthodox small states.

BALKAN NATIONAL AMBITIONS AND THE 'ALBANIAN' QUESTION

The formation of these alliances and the motivations of the parties involved have been well explored and documented.[68] For the purpose of this study, it is necessary to focus on those ambitions to 'Albanian' territory, and on the rivalries between the states, that had an impact upon the Albanian question. Some studies have considered the importance of Albanian activities in promoting the formation of the League, but usually as the trigger, or as an accelerant in the later stages. In reality, Albanian activities seem to have played a more influential role. The Albanians may not have been calling for independence, or even very forcefully for autonomy, but the suggestion of either goal was viewed with much anxiety by the governments of the other Balkan small states. The governments of all the League states appear to have been perturbed by Albanian claims for autonomy, out of fear that this would be detrimental to their irredentist ambitions and historic claims in the area that the Albanians were now claiming as 'Albania'. Nascent divisions between the Serbs and the Albanians appear to have been accentuated by the rise in Albanian national activities, and by the Serbian response to secure their own national ambitions in these areas, especially Kosovo. Meanwhile, as early as September 1911 (at least), officials in Sofia articulated to the Russian government their concerns about the significance of a future Albanian revolt. They feared that it would prove a major block to Bulgarian ambitions, especially if it resulted in autonomy (independence was not considered) for those Albanians living in the Kosovo and Monastir *vilayets*. Typically, the four Balkan League governments resented any privileges being given to the majority Muslim population that were not likewise afforded to the Christians. The Bulgarian Prime Minister, Ivan Gueshov, was under particular pressure to ensure that any such advantages were also accorded to the Christian populations.[69] But the League governments were even more concerned by the appeals by Christian Albanians for the protection of their rights. If these concessions were granted, this would negate the possibility of these states interfering themselves, or of persuading the great powers to do so, as had occurred in previous advancements in their respective nationalist programmes. The Serbs were particularly disturbed by references to 'ethnic Albania', because this directly opposed their claims to 'Old Serbia' and a coastline on the Adriatic. Bulgarian officials were anxious that portions of the Monastir *vilayet* should not be included within an 'autonomous Albania', and even more anxious that the demand for reform in 'Albania' might lead to corresponding disturbances in 'Macedonia', and to the people there (the term Macedonians not being used) claiming similar concessions for themselves. British officials therefore predicted that there was every possibility that the continuing Albanian activities in 1912, especially their demands for autonomy, would lead to action by the other Balkan state governments to prevent it from materialising.[70] Thus the success of the Albanian national movement was clearly linked with the level of success of the other Balkan state national aspirations, which were designed to upset the system, and to prevent the realisation of Albanian national aspirations. The rapid radicalisation of Albanian activities in the summer of 1912, and the spread of the uprisings to the Vardar valley in Macedonia, confirmed the fears of the Balkan states.[71] They pleaded with the Russian government, as the protector of the Ottoman Empire's Orthodox population, to intervene and secure the same rights for the Empire's Christian populations as those being granted to the Christians and Muslims in Albania, but this remained a double-edged sword.[72] None of the Christian states wanted such concessions to be made. The Christian states accelerated the development of alliances between themselves, and resolved that they would act swiftly to prevent Albanian gains, rather than relinquish their own ambitions. They were confident that they would be successful, because the Italo-Turkish war had illustrated that the great powers no longer considered Ottoman territory as inviolable, and were prepared to accept an alteration of the territorial integrity of Ottoman territory, and of the balance of power in the region.

All four League states had ambitions in the territory claimed by the Albanians. As Farrar has shown, the ambitions of the League in 1912 were generally a combination of nationalism, apathy and aggression.[73] In the simplest terms, the four states claimed parts of 'Albania' for 'national' reasons because this territory was considered part of their respective 'historic nations'. Yet strategic and economic considerations were also important. They were all agreed that they needed to overcome the rivalry between themselves, because individually none of them was strong enough to defeat the Porte and realise any of their national and other ambitions.

The Serbian claims were the most important for the Albanian question. The Serbs sought to acquire that territory in northern Albania that they considered ethnically and historically theirs, as part of 'old Serbia'. On these grounds, they claimed territory as far south as the Drin river, and including the *sanjak* of Novi Bazar, the Kosovan plain and the *vilayet* of Scutari (all of which the Albanians considered part of northern 'Albania'), and northern and western Macedonia. Economic motives were also crucial. Serbia sought to gain 'Albanian territory' to obtain an Adriatic coastline, and to overcome the problems caused by its landlocked position, especially its economic dependency upon Austria-Hungary for trade. Serbian aspirations therefore stretched as far south as the town of Durazzo, which was considered the ideal location for a suitable Serbian port, or, alternatively, the ports of San Giovanni di Medua or Alessio, which were further north. Serbian officials were prepared to go to great lengths to secure Durazzo, which has been termed the 'all or nothing port'.[74] When the war broke out, Serbian King Peter proclaimed it a 'Holy War to free our brethren and ensure a better future.'[75]

Greek claims to Epirus were next in importance for the Albanian question, because they conflicted with Albanian claims in the Koritza and Monastir *vilayets*. The Greeks also sought gains in eastern Thrace, especially Salonika, and in southern Macedonia. In all three locations, religion, history, and economic and strategic considerations were important.[76] The 'Albanian' areas claimed by the Greeks were home to the vast majority of Orthodox 'Albanians'. The Greeks claimed, in line with their view that religion was synonymous with nationality, that, regardless of the language these people spoke, and even admitting that many spoke only Albanian, their religion (Orthodoxy) and Hellenic sentiment made them Greek. Greek claims largely complemented Serbian ones, in that they focused on 'southern

Albania', whereas Serbian claims centred on 'northern Albania'. It was thus considered unnecessary to make a formal agreement. The Skumbi river, the traditional divide between the Gheg and Tosk regions, provided a sufficiently accurate division between the extent of the maximum claims of the two states in 'Albania'. The Greek and Serbian governments, often in cooperation, worked actively to enhance their claims to this territory, and appear to have been equally determined to suppress an Albanian nationality, which was contrary to their ambitions. The Serbs used a two-pronged approach, deploying guerrilla warfare in northern Albania, but also making alliances with a number of prominent Albanian chieftains, most notably Isa Boletin, in an attempt to disrupt Albanian unity and nationalist-inspired initiatives. The Greeks, meanwhile, attempted to upset the Albanian national programme in the south by an ecclesiastical and educational policy designed to reinforce Christian and Muslim divisions.[77] The ambitions of both Serbia and Greece clashed with Bulgarian ones, especially in 'Macedonia', and Serbian ambitions also conflicted with Montenegrin aspirations in 'northern Albania'. These rivalries had seriously hindered the development of the League, and they would continue to be significant.[78]

Montenegrin ambitions regarding Albanian territory were the third most important. Montenegrin ambitions centred on the town of Scutari, which had been the centre of the medieval Montenegrin kingdom, and also on the *sanjak* of Novi Bazar, possession of which it desired to provide a coterminous frontier with Serbia, and thus reduce its own isolation. The possibility of financial and military assistance was also attractive. As the smallest of the four League states, numerically fewer than the Albanians and with a less secure relationship with the great powers, including their Russian Slav patron, Montenegro was weaker than the other small Orthodox states. The largest Montenegrin problem arose because of the incompatibility of its claims with those of Serbia. Although the Serbs and Montenegrins were religiously and linguistically similar, their historical separation had produced many divisions, and their leaders were bitter rivals for the leadership of the Serbian 'race'.[79] Their animosity was so great that the Russian government had warned against any form of Bulgaro-Montenegrin agreement. After such an agreement was signed, the Montenegrin and Bulgarian governments thought it necessary to keep it secret from officials in Belgrade.[80]

Bulgarian aspirations to Albanian territory were important for two reasons. Bulgarian ambitions focused on territory in Macedonia and Thrace, in pursuit of the restoration of the frontiers allocated to it at San Stefano, but Bulgaria also sought territory as far west as Lake Ochrida and including the important town of Monastir, which was claimed by the Albanians. These claims also clashed with Greek and Serbian claims. Although they did not give up their claims to this territory, Bulgarian officials hoped that, if they could focus Serbian and also Greek attention on 'Albania', then they would be able to make significant gains for Bulgaria in Macedonia as recompense.[81] This prospect was not very likely because the Greeks and Serbs were not willing to forgo their ethnic, historic and strategic claims to Macedonia in order to satisfy the Bulgarians. Greek-Bulgarian rivalry was so intense that it was not possible to conclude a territorial agreement, except for Crete and the Aegean islands, where the Bulgarians had no ambitions.[82]

In the light of these rivalries and conflicting ambitions, the establishment of the League was a remarkable achievement. However, it proved possible to subsume these animosities temporarily, in an attempt to overcome the perceived greater threats posed by Albanian nationalism, and a possible strengthening of the Ottoman Empire in Europe, if Albanian autonomy within it, and concessions to the Christian minorities, were granted. At the outset of the first Balkan war, all four states, even the Montenegrins, had better prospects of securing their national goals than the Albanians. These states already had an established position within the great-power system, and therefore an outlet by which to elucidate their claims. More importantly, the Slav states retained the support of Russia and Greece the French, and, increasingly, the Germans.

IMPLICATIONS FOR ALBANIAN 'NATIONALISM'

In response to the outbreak of the first Balkan war, the Albanian nationalists reaffirmed the centrality of ethnicity to Albanian nationalism, and used both diplomatic and military force to back up their claims. It was observed that the threat posed by the Balkan League drew the Albanian Christians and Muslims closer together, in an effort to prevent partition.[83] There was considerable confusion and disagreement amongst the Albanian nationalists concerning the most appropriate course of action necessary to achieve this. There was still no universally recognised authority strong enough to direct such an intricate policy, and to override independent local action.[84]

On the military side, the most significant initiative resulted from a meeting of a number of leading nationalists in Uskub, on 14 October 1912. A policy of neutrality seemed desirable, because the Albanians hoped that a 'distinctive policy' would establish their 'racial individuality', but this 'distinctive policy' was not advocated or pursued. As Skendi has shown, the Albanians decided to pursue a policy that was distinctive not in itself, but in its motivation. It was decided that they would fight on the side of the Ottoman Empire, but would fight for themselves, not for the Porte. They considered this the only way in which they could successfully defend their territory and prevent the partition of 'ethnic Albania' (the four *vilayets*). In October 1912, the Albanians had the inherent advantage of the possession of this territory, which they believed that they could maintain only through war. Their declaration was presented to the Porte and the great powers on 16 October 1912.[85] It had still proven impossible to achieve a single unified 'Albanian' policy: for instance, many Kosovan Albanians, under Boletin, fought with the Serbs in Kosovo, whilst the Catholic Malissori tribesmen, after assurances from King Nikita that he had no designs on Albanian territory, and was solely determined to free his borders of Ottoman Turks, fought with Montenegrin forces.[86] The Porte responded by trying to exploit this co-operation, in the hope of inciting religious fanaticism amongst the Muslim populace. In response, the Uskub meeting appointed a delegation to detach the Catholic tribesmen from the Montenegrins, but such action proved unnecessary. The Malissori felt like pawns rather than allies and quickly abandoned the conflict and returned to their mountain homes. Most Albanian patriots pursuing other tactics soon arrived at similar conclusions regarding the duplicity of the Greeks and Slavs, and agreed that the League states were more dangerous to Albanian aspirations than their Ottoman predecessors. Consequently, even those Albanians initially willing to work with the League soon came to resist its approaches.[87]

Albanian fears were quickly realised when the League secured a series of sweeping victories. Despite ending the Italo-Turkish war, in order to concentrate on fighting in the Balkans, the Porte had proven unable to send troops from Tripoli, because of the Greek blockade. This resulted in only 320,000 Ottoman troops facing a combined League force of 700,000.[88] The Ottomans sued for peace, and at the beginning of December 1912 an armistice was signed. The League had fulfilled all its ambitions, and surpassed many of them. The British Ambassador in Vienna, Sir Fairfax Cartwright, wrote of the League's outstanding success: 'Tomorrow she will want to annex Bosnia Herzegovina.'[89] When the armistice was signed, the League occupied all Ottoman territory in Europe, except for the four cities of Constantinople, Adrianople, Scutari and Janina. The last two were held by 'Albanian' forces and were claimed by the Albanians as part of Albania.

Albanian diplomatic initiatives, above all the efforts to gain great-power support, proved more significant than their valiant military efforts. As a smaller and weaker nationality in an ethnically contested zone, these military efforts needed the support of the bigger and stronger great powers, in order to increase the strength of the small nationality diplomatically, and possibly militarily too, relative to the League states. With the start of the war, and above all with the rapid success of the League, Ismail Kemal had intensified his efforts to secure great-power support for the Albanian national movement. To this end, on 5 November 1912, he helped organise a meeting of the large Albanian colony in Bucharest, at which it was decided to establish an executive committee that would become responsible for governing their country. It was decided to send a commission to Europe to advocate the Albanian national cause. However, even this meeting fell short of specifying whether Albania would be autonomous or independent, because any such decision depended upon future developments, and upon the stance adopted by the great powers' representatives.[90] The Albanian representatives seemed unwilling to take the lead in their own national movement, and were instead willing to defer responsibility to the great powers, in accordance with their position in the concert system. They did this because they genuinely believed that the great powers would act honestly, both in the Albanian interest and on the merits of the case. They naively believed, therefore, that the powers would automatically support Albanian ethnic nationalism as the Albanian patriots had envisaged it, and would make the best choice for the Albanian people. Such an attitude is indicative of Paskal Milo's comments about the weaknesses of the Albanian political class in this period, and in particular their inexperience in external relations with the great powers.[91] It took some time for most Albanian representatives to realise that the interests and aspirations of the two groups, even the so-called disinterested powers, were not necessarily the same as their own.

However, Ismail Kemal succeeded in securing approval, from this section of the diaspora, of the importance of great-power support for Albania's future. He then proceeded to Vienna to plead his people's case. Disappointingly for Ismail, the Foreign Ministry in Vienna limited itself to no more than generalities, but in Budapest Ismail was received much more warmly, by Count Leopold Berchtold, the Austrian Foreign Minister. Ismail Kemal stated that the Albanians were determined to maintain the integrity of their country, and that, along with other Albanian chieftains, he intended to produce a memorandum of aspirations to be sent to the great powers. Ismail Kemal later wrote that Berchtold approved of his views relating to the Albanian national question.[92] By the time Ismail Kemal arrived in Valona, on 26 November 1912, to take part in a national convention along with eighty-three delegates from across Albania, there had been a dramatic shift in Albanian nationalism in favour of a policy for independence. The convention opened two days later, with Ismail presiding. His proposals for the proclamation of an independent Albania, as the 'only way for the salvation for the Albanians', were all enthusiastically accepted: they were the election of a senate to control and aid the government, the formation of a commission to be sent to the great-power capitals to defend Albanian rights and a provisional government under Ismail Kemal's presidency. The delegates hoisted the flag of Skanderbeg, and designated it the 'national' flag.[93]

Before the first Balkan war, such a step would probably have been unnecessary and it was certainly desired by only a small minority of nationalists, primarily those living abroad, who had experienced more liberal and democratic institutions at first hand. The war had showed that the Albanians needed to seek a viable alternative to Ottoman protection, if a distinct and separate Albanian entity and identity were to survive. They opted for independence, but this meant, significantly, independence under the protection of the great powers. Despite their considerable and valiant resistance and resilience, it was obvious that they would be unable to withstand their larger, expansionist and predatory neighbours indefinitely. It seems that this recognition was the crucial factor that enabled Ismail Kemal to convince the national convention to decide, finally, on independence, rather than the earlier, albeit still recent, goal of autonomy within the Ottoman Empire.

GREAT POWER RESPONSES

Meanwhile, the great powers had also responded to League activities and the increase in Albanian nationalist activity, albeit somewhat slowly. On 8 October 1912, the day that the war started, Russia and Austria-Hungary, the two flanking Balkan powers, and those with the most extensive interests in the region, issued a statement that the League must not overturn the Berlin Treaty, and that the war must not result in any territorial changes. Reiterating Article Three, they urged the Porte to undertake reform of the administration of Turkey-in-Europe, in the interests of the people living there. This stance was intended to resolve the claims of the Ottoman Empire's Christian subjects. The great powers understood that this would not infringe upon the Empire's territorial integrity. Events had moved too quickly, and the declaration arrived too late to preserve the *status quo*.[94] The alternative French idea of a '*protocle de désintéressement*' was rejected because the Austrian, Russian and Italian governments were not prepared to accept a *carte blanche* change to Balkan frontiers in an area where they had paramount interests at stake. Above all, the Ballhausplatz feared Serbian pretensions to an Adriatic outlet there, and Sergei Sazonov, the Russian Foreign Minister, was anxious about further joint action with the Austrians alone.[95] The powers agreed that the map of the Balkans, which the great powers had constructed at the Congress of Berlin, could be redrawn, but that the League would be permitted to do this themselves only in areas where the great powers had no pre-eminent interests. The Berlin Congress had established the principle that all future settlements must protect the rights of small nations and promote self-determination, but only to the extent that they did not contravene or interfere with great-power interests or the balance of power, as was the case in the Albanian littoral. Additionally, there were fears that the war, even if localised, might spread to Ottoman territory in Asia Minor, and result in the great powers being drawn into a scramble for Ottoman territory there, which British officials were especially anxious to avoid. Grey also wished to avoid exerting too much pressure on the new liberal government in Constantinople.[96] The great-power states therefore took control of consideration of the Albanian question. In the next twelve months, the role played by Albanian representatives and those of the other small states would be much reduced.

In reality, great-power involvement, especially by the Russians, had taken place much earlier, whilst not keeping French and British colleagues informed. It appears Sazonov played the role of power broker, and was far from stabilising or balancing the Balkan system.[97] He had intended to use the rapprochement of the Balkan states to form a bloc that could be used to counter-balance the Ottoman Empire and to neutralise Austrian pretensions, following the annexation of Bosnia-Herzegovina (1908-09). This would strengthen Russia's position in the region, especially its designs on Constantinople, the Dardanelles Straits and a warm seaport in Europe, which its Entente partners (Britain and France) still refused to recognise.[98] Sazonov claimed that he intended the alliance system to be defensive. He was concerned lest the conflict between the Porte and the Balkan states could not be localised, and that Austria might then be drawn in: the very scenario that occurred over Austrian interests in the Albanian question. Still smarting from the disaster against the smaller Japanese state (1904-05), and uneasy about the solidarity of the Entente, Sazonov did not feel sufficiently confident about Russian prospects in a major confrontation with the Austrians.[99] Sazonov does not seem to have taken into account the alternative priorities and agendas of either Russian officials or the Balkan governments, neither of which could be relied upon to be subservient to official Russian designs.[100] However, it can be questioned whether Sazonov's motives were as 'defensive' as he claimed at the time, and they seemed more designed to temporarily appease the other great powers.[101] As one British official observed, the Russians were unlikely to stand 'idly by' and let Austrian forces 'crush' their Slav protégés.[102] The policy of a great power can therefore be seen to be modified, even determined, by the actions and policies of smaller states, even when there is a disparity between them. Such a disparity might even make the smaller state stronger, if it was encouraged to be more assertive in its own national interests, rather than looking to the great power for guidance. In proclaiming independence, the Albanians likewise 'forced the hand' of the Austrians. The great power then either needed to support them, or to relinquish its great-power ambitions.

Austrian interests were to be decisive for the Albanian question. With the Balkan League besieging 'Albanian' territory on all fronts, the Albanian nationalists determined that the fate of the Albanian question depended upon the great powers. On 21 November 1912, representatives from the Albanian colony in Constantinople had presented a petition, on behalf of all Albanians, Muslim, Orthodox and Catholic, to the 'Great Powers to intervene and preserve the territorial status quo of Turkey-in-Europe as far as it affected the position of Albania'.[103] This eventually provided the necessary excuse for the great powers to intervene, although the indications were that such action would have been taken anyway. The extensive gains by the Balkan League had made it clear that the great powers would be unable to maintain the *status quo*, but the impact of these acquisitions on great-power interests was too great to be ignored. Without this intervention, an independent or even autonomous Albania could not have been created, for it would have been only a matter of time before the Albanian forces succumbed to the League's onslaught. Thanks largely to Austrian efforts, based mainly on self-interest, the Albanian appeal to have the matter settled by the European great-power concert was successful. Cartwright wrote that:

> the Albanians were determined to maintain their country. They would fight to the bitter end rather than allow their country to be dismembered. If Servia is allowed to absorb a large portion of Northern Albania it will be followed by a continual state of unrest and insurrection until Austria and Italy are forced to intervene.[104]

The other great powers agreed to settle the Albanian question in concert between themselves, in order to prevent Austrian military action, which would also have resulted in Russian involvement, to protect its Slav protégés and its own Balkan interests. The prime mover in great-power thinking was concern for their respective great-power interests, and the desire to maintain the balance of power in the Balkans and the Adriatic, rather than any recognition of or support for Albanian national sentiment. Nevertheless, Albanian representatives had been influential in aligning the Albanian national question with these great-power interests, and thereby defeating the aspirations of the Balkan League states, which, although small themselves, were stronger than the Albanians, especially when acting collectively.

On 16 December 1912, representatives from the League, the Ottoman Empire and Romania, along with an Albanian delegation, met at St. James' Palace in London to discuss peace terms. Fighting continued sporadically in the Balkans and the negotiations were slow and protracted, but eventually, under much great-power pressure, the Treaty of London was signed (30 May 1913). This left many parties dissatisfied, and helped precipitate the second Balkan war, at the centre of which was a Greco-Serbian partnership, supported by Montenegro, Romania and the Ottoman Empire, against Bulgaria. The Treaty of Bucharest (10 August 1913) concluded the war and produced a number of revisions—mostly to the detriment of the Bulgarians, and none affecting the Albanian question, which remained outside the remit of the small states. The ambitions of the Christian Balkan nation states had resulted in two major wars, Serbia had doubled in geographical size and its population had increased by fifty percent.[105]

Conclusions

The success of the Albanians in their calls for autonomy had been a major consideration in the formation of the Balkan League, especially the League's decision to engage in war against the Ottoman Empire. The neighbouring Balkan states feared that, if the Albanians were successful in achieving their national programme, they would settle down and support the Ottoman regime. This would help stabilise the balance of power in the region, the opposite of what the Christian small states sought to secure their own national aspirations. More importantly, any Albanian success would prevent the Balkan League from intervening and claiming this territory for themselves. As Joseph Swire argued as early as 1929, the League states therefore desired to act to prevent the settlement of the Albanian problem, and to deny the possibility of concessions spreading to other parts of the

Empire, especially Macedonia.[106]

In turn, the threat posed by the Balkan League to Albanian national and local interests had finally managed to weld together the disparate groupings. Ismail Kemal and Hasan Prishtina led the movement to gain great-power support for the Albanian national cause, especially amongst the Austrians. The first Balkan war was the factor that finally pushed the Albanians to affirm the need for independence, and to work together, irrespective of their other differences. Besides the external threats that advanced the national movement, the other key unifier was the Albanian spoken language, which was the one common bond between the various groups. That they spoke Albanian was what made them different to the Slavs, Greeks, Turks and other ethnic groups in the region, and this was the basis upon which they determined to base the independent state they proclaimed. To achieve this, they needed great-power support to defeat the ambitions of the Orthodox Christian small states, who already held an established, albeit low-level, position in the international system, had a great-power patron and were much stronger than they were. Cartwright was convinced that the activities of the Balkan League, and to an important but lesser extent those of the Young Turks before, did more to advance the Albanian national movement than the previous thirty years of cultural initiatives. As he maintained up to the outbreak of the first Balkan war, he could still write that, if the Young Turks changed their policies towards the Albanians, 'the Albanians might become its staunchest supporters… Their loyalty is unquestioned; they demand only the right to develop within the limits of the Ottoman Empire.'[107]

Chapter 2

Initial Independence:
great-power interests and Albanian boundaries during the Balkan wars and London conferences

The Ambassadors' Conference in London (1912-13) was initially convened by the great powers, in an attempt to impose a settlement on the belligerents of the first Balkan war, and to prevent the conflict from escalating into a general European war. As part of this effort, the ambassadors had responsibility for determining whether Albania would be independent, and for delimiting Albanian boundaries. They decided to base their decisions on ethnography, which, in line with concurrent views on ethnicity corresponding to nationality, for them meant language, and specifically the mother tongue of the population or the language spoken within the family.[108] Any territory where Albanian was the majority spoken language was supposed to become part of a new Albanian state. However, the great powers were not entirely committed to these 'ethnic' objectives. They compromised them in the light of their own political interests, and espoused ethnographical arguments only when these supported or reinforced their own strategic ones.

Language Nationalism and Ethnic Boundaries

The Ambassadors' Conference consisted of representatives of what were then the six European great powers: Russia, France and Britain, the so-called Triple Entente, on the one hand, and Germany,

Austria-Hungary and Italy (the Triple Alliance or Triplice), on the other. It declared that Albanian boundaries would be based on scientific principles or ethnography. In the late nineteenth and early twentieth century, European ethnographers worked for a systematic representation of peoples and their codification, according to their interpretations of 'race' and ethnicity. This began with the cartographic mapping of ethnic and 'racial' groups and characteristics, although maps showed huge variations.[109] With the advance of nationalism in eastern Europe, there was a need to trace such boundaries on the ground and on maps. Fredrik Barth and Katherine Verdery have considered the complex relationships between ethnicity, nationalism, nation-state formation and borders.[110] However, there are still few studies of the practicalities of defining ethnic boundaries in political terms. Boundary delimitation in the era before World War One was closely linked to these contemporary concerns for 'ethnic frontiers'. In 1913, the problem was how to define the 'nation' or a nationality.[111] The western powers tended to follow the western liberal/civic tradition, which did not distinguish between the concept of a person as a member of a 'racial' group and as a citizen of a state.[112] However they realised that such a conception was never going to be practical in eastern Europe, given the ethnic mix there. Thus by 1913 the great power representatives had adopted a German, or ethnic primordial, view of national determination, based on factors such as 'race', language, culture, religion, historical allegiance and geography. For the ambassadors in London in 1913, language became the favoured principle. There appears to have been a tacit assumption that the speakers of each language constituted a 'race' and community, and therefore had the right to become a nation, separate from other communities or 'races'. The great power representatives thought that language was an objective criterion, and one that would be relatively easy to determine. In south-eastern Europe, language was increasingly considered a self-evident marker. Seemingly unrelated languages (Albanian, Greek, Romanian and Slavonic languages) were viewed as clear cultural or ethnic boundaries that could be mapped to determine where the political frontiers should be.[113] Albanian was recognised as an Indo-European language but, like Greek and Armenian, as one that formed its own branch and had no close links to any other. This view of language was especially important for the Albanians because of their religious and cultural divisions.

Great Power Interests and Objectives

The great powers, particularly Austria and Italy, strongly resisted such a large scale alteration of Balkan frontiers, as the Balkan victories called for, especially because it would advantage Russia's Slav protégés. Yet considering the scale of the League's victory, changes to the frontiers were unavoidable. Therefore it was decided that the London ambassadors of the great powers would meet to discuss questions of interest: Serbian access to the Adriatic, Albanian independence, Albanian frontiers and the Aegean islands. The prime position of a future Albanian state, situated on the eastern Adriatic littoral, especially at Valona and the Otranto Straits (between Corfu and the eastern Adriatic coast, considered equivalent to Gibraltar for the Mediterranean), and less than sixty miles from the Italian coast, made Albania a vested Austro-Italian interest. Neither state wanted a Russian satellite entrenched on the eastern Adriatic, a view with which the British concurred. The other great powers agreed to an ambassadorial conference in order to avoid a probable war between themselves. They hoped that the meeting would speed up geopolitical discussions by minimising formality, misunderstandings and other complications. None of the representatives had any particular Albanian expertise. London was chosen because of objections to the other capitals. Throughout the Conference all the representatives remained in close contact with their respective foreign ministries, which largely directed the deliberations. By so doing, the powers had decided to resurrect the 'concert of Europe', that traditional nineteenth-century means of diplomacy whereby representatives of each power met in one country to discuss and reach agreement on disputes, most notably in the 1815 (Vienna) and 1878 (Berlin) Congresses. Concert diplomacy had the advantage of enabling negotiations to be conducted more quickly, by reducing the inevitable complications, misunderstandings and delays that arose in carrying out negotiations between capitals, particularly when dealing with a situation that might escalate at any moment.[114]

Of all the great powers, Austria-Hungary had most interests at stake at the Conference and in the Albanian question. This explains why the Ballhausplatz had taken the most active interest during the first Balkan war, had been the first power to realise that the *status quo* could not be maintained and had been so instrumental in establishing the Conference in the first place. Austria was the traditional protector of the minority Catholic population in the Balkans, particularly in northern Albania, and could consequently claim to be genuinely acting in the interests of nationality and ethnicity, which had been established as the basis for future settlements in 1878.[115] National and moralist arguments were used only when it suited Austrian interests to do so. Strategic and economic concerns were more important. Economically, Austria was the largest exporter and importer to and from the western Balkans. Strategically, the Ballhausplatz advocated a small Albanian state because it was more interested in the northern coastal regions (Scutari) than in inland Kosovo or the southern areas conflicting with Greek ambitions. A smaller Albania could more easily be made dependent upon Austria.[116]

More significantly, the Habsburg Empire, like the Ottoman Empire, was a huge polyglot empire, encompassing at least eleven different nationalities. Austrian officials feared that the Ottoman fallout would spread to its territory, and incite the Serbs there to unite with 'mother Serbia' to form 'Greater Serbia'. Consequently, Austrian policy attempted to control the reallocation of Balkan territory, and to prevent the spread of Serbian or Slav nationalism into Austrian territory. As long as Serbia remained landlocked, this task was all the easier, because a substantial proportion of its trade had no alternative but to pass though Austrian-controlled territory. Austria's key objective was to prevent Serbian access to the Adriatic, hence the formal annexation of Bosnia and Herzegovina (1908-09), and its pre-occupation with opposing Serbian claims to northern Albania. A Serbian Adriatic outlet would endanger not only Austria's economic and commercial interests but also its strategic ones: the Adriatic was Austria's only access to the Mediterranean. The Austrians already had to share the Adriatic with Italy but they did not want to share it with a third power that, through control of the Otranto Straits, would have the potential to close the Adriatic to Austrian vessels, both commercial and military. This was particularly worrying in the event that a Serbian port became a Russian naval base.[117] Therefore, by October 1912, the Ballhausplatz had resolved to prevent either a small state or a great power obtaining a foothold on the eastern side of the Adriatic. To further this policy, Austrian officials began calling for the creation of an independent Albanian state.

At the end of 1912, the Ballhausplatz took the decision to achieve its objectives through diplomacy and not war. This was for several reasons. The Austrians were not confident that they would secure Italian support, but they were convinced that the Russians would secure French assistance. (This very situation materialised in July 1914.) Even more worryingly, the Ballhausplatz was not assured of German support. When Theobold von Bethman-Hollweg, the German Chancellor, had announced the re-signing of the Triple Alliance Treaty (1912), he had declared that Germany must leave it to its Austrian ally to realise its Balkan aspirations alone. A further complication in this dynamic was that the Dual Monarchy had to take into account both Austrian and Hungarian sentiment: the former favoured conciliation, whilst the latter favoured force to deal with this 'Slav problem'.[118] The Austrian great power therefore supported Albanian nationalism because the Ballhausplatz viewed it as a counterweight to the other Balkan small state nationalisms, especially the Slavs. The Ballhausplatz was prepared to work within the concert system because it needed the support of other great powers to defeat the threat posed to Austrian interests by the Balkan League small states.

Italy was the only other directly interested power. The Consulta, the Italian Foreign Ministry, had for some years been attempting to expand into the Balkans, particularly economically and culturally. The Italian Foreign Minister, Marquis Antonio di San Giuliano, had first-hand knowledge of Albania, and had written a book on the area.[119] After Austria, Italy was the principal importer and exporter in Albania, and accounted for twenty-five percent of goods leaving Scutari and thirty percent from southern Albania. The *Servizi Maritime* carried Albanian mail, the Puglia Line served northern Albanian ports, there were Italian financial houses in Durazzo and Valona, and in the latter the *Società Commerciale d'Oriente* ranked as the official bank. There was a large Albanian diaspora in Italy, especially in Sicily, and a Chair of Albanian had been established at Naples University. In 1910, there were seven Albanian communes in Sicily (50,000 people), and seventy-two in mainland Italy (152,000).[120] Italians had been instrumental in founding schools and missions in Albania. Although Italian expansion had focused predominantly upon southern Albania, it inevitably brought about some conflict with the Austrians, especially regarding control of the Otranto Straits.[121] As early as 1906, Brailsford had accurately predicted that this Austro-Italian rivalry was so great that either power would go to war to prevent the other acquiring so dangerous an advantage as the possession of the Albanian coast:

> One hopes that this rivalry may mean checkmate to the ambitions of both powers... Autonomy has become a practical policy because the rivalries of the two great powers which aspire to its possession are acute and incompatible.[122]

This was particularly true for Italy, the weaker of the two powers. For the Italians, the old dictum held true: only two conditions between Italy and Austria were possible - alliance or war.[123] At this point the Consulta chose alliance. Italy had only just completed a difficult war against the Ottoman Empire in Tripoli, and did not desire to become embroiled in another major conflict so soon afterwards, especially with Austria, whom the Italians considered likely to gain German support. Even a conflict in which Italy fought alongside Austria, was likely to be to Austria's advantage and Italy's detriment. Albania was an area on which Italy and Austria could agree: they had signed an agreement regarding Albania in 1901, reaffirmed it in 1909 and, in 1912, incorporated it into the Triplice.[124] Through these agreements, the Consulta sought to prevent another power acquiring control of the Albanian littoral on the eastern side of the Adriatic, less than forty miles from the Italian coast at the narrowest point. Perhaps, in the future, the ultimate goal—Albanian territory divided into Austrian and Italian spheres—might be achieved, but in the meantime the Consulta was prepared to work with the Austrians for the creation of an independent Albania that touched the Adriatic. This was a much better option than it becoming Slav, Greek or Austrian. In 1912-13, the divergent interests of Austria and Italy could be ignored in the short term in order to oppose the Hellenic and Slav threat, which at that moment appeared more pressing.[125]

The German government was prepared to follow the line taken by its alliance partners, although with the further complication that it would then need to resolve any disagreements between Austria and Italy. Throughout the Conference, the Wilhelmstrasse's main priority was to ensure that the divergent interests of its alliance partners were minimised, and that the Triplice remained intact. The latter was especially important because of press reports encouraging the Italian government to move toward the Entente, and the extensive Slav (and therefore Russian) gains made in the Balkan wars.[126] Herr Alfred Kiderlen-Wächter and, later, his replacement as Foreign Minister, Gottlieb von Jagow (on 31 December 1912, following Kiderlen's death), were prepared to work with Grey, especially in the earliest stages of the concert, to help facilitate compromise. Officials were particularly keen to follow a peaceful course following the Grey-Lichnowsky exchanges of 3-4 December 1912, in which Grey had stated that Britain would support Russia in a military confrontation. The Wilhelmstrasse had responded with support for Austria. This resulted in the infamous war council meeting of 8 December 1912, at which the German general staff concluded that two more years were needed before they would be ready for war.[127]

Of the three Entente powers, Russian interests were the most directly affected by the questions under discussion. Russian policy consistently had the objective of protecting and promoting the interests of fellow Slav nations in the Balkans, especially Serbia and, in so doing, furthering Russia's stature and interests and diminishing that of its Austrian rival.[128] The Bosnian annexation crisis had highlighted just how dangerous Austrian pretensions to hegemony in the Balkans could be. Sazonov sought to use Russia's protégés to counter this, hence Russia's patronage of the Balkan League. In the Ambassadors' Conference, this meant promoting Serbian interests. Sazonov consequently argued that the victorious Balkan states should be able to keep the spoils of their victories, and that this should outweigh any national sentiments. Sazonov was under immense pressure, both publicly and politically, to forward the 'pan-Slavist' ideal, but he found that in reality his policy was compromised, for two reasons. Sazonov feared that if Russia held out for concessions for Serbia in northern Albania, and especially the Adriatic outlet, this might push Austria and Italy closer together, which he wished to avoid lest it lead to even greater Balkan problems. Secondly, he was apprehensive about the position of Britain. He felt secure of French support through the 1894 Franco-Russian Alliance. With Britain, despite Triplice fears about the Entente growing closer together, Sazonov considered

Russia had 'no tie of any kind', because the Entente related solely to their empires and colonies, and made no mention of Europe. Additionally, Russian policy underwent considerable revision during the period of the Conference. The expansion of Russia's protégés, both in territory and population, meant that they were not as insecure as they had been during the Bosnian crisis, and not so dependent upon Russia support.[129] Consequently, Sazonov felt able to communicate to Belgrade that he would be unable to offer any active opposition to the creation of an Albanian state, despite this being contrary to Serbian interests[130] and long-term Russian ones.

French actions, despite there being no real threat to France, appeared even more pro-Slav than Russian ones, and explain further why there were no Russian fears of French opposition. Grey had accurately surmised that the French Ambassador to London, Paul Cambon, was not altogether happy with Grey's conduct, and was fearful that it might lead to a loss of Russian prestige, that it might impact unfavourably on the Triple Entente, and that Grey should have shown more partisanship.[131] The French were prepared to follow the lead taken by Russia in negotiations. On some questions, most specifically in southern Albania, where Russian interests were not as great and because of French interest in Greece, the French took the lead. The French attitude was summed up in a communication from the ardent pan-Slavist Count Nicholas Hartwig, the Russian Ambassador in Belgrade (1909-14), to Sazonov:

> France, in complete agreement with Russia, is ready to aid Serbia in realising her national aspirations. Paris…is in deep sympathy with the Serbo-Bulgarian Alliance and sees in it a strong barrier against Austro-German encroachment.[132]

Throughout the Ambassadorial Conference, and afterwards, Grey was frequently criticised by his Entente partners for not supporting them more. The Russians, in particular, were infuriated by their apparent inability to interest Grey in Serbian claims. Grey asserted that he felt Count Alexander Benckendorff, the Russian Ambassador, was satisfied with his policy as it was intended to get fair terms and secure peace, was not indifferent to Russian friendship and did not intend to enact a rapprochement with the central powers. In reality,

Grey's actions were designed to pursue four key British objectives. Only on the surface did Grey appear to pursue a neutral line. Grey was motivated, firstly, by the desire to ensure a European peace, and for Grey this meant maintaining the balance of power. He wanted policies that Russia and Austria could agree upon, regardless of the technicalities, or merits, of the case.[133] Equally important, although in some respects contradictory, was the necessity to maintain and preserve the Entente. Whitehall had no direct interests in Albania. If able to pursue an independent policy, it would apparently have favoured the establishment of an independent Albania, as long as good government could be assured. This was not possible because Russian and French opinion had to be considered. Despite their appearance of being non-committal and of pursuing a neutral policy, Grey and Richard Haldane, the War Minister, believed it was really necessary to commit Britain to the Entente.[134] The fear was not so much that war would break out, but that Russia might leave the Entente and join the central powers, thus resurrecting the *Dreikaiserbund* (Three Emperors' Alliance) of Russia, Germany and Austria. Whitehall did not yet consider Britain ready for war. Hostilities needed to be avoided, or at least postponed.[135] British policy was also determined by a third further complicating factor: British actions in Albania, a predominantly Muslim country, were perceived as likely to have an impact on Muslims elsewhere in the British Empire, especially India, where Britain was trying to enlist Muslim help against disparate Hindu elements. Sazonov, in particular, cited this as the prime reason why he had failed to secure Grey's support for his plans to divide Albanian territory between Greece and Serbia.[136] In one further important respect, British interests were contrary to Russian. Whitehall was concerned lest the Serbian Adriatic outlet should in time become a warm-water Russian naval port, potentially endangering British naval supremacy, as the southern Russian fleet would then no longer be confined to the Black Sea. Grey was equally perturbed by the prospect of Italy gaining permanent possession of islands in the Aegean, thus endangering British interests in the eastern Mediterranean and the Suez route. Events contrived to allow Grey to follow this policy. Once the concession of the Albanian state had been made and the urgency of the situation had been diffused, none of the countries wanted war. After the Agadir Crisis

(1911), the German government was prepared to work to moderate Austrian opinion, the Russians did not want another humiliation after Japan (1904-05) and Bosnia-Herzegovina (1908-09) and the French did not want trouble over a Balkan dispute that was not their concern. Therefore Grey's role of mediator became consistent with maintenance of the Entente. Consequently, when a concession was made, it was not used as a diplomatic 'score' but as a reason for urging the other side towards moderation and concession. Grey felt that he had secured the confidence of all the ambassadors, and even secured a strong personal relationship between himself and Sazonov, because the other states did not feel that he was trying to increase the prestige of British diplomacy.[137] In reality, Grey was not as disinterested as it first appeared, but rather worked consistently to safeguard British interests, especially the preservation of the Entente, British naval power and the balance of power.

Ambassadors' Conference (1912-13)

On 17 December 1912, with Grey in the chair, the first meeting of the Ambassadorial Conference took place, although much important work also occurred during informal discussions. The other powers were represented by their ambassadors in London: Count Alexander Benckendorff for Russia, Paul Cambon for France, Count Albert von Mensdorff for Austria, Prince Karl Marx Lichnowsky for Germany and Count Guglielmo Imperiali for Italy. They met formally sixty-six times, with the final meeting on 11 August 1913. The Conference was never officially closed. As Grey later commented, they just stopped meeting, having adjourned for the summer break. They did not reconvene because the urgent necessities that had first brought them together were no longer threatening European peace. Many differences were left unsettled, but the relations between the great powers had been deprived of those dangerous elements that had dominated late 1912.[138]

As early as the first meeting, an independent Albania was recognised as a new political entity, but, as Richard Crampton argued, the principle had never really been in doubt.[139] Although the Albanians had declared independence, local events had only a limited impact on the great power discussions. That the powers were able to achieve consensus on this issue was due largely to the groundwork that had been laid in preliminary discussions. The Ballhausplatz had been insistent that Albania should be created, and when the German and British governments also supported this course, the Russians acquiesced, not feeling the issue important enough to go to war over. As Benckendorff wrote to Sazonov in early November 1912, 'the standpoint of the "Balkans for the Balkan peoples" will surely also be applied to the Albanians'. As early as 1897 the Austrian government had been assured of Russian support for an independent Albania.[140] By agreeing to Albanian independence, and diminishing its championship of Serbian and Montenegrin claims, Russian officials hoped to protect their geo-political position by preventing greater Austro-Italian co-operation. Therefore Hartwig was instructed to reduce Serbian enthusiasm for gains in northern Albania.[141] There was an acknowledgment, as Mensdorff argued, that unless Albania was made 'autonomous and "viable": that is to say large enough to have a separate existence' it would easily succumb to its neighbour states. However, the ambassadors agreed that Albania was not to be fully independent but autonomous, under the sovereignty or suzerainty (still to be decided) of the Sultan, and the powers would commit themselves to a neutral guarantee. These decisions were later revised to make Albania a fully independent state, with the Sultan being replaced by a separate prince.[142]

At the first meeting, it was agreed that Serbia would be denied access to Adriatic territory in northern Albania, despite this being one of Belgrade's major motivations. Instead Serbia would have access via rail links to a neutralised port, although the port was left unspecified, as the Austrians had ruled out Grey's suggestions of San Giovanni de Medua, or the decision being left to a commission.[143] From Grey's perspective, he had facilitated a satisfactory compromise and one that preserved Britain's paramount interests, above all naval ones. The same day he naively wrote to Cartwright that Serbian difficulties regarding an Adriatic outlet have 'completely disappeared'.[144] The solution satisfied nobody except Grey. The Austrians were dissatisfied that Serbia should have any access at all, although the grave threat of Russian use of the port had been removed, whilst Grey was forced to placate Sazonov by assuring him that, in future discussions regarding the northern Albanian boundary, Austria must yield.[145] This decision also produced severe delays in the ensuing conference proceedings, as the Russians persistently rejected compromises in other areas. From 1913 onwards the Serbs would also make a number of efforts to secure the port that had been denied them.

The issue of Albanian boundaries proved far more controversial from the outset, despite proclamations that they would be based on ethnography. At the first meeting, it was agreed that Albania would share borders with Montenegro in the north and Greece in the south, but it was not decided whether to leave the frontiers of Greece and Montenegro unchanged.[146] Three days later, Benckendorff and Mensdorff each introduced their boundary proposals, which were significantly different (Appendix B). Mensdorff proposed an Albania based, he claimed, on ethnographical lines. However, the suggested territory was considerably smaller than the 'ethnographic' state declared by the Albanians. Benckendorff, on the other hand, proposed only a truncated coastal strip to form a central Muslim Albania. He insisted that the territory north and east of the Skumbi River was predominantly Slav (Serb and Montenegrin) and that south of the river was Greek.[147] Clear power-political divisions emerged. Mensdorff, supported by his German and Italian colleagues, pursued Vienna's interests by advocating a pro-Albanian case, whilst Benckendorff, supported by his French associate, promoted the interests of Serbia and Montenegro. Grey was criticised by his Franco-Russian colleagues for never heeding their requests to co-ordinate Entente demands. For the most part, he performed his allotted role as mediator.[148]

Northern and North-eastern Boundary

The town of Scutari was the most contentious issue on the northern boundary. Mensdorff claimed it for Albania for economic reasons, arguing that it was the major market town, and crucial to the livelihood of farmers in northern Albania. Ethnically, he claimed, Scutari was predominantly Catholic in religion and Albanian in spoken language and sentiment, and he cited in support the staunch defence of the city by Albanian forces (admittedly under Ottoman auspices) against Montenegrin assaults.[149] Benckendorff countered that Russia had already compromised in other areas, most notably in agreeing to deny Serbian Adriatic access. He claimed Scutari for Montenegro for economic but, especially, historical reasons: Scutari had been the centre of the Montenegrin kingdom in the fourteenth and fifteenth centuries.[150] Little progress was made until 22 January 1913. Grey, hoping to prevent a breach, attempted to facilitate a compromise by proposing to link Scutari with the other major northern towns of Ipek, Prizrend and Djakova.[151]

Discussions remained exceedingly tense, but Berchtold, directing Austrian policy from Vienna, encouraged Mensdorff to moderate their position, as it seemed only a matter of time before the Montenegrin forces would enter Scutari. Throughout January and February 1913, Mensdorff offered the Kosovan plain, the Visoki Decani Orthodox monastery (despite claiming it was in a predominantly Muslim and Albanian speaking area), and a procession of northern towns, most notably Ipek, Dibra, and Prizrend, the place where Albanian nationalism had first emerged in 1878 (Prizrend League), in exchange for Scutari becoming Albanian. This was despite Berchtold's earlier assertions that no town with an Albanian-speaking majority would be excluded, and despite Vienna's long-term objective of keeping the Serbs and Montenegrins without a coterminous frontier in the *sanjak* of Novi Bazar.[152] Serbian officials consistently opposed Austrian claims that Djakova and other places were 'Albanian', and claimed that the Albanians were 'really' Serbs by origin, and had only converted to Islam for Ottoman protection (Arnautaši thesis).[153] These 'ethnographic' arguments proved unnecessary. The Kosovo decision was a relatively simple one for all ambassadors. Without going to war, the great powers would not be able to remove the Serbian forces in possession of most of the *vilayet*. At this stage, no great power was prepared to risk war with, or on behalf of, Serbia, especially for one of its most treasured gains in 'Old Serbia'.

No agreement was reached because Benckendorff insisted on gaining Djakova for Serbia, which, as the Serbs claimed, was an integral part of 'Old Serbia' because it had been the episcopal see of the famous Bishop Strossmeyer.[154] Eventually, on 21 March 1913, Mensdorff offered Djakova for Scutari. Not only did he consider Djakova essentially Albanian and Catholic, it was also the town in northern Albania where Albanian nationalism was strongest. Berchtold had instructed this changed position, arguing that humanitarian considerations, resulting from the sordid conditions in Scutari, now outweighed any political and ethnographical concerns.

In reality Berchtold had staked his own reputation and position on securing Scutari. He was under considerable domestic, political and public pressure to live up to his commitment to prevent the Slavs from gaining this key town.[155]

The powers may have 'compromised', but Montenegrin King Nikita had other ideas. On 23 April 1913, Montenegrin troops finally managed to secure Scutari, thus threatening to upset the settlement in London. Nikita was persuaded to withdraw his troops with promises of financial assistance and threats of military intervention. Once this crisis was over and the major 'prizes' were determined, the ambassadors agreed to delimit the rest of the northern frontier by appointing a boundary commission consisting of experts from the region. Similar frontier disputes had been settled in much the same way (Eastern Rumelia 1880-1; Greco-Turkish frontier 1897; Bulgaro-Turkish frontier 1913).[156] Grey had initially proposed setting up an international commission to determine the frontier in November 1912. The following months of frustration and anxiety apparently confirmed his belief that such a commission would be the only possible way to settle the boundaries.[157] However, the pre-allocation of towns would inevitably hinder the commission's ability to produce an ethnographic frontier.

Problems materialised before the commission began its work. Berchtold refused to allow the Austrian representative, Colonel Mietzl, to participate unless Scutari was unequivocally committed to Albania. This inadvertently had what Edith Durham, travel writer and later Secretary-Treasurer of the Anglo-Albanian Society, called the 'criminal effect' of giving the Serbs sufficient time to distort ethnography by clearing districts of Albanians to give them a Slav majority.[158] These activities also gave the Ballhausplatz sufficient excuse to intervene. Viennese officials grew increasingly disillusioned with the concert system, and sent an ultimatum (couched in similar language to the more infamous one nine months later) to Belgrade on 18 October 1913, demanding Serbian withdrawal from the disputed areas within eight days, and warning that non-compliance would result in 'necessary measures' to enforce it.[159] This unilateral act unsurprisingly generated much hostility, but none of the other great powers dared support the Serbs, believing that they would risk war with Vienna if they did. Lacking any potential support, Belgrade withdrew its troops from the disputed zone.[160]

Southern Boundary

Meanwhile, contentious conference discussions regarding the southern Albanian frontier had also occurred. The alliances of the great powers determined once more their positions on the disputed points. As with the allocation of the Kosovan plain to Serbia, it had been quickly decided that the Greeks would gain southern Epirus, including the important town of Janina. Discussions therefore centred on whether the Greeks would also gain what they called northern Epirus, or whether this territory would instead become southern Albania. According to the official statistics of the Greek Government (1913), northern Epirus consisted of the former Turkish *kazas* of Koritza, Starovo, Kolonia, Argyrocastro, Khimara, Delvino, Telepeni, Premedi, Pogonio and Philiataes.[161] Imperiali led the Triplice's support for Albanian claims, supposedly because of more extensive Italian cultural and economic relations in southern Albania. Cambon led the representatives of the Entente in support of Greek interests. Cambon was instructed by the Quai d'Orsay (French Foreign Ministry) to do so because of French financial links with Athens and its classical heritage. However, Cambon's diplomacy was also an attempt to curtail Berlin's attempts to exploit the German ancestry of the Greek King Constantine for its own advantage. This in itself complicated the German position, because they did not wish to offend Constantine. Benckendorff was apparently instructed to let Cambon take the lead, because the Russian government had only minimal interest in the non-Slav Greeks, and was keen to avoid a direct confrontation with the Consulta. The ultimate aim was to court Italy away from the Germanic powers.[162]

Discussions started in March 1913. The most crucial disagreements proved to be over the important and strategic towns of Argyrocastro and Koritza, and the forty-mile coastline opposite Corfu that forms the Corfu Straits. Through control of the Corfu Straits it was possible to effectively close the Otranto Straits at the mouth of the Adriatic.[163] Possession of both sides of the Corfu channel would give a great strategic advantage, because of the narrow exits and the good shelter for all classes of vessels of a fleet watching the exit lanes. Cambon argued in favour of handing over territory as far north as

Cape Kefalu (north of the northern-most point of Corfu) to Greece, thus giving Athens possession of both sides of the channel and, therefore, control of the Straits. He asserted that Koritza was a centre of Greek learning and that the educated people of the district were Hellenic in sympathy. However, even contemporary ethnographers sympathetic to Greek claims considered the town Albanian.[164] Cambon also argued that the Orthodox population should go to Greece, as it was unfair to leave them in a majority Muslim state. Again, strategic considerations were far more important. Greek officials felt that difficulties in communications between the territories of southern Epirus and Macedonia, over the Pindus mountains, which Greece had acquired after the Balkan wars, could only be overcome by a road that passed through Koritza. The Greeks claimed Argyrocastro on the basis of supposed ethnic reasons, considering the area Hellenophile, but strategic factors must certainly have been the principal determinants. Argyrocastro town was an important centre commanding the route from Janina to Valona, but, above all, possession of Argyrocastro would effectively shorten the Albanian frontier and give Greece control of the Corfu channel, although such *realpolitik* was not mentioned in the discussions.[165]

The Triplice ambassadors did not accept this. Mensdorff argued that cession to Greece would place Austrian vessels in jeopardy because all the Austrian ports were in the Adriatic.[166] Imperiali and Mensdorff instead proposed drawing the border twelve kilometers south of Santa Quaranta, at Cape Stylos in Phtelia Bay. This would have included Koritza, Argyrocastro, the road from Argyrocastro to Delvino and Santa Quaranta (the port that served Argyrocastro) within Albania.[167] Although Koritza had been an important centre of the Albanian cultural and literary movements in the nineteenth century, and had a number of Albanian schools, neither ambassador cited ethnographic arguments to any large extent. They insisted that the Corfu channel had to remain neutral with the mainland going to Albania, whilst Koritza had to be included in the new state in order to limit the coterminous frontier between Serbia and Greece. This further perpetuated Serbian economic dependence and supported Austrian policy, which considered northern Albania a block to Serbian Adriatic access.[168]

Grey, once again, found himself in the role of mediator. He

proposed delimiting southern Albania by a boundary commission, and compensating Greece for Albanian gains there with acquisitions in the Aegean islands, which were at that point under Italian occupation, following the Italo-Turkish war.[169] This provides an obvious example of how Grey used the Ambassadors' Conference to protect British interests: although he had little interest in the Albanian issue, Grey sought to use it to remove Italian control of the Aegean islands. He feared that the Italian-controlled islands threatened Britain's naval power in the eastern Mediterranean, especially given their proximity to the Dardanelles and the Suez Canal. Imperiali immediately rejected the Aegean part of the proposal, but agreed to the establishment of a commission, albeit with certain provisions designed to safeguard Triplice interests: Koritza, Cape Stylos, and the southern shore of Lake Ochrida were confirmed as parts of Albania.[170] Despite these provisions, the southern commission had far greater scope to produce an ethnographical settlement than the northern commission, because fewer southern disputed areas had been pre-determined.

Albanian Boundary Commissions (1913–14)

The precise details of how the Albanian boundary commissions were constituted and operated remain vague. Each power selected its own delegate. The northern commission consisted exclusively of military officers, whilst both military and civil (consular) officials were members of the southern commission. The delegations that were most interested in the discussion of Albania's southern borders (Austria, Italy and France) each brought two members, but had only one vote. The nature of the commissioners' 'expertise' is questionable. None had an 'ethnographic' background, no information indicates whether any spoke Albanian, but the majority had some experience of service in Balkan, Ottoman or Adriatic territory. For example, on the southern commission, Colonel Goudim-Levkovitch was the Russian Military Attaché at Athens, but Major Thierry, member of the German Staff, had no apparent Balkan experience. Balkan knowledge was not necessarily an advantage or evidence of expertise, as the examples of Constantine Bilinski and Consul N. Labia, the Austrian and Italian delegates on the southern commission, show. Both had previously been consuls at Janina, where they had been subject to much criticism because of their anti-Greek views.[171]

Both commissions seem to have received fairly limited instructions by the Conference. They were to proceed on an ethnographic basis (mother tongue), and were instructed not to accept plebiscites, petitions or other public manifestations as evidence of nationality, probably to prevent interference by interested parties.[172] The southern commissioners added further stipulations to this purpose: delegates should not meet Greek or Albanian deputations, they should not be escorted by any Greek or Albanian officials and the escorts must remain outside any villages examined.[173] The British representatives apparently received very few additional instructions, although the representatives of the more interested powers were probably better equipped. The two British representatives complained they had not received any instructions, apart from the Conference protocols, and that they needed a decent map. It was only after repeated appeals from the commissioners that topographers were sent to aid their work. The commissioners had cited the inadequacies of existing topographical maps, and the ambassadors were not able to agree on an official version.[174] Both commissions ultimately followed a common pattern in their work: interviewing and questioning people in the disputed villages, and then meeting to discuss their findings. The rules of procedure were theirs to decide.[175] The commissioners communicated with their respective capitals by telegram and surface mail, wherever either was available. The remoteness of many of the areas under investigation led to inevitable delays and sometimes complications, as information did not arrive. Colonel Edward Granet, British delegate on the northern commission and former Military Attaché in Rome, wrote that he found unforwarded correspondence waiting for him at Scutari.[176]

NORTHERN COMMISSION

The northern commission started work at the end of October 1913 at Lin, on the northwestern shore of Lake Ochrida.[177] Problems soon emerged. The opinions of the commissioners largely mirrored those of their respective ambassadors in London, with geopolitical objectives superseding ethnographic 'findings'. The Russian representative, General de Potapov, and his French colleague argued in favour of Serbian claims, while the Triplice representatives opposed them. Granet, whom Whitehall had believed would take a conciliatory position, increasingly considered the Franco-Russian claims so extravagant that they could not be taken as a serious basis for discussion. He subsequently came to support proposals advocated by the Triplice commissioners. The Serbian Ambassador in London complained that Granet had 'no will of his own' and always sided with the Triplice, counter to Entente interests.[178] At the town of Prizrend, ambiguities in remit intensified animosities. The delegates were attempting to delimit the frontier between the 'districts' of Prizrend and Luma (the areas surrounding these main towns being named after them), but disagreements emerged over the definition of a 'district'. Was it to be an ethnographic area, as the Italian and Austrian delegates argued, or was it an administrative area (the former Ottoman *kaza*), as Potapov claimed?[179] Eventually, the Triplice representatives and Granet moved from their original position and advocated a frontier based on current Serbian outposts that were able to defend the town of Prizrend. Although they admitted that this would leave a considerable number of Albanian speakers in Serbian territory, they found that strategic and geographic considerations outweighed their ethnographic objections. Potapov argued for a compromise far in excess of this, though his precise proposal remained unclear.[180] With the 'district' issue still not resolved, the commission adjourned in December 1913 until the spring, because of bad weather and the need to return before roads became impassable.[181] The new Albanian kingdom was established in March 1914, although the northern territory was still without fixed frontiers. The Serbian outposts effectively became the *de facto* frontiers but this was not formally endorsed by the powers.

When the commission resumed its work in Scutari, in April 1914, the same divisions persisted. These proved so severe that Granet communicated to London his doubts as to whether they would ever arrive at a 'definite and honest conclusion'. Granet's inability to distance himself from the inter-personal issues within the commission appears to have been a considerable factor constraining his influence on the proceedings. Perhaps the most damaging decision the northern commission made, and one contrary to their original directives, was to agree upon a policy of 'compensations': an Albanian (Austrian) gain to be offset by a Serbian (Russian) one. They had begun visiting, in turns, sections of the disputed frontier, in order to decide on the merits of each section. However, the lengthy discussions and the inability to reach agreement resulted in the acceptance of a scheme that considered the visited sections simultaneously. The Dibra and Lake Scutari questions were considered in this way, but no agreement was reached.[182] The discussions on Vermosh and Velepoja in Gusinje, mountainous regions in the disputed Albanian-Montenegrin frontier, proved particularly pertinent. Potapov argued that these had been promised to Montenegro, but the Triplice commissioners maintained that the London peace agreement (between the Balkan League and Turkey) had unequivocally stated that any territory belonging to the Albanian-speaking Clementi tribes should become part of Albania.[183] Negotiations took on an increasingly tense political tone, and relations deteriorated to such an extent that Granet communicated to London that only a change of commissioners could break the deadlock and produce results. Whitehall did not support him. It did not want to jeopardise more important objectives elsewhere by proposing a course that would offend the other powers over a marginal British interest.[184] By August 1914 the commission had still not finished, but with five of the six great powers at war its operations ceased.

SOUTHERN COMMISSION

The southern commission began its work at Monastir, on 4 October 1913. Obstacles soon materialised: in 58 days the commissioners visited only six villages and interviewed 14 people. Athens was repeatedly accused of attempting to influence decision-making with the use of extensive propaganda and subversive initiatives. The commission reported a so-called 'Sacred Legion' which cried 'union or death' at every opportunity, and the presence of irregular troops that were used to ensure that all doors of Christian homes remained closed to conceal the Albanian speaking women inside, or so it was believed. Lieutenant-Colonel Charles Doughty-Wylie, the British representative and commission chairman, reported that houses were painted in the Greek colours of blue and white, and that the church bells rang whenever the commission arrived at a town or village. He believed that this was meant to reinforce the Christian (Orthodox) and thus supposedly Greek nature of the town. He wrote that the commissioners were always greeted either by a hostile crowd, clamouring for union with Greece, or by school children speaking Greek and waving Greek flags.[185] The inference was that the 'Greeks' were orchestrating these welcome parties. The suspicion of the commissioners seemed verified on one visit, when a group of children appeared to speak Greek. However, when the senior Austrian delegate, Bilinski, threw down a handful of coins, they all started squabbling in Albanian.[186]

The commissioners appear to have realised the grave deficiencies in using language as the solitary criterion to determine ethnography. Many people in the region were bilingual or trilingual, and spoke Albanian in their homes (mother tongue), but Greek for business or general communication outside the home (lingua franca), whilst Turkish was the official language, and some also spoke Vlach or a Slavonic dialect. This bi-or multi-lingualism seems predictable considering that there was no separate Albanian Church, no agreed written language until 1908, and that the teaching of Albanian had only recently been allowed in schools. Additionally, the commissioners discovered that within the family, the younger generation, particularly male members, commonly spoke Greek. The commissioners surmised that this phenomenon was a result of economic necessity: Greek was the language of trade, whereas Albanian had no wide commercial usage. On the other hand, the older generation, especially women, spoke Albanian. In response to this discovery, Doughty-Wylie recorded that the junior Italian delegate, Captain Fortunato Castoldi, proposed that only old people should be examined, although this was not borne out by the official commission reports. Doughty-Wylie, in his position as commission chairman, telegraphed London to petition that language not be the sole criterion, but that nationality, geographical features and economic and strategic considerations should also be considered.[187]

On 30 October 1913, supposedly in response to Greek attempts to mislead the commission, and less than two weeks after the *démarche* to Belgrade, the Austrian and Italian governments sent a bilateral ultimatum to Athens. It stated that in any village in which the southern commission met with Greek interference, the commission would be instructed to regard the town as Albanian; and if the commission failed to finish by the end of November, the Greeks would be compelled to leave by 31 December 1913.[188] This received a hostile reception in all the Entente capitals. For instance, Grey's first response was to withdraw from the Albanian commissions altogether. He eventually decided against this in order to protect the related British strategic interests in the Aegean.[189]

Nevertheless, on 13 November 1913, Doughty-Wylie informed the other commissioners that they had been authorised to proceed on the new basis of *'seulement la nationalité, mais encore la situation économique, stratégique et géographique'*.[190] On this basis he proposed a frontier, roughly midway between the French and Italian proposals. It started at Cape Stylos in the west and finished, although not definitely fixed, near the point where the Koritza district met the Grammos Mountains. The proposal received a favourable response.[191] The commission made considerable progress during the next month, possibly due to the death of Bilinski, who appears to have been very vocal in opposing any concessions to the Greeks. The main stumbling block to any agreement remained the allocation of the district of Argyrocastro. Vice-Consul Buchberger, the junior Austrian delegate who replaced Bilinski, and the Italian representatives, remained determined that the area should be settled on an ethnographic basis, and that the frontier at Argyrocastro be *'juste et équitable'*. Buchberger claimed that of the 25,000 inhabitants, 14,000 were Muslim and 11,000 Orthodox, with the majority speaking Albanian. The French and Russian delegates opposed this.[192] It was decided to postpone the decision until they visited the area on 10 December 1913. It was then agreed that, except for three villages (Policani, Skoriazes and Sopiki), the Argyrocastro valley was predominantly Albanian, but that it would not be possible to draw the frontier in such a way as to include the aforementioned villages within the Greek mainland. Goudim-Levkovitch considered this regrettable but agreed, on condition that Greece was compensated for the loss of these three villages. The Italian delegates then proposed to move to Florence in Italy to finish their deliberations on the basis of Doughty-Wylie's directives, using the maps of the Geographical Institute in Florence.[193]

Having surmised that the commission would advocate a frontier largely to Albanian advantage, Eleftherios Venizelos, the Greek Prime Minister, protested directly to Grey.[194] He threatened to resign on 10 December 1913, unless Greek claims were settled satisfactorily. Grey perceived that Venizelos was under considerable domestic pressure not to lose either northern Epirus or the Aegean islands. Grey was also aware that, although Venizelos was probably the only Greek statesman who could withstand the political consequences of the loss of northern Epirus,[195] his position would be extremely tenuous without a resolution of the Aegean dispute. Consequently, on 12 December, Grey willingly revived his proposal of a 'simultaneous resolution' of the Aegean islands and northern Epirus disputes.[196]

Before the remaining powers responded on 17 December 1913, the southern commission concluded its operations. It reported its findings three days later in a report which became known as the Florence Protocol, recommending, with minor rectifications, the frontier proposed by Doughty-Wylie, starting at Cape Stylos and finishing at Lake Ochrida, and ceding both Koritza and Argyrocastro to Albania, but Konitza to Greece (Appendix C). The majority of the disputed towns were left to Albania. On 31 December, the Triplice replied to Grey's proposal to link the southern Albanian and Aegean questions, stating that they preferred to acquiesce in the Florence proposals, which all six great powers and the Albanian provisional government eventually accepted. Only Venizelos and the Greek representatives raised objections. The Entente seemed to have an unofficial understanding that Greece would get the islands if Stylos and Koritza became Albanian, despite the Triplice having rejected this when Grey first touted the idea. Greece eventually gained all Aegean islands, except for three which were returned to the Ottoman Empire.[197] Additionally, on 18 June 1914, the Greeks issued a Royal Decree ceding the island of Saseno in Valona bay to Albania.[198] The island had become Greek in 1864 as part of the Ionian Islands settlement, despite being much further north in the Adriatic. It was uninhabited and without running water, but was important because of its position at the head of the Otranto Straits and proximity to the Albanian mainland. Its transference to Albania was deemed necessary for Albanian, and also Italian and Austrian, strategic security.

Conclusions

According to the Carnegie Report investigating the Balkan wars, the new Albanian state comprised 11,317 square miles. This included 3,922 square miles from Janina *vilayet*, 3,529 from Monastir, 2,970 from Scutari and 896 from Kosovo.[199] This was far short of the vision of an ethnographic Albania envisaged by the Albanians, but it did represent a fairly even compromise between the Russian and Austrian proposals of December 1912. As Grey wrote in February 1913, 'if a good settlement of Albania would mean war between two or more great powers, and an inferior settlement would secure peace between them, the latter has to be preferred.'[200] In this sentence, Grey clearly illustrated his true motivation in the discussions he was to chair at London. He later wrote that 'the [Ambassadors'] Conference had not settled anything, not even the details of the Albanian boundaries, but it had served a useful purpose'.[201] By this, he meant avoiding war between the powers, preventing Russia from moving towards the Triplice and safeguarding British sea power. Throughout the Conference and the resulting commissions, Grey's apparent impartiality and pragmatic approach, combined with his sense of ingenuity and inventiveness, had contrived to produce compromises on which he could convince Russia and Austria to agree. As a bi-product, the new independent state of Albania had been created. However, as Grey was fully aware, the results of these compromises were far from perfect.[202] British policy was thus clearly in line with defensive realist rhetoric. British representatives oscillated between the two coalitions trying to create a balance, both in the Balkans and more widely. Britain believed that an enlarged Serbia with Adriatic access, coupled with the benefits for Russia of warm ports, would fundamentally upset the balance of power in the region, if not throughout Europe. Sazonov was also constrained by the system. He felt unable to stop the tide towards an independent Albanian state without causing great power conflict. The creation of Albania was about making a new balance in the Balkans and Adriatic, and therefore preserving great power interests and the system as a whole. The geo-political factors were clearly more important than the proclaimed ethnic rationale. Robert Vansittart, then a junior clerk in the British Foreign Office, but already with substantial overseas service behind him and with a distinguished diplomatic career ahead of him, offered a forlorn but accurate comment on the role of ethnographic criteria in the delimitation of Albanian boundaries: 'In outlining the frontiers of Albania it has been often necessary to disregard ethnography for larger reasons; but there is no reason to disregard it unnecessarily.'[203]

Chapter 3

Experiments with Self-government: provisional authorities, the international control commission and Prince Wilhelm of Wied

This chapter explores the period in Albania after independence and before World War One, including the provisional regimes, the international commission of control established by the Ambassadors' Conference to prepare the state for a permanent regime, and the first Albanian kingdom. The new state officially came into existence on 7 March 1914, with the arrival of the *Mpret* (literally in Albanian 'king'). From its inception, the newest 'nation' in Europe, and the world's first predominantly Muslim one, faced insurmountable problems. Within six months of his arrival, the *Mpret* fled the country, never to return. During this period the Albanian nationalists failed to assert themselves, because they were unable to agree on any vision of what an independent Albania meant or might mean. Instead local traditions, interests and rivalries, especially religious and geographical ones, came to dominate. Meanwhile, the great power solidarity, especially Austro-Italian, which in 1912-13 had been so crucial in the creation of an independent Albania, unravelled as these powers returned to their previous policy of competition and rivalry. In turn, the new Albanian state began to dismantle.

Ismail Kemal's Provisional Government and Rival Regimes

At Valona (November 1912), a provisional government, under

the Presidency of Ismail Kemal, had been established to govern the country until the powers had decided on Albania's future.[204] Throughout 1913, the provisional government took some impressive steps. Most significantly, it established an independent Albanian Muslim church, and appointed a patriotic Albanian, Muslim Mufti, as its head, thus breaking allegiance to the Ottoman Sheik-ul-Islam. Jurisdiction over civil cases was passed to the civil courts, and a jury system was introduced for criminal cases. These initiatives were not radical enough for many nationalists, especially those from the United States, who had greater experience of liberal and revolutionary traditions. In other areas, progress was severely limited. By the end of 1913, Albania remained without any international recognition by other states (above all from the great powers, Balkan neighbours, and the Ottoman Empire).[205] The lack of Austrian and Italian recognition was perhaps the most surprising and damaging. Foreign states occupied much of what the provisional government considered 'Albanian' territory: Serbs and Montenegrins in the north; Greeks in the south; an international force at Scutari had replaced the Montenegrin forces there. Propaganda hostile to Ismail Kemal's government prospered, and numerous schemes to replace the previously popular President materialised. It was alleged that he aspired to the Albanian throne himself, and he was accused of accepting bribes and being subservient to Italy. His rivals, especially Essad Pasha, did everything to promote these accusations.[206]

Throughout 1913, support for the government dwindled. There had been problems with its composition from the start. Key nationalists were not part of the new regime. Mehmed bey Konitza and Philip Nogga, both Albanian representatives to the London conferences, were still pre-occupied overseas, and other influential leaders, especially Bib Doda, had retired from national politics. In September 1913, eighteen committee members presented Ismail Kemal with a document detailing the faults and shortcomings of the provisional government.[207] Many ministers resigned, perhaps most notably Mehmet Pasha of Kalkadelen, the Minister of War, who had been so influential in maintaining stability and the *besa* (meaning 'pledge', and when it is in operation no Albanian, not even one carrying arms, will injure another). Harry Lamb, the British delegate on the international control commission, and former British

Consul at Salonika, maintained that these defections meant that Ismail Kemal had to seek less well-known, less able and often tainted functionaries to serve. This further reduced the credibility of the government it was intended to bolster.[208] The government became increasingly dominated by Muslims, especially the feudal beys. This generated mistrust and uncertainty amongst Orthodox Christians and Catholics, many of whom had been amongst the most nationalistic during the 1912 campaigns. Lamb considered Ismail Kemal's failure to gain the confidence of the Malissori and Mirdite Catholic tribes in northern Albania particularly damaging.[209] Although these problems were harmful, they are fairly typical of provisional regimes, which tend to be weak and prone to attack from opposition, because they are often temporary and based on dubious legitimacy.

The provisional government had many rivals for its authority: these were associated with the tribal, religious and geographical divisions, which independence had not rendered irrelevant. Greek troops controlled large areas of northern Epirus assigned to Albania. In the north, an international force was stationed in Scutari, under the leadership of British Colonel George Phillips. Many northern tribesmen remained indifferent to the whole independence project. Mirdita remained virtually a separate entity, despite the heroic efforts of the Mirdites during the first Balkan war. In December 1913, Ismail invited Bib Doda to become Vice-President of the provisional government. This was a direct attempt to link Mirdita with the provisional government's zone of control. Ismail hoped that the arrangement could be used to extend the provisional government's influence and authority over a wider area of northern Albania. Although he accepted the offer, Bib Doda ruled precisely as he had done before: he never left Mirdita, and he played no active part in the government. Thus, as Lamb wrote, his hypothetical allegiance was 'practically worthless'.[210]

Potentially the greatest internal challenge came from Essad Pasha's so-called 'Senate of Central Albania'. Essad was an influential pasha who dominated much of central Albania from his base around Durazzo and Tirana, where he had the support of many of his tenants, *redrifs* (a form of personal bodyguard), Muslim clergy and Bosniaks (Muslims from Bosnia). He was exceedingly critical of the provisional government. Ismail had offered Essad the position of Interior Minister, in an attempt to curtail his activities and gain control of Essad's demobilised force (estimated at 9,000 men). Essad refused to acknowledge the provisional government's authority and instead established a rival Senate, with himself as President, on 16 October 1913. This occurred on the same day as the first meeting of the international control commission, and it illustrated Essad's determination not to submit to its authority either. Essad's Senate consisted of his friends, family and supporters. It was less representative than the provisional government, but it was successful in gaining support from people across Albanian society, including those who had previously opposed this notoriously self-obsessed and unscrupulous schemer, because of what were considered his well-founded criticisms of provisional government activities.[211] Eventually fighting broke out between Essadists and supporters of the provisional government.

International Control Commission

With the provisional government stumbling, the powers dithered over what to do with the new state. By March 1913, they had decided that, instead of placing Albania under the sovereignty, or suzerainty, of the Sultan, and the inevitable complications for the Balkans that might result from having a Muslim head of state, a European Christian prince should rule.[212] Albania would therefore be independent rather than autonomous. An international control commission, consisting of representatives of the six great powers and, unlike the two boundary commissions, an Albanian representative, would govern Albania until the arrival of the prince, facilitate the transfer to his authority and assist him in running the new state for ten years. By the end of July 1913, an even more detailed formula had been worked out, by which Albania was to be guaranteed by the six powers. It was to have a civil administration that would be run by the control commission for six years, with a further preliminary six months to enable the commissioners to determine the details, and Dutch officers to command the gendarmerie. On Russian insistence, Grey agreed to prevent any Catholic officers from participating, lest they prove susceptible to Austrian or Italian influence. Grey insisted that the Entente keep this resolution secret in order to avoid repercussions, thus clearly illustrating that on occasion he too acted outside the concert.[213] The flag of Skanderbeg was recognised as the official Albanian flag because, Grey believed, it was universally popular amongst Albanians.[214]

The control commission arrived in Albania in October 1913. It faced problems from the start. Lamb wrote that the commissioners were hampered in their activities because of the needs of their own respective governments to decide whether to recognise and work with the provisional government, and the other regional authorities existing *de facto*. This decision was deemed necessary, if the commission was to work successfully with them and manage to bring the country under control, and to unite it under one single administration, ready for the arrival of the new ruler.[215] The commission held its first meeting on 16 October 1913. It was agreed that each delegate would hold the presidency of the commission in turn, for one month at a time, *à tour de role*. From the first meeting, divisions became apparent. This great power rivalry, which would prove to be the major destabilising factor in the new state, emerged at an early stage. The trivial issue that produced the first controversy centred on the admission of an Albanian delegate to the commission. Disagreement materialized over how this delegate should be chosen. The Italian delegate, Alessandro Leoni, suggested that the decision be left to the provisional government. Lamb maintained that it was doubtful whether he would be recognised as the 'delegate of Albania' anywhere outside Valona, where the provisional government had control, and particularly north of the Skumbi river. Lamb favoured some form of election or popular selection, possibly by the four or five major municipalities. If that was considered too difficult, he would accept a selection by the commission itself.[216] The Russian and French delegates argued for selection by the commission, but the Triplice representatives remained adamant that the task should be entrusted to the provisional government. According to Lamb's account, they believed it possible to influence the government's decision. After several meetings, it was agreed that the commission would select the delegate, but on the proviso that this would be temporary, and that a permanent appointment would be made after the establishment of the future Albanian government. On 30 October 1913, Mufid bey Libohova was selected as the Albanian delegate, and resigned his position as Minister for Foreign Affairs in the provisional government to do so. This arrangement satisfied both sides—a control commission decision but a provisional government man—yet Mufid made it clear that he would not be controlled either by the provisional government or by Ismail Kemal.[217] It is interesting that being the Albanian delegate on the control commission was considered a more important and influential position than that of Albanian Foreign Minister, presumably because Albania had still failed to establish diplomatic relations with any other state. The decision was significant because a representative of a small state had been invited to sit as part of the concert, albeit at a low level. Inevitably he proved far less influential than his great-power colleagues.

In Search of a Prince

The major problem facing Albania at this point was uncertainty about the state's future, and above all the delay in having a new ruler appointed. There was much consensus on this point, but for different reasons, and with diverse ideas about who would be a good choice. Ismail claimed that only the appointment of Albania's monarch could stem the violence that was becoming endemic in the country. He blamed the provisional government's lack of progress and acceptance on the powers' failure to determine Albania's future, and specifically on their delay in appointing a prince. Essad pressed its urgency too.[218] His claim seemed largely political rhetoric, aimed at undermining Ismail. His earlier statements and subsequent actions indicate that he had no intention of submitting to rule by anyone else, and instead coveted the Albanian throne himself. The British representatives in Albania (Lamb, Doughty-Wylie, Granet and Phillips) all seemed particularly anxious. Lamb and Doughty-Wylie, for instance, made repeated appeals to the British Foreign Office to hasten the ruler's announcement and arrival. They were both convinced that this was the most effective way to reduce divisions and uncertainty amongst the Albanians.[219] In London, Aubrey Herbert and other members of the Albanian Committee exerted political pressure continuously.[220] As early as May 1913 (while the Conference of Ambassadors was still in session), Herbert had written to Grey stressing the importance of selecting someone with the right qualities as the Albanian prince. According to Herbert, if the prince was to succeed in uniting the Albanians behind him, then it was important to select a Protestant and a man of 'considerable stature', because the Albanians respected a 'tall man'.[221]

After the conclusion of the London conferences, the six powers devoted much time to discussing the future ruler of Albania, but they ultimately agreed to leave the decision to the Ballhausplatz and Consulta.[222] Officials in the Ballhausplatz wrote that they were concerned about the delay in appointment, lest the situation became permanent, but difficulties had arisen because of concern that the prince might lead Albania into a particular sphere of influence.[223] A formidable list of candidates was proposed. These included Aladro Caŝtriota, of the Albanian colony in Italy, who claimed descent from Skanderbeg, Prince Ghika of Romania and Prince Arthur of Connaught, who was allegedly favoured by many Albanians. However, all three were rejected on the grounds that they might lead Albania into a hostile orbit. The powers also debated whether the prince should be Christian or Muslim. Eventually, a Christian prince was agreed in order to protect the rights of the Christian minorities, and also in the hope that Albania would become a European state and not a vassal of the Ottoman Empire. The nominations of Princes Burhan Eddine and Abdul Medjid of the imperial Ottoman dynasty, and Prince Ahmed Fuad Pasha of Egypt, who was a descendent of the early nineteenth-century hero Ali Pasha of Tepelena, were therefore rejected.[224] The great powers were continuing with the realist policy nurtured during the Ambassadors' Conference, of maintaining the balance of power by using the European concert to contain the ambitions and strength of their protégés, satellites and partners.[225]

A 'compromise candidate' was agreed upon. He was the Lutheran German Prince Wilhelm of Wied, a third son, captain in the German army and nephew of the Queen of Romania, who had pressed his candidature.[226] In so doing, the great power representatives followed the pattern, employed during the nineteenth century, of giving new Balkan states German Protestants as their rulers. However, the new Albanian state received far less international support than its Balkan counterparts had when they had gained independence. When Greece and Bulgaria became independent and were put under a foreign (German) prince, the then great power representatives gave them sufficient military support to enable the new rulers to maintain order until a native army could be organised. Albania was provided with no

international forces, except those at Scutari, who were ordered not
to leave the town, plus fifteen Dutch officers, under General Willem
de Weer, who had responsibility for organising the gendarmerie.[227]
The powers were already reneging on their commitment to the
establishment of a viable Albania and undermining its chances of
success. Edith Durham claimed that Wilhelm was chosen specifically
because selecting a man of limited ability made it easier to get rid of
him later.[228]

Initially Wilhelm seems to have made sensible decisions, designed
to safeguard both his own future and the new regime. At the end of
December 1913, Wilhelm provisionally accepted the throne but only
on certain conditions, namely guarantees for a great power loan, his
Civil List and an assurance that Essad Pasha recognised the 'will of
Europe'. The British Ambassador in Berlin wrote that other conditions
included that the scheme of organisation for the administration of
the country was subject to Wilhelm's approval and that an agreement
by which all the great powers approved his candidature was first
obtained. On 6 February 1914, Wilhelm announced his acceptance
of the throne. On 21 February in Neuwied, he received a deputation
of representatives from throughout Albania led by Essad Pasha, who
had travelled to Germany to formally offer him the throne.[229]

Wilhelm wisely refrained from taking up the throne until
the internal situation had improved. This may indicate that he
was not as inept as some have claimed.[230] Problems and divisions
within the country had escalated. The Young Turk government had
resolved to restore Ottoman suzerainty over Albania. In October
1913, the Porte sent Major Bekhir Grebeneja, together with several
followers, to Albania with the idea of propagating the idea of the
Albanian-descended Izzet Pasha, the Ottoman Minister of War, as
a Muslim prince.[231] At the time, it appeared that an arrangement
had been reached with Ismail, and that the President had broken
Albania's neutrality.[232] One Whitehall official described the affair as
reminiscent of the Jameson Raid in southern Africa. The intention
seems to have been to make it appear that Ismail had consented to
the Turks bringing arms and military forces to Albania, and to Izzet
Pasha as prince, in exchange for Albania (under Ottoman sovereignty)
regaining those districts that the London Conferences had ascribed
to Serbia, Greece and Montenegro. On reflection, the British

Foreign Office determined that it appeared more likely to have been a plot to ensnare Ismail. Nevertheless, it succeeded in diminishing Ismail's credibility, as his enemies had presumably intended. On 11 January 1914, Ismail declared his intention to hand over the Valona administration to the control commission if Essad also surrendered his authority to it.[233]

The control commission agreed to assume control until Wilhelm's arrival, considering this the best way to stem the mounting disorder and violence. On 22 January 1914, the provisional government abandoned its powers in favour of the control commission. Ismail Kemal retired to Nice and never returned to Albania.[234] The commission invited Essad to resign. He refused. Essad objected to being treated in the same manner as Ismail, who had been dismissed for his involvement in the Bekhir affair. In response, the commission stated that Essad Pasha would be removed, by force if necessary. Eventually, on 3 February 1914, Essad did resign but, significantly, only on the proviso that he would lead the delegation to Neuwied to welcome Wilhelm, and formally offer him the crown, an accession that he had until then persistently opposed. Lamb considered this condition far from satisfactory but saw no alternative, in the light of Essad's perceived support and strength in Albania.[235] The international administration in Scutari was also removed, although a military force remained. The control commission had managed the considerable achievement of successfully linking under one administration all Albanian districts allotted to it, except Koritza and Argyrocastro, which remained under Greek occupation. By the start of Wilhelm's reign, in March 1914, the situation appeared promising and the commission delegates had reason to be confident. Such optimism proved ephemeral.

Wilhelm's choice of capital (Durazzo) created a multitude of problems, above all by aggravating the rivalries between the various Albanian factions. Wilhelm insisted on landing at Durazzo, despite having received advice against doing so. He considered the port one of the chief towns in Albania, and one where he would have the use of a suitable residence without being dependent on any prominent Albanian. He resisted alternative proposals to arrive at Scutari, because of its proximity to the Montenegrin frontier, despite the protection that the international forces could provide there, or at Valona, because it had been the provisional capital.[236] Lamb had

persistently warned against the advisability of Wilhelm landing at
Durazzo, especially under Austrian auspices, because he considered
that this would seriously jeopardise the Prince's chances of
establishing a stable national administration. It would give Albanians
the impression that he was under the influence of Essad Pasha,
and thereby promote Essad's prestige relative to other authorities,
especially the provisional government, and even Wilhelm himself. It
was alleged that Wilhelm had entered into a secret arrangement with
Essad to land at Durazzo, and that this had been Essad's intention in
leading the Neuwied expedition. However, no evidence has survived
to confirm or disprove this.[237] Lamb favoured Wilhelm disembarking
at Scutari, where he would be under the protection of the international
forces, and then embarking on a tour of the country.[238] Nevertheless,
on 7 March 1914, Wilhelm sailed from Trieste to Durazzo, which
he declared as his capital, much to the jealousy of both northern and
southern Albanians, who preferred Scutari and Valona, respectively.
The majority of Albanians rejoiced at his arrival. Here was their
'Skanderbeg' to end all their problems, and they declared him *Mpret*
or king, although the great powers recognised him only as a hereditary
prince. However, he was not to bring the much-anticipated happiness
and prosperity to his new subjects.[239]

The New Albanian Kingdom: royal shortcomings and external threats

Wilhelm's honeymoon period was short-lived. With his arrival, the
control commission transferred its powers to him, but remained in
an advisory capacity. On 10 April 1914, a scheme of organisation was
drawn up and signed by Albanian representatives and control commission delegates. Religious complaints surfaced almost immediately:
Muslims hated a Christian prince, and as a Lutheran he satisfied
neither Catholics nor Orthodox. Wilhelm then made a number
of errors. He failed to tour the country, which made it difficult for
him to exert his authority, and ensured that the early optimism soon
diminished. He was criticised for wasting money on such things as
the High Court of Appeal when there were only fledgling law courts,
the appointment of school inspectors when there were few schools,
and the maintenance of ministers to other countries who never even
left Albania. In contrast, the gendarmerie, arguably Albania's most
urgent requirement, received only modest funding.[240]

Wilhelm formed his cabinet on 17 March 1914. It was universally unpopular. Only two of its members had recently been resident in Albania, its members were considered too steeped in Ottoman government methods and the landowning Muslim class was over-represented. Many did not speak or write Albanian, although the Albanian spoken language was supposedly the cornerstone of the Albanian state. Turkhan bey Pasha, who had enjoyed an illustrious career in the Ottoman diplomatic corps, was chosen as Prime Minister. He had not lived in Albania for many years, nor had he been involved in the nationalist movement. He was suspected by some of having leanings towards Russia, following his service there, by others of having Ottoman sympathies, and by others of being an Italian agent. Even Hasan Prishtina was criticised by Lamb as a 'mere puppet in the hands of Essad', although the two men usually took opposing positions. The most controversial appointment was Wilhelm's choice of Essad Pasha, who, in a complete volte-face, had now come around to 'support' Wilhelm, as Interior and War Minister (and effective Prime Minister). Many nationalists considered him a traitor, primarily because of his role in the Scutari capitulation to Montenegro (April 1913), and few trusted him. Durham, in one of her more accurate assessments, pointed out that Essad believed that by ingratiating himself with Wilhelm he could become effective ruler and perhaps usurp power. Conversely, Wilhelm considered it the lesser evil to bring Essad into the government, in the hope that he could contain his activities.[241] Essad's appointment as Interior and War Minister was particularly significant, because it gave him control of those limited forces and munitions that the state did possess, and made the Prince even more dependent upon him. Essad soon obtained the upper hand. He managed to keep Wilhelm 'prisoner' in Durazzo, and prevented him from touring the country as the Albanians and the British representatives had urged.

Responsibility for Albania's continuing problems was not solely Wilhelm's, a view to which even his critics subscribed. Durham wrote that 'We may blame Wied for his incompetence, but only a man of unusual force of character could have made headway against the powers combined against him'.[242] Lamb wrote to the Foreign Office that, despite repeated appeals for financial and military support, Wilhelm had not received the assistance he so desperately needed. He went further, claiming that the great powers had failed to live up to their earlier pledges and commitments to him.[243] British officials in Whitehall, if not Albania, were now lukewarm about the new Albanian experiment the powers had sponsored. Grey, who had been crucial in maintaining the European concert in London regarding Albania, seemed to lack confidence in Wilhelm's abilities, and expected him to fail in his appointed task. He noted that, despite being keen and eager to learn, Wilhelm had no knowledge of Albania, its tribes or its customs, and he lacked sufficient skill to rule the turbulent country.[244] Even supposedly disinterested powers were already reneging on their promises to the new sovereign, especially since the initial crisis had been resolved. Albania was no longer considered capable of disrupting the great power, Balkan or Adriatic balances.

In early 1914, intervention and plotting by Albania's rivals revealed itself most clearly in Greek interference in southern Albania. Although the Greeks denied responsibility, and Sir Francis Elliot, the British Ambassador in Athens, supported this view, Greek involvement was extensive. Lamb reported on the frequent visits to Corfu of Christaki Zographos, a former Greek Foreign Minister who would return to that post in 1915. The development of events clearly illustrated that the Greeks were not prepared to leave their 'countrymen' to the 'mercy' of the Albanians.[245] Before Wilhelm's arrival, a 'national' revolt had started in northern Epirus. On 22 February 1914, a meeting of the representatives of all the occupied provinces, at Argyrocastro, had proclaimed that the Epirotes would resist by force of arms any attempt on the part of the Albanian gendarmerie to 'violate their territory'. They also announced the establishment of the 'Provisional Government of Autonomous Northern Epirus' under the presidency of Zographos. This was notified to the president of the control commission in a telegram from Corfu received *en clair* on 28 February 1914. Despite all claims that this was a 'national insurrection', in reality there appears to have been only an infinitesimal number of the 'native' population involved, the majority of whom had previously served in the Greek army or had been imported from Greece, including prisoners recently released from Cretan jails. This was followed by a declaration of the independence of autonomous 'northern Epirus' at Argyrocastro, on 2 March 1914, presumably orchestrated to pre-empt Wilhelm's arrival and the establishment of the new kingdom. To conceal their complicity, the Greeks had withdrawn their troops the day before (1 March 1914), although they had left a number of troops in Koritza for 'treatment'.[246] Appendix D gives an indication of towns covered by the 'northern Epirote' insurrection.

Venizelos was under considerable pressure from the Epirotes, the Greek public and the political opposition to help the insurgents but, at this time, Greece was in no position to enrage the great powers. Therefore, in an attempt to assuage both sides, Venizelos appealed to the powers to ensure linguistic and religious safeguards in northern Epirus, and did so again four weeks later. The powers took two months to respond. This delay added to the uncertainty, confusion and anxiety. In their reply, on 24 April 1914, the powers urged the Albanian government to implement the guarantees and to include local elements in the gendarmerie.[247] Meanwhile, on 6 April 1914, the Greek troops left in Koritza for 'treatment' had escaped and started a further revolt, and were joined by Greek partisans and 'Epirote' bands. To defend the town, there were only fifty gendarmes and their Dutch officers. Within a few hours, the public buildings and vantage points were in Greek hands. Wilhelm was keen to lead forces against the Epirotes, although these 'forces' amounted only to armed civilians and 2500 gendarmes under the Dutch officers. Such an action would have enhanced Wilhelm's prestige in Albanian eyes, but he was prevented from taking it by Essad, the Italian forces in Durazzo and the majority of the control commission delegates. Essad and the Consulta feared that Wilhelm's involvement would jeopardise their plans, and, according to Lamb, the commission members dreaded the potential outcome of any military action for the inexperienced Albanian forces, especially because the Greeks had announced that they would invade if there was any regular military action by the Albanians, which in turn would probably have resulted in Italian and Austrian intervention. Meanwhile, Essad had announced his intention of sending a force to southern Albania (northern Epirus). Wilhelm saw the danger in this move but he dared not oppose it. The commission concluded that the only way to avoid a bloodbath was to offer concessions. The great power governments agreed to approve whatever was decided upon by their representatives on the ground, on condition that there were no boundary modifications, thus ensuring that their interests were protected. The Albanian government also agreed to negotiate, and invited the control commission to act as mediators.[248]

The control commission delegates met the insurgents at Santa Quaranta in an attempt to stop the resistance, but then proceeded to Corfu because of the less intense political climate there. Negotiations took place between 9 and 17 May, and resulted in the Corfu Protocol of 18 May 1914. This ceded a level of autonomy to the Epirotes, who were to be under the nominal hegemony of Wilhelm, and provided for the recruitment of local elements into the gendarmerie, and the teaching of Greek in schools. The Albanian government in Durazzo accepted this at the end of June 1914, as did the autonomists, with much reluctance, a month later.[249] Although it accepted these provisions, the Albanian government did not accept the right of northern Epirus to have a separate administration, but took the view that Albania was in no position to go to war against Greece. Meanwhile, for the Greek side, the local autonomy option represented a considerable modification of their former position. This option was pursued for two main reasons. Firstly, Greece needed the support of the Orthodox Albanians and, contrary to Greek ambitions and their religious affinity, it was becoming apparent that the majority desired to be Albanian not Greek.[250] Secondly, union with Greece was not yet possible because it would have resulted in considerable opposition, if not intervention, by Austria or Italy. Therefore, in opting for local autonomy, the Greeks, as opposed to 'Epirotes', managed to circumvent both the Albanian responses and great power interests, and simultaneously secured Greek dominance and interests in the region. Lamb was not blind to this trick. He wrote to Grey that the Greeks understood that the arrangement 'simply smoothes the way for a speedy annexation of northern Epirus'.[251] Elsewhere, the great powers had been primed to modify their former plans for Albania because they were not prepared to go to war with Greece, whom even Germany and Britain did not wish to offend. The start of World War One meant that the great powers never formally agreed to these resolutions.

Austro-Italian Rivalry and the Collapse of Wilhelm's Regime

The greatest threat to Albania came not from its Balkan neighbours but from the great powers. Lamb made numerous complaints about his fellow commissioners. He carped that only he made decisions for the Albanian state based on the best interests of the Albanian people, and that the other commissioners were more concerned to consult 'back home' to ensure that their decisions safeguarded their respective geo-political interests.[252] Durham went further, alleging that only Germany and Britain had ever intended to act honestly. She considered Leon Krajewsky, the French representative, one of the worst, and accused him of being even more pro-Slav than the Russians.[253]

Great power rivalries dominated the commission and in turn undermined the state, regardless of any individual intentions. The first example centred on the question of the Albanian Bank. As early as September 1913 (before the arrival of the international commission), the Austrian and Italian representatives made an agreement with the provisional government, in an attempt to gain exclusive rights in the Bank and the consequent influence in Albania. The Entente commissioners argued that the provisional government had no right to make this agreement, and that the Albanian Bank must be international on the same lines as the Moroccan Bank that had been established by the Algiers conventions (1911). Eventually, and with help from Jagow, Grey ensured that the Bank would be international.[254] Elsewhere, the Entente powers were no less complicit in their duplicity to undermine the new state. They refused to subscribe to the loan that was necessary to implement reforms, and to rebuild and establish Albania on a secure footing. All the powers refused to send the troops necessary for stability and security.[255] After the great power controversy over the larger Balkan crisis had subsided, most of the governments returned to a policy of ambivalence towards Albania, or to the pursuit of their longer-term ambitions.

Richard Bosworth has maintained that Albania continued to be the major consideration for Italian policy makers, to the extent that the Sarajevo crisis was viewed as merely adding to the 'graver continuing problem in Albania', and that Marquis Antonio di San Giuliano, the Italian Foreign Minister, intended to act 'honestly' regarding Albania. Sir Rennell Rodd, the British Ambassador in

Rome, maintained at the time that the alleged Italian intrigue in Albania must be 'quite unauthorised' because the continuance of an independent Albania was the Consulta's 'only weapon' against Austrian aggression.[256] In practice, Italian actions seem far removed from this idealised policy. Contrary to Bosworth's analysis and Rodd's observations, and perhaps the Foreign Minister's intentions, Italian efforts in practice sought to undermine and destabilise the newly independent Albania, and to replace the fledgling regime. What Rodd does not seem to have appreciated is that an Italian-controlled Albania would be an even better weapon. This breakdown in Austro-Italian solidarity, which had been so instrumental in London, was enormously damaging to the new state's, and Wilhelm's, chances of success.[257] The Austro-Italian objective in creating Albania had been to prevent Serbian access to the Adriatic and, in turn, effective Russian access. With this objective achieved, both states returned to their traditional rivalry in Albania, and both connived and intrigued to become the dominant force in the new state. Wilhelm later wrote to Swire that he considered the fallout to have started over issues outside the Albanian problem, and even went so far as to link the change in attitude to the fear that a great power war might break out. This theory becomes credible only from July 1914 onwards. In reality, it had been a very venturesome arrangement, born out of expediency and the great Slavonic (Russo-Serbian) threat. In mid-1914, the situation deteriorated rapidly, particularly as the French, Russians and their protégés exploited the feud. Having persistently opposed the establishment of an independent Albania, these forces were exceedingly willing to undermine it.[258] However, Austrian and Italian actions were to prove far more divisive and destabilising.

In May 1914, whilst the Corfu negotiations were still ongoing, a series of minor disturbances in central Albania, especially in the Shiak region, a small rural area between Durazzo and Tirana, proved impossible to contain. They had begun as traditional Albanian grievances, but they soon escalated and had profound implications for the national regime. Reports had emerged of armed men concentrating near Shiak. There was nothing exceptional about these reports, but the (potentially) volatile situation appears to have intensified, although other similar ones did not, because of personal differences in the Durazzo administration. Amid accusations that he was conniving with the insurgents and diverting military supplies in a plot to overthrow Wilhelm, Essad was arrested on a charge of treason and imprisoned aboard an Austrian cruiser. The Austrians and the Dutch Major, Johan Sluyss, appear to have instigated his arrest because they feared he would obstruct Austrian plans in Albania. They therefore took advantage of the temporary absence of both Leoni and Baron Carlo Aliotti, the Italian minister in Albania, from Durazzo. But the Italians soon turned the situation to their own advantage. Leoni, who had returned from the Corfu negotiations, and Aliotti, who had returned from Rome, persuaded Wilhelm against a court martial. Essad was released into Italian custody and subsequent exile.[259]

This outcome aggravated the situation and damaged Wilhelm irrevocably, although he had tried desperately to assuage both sides. To ordinary Albanians he appeared weak, and unable to restrain his rivals and maintain law and order. As Captain Duncan Heaton-Armstrong, the Prince's Irish private secretary, commented, Wilhelm's decision, which neither acquitted nor condemned his late most powerful minister, made an exceedingly bad impression on his loyal subjects; they considered that the King had robbed them of their prey and allowed himself to be outwitted by the Italian diplomats, who were generally believed to be Essad Pasha's allies.[260]

Meanwhile, Essad's *redrifs* and many of his relatives joined the Shiak insurgents in protest. According to Heaton-Armstrong, the rebels consisted primarily of disenchanted peasants whose (perhaps unrealistic) dreams had not been fulfilled by the Prince's arrival. Their initial demands had been based on local customs and rights. Various outside sources (Serbs, Ottoman Turks, Essadists, Epirote autonomists) then sought to exploit the revolt for their own purposes. Propaganda flooded into Albania. The most influential argued that Wilhelm was seeking to destroy Muslim rights, and that a Muslim prince was needed for protection. By the end of the month, a revolution had been proclaimed, the Ottoman flag had been hoisted and a series of demands issued. These included, most notably, the restoration of Ottoman rule or else the appointment of another member of the Ottoman royal family, and the reappointment of the Sheik-ul-Islam as Chief Mufti.[261] It is significant that the religious component was so prominent in this rebellion. In the independence campaigns, and in opposition to the claims of their Balkan rivals, the Albanians had persistently downplayed their religious differences in order to appear united and gain independence. In 1914, outside forces were soon able to exploit these differences for their own goals. The insurgents soon surrounded Durazzo. To oppose them, the Prince had only a small number of gendarmes, Dutch officers and foreign volunteers, and Bib Doda's Mirdites. The latter refused to fight and break the *besa*. The Prince's prestige depended primarily upon the support that he had from the powers. In this case, they all refused to give him either material or monetary aid.[262]

On 23 May 1914, the actions of another Dutch Officer, Captain Saar, provoked the final phase. Saar had been sent to meet the insurgents, but, seemingly ignorant of Albanian customs, whereby most Albanians carried arms although a man who had given his *besa* would not use them, he mistakenly fired on a group of Albanians. It appeared to many Albanians that the Prince's troops had broken the *besa*. According to Lamb, it also confirmed rumours that Wilhelm intended to massacre the population. This prompted even more people to side with the rebels.[263] The rebel leaders proclaimed that they did not trust or recognise the Prince, and insisted on meeting only great power representatives (in effect, the control commission delegates). They met three times but with little success. Wilhelm seems to have received poor advice—perhaps a reflection of the other priorities that his great power advisers had. The commission delegates repeatedly urged Wilhelm to leave Durazzo, and he repeatedly refused to do so. With shells bombarding the town, Wilhelm was persuaded to escort his family to safety on an Italian ship stationed in the harbour. Wilhelm had proclaimed his intention to return to the palace, but once he was on board the Italians seem to have taken the matter into their own hands. The ship raised anchor and sailed out of port, with Wilhelm aboard.[264]

In these events, there were three determining factors: Essad Pasha; great power actions, above all Austro-Italian; and Wilhelm. It was alleged that Essad had been scheming with the rebels and Italians to provoke an incident and seize the throne for himself, but such allegations were never proven.[265] Swire's allegation that the Italians were reluctant to hold a full investigation, for fear of it revealing Italian duplicity, is most likely correct but cannot be taken as self-evident. The same is true of the accusations made following Essad's departure. Despite persistent allegations that he was promoting the insurrection from abroad (financially, materially and with propaganda), nothing was ever proven. According to Heaton-Armstrong, whilst Essad was too clever to leave any 'incriminating documents' in his own possession, even those documents that were sequestered were never examined and eventually returned to Essad.[266] Like other Albanian leaders (such as Turkhan Pasha), Essad seems to have been a pawn of the great and lesser powers. Had the Italian officials wanted, they could most probably have restrained him. During his arrest and imprisonment Essad appears to have been completely helpless, dependent upon the whims and actions of great power superiors.

Austrian and Italian actions and rivalry were far more important. The Italians and Austrians were split and working against one another, and against Prince Wilhelm. The response to the Sluyss-Essad confrontation was the first significant indication (on the surface at least) of the conflicting and divergent objectives of the Triplice allies in Albania, and of the breakdown of Austro-Italian solidarity. Accounts differ greatly, but it appears that the main controversy arose because the Austrian representatives, anxious at their deteriorating influence in Durazzo, had attempted to use the altercation, and the absence of the commission delegates and Aliotti, to secure the dismissal of Essad and to enhance their own position at the expense of their Italian rivals. Lamb wrote to Grey that the Austrians were able to profit from the absence of the Italian representatives (Aliotti and Leoni) in Durazzo, and had succeeded in momentarily eluding the vigilance of the Italians. The Italian *Chargé d'Affaires* (Castoldi - who had previously been the junior representative on the southern boundary commission) allowed himself to be duped into acquiescing in what was to be done. On their return, Aliotti and Leoni immediately succeeded in turning the incident to Italian advantage, by conniving for the release of Essad into Italian custody, and thus again relegating Austrian influence and advantage to second place.[267] Following Saar's *faux pax*, the Italians in turn exploited the Durazzo bombardment. By 'imprisoning' Wilhelm offshore, they dealt the Prince's dwindling credibility as sovereign another blow. He appeared to have abandoned his people.[268] In reality, he was offshore for only

one night, and even that not at his own behest. Nevertheless news
of his departure spread quickly throughout Albania and Europe.
Sir Rennell Rodd, the British Ambassador in Rome, reported the
extent to which the Consulta had retracted from its earlier position
of support for the new Albanian state. He wrote that San Giuliano
believed that there was no longer any hope of maintaining the Prince,
and that the commission (on which Leoni was still influential) should
take control of the administration, but this change in Italian policy
had obviously come about much earlier.[269] Heaton-Armstrong and
Durham (who were both in Durazzo) wrote that the Italian forces
supposedly defending Durazzo were repeatedly seen signalling to the
insurgents. Yet the Dutch officers were unable to remove the Italian
forces. The Dutch officer who first detected this Italian duplicity was
himself forced to resign. This is perhaps indicative that Holland too
as a small state was unable to carry much weight in the great power
system, and despite the Dutch forces supposedly representing the
European concert.[270]

Wilhelm's role was the most interesting. There were times when
he could have acted more decisively. Heaton-Armstrong's forlorn
comments about Wilhelm's military failings, despite his training
in the German army, and the decision to send Essad into exile, are
intuitive examples.[271] However, Wilhelm seems to have received
extremely poor information and conflicting advice. According to
Heaton-Armstrong, he was often left isolated and without support.
This was in spite of Wilhelm desperately needing counsel because he
found himself in situations of which he had no experience. Heaton-
Armstrong also recorded that many of Wilhelm's 'better' decisions,
for example regarding the defence of Durazzo, were blocked by
other members of the administration.[272] Wilhelm's role in Essad's
arrest remains ambiguous. It is unclear whether he authorised the
pre-emptive strike, or acquiesced only after Essad had been arrested.
According to Lamb, Wilhelm did not authorise the use of guns.
Lamb therefore placed greater culpability on Sluyss and the Austrian
officials.[273]

Descent into World War One

The Italians continued working to undermine Wilhelm but none of
the other powers sought to help him. Between May and July 1914,

Wilhelm repeatedly appealed to the great powers for military and
financial assistance. He blamed the current situation on the failure of
the great powers to settle the Epirus question in line with their own
decisions in London, and their subsequent unwillingness to help him
in his difficulties.[274] Lamb and Phillips sent numerous appeals to the
British government that this was the only way to save the Albanian
situation. On each occasion, they were informed of the impossibility
of sending troops or other assistance. The Foreign Office maintained
that morally Britain was not in a position to help, and that practically
it was physically impossible to assemble an expeditionary force large
enough to be effective in Albania. Furthermore, there would also be
complications for the concert if the powers were forced to resort to
arms to uphold the Albanian regime.[275] Faced with these obstacles,
the Prince's position became increasingly untenable.

By August 1914 and the start of World War One, Wilhelm's
position had deteriorated further. One by one, the great powers
withdrew their representatives from Albania. From a great-power
perspective, they had more important things to deal with than
Albania. With the assassination of Archduke Franz Ferdinand, even
the Austrians, until then Wilhelm's most vehement supporters, albeit
for motives of self-interest, became uninterested in Albanian affairs.
The international squadrons in the Bay of Durazzo were the first
to be withdrawn. Italy (still neutral) was the only power to remain.
With the outbreak of war, Phillips and his international force were
evacuated from Scutari. A Council of Consuls of the Powers was
left to supervise the administration of the town and district.[276]
Diplomatic representation was withdrawn from Durazzo. This
inevitably had consequences for the working of the commission.
Grey ordered the withdrawal of Lamb on 12 August 1914, the day
on which Britain declared war on Austria. By then the German
and Russian representatives had already departed, leaving their
votes with the Austrian and French members, respectively, and the
Dutch mission left on 7 August. The Italians repeatedly urged the
Foreign Office to keep Lamb in Albania, arguing that the whole
control commission would dissolve if he left, and that the Albanians
would regard this as a desertion of the Prince by the great powers.
This would in turn create a new set of difficulties for the remaining
powers.[277] Meanwhile, the administration remained short of funds.

The Consulta, who together with the Ballhausplatz, was responsible for administering the promised loan, refused to authorise the commission delegates to pay the remaining sums. Instead, Aliotti demanded that Italy receive fishing, telegraph and other concessions in exchange for them.[278] The Austrians refused to help Wilhelm for fear of offending the Italians, who had remained neutral in the war. Only at this late stage, and when a greater emergency required it, did Austro-Italian co-operation re-emerge.

With the control commission went the last hopes for Prince Wilhelm's regime. His supply of funds finally ran out on 13 August 1914, and the remaining representatives of the commission urged him to leave. He refused to do so, although he did send his children back to Germany on 22 August 1914, with Heaton-Armstrong. The Prince's intransigence caused his opponents great annoyance. He was finally convinced to leave following the firing of shells into Durazzo. He departed, with his wife, on board the Austrian ship *Misurata*, on 3 September 1914. He never formally abdicated or renounced his rights to the throne, and he declared that his thoughts would always be with Albania. He entrusted his possessions and the palace to the commission under the presidency of the Italian Consul.[279] He asserted his desire to return to the throne with the conclusion of war, and the Austrians promoted his candidature. The Albanians, almost all of whom appear to have interpreted his departure as his abandonment of them, made it clear that they did not want him to return. Wilhelm kept his promise not to return unless the Albanians desired it.[280]

Conclusions: a failed experiment?

The Albanians had united in 1912, only to proclaim independence when the various factional differences (religious, linguistic, geographic, tribal, and lifestyle) were minimised by the threats caused by the first Balkan war. When these threats declined, Albanian schisms resurfaced. From the autumn of 1913 until the outbreak of World War One, these important issues were not dealt with, as an independent and self-governing Albania came into being for the first time. Internal and external rivalries and intrigue sought to undo what had been established, and threatened the very nature of the Albanian state. The appetites of the great and small powers that had an interest in Albanian territory resurfaced, as did Albanian differences, as varying groups sought to assert their authority, or protect their traditional rights, privileges and influence. This rivalry was not about balancing, but was instead designed to upset, or even destabilise, the international system. With the advent of the war, these pressures increased even further. The concert that had worked so hard for Albania's creation, and that had been preserved using the Albanian question, was now broken. It was no longer a check on the ambitions and rivalries of Albania's enemies. Significantly, it was not the Albanian question, which had for so long tested the principles of European concert diplomacy, but events elsewhere in the Balkans that eventually brought down the concert and provoked the European war. When the Albanian question no longer threatened peace between the powers and the great-power balance, the powers abandoned Albania. Simultaneously, Albania's 'friends' were no longer in a position to protect it. As Durham wrote, 'The infant state of Albania was to be flung to the wolves to save its elders'.[281]

At the point of proclaiming independence, the Albanians were only in phase A of applying Hroch's model of the national awakenings of small nationalisms.[282] During their independence experiment, they were not able to progress into phases B or C. During the brief provisional government and Wied's reign, there seem to have been few, if any, initiatives to advance the nationalist movement. Instead counter-national ones, often based on Islam that, as Hastings argues, were the 'inhibitor of nations', were able to gain the ascendancy.[283] The small band of nationalists and the larger bulk of the population were not ready to withstand the pressures that came with statehood, not least the external ones to which they would be subject. Faced with these obstacles and the varying intentions of some great power representatives, the nationalists found that they were unable to create 'Albanians'. Wilhelm was repeatedly accused of not understanding Albania or Albanians, and of not being strong enough to take control. He has therefore been given much blame for the failure of the first independent Albania. In reality, although Wilhelm did not help foster phase B of Albanian nationalism (for example, he chose few nationalist leaders for his cabinet), he often showed considerable foresight. For instance, he once remarked that 'if Albania is to be ruled peacefully, three persons ought to be hanged: Ismail Kemal,

Essad Pasha and myself. If all three were dead, Albania would fare much better'.[284] However, outside pressures and the growth of counter-national forces were far more influential in the demise of an independent Albania. Faik Konitza probably summed up Albania's predicament best:

> It is clear that, above all else, Albania has the failing of being friendless and defenceless, and of being where it is, an easy gift placed along an important route. And she has another failing, which is considerable...that of being tiny in size.[285]

Ismail Kemal bey Vlora, President of the Provisional Government, declaring the independence of Albania, 28 November 1912

The house in Valona where Albanian independence was proclaimed on 28 November 1912. (It is now the Independence Museum.)

Above: Essad Pasha
Left: Isa Boletini

Ismail Kemal bey Vlora

Turkhan Pasha *(left)* and Bishop Luigi Bumçi *(right)*, who both represented Albania at the Paris Peace Conference, 1919-20

Delegates to the Ambassadorial Conference in London 1912-13

Sergei Sazonov, Russian Foreign   M. Paul Cambon, French
Minister 1910-17   Ambassador to Britain 1898-1920

Aubrey Herbert MP

Count Leopold von Berchtold,
Austro-Hungarian Foreign
Minister 1912-15

M. Edith Durham

Count Alexander Benckendorff, Russian
Ambassador to Britain 1903-17

Sir Edward Grey, later Viscount Grey of
Fallodon, British Foreign Secretary 1905-16

Dr Mihal Tourtoulis

Prince Karl Max Lichnowsky, German
Ambassador to Britain 1912-14

Three contemporary cartoons depicting the London Conferences
1912-13

Glühlichter]   [Stuttgart.
The Albanian to the Austrian and Servian :
"You wish to bring to me culture and peace, and that is
why you are fighting together about me."

Minneapolis Journal.]
The Bone of Contention.

Le Cri de Paris.]   [Paris.
The London Conference at Work.

Hasan bey Prishtina   Philip Nogga

Hasan Riza Pasha, Essad Pasha and defenders of Shkodra, 1913

Prince Wilhelm of Wied, Albanian 'Mpret' March-September 1914, with Princess Sophie his wife

Prince Wilhelm, Princess Sophie and members of the Albanian cabinet in attendance at Neuwied when Prince Wilhelm was offered the throne of Albania

Prenk Bib Doda (in white jacket) in Mirdita with Dutch gendarmerie and Albanian soldiers, 1914

Members of the International Control Commission of Albania in Valona, 1914

July 4 1918: Bishop Fan Noli and other European leaders meet President Woodrow Wilson at Mount Vernon. In the photograph Fan Noli is in the second row, in ecclesiastrical collar, just to the right of Woodrow Wilson

Chapter 4

The Entente Powers and the Projected Partition of Albania: the attempt to form a Balkan alliance (1914-15)

When she left Albania in 1914, Edith Durham noted what people had said to her: 'Now that the powers are busy fighting each other, they will leave us free to manage our own affairs.'[286] The international forces left quickly, but Albania did not cease to occupy the attention of the great powers. It was perceived as having a key role to play in any future Balkan settlement. Both sides in World War One were ready to barter away Albanian territory in order to gain allies in the Balkans. The instability in Albania gave the neighbouring Balkan states and the interested great powers a situation that they could exploit in their own interests, and so overturn the decisions so laboriously achieved during the London conferences. Moreover, the situation created by the war was entirely new. Austria, whose attitude and policies had been so instrumental in the formation of Albania, was the enemy rather than the partner of the Entente powers. The latter were now free to pursue their own power-political and military objectives. The establishment of independent Albania in 1913 had been the compromise that reconciled the competing interests of the great powers, and preserved their concert. With the collapse of that concert into war, the existence and the interests of this small, fledgling state were expendable. Britain ostensibly entered the war of 1914 in order to uphold the 1839 guarantee of Belgian neutrality. But significantly, there was no parallel commitment to uphold Albanian neutrality, even though it had been internationally agreed only one year earlier. Despite Britain's rhetorical justifications of the decision for war being all about protecting the rights and independence of small nations, Grey's previous policy of self-determination for Albania was soon abandoned under the exigencies of war. Instead he pursued a strategy of using Albanian territory as an inducement to attract potential allies. Those interested parties were able to revive their expansionist appetites—hence the renewed constellation of acquisitive states: Austria, Italy and Albania's Balkan neighbours.

From the start of the war, both sides entered into negotiations with the neutral Balkan states of Greece, Bulgaria and Romania, in an attempt to recruit them, or to at least secure their neutrality. None of them negotiated with Albania. In the Balkans, the Entente powers desperately needed to provide help and support to Serbia, but Serbia's landlocked position made it difficult for them to deliver this themselves. The British doubted whether they could supply armaments or ammunition to the Serbs. Even if they could provide them with money, it was not clear that it would be possible for the Serbian government to purchase anything useful.[287] Serbia needed above all a Balkan ally or, better still, the re-formation of a Balkan alliance such as had operated during the Balkan wars. In the case of Bulgaria, this could only be achieved by territorial concessions, and in reality these were only possible in Macedonia, at the expense of Serbia.[288] Bulgaria had been left embittered by both Serbia and Greece following the 1913 Treaty of Bucharest, but Serbia was hardly likely to give up its Macedonian spoils willingly. Therefore, the Entente formulated a policy whereby they would offer Serbia territory in northern Albania, and in particular the prized asset of an outlet on the Adriatic. This would recompense Serbia for surrendering territory in Macedonia to Bulgaria. Since the creation of Albania had originally been an Austrian idea to keep Serbia away from the Adriatic, the fact that the Entente powers were now at war with Austria made the abandonment of Albania easier to contemplate.

Preliminary Negotiations

Throughout the war, diplomatic negotiations over alignments in the Balkans were probably more complex and drawn out than negotiations anywhere else: the actions of one state affected the actions of the others; there were ancient antagonisms and bitter rivalries to overcome; states were unwilling to commit to either side without knowledge of their neighbours' actions or guarantees by the powers. From the start, Entente diplomats, especially Sazonov, argued that Greece was the crux of any successful confederation scheme: if Greek support was gained, Bulgarian support would follow as a natural consequence.[289] There was hope that the Greek government, still obligated to Belgrade by its 1913 Treaty obligations, by which Greece was bound to support Serbia if Serbia was attacked by a third power, would fulfil these commitments and join Serbia, with resulting knock-on effects on the actions of the other Balkan states. Initial signs appeared promising. Following entreaties, Venizelos offered unconditional support to the Entente. Venizelos feared that, unless Greece joined Serbia, the Entente powers might return the Aegean islands to the Ottoman Empire, in exchange for Ottoman neutrality. Although the Entente had initiated the conversations, its members felt unable to accept the Greek offer, fearful of the response such a step might invoke in neutral Constantinople. Perhaps the best chance of acquiring Greek assistance was consequently lost. David Lloyd George, future British Prime Minister and then Chancellor of the Exchequer, later claimed that this decision was 'a stupendous error of judgment', and may have prolonged the war by a whole two years.[290] From then on progress was agonisingly slow.

It is doubtful whether Venizelos could have brought his offer to fruition. His position was complicated by the attitude of the Greek King. Constantine, influenced by his German ancestry and wife, and the views of the General Staff, had a passionate belief in the superiority of German militarism, and was convinced of an ultimate Germany victory. He had no sympathies for the Entente, and no desire to help the Serbs in a conflict against Germany. However, he did recognise Greece's obligations. The Entente foreign ministers believed this would be useful in preparing public opinion for the confederation. They consequently pledged help for Greece against Bulgaria, if Greece stayed neutral or joined the confederation. Attitudes in Athens were largely dominated by fear of any retaliatory action by the Bulgarian government. William Erskine, a British official in Athens, appears to have had a fairly accurate perception of Greek attitudes, especially in comparison to his superiors in Whitehall. He reported that, in his view, the offer of the whole of southern Albania up to the Skumbi river (north of the territory Greece claimed), without Valona, would be insufficient to gain Greek entry.[291]

Italian attitudes and interests were also paramount in British thinking. Many British diplomats considered that, as Italy was the only neutral power, its preoccupation with Albania (in particular its strategic, economic and cultural interests in southern Albania) could prove a key obstacle to the re-formation of the Balkan states' confederation. Grey claimed that Italian intervention would be 'the turning point in the war', because of the perceived impact it would have on the other neutral states, especially Romania.[292] The Greeks were concerned lest the Italian attitude should prove a block to their aspirations, especially in northern Epirus, as it had been in the 1913 London conferences. However, on 20 August 1914, Grey dismissed his colleagues' fears. He stated that, as far as he could ascertain, Rome was showing no interest in Albania, made no mention of anything affecting Albania, except Valona, and did not even claim Valona. He went so far as to suggest that Italy might accept 'international status' for Valona, in the same manner as Tangiers, in which all the powers interested in the Adriatic could participate. Grey urged Athens to uphold the Corfu agreement of May 1914, and warned against any designs upon the town of Chimara.[293] From the outset Grey, who had been so instrumental in establishing an independent and viable state of Albania, was willing to dismember it in the interests of British wartime policy. Yet it soon became clear from the corresponding Italian negotiations, especially Italian actions regarding the island of Saseno, that Grey's initial view had been short-sighted.

The negotiations between the Entente powers and the Italians were closely related to those with the Balkan states. The Italian government asserted that, as Austria had attacked Serbia, Italy was not obliged to invoke the Austro-Italian Alliance, because Austrian actions were in violation of Clause Seven, which forbade territorial changes in the Balkans without Italian approval.[294] As a result, the Central Powers and the Entente vied for Italian support and intervention on their sides. From the onset of hostilities, Italian policy makers acted to preserve Italy's paramount interests, and sounded out Entente representatives regarding the prospect of

Italian co-belligerency. They feared that the war would change the equilibrium in the Adriatic, and possibly in the Mediterranean too, thus endangering Italian strategic and naval interests there and in the Balkans, especially the Albanian littoral.[295]

Negotiations started as soon as the war began. The Italian representatives expressed their sympathy with the Entente cause of ending German military domination of western Europe, and hinted at the possibility of entering the war on the Entente side. Russian documents show negotiations with the Italians earlier than most western accounts allow for. As early as 1 August 1914, Sazonov had endorsed Raymond Poincaré's, the French President, suggestion that they should attempt to attract Italy by offering Valona and 'freedom of action' in Albania. This was in spite of the latter being beyond proclaimed Italian ambitions at that point.[296] Marquis Andrea Carlotti, Italian Ambassador in newly renamed Petrograd, had included the annexation of Valona amongst Italian claims in order to secure 'a preponderant position' in the Adriatic.[297] As Paul du Quenoy wrote,

> Russian diplomacy thus encountered a difficult situation. Having entered the war ostensibly to protect Serbia and Slavic interests in the Balkans, Russia had already offered Italy, a 'preponderant position' in the Adriatic, anchored in Rome's possession of Trieste and Valona.[298]

By 10 August 1914, Sazonov had proposed an agreement including the annexation of Valona by Italy, as he was anxious for Italian intervention at the earliest opportunity.[299] In these opening exchanges, the position of Albania was considered important but still marginal. The chief interest was Valona. Italy was prepared for Valona to be not only neutralised, but perhaps even internationalised, with all the Adriatic powers taking part in the administration. Italian officials claimed that they would not object to the division of the rest of Albania between Serbia and Greece, but on condition that the whole Adriatic coast from Mount Stylos to the mouth of the Boyana was neutralised. These initial proposals represented a complete change in Italian policy from the 1913 Ambassadors' Conference, but they supported longer-term policies that coveted expansion into the eastern Adriatic.[300]

The negotiations were slow and uneven. Grey refused to countenance what he considered 'hypothetical negotiations', despite pressure from Sazonov on the necessity of Italian entry.[301] Despite his insistence that it was an inopportune moment to press the Italians to abandon their neutrality, Grey was fully aware, from reports by Rodd, still British Ambassador in Rome, that the Consulta had decided to join the Entente and was merely awaiting a decent pretext to take up arms against Austria.[302] For the time being, discussion amongst British policy-makers centred on what might furnish the necessary excuse. Most believed that a much greater threat to Italy than the protection of its interests in Albania would be needed. Sir Eyre Crowe, British Assistant Under-Secretary for Foreign Affairs, considered that only seeing Bosnia, Herzegovina and Dalmatia all 'in a blaze' would induce the Italians to help Serbia and Montenegro.[303] Others within Whitehall took a different view, and considered that the Albanian position might win over the Italians. This was particularly true since San Giuliano had hinted at the importance of Albania when he had commented that the timetable would depend upon 'the march of events on the other side of the Adriatic'.[304] As Sir George Clerk, then a senior clerk in the Foreign Office, remarked, it was hoped that, although Albania might now have become a secondary issue in European international affairs, it was definitely true that 'Valona may yet provide cause for war between Italy and Austria'.[305] Evidence suggests that some form of Entente action in the Adriatic may indeed have induced Italian intervention. In September 1914, Grey, Rodd and Sir Francis Bertie, British Ambassador in Paris, all proposed action in the Adriatic, including the destruction of the Austrian fleet there, to induce Italian involvement. The idea was eventually dropped because of Franco-Russian opposition.[306]

The First Occupations of Albania

Throughout September, discussions continued but they remained low key because officials in Rome and Athens still refused to agree formally to intervention. Within one month, the Italians and Greeks had both acted to safeguard their Albanian interests. The departure of the Albanian sovereign and great power representatives, the disintegration of the Albanian state and dispersal of the small gendarmerie gave the interested parties (Italy, Greece, Serbia and Montenegro) ample opportunity to use the situation to their advantage. The Greeks, still neutral, were the first to respond. By the beginning of October 1914, the situation in northern Epirus was deteriorating partly, it was believed, due to the complicity of the Epirote police. The British relief mission, under Mr Duncan, had been forced to leave. It was reported that Muslims in Argyrocastro were threatened with massacre, and that the Greek-speaking (mainly Orthodox Christian) populations were convinced that Athens had approved such an extermination of 'non-Greek' (Muslim) elements. It appeared that all respectable members of the Autonomous Northern Epirus government, including Prime Minister Zographos, were powerless. This inevitably gave the Greeks the 'opportunity' that they had been seeking to intervene. Initially the Consulta objected to any Greek action, allegedly to protect the decisions in London, but undoubtedly out of fear of any Greek designs regarding Valona.[307] The Italians claimed that, as the only great power signatory of the statutes creating an independent Albania not involved in the war, it was their responsibility to prevent the occupation of Albanian territory.[308] Venizelos sought to gain Entente support for an occupation to protect the Greek population from violence by Muslim irregulars. However, he stressed that Greek intervention would go ahead even without this.[309] In response, Grey, trying not to lose Italian goodwill, attempted to reach an agreement with the Italians. He did not see how Britain could support this move otherwise. The Consulta replied that it would make no objection to a Greek occupation of Argyrocastro to 'restore order', as it too might need to do so at Valona, as long as it was understood that the London resolutions still generally held good. Antonio Salandra, the Italian Prime Minister, deputising at the Foreign Office following San Giuliano's death, refused to acknowledge the agreement formally or publish it. Whitehall believed this was for fear of the impact it would have on the Muslim Albanians, particularly Essad Pasha, whom Whitehall suspected had a tacit understanding with the Consulta. Rodd advised that the Consulta was prepared to communicate with Athens, but only by using London as an intermediary, and on the understanding that no official agreement would be reached.[310] Salandra stated that he preferred any Greek action at Argyrocastro to pre-empt Italian action at Valona, but he stressed that this would not necessarily occur, even if the Greeks occupied Argyrocastro.[311]

The Greeks agreed to these conditions, and were satisfied that their occupation could be used as a pretext for an Italian occupation of Valona.[312] Whitehall also secured an agreement that the Consulta would not confer with Vienna or Berlin, but, considering that the Italians had already gained agreement for intervention from them, this was an easy promise to make.[313] The Entente also stated that they were prepared for the Serbs to occupy northern Albania, but the Serbs declared that they had no current interest in doing so, unless attacked by Albanian bands. By contrast, the Entente leaders persistently refused to sanction a Montenegrin occupation of Scutari, primarily because they viewed such initiatives as detracting from help for Serbia. Nevertheless, as early as 8 August 1914, Montenegrin forces had unofficially occupied Mount Tarabosh, overlooking Scutari, in an initiative to secure the territory that the powers had denied them at the London conferences.[314]

Greek troops crossed the southern Albanian border in October 1914, officially re-occupying all of southern Albania, apart from Valona, and establishing a military administration by 27 October. Four days later, supposedly in response to the Greek occupation and to Ottoman intrigues, and to uphold Albanian neutrality, Italian troops as a 'cautionary measure' occupied Saseno Island. They established a 'sanitary mission' at Valona to provide relief for the inhabitants, especially the foreign nationals. The Consulta argued that Ottoman intrigues would undermine Albania's future stability and were in the Austro-German interest, following the Ottoman Empire's entry into the war (2 November 1914). Therefore they proposed boarding and searching all vessels flying Greek or Ottoman flags, to prevent the landing of arms and ammunition in Albania.[315] Saseno was the closest Italian forces could get to the Albanian mainland without occupying it. It was believed that it would provide an ideal base from which to search any vessels. The move clearly illustrates the importance of the Albanian littoral to Italian policy makers. Their actions placed the Consulta in a supreme position, if events were to develop in a way that 'forced' them to intervene. This would also enable Italy to control the Otranto Straits, and therefore access to the Adriatic. For this policy, the Consulta obtained unanimous Entente support, although Petrograd was prepared to accept it only as long as traditional French interests and operations in the Adriatic were not compromised.[316]

The Saseno occupation was an incredible achievement and it would play a significant part in subsequent negotiations. Baron Sidney Sonnino, soon to be Italian Foreign Minister, later claimed of the incident: 'They [the Entente] would swallow anything rather than risk pushing new forces into the arms of their enemies.'[317] Moreover, as San Giuliano had earlier predicted, the occupation of Valona would remove it from the bargaining table. It would require both the Entente and Central Powers to make more substantial offers to secure Italian intervention. Surprisingly, yet crucially, all the Entente representatives appear to have failed to realise this, and in so doing they made a calamitous error.[318] Instead of making Italy more receptive to a possible intervention, as intended, the Entente would now have to offer more to secure it. In late September 1914, Carlotti had already taunted Sazonov that the Italian entitlement to Valona (on the basis of the decisions made in London, and to protect it from aggressors) would grant the Italians 'absolute mastery' of the Adriatic.[319] None of the Entente negotiators seem to have taken the hint.

Sazonov's Balkan Initiatives

The Ottoman Empire joined the Central Powers, declaring war on 29 October 1914. This made the Serbian position even more precarious because it created the possibility of a joint Austro-Ottoman offensive against Belgrade. From early November, Sazonov took the lead on the diplomatic front. In his first proposal, Sazonov was prepared to offer Bulgaria the so-called Enos-Midia line in exchange for Serbian Adriatic access in northern Albania, Bosnia and Herzegovina. Greece would be confirmed in the possession of northern Epirus and the Aegean islands.[320] The Entente had still not gone far enough to satisfy the Bulgarians, who re-asserted their decision to remain neutral.[321] Grey, in a reversal of his attitude in 1913, seems to have decided that the powers had made a mistake in shutting Serbia off from the sea: he was adamant that Serbia must have access to the Adriatic in northern Albania. Grey saw this as the answer to inducing officials in Belgrade to cede territory to Bulgaria in the east, the offers of which the Entente needed to increase, in order to compete with Austro-German ones.[322] To further this proposal and overcome Serbian objections, the French proposed to negotiate directly with the Bulgarians, without notifying or communicating this to the Serbian government. This was more than Sazonov or Grey were prepared to countenance.[323]

Meanwhile, the ability of the Entente to persuade the Greek government to contemplate concessions had greatly diminished. Venizelos was not prepared to give up the solitary town of Cavalla in eastern Thrace to secure northern Epirus. The latter was no longer as attractive as a means of compensation because the Greeks were now in possession of it.[324] As a result, the Greeks became increasingly intransigent, refusing to make any concessions to Bulgaria but claiming compensation for any Bulgarian gains in Thrace. News soon arrived that the Serbs had occupied Albania as far south as Elbasan, although they stressed that this was only 'provisionally' to ward off Albanian incursions, and was not indicative of designs on Albanian territory. The Entente feared that such action would give Montenegro the excuse to seize Scutari and provide a similar pretext for Bulgarian operations in Macedonia, which the Entente wished to prevent at all costs.[325]

Securing Bulgaria's immediate intervention against Austria was considered the top priority to protect Serbia from a crushing defeat. To achieve this, the Entente needed to guarantee Sofia the Enos-Midia line, and even the districts in the 'contested zone' in Macedonia promised under the 1912 Serbo-Bulgarian convention. They also needed to allow for a coterminous Serbo-Greek frontier.[326] Sazonov attached great importance to the fact that Greece and Serbia needed a common frontier. He argued that this, together with Bulgarian territorial aspirations, could be achieved only at the expense of Albania. He had always opposed Albania's creation, and argued that recent events had confirmed that its independence was untenable. Sazonov detailed the precise line that the Greco-Serbian frontier should take. It would start at Pogradec, would pass by the watershed of the rivers Skumbi and Deval and go south to the Adriatic at the mouth of the Skumbi, although Valona would be left to Italy. By acquiring the fertile region of Durazzo, Shiak, Cavaya and Tirana, Serbia would receive some material compensation for the loss of Macedonia, whilst Greece would gain Albanian territory further north than that defined as northern Epirus, including Berat and Elbasan. Even ethnic considerations were invoked for this division, as the Skumbi represented the traditional division between Ghegs and Tosks. Despite some French support, officials in Whitehall did not give this scheme much credence. Their objections centred on their belief that Venizelos would refuse the proposal, and not accept the allocation of Monastir to Bulgaria. They also believed it would be violently opposed by the Serbs and Albanians, especially the northern tribes, and that no definite acceptance by a Balkan state would be achieved if Sazonov kept putting forward one new idea after another. The Balkan leaders would merely wait for the next one to see how it differed, hoping for and expecting improvements.[327]

Nevertheless Sazonov continued to draw up Balkan schemes. He argued that Austrian objections (during the Ambassadors' Conference) regarding Albania were no longer relevant, that an enlarged Bulgaria should no longer be feared and that the precise details should be left to Russian arbitration, in accordance with the 1912 Serbo-Bulgarian agreement. By the end of November 1914, Sazonov was prepared to accept a guarantee of Bulgarian neutrality as the price.[328] Grey was not prepared to go beyond the proposals formulated in mid-November. Although prepared to offer Bulgaria compensations up to the Enos-Midia line and to secure Serbian access to the Adriatic, Grey refused to countenance the partition of Albania between Greece and Serbia, insisting that this would arouse Italian objections because the Consulta would feel shut off from securing its interests in the Adriatic. British ministers were urging that Bulgarian neutrality must be secured, as they believed its delay was preventing the Greek and Romanian governments declaring their allegiance to the Entente. Consequently, Grey urged that the Bulgarians should be pressed for a reply, and Sazonov proposed to guarantee the Greeks against a Bulgarian attack.[329]

On 5 December 1914, the Entente offered Greece the whole of northern Epirus, except Valona. Venizelos refused. He was insulted that Greece should be offered so small a cession of territory, and stated that the whole of northern Epirus meant less to him than the possession of Cavalla, whilst the Bulgarians were to receive vast territories for nothing more than neutrality.[330] The internal Greek situation had developed in a way that necessitated the maintenance of Greek neutrality. Royalist circles were becoming increasingly pro-German; Venizelos and his supporters were becoming more vehement in support of a pro-Entente policy; the occupation of northern Epirus had in itself produced problems. Members of the Greek parliament and public were attacking their government for leaving northern Epirus under a military administration, instead of incorporating it into the ordinary civil regime. There was a realistic danger of further Greek manoeuvres, especially as Venizelos had sounded out the Consulta as to a possible advance on Berat, a significant town in central Albania.[331] Despite the Greek rejection, a further Entente offer was forwarded to Sofia, but this too was rejected. The Bulgarians repeated their commitment to remain neutral, but added that they might be convinced of the necessity of participation on the Entente side, if a more definitive and substantial offer was made. This did not materialise.[332] The Entente remained desirous of Greek support, fearful that without it the whole confederation scheme would collapse.

Before any further offers could be made, the position regarding Albania was transformed by the Italian occupation of Valona, and its hinterland, on 26 December 1914. The Consulta reported that they had heard gunshots in the port on Christmas Day, and had received an appeal from the Albanian government at Durazzo, which presumably meant Essad, for them to occupy. They claimed that the move was necessary to defend Albanian neutrality and to oppose the policy of the Ottoman Empire. The official explanation stated that disorder, around Durazzo, had spread to the neighbourhood of Valona. Sonnino added that the occupation was only 'provisional' and that the Consulta had no intentions of further action.[333] There is considerable evidence to dispute these assertions. The Consulta had already been pressing the Porte to recall the Ottoman officers, whom it blamed for fomenting agitation in Albania. The occupation was also a direct response to reports of expected Austrian action in the eastern Adriatic, because of the absence of the Montenegrin army. It is reasonable to suppose that Italian action would serve as a reminder to Vienna that Italy had interests in Albania, and the Balkans in general, that it wished to protect, and was prepared to do so by force if necessary. Conversely the American Ambassador in Italy, Thomas Page, wrote of discussions between the Consulta and the Central Powers regarding Italian action 'for the purpose of upholding the agreement concerning Albania'. This was in order to divert 'public opinion from its attitude toward the Triple Alliance' and because 'The

Entente powers would understand, probably to their discomfiture, that the Triple Alliance is still working together.'[334] Italian documents are even more illuminating. They attest to Sonnino's direct involvement three days earlier, when he had sent details to Aliotti to provoke 'a local incident to facilitate intervention and the opportunity to execute our plan'.[335] Most of all, the occupation ensured the removal from the bargaining table of the most obvious acquisition that either side could offer the Italians in return for intervention. Despite all the protestations that Italian troops would not advance further than Valona, Italian actions remained highly suspect. The Balkan states became more aggressive in their pursuit of Albanian territory, keen to stake out their claims before Italian forces were able to prevent them. Reports materialised of a Serbo-Greek understanding regarding Albania: if the Albanian tribes attacked the Serbs, then the Greeks would create a 'diversion' in the south.[336]

From the beginning of January 1915 information emerged, detailing the likelihood of an Austrian offensive against Serbia and Austrian agitation in Albania. This made help for Belgrade even more imperative.[337] It prompted the Entente to resume Balkan negotiations: the importance of Albanian territory within them declined, particularly for the Greeks. Clerk commented that, as far as Balkan territory went, Athens had practically nothing more to hope for in the war. Northern Epirus was already to 'all intents and purposes hers', the Consulta showed signs of preventing a further Greek advance, for example northwards to Berat, and Sofia would eventually form a barrier between Greece and Serbia in Macedonia. The Bulgarians would probably also try to seize Cavalla, to which the Greeks were resolutely opposed. In addition no more offers of Albanian territory could be made. Théophile Delcassé, the French Foreign Minister, refused to do anything that might offend the Consulta. Instead, the Entente sought to find payment for Greece outside the Balkans, and eventually settled upon Smyrna, because Ottoman possessions had become bargaining tools, following the Ottoman entry in November 1914.[338] These initiatives failed because opposition from Constantine resulted in Venizelos resigning on 6 March 1915.[339] Despite the loss of the most passionate Greek advocate of the Entente cause, relations between the Entente and Greece remained good. There were indications that the new Greek government might agree to join them, although most likely this would not include the restoration of a Balkan bloc. The final reply came at the beginning of May 1915.[340] By this point the situation had been completely transformed by Italian entry into the war.

Italian Entry and the Partition of 'Albania'

The initial interpretation, that Italian neutrality was merely a means of playing for time in order to extract the highest price from the highest bidder, has long been discounted. In reality, the Consulta had quickly surmised that its irredentist ambitions could be secured only by entry on the Entente side. Any alliance with Austria, or even neutrality, was unlikely to produce the desired results. The true tenor of Italian intentions became obvious when the Consulta asked for concessions from the Entente in exchange for intervention, although they had asked for the same concessions from the Central Powers in exchange for mere neutrality. The Consulta simply spun out negotiations with the Austrian government until it was possible to extract the necessary concessions from the Entente.[341] By the middle of February 1915, the Austrian negotiations had reached an impasse, and Rodd was able to report that he believed the Consulta had definitely decided to join the Entente.[342] The position of the Balkans, if not Albania specifically, was crucial. Since the beginning of the conflict, there had been reports of the impact that a Balkans expedition might have on Italian thinking. As Clerk maintained, the Italians were waiting for the Dardanelles campaign before acting. By the end of February 1915, and the start of the operation, Rodd too was urging that the time had come 'to speak more plainly' in Rome, but it was decided, once more, to wait for the Italians to make the first move.[343]

Eventually, on 4 March 1915, Imperiali approached Grey as to a possible agreement. Any such agreement would have several Albanian clauses, albeit as part of a much wider settlement, predominantly in the Adriatic. The Albanian clauses centred upon Valona, but also the creation of a 'Muslim state' in the central Albanian lowlands (the area inhabited almost exclusively by Muslim Albanians) as an Italian protectorate. In addition it was proposed that any part of the coastline annexed by Greece or Serbia, which *de facto* meant the rest of the Albanian coastline, should be neutralised.[344] The central Muslim state stipulation probably arose from Italian treaty obligations with

Essad Pasha. This territory represented Essad's power base and would also exclude many nationalist elements (Orthodox Albanians in the south and northern Catholic tribes), who had both opposed him in the past. Throughout the negotiations, the Italians tried to obtain as much as possible, the Russians attempted to stop them. The British worked for compromise, in accordance with contemporary ideas about the balance-of-power and British naval interests. Neither Whitehall, nor any of the Entente or Italian negotiators, foresaw the collapse of Austria-Hungary. Whitehall feared Italy replacing Austria as the dominant power in the Adriatic and western Balkans. Therefore, it deemed it necessary to increase Serbian acquisitions to provide a counterweight, and to make additional commitments to the Serbs as an alliance partner. Conversely, the Foreign Office did not want to see Serbia, especially a Russian-dominated one, sufficiently enlarged to upset the balance of power in the Balkans and Adriatic to Russian advantage. Ideas of self-determination, especially relating to the Albanians, were not considered.

Although the majority of the Consulta's demands proved uncontroversial, the negotiations did not run smoothly. Sazonov had became increasingly resistant, largely because he realised that Italian aspirations in Dalmatia were in contravention of Slav interests, and this led to a re-evaluation of the possible help Italy could provide. Sazonov advised his ambassadors in London and Paris to repeat his conviction that Italian aspirations should be 'proportional' to their assistance, and not solely against Austria-Hungary.[345] Sazonov desired to exclude Italy by defeating Italian ambitions in the eastern Adriatic, but eventually Franco-British pressure lessened his objections. The obstructive Russian Ambassador in Rome was also replaced to facilitate negotiations.[346] Grey thus found himself once more in the role of mediator. At the beginning of March 1915, Whitehall and the Quai d'Orsay acknowledged complete recognition of the Russian government's claims to Constantinople and the Dardanelles straits, despite this being in contravention of the long-term interests of both.[347] Grey had insisted upon the importance of this, to 'remove Russian suspicions as to our attitude and to get rid of the Russian objections to the participation' of Italy and the Balkan neutrals.[348] Nevertheless, Russian objections consistently threatened to jeopardise Entente chances of securing help from the neutral states, especially Italy.

Sazonov's objections to the Albanian settlement were considerable and played a major role in the discussions. He passionately disapproved of creating a central Muslim state, believing it would be completely impractical, and was adamant that the whole of Albania should be partitioned between Greece and Serbia. He continued to oppose any scheme that included blocking Serbian access to the Adriatic, but he accepted that Serbian and Montenegrin ports could be neutralised.[349] All these issues had an impact upon Serbia's potential Adriatic access, and therefore on Russian use of any Adriatic ports.[350] Delcassé also opposed any future Muslim Italian-controlled state in Albania, and even the neutralisation of the Adriatic coast: this could be prejudicial to Serbian commercial expansion and have severe implications for Serbian morale.[351] Grey, on this issue, as on so many others, held a position halfway between Rome, on the one hand, and Paris and Petrograd, on the other. Grey's personal views were immaterial: he considered Italian intervention crucial. He stated that, although he had no principled objections to the creation of an independent Muslim state, he believed that there would be great difficulties in sustaining the state in practice.[352] Attempting to bring the sides closer together, Clerk proposed that the idea of the 'state' was a matter of detail that should be left for discussion. He added that, although the Italian claims were considerable, it might be worthwhile to meet their wishes, albeit only after some 'opposition'.[353] Eventually, Delcassé was convinced by British arguments, as he too was desirous to avoid further delaying Italian entry. He agreed to accept the Italian proposal, including 'in principle' any British suggestions regarding Albania.[354] Under immense diplomatic pressure, Sazonov too gradually, and grudgingly, lessened his objections. He conceded the recognition of Italy's outright annexation of Valona and the Muslim state idea, albeit with certain modifications and stipulations. It was in these that controversy persisted. Sazonov maintained that, whilst Durazzo was to be the capital of the Muslim state, the seaboard territories generally would need to be placed under Italian rule. More significantly, he insisted that a central strip of Albanian territory should be left to provide Greece and Serbia with a conterminous frontier.[355]

Although Sazonov considered other parts of the Adriatic, as the home to native Slav populations, more important than Albania, he held out on negotiations regarding Albania; but in other areas, including Dalmatia, he was prepared to compromise. Sazonov insisted that, if the Italians wished to annex the Dalmatian coast from Sebenico northwards, they must abandon their pretensions to Albania, whilst keeping Valona. Dalmatia was most definitely Slav but it was also home to non-Orthodox Catholic Croats and Slovenes. Sazonov was prepared to make concessions at the expense of the Croats and Slovenes, but not of his protégé Orthodox Serbia, whose claims focused on northern Albania. Eventually, Sazonov chose to grant the Italians two Dalmatian ports rather than make concessions in Albania. Sazonov was prepared to go so far as to threaten that, if the Italians did not join the Entente 'soon', all promises might be withdrawn. He also continued to argue vehemently against the Muslim state, claiming that it could not be self-sustaining. He was only prepared to give Italy this claim, including Durazzo, if it abandoned claims further north, together with Spalato which, he argued, must become Slav. Later he relented to some extent, maintaining that Spalato could be neutralised and that Italy could retain the Dalmatian islands for strategic reasons.[356]

The Italians succeeded in holding out, arguing that if the proposals were rejected then Italy would not enter the war, because its object was to make the Adriatic secure. If this objective was jeopardised, its operations would be futile. It was not so much fear of Austria but fear of Russia that dominated Italian thinking. The Consulta feared that, after the war, Austria-Hungary would be replaced by Russia as the dominant power in the Adriatic, if not the Mediterranean, through its position in the Balkans, including above all an enlarged and strengthened Serbian protégé. The Italians considered that only Pola, a port in Istria, could provide an adequate guarantee of security. Valona, despite all perceptions to the contrary and the former Italian interest in the port, was a far lesser prize. Since its occupation, it had been discovered that, without a massive works programme to convert it into an adequate naval base or defensive station, Valona would not be able to secure the Adriatic. Rodd insisted that he did not believe that the Consulta would really break off negotiations. However, an increasing number of reports were materialising, and from 'credible sources', thus they could not be dismissed as Italian propaganda or intrigue, that the Consulta was about to conclude a definite agreement with the Ballhausplatz.[357] More crucially, disastrous news from the Dardanelles, at the end of March, made the signing of any agreement all the more imperative for the Entente. Sonnino considered himself in a stronger position. He had received a firm indication that Grey would not support the prospect of a Russian client state in the Adriatic, considering such an eventuality as potentially dangerous to Britain as to Italy. Sonnino had notified his ambassadors that Rodd had informed him that, from 'the military viewpoint England has interests in common ... military predominance in the Adriatic is of primary importance'.[358]

At the beginning of April 1915, Grey announced that, because of his failing eyesight, he was to take a rest. He passed over control of the Foreign Office to Herbert Asquith, the British Prime Minister. This news, coming at such an impasse in negotiations, could not fail to impact on both Sazonov and Sonnino. Sazonov was particularly disturbed. He greatly valued his personal relationship with Grey. He considered that his recent acquisition of British support for Russian designs on Constantinople would not have been achievable without this relationship. He feared that another foreign secretary would not feel obliged to abide by it. He was informed only indirectly of Grey's departure.[359] He therefore moved to bring about a quick resolution of differences with Sonnino. Under these circumstances, Asquith was able to secure that agreement which had so eluded Grey.

This agreement had something for both sides. The Italian government would be responsible for Albanian representation in foreign affairs of the small Muslim state version of Albania. The Entente ensured that the hinterland of such a 'state' would be limited to the east, to provide a territorial connection between Greece and Serbia, west of Lake Ochrida.[360] From the British perspective, this arrangement served two purposes: it would help to maintain the balance of power and it would ensure that the Serbs would not be dependent on the Adriatic for their maritime outlet. Serbia's landlocked position had placed it in a precarious position, and had prevented the Entente providing help and supplies. Under the terms of the Pact, Clauses Five, Six and Seven related to Albania. Most significantly, Valona and Saseno were to go to Italy in full sovereignty, the coast was to be neutralised as far south as Cape Stylos, thus neutralising the Corfu straits, and the Albania created in 1913 was to

be tri-sected between Serbia and Montenegro in the north, Greece in
the south and a small neutralised Muslim state under Italian tutelage
in the centre.[361]

In the final stage of discussions, Sazonov and then Sonnino and
Salandra raised new objections. Grey, returning after his recuperation,
finally brought his full weight to bear on the proceedings. Together
with Delcassé, he persuaded Sazonov not to insist on Italian entry by
1 May 1915, and he persuaded the Consulta, against its wishes, not
to delay signing until 2 September 1915.[362] Although other areas of
the settlement remained more important, the Albanian question was
particularly time-consuming because the Italians raised several new
objections. The Italians modified their position regarding Article
Seven. They suggested that the frontier question should be left
open, and objected to the definition of Lake Ochrida as the point
from which the Serbo-Greek frontier should start. Grey countered
by arguing that there were several points of drafting where the
Entente had considered improving the text, but had dropped these
to save time. His main argument centred on a threat to a key Italian
ambition. If the Consulta pressed the definition of the territorial
connection in eastern Albania, the Entente powers would need to
raise the definition of the Dalmatian hinterland already assigned to
Italy. Grey argued strongly that the Italians should not press for a
weakening of Article Seven: such an action would lead to a double
loss of time and make it necessary to discuss two more changes. He
also stressed the effect on morale of Italy entering the war at the
earliest opportunity.[363] In response, Sonnino relented, stating that he
now accepted Grey's point of view, together with the points raised by
Sazonov, and hoped that signing could take place immediately.[364] The
projected gains in Dalmatia had proved more attractive than those
in Albania, and Sonnino dared not jeopardise them. The Russians
likewise waived raising any new points as to the Albanian hinterland,
and Sazonov stated that he was now content to leave any necessary
redrafting to Grey.[365] The final Pact of London was eventually signed
on 26 April 1915, and the signatories deliberately did not call it a
treaty, to avoid it requiring parliamentary approval.

The final version with reference to Albania included Valona,
Saseno and surrounding territory, sufficient for defence, going to
Italy in full sovereignty (Article Six). Secondly, it provided that

Italy should obtain the Trentino and Istria (Article Four) together with Dalmatia and the Adriatic islands (Article Five). Thirdly, providing the central portion of Albania was reserved for the establishment of a small autonomous neutralised state, Italy would not oppose the division of northern and southern Albania between Montenegro, Serbia and Greece, should France, Britain and Russia so wish (Article Seven). The coast from the southern boundary of the territory around Valona assigned to Cape Stylos was to be neutralised. Clauses regarding Italian representation of Albania in foreign affairs, and the coterminous Greco-Serbian frontier west of Lake Ochrida, were also included.[366] Less than two years earlier, Grey and the same Italian, French and Russian Ambassadors had represented four of the six great powers who had created, delimited and guaranteed an independent Albanian state. By the end of April 1915, they had negotiated Albania's complete dismemberment. Italy formally entered the war against Austria, and severed diplomatic relations with Germany, on 23 May 1915, although it did not declare war on Germany until 28 August 1916. The Consulta was highly satisfied with the terms, for it had finally secured the long-coveted foothold in the Balkans, and far-reaching territorial concessions elsewhere in the Adriatic. As Salandra later claimed, and there were many who would agree with him, the Pact was 'the greatest, if not the first, completely spontaneous act of foreign policy executed by Italy after the Risorgimento'.[367] Sazonov remained highly dissatisfied.[368]

Interventions and Albania's Strategic Position

Although the Pact was not published, there were strong suspicions that it existed and that its scope covered 'Albania'. The agreement revived long-held suspicions of the Italians in Belgrade and Athens, and heightened their mistrust of the Entente: the Serbs regarding Italian claims to Dalmatia, and the Greeks regarding Asia Minor.[369] The possibility of Serbian and Greek gains elsewhere had diminished, and without the possibility of these as trade-offs, the ever-dwindling prospect of the confederation scheme may have been rendered inoperable. In reality, although the Balkan states did not know this at the time, the Italian agreement was very much in line with the confederation proposals. Throughout the Italian negotiations the Entente leaders, especially Sazonov, had been determined to ensure the Balkan scheme, and insisted in particular on ensuring a sufficient Greco-Serbian frontier in Albania and a Serbian Adriatic outlet in northern Albania.[370]

Negotiations for the formation of the Balkan alliance had been continuing. At the start of August 1915, the issue of what to do with Albanian territory became prominent. The Consulta had formalised those concessions it was prepared to grant Serbia and Greece in Albania, and upon which subsequent offers of territory in Macedonia to the Bulgarians could be based. The definition, and determination, of the Greco-Serbian frontier in Albania proved very contentious. Under the Italian Pact, the arrangements for this had not been specified, in order to secure Italian co-operation. Sonnino was resolute not to see Austria replaced by another dominant power in the Adriatic. Sazonov was determined to secure the largest possible Adriatic frontage for Serbia, and for the Serbo-Greek frontier to be as long as possible, to secure rail and other communications. Sonnino wished to limit this in order to maximise the scope of the central Albanian state.[371] Conversations continued on these lines until news arrived that the Bulgarians wanted an announcement from the Allies that Serbia had consented to the proposals regarding Macedonia.[372] The Allies had not secured the necessary concessions from the Serbian government for fear of aggravating the delicate Serbian political situation. Nevertheless, on 3 September the Allies offered Bulgaria the Enos-Midia line and the 'contested zone' in Macedonia, if Bulgaria entered the war against the Ottoman Empire. The Allies were prepared to disregard Serbian sensibilities in a desperate attempt to prevent Bulgaria aligning with the Central Powers.[373] On 22 September 1915, however, Bulgaria mobilised in support of the Central Powers, and declared war on the Allies on 12 October 1915.[374]

Following Bulgarian entry, Serbia's position quickly deteriorated. This, in turn, had an impact on the diplomatic front. It rendered the idea of the Balkan confederation null and void. Conversely, there was no longer any need to offer Bulgaria compensation in Macedonia, and the resulting compensation for Greece and Serbia elsewhere, including Albania. More critically, Serbia was now surrounded on three sides by enemies, and the long-feared decisive onslaught had arrived. This made any form of Balkan agreement all the more expedient. It also made the position of 'Albanian' territory even more important. Bulgarian entry also revived the issue of Greek treaty obligations. A Balkan alliance on the terms of the first Balkan war was no longer possible, but the Allies still held out hope of establishing one similar to that of the second Balkan war. This was directed against Bulgaria and based on a Greek-Serbian-Romanian partnership. As early as 17 September 1915, the Allies had proposed the idea of a Balkan bloc aimed against Bulgaria. At that point, they still hoped that the proposal would secure at least Bulgarian neutrality.[375] Allied offers to supply 150,000 troops to Salonika, which Serbia was obliged to send under the 1913 Treaty, and even the cession of Cyprus by Britain, were insufficient to prompt the Greeks to intervene. The Athenian government insisted upon, at most, a policy of benevolent neutrality.[376]

The Greeks once more exploited the military situation to their advantage in northern Epirus. The Prime Minister, Stephanos Skouloudis, issued a proclamation stating that the Greek return to northern Epirus was a success of the highest importance (*kiryx* or first order), and implemented a series of administrative reforms. The Athenian press announced a Royal Decree reuniting northern Epirus with the Kingdom of Greece. In the December 1915 Greek elections, the northern Epirotes, inhabitants of territory still officially part of the state of Albania, were allowed to vote and to return deputies to the Greek parliament. On 11 January 1916, the elected representatives took up their seats at the opening of the new Greek parliament. This last step proved too much for the Allied representatives. In spite of the necessity of gaining Greek assistance, the Allies, under Italian influence, and in view of the plight of the Serbs, were not prepared to so blatantly offend Albanian sensibilities. They demanded an explanation from Athens, and declared that such moves were not in line with the decisions of the great powers regarding Albania. The Greeks protested at the Allied demands, claiming, in particular, that it was necessary to give the northern Epirotes a voice, as taxes were levied upon them. Nevertheless, the Greeks were eventually forced by the Allies to exclude the northern Epirote deputies.[377] With their troops now positioned at Salonika, the Allies were much better placed to ensure that their demands were met.

Under attack from three sides, somewhat ironically, the Allies decided that 'Albania' would be Serbia's salvation. An Adriatic Mission was instituted to supply the Serbs through Albania, and help was sought from the northern tribes to facilitate it. Grey went further. He proposed bringing the Albanians within the Balkan confederation. He argued that, to ensure their participation, it would be necessary once more to secure Albanian independence. Despite acknowledging many problems (above all in determining with whom to negotiate, and the need to give guarantees about Scutari), Grey considered this the best solution under the circumstances. Grey was sceptical that the scheme would be successful 'without offering the Albanian tribes anything except food and good words and bribes'. He was not prepared to go so far as defining any frontiers for a future Albanian state, as this would inevitably create too much disagreement amongst the Allies and opposition from Albania's neighbours.[378] Delcassé and Sazonov vetoed the scheme. In so doing, Sazonov argued in favour of an Italian protectorate for the whole of Albania—the very policy he had vehemently opposed in the discussions over Italian entry. He now considered this a lesser evil than an independent Albania.[379] But, as one official pointed out, they were tied by the 'Gordian knot' of the London Pact, especially in relation to Valona.[380] British thinking about Albania was determined by that of its alliance partners. Any moral sentiment was discarded for the harsh reality of wartime *realpolitik*. With Albania's chief proponent Austria now the enemy, the Entente was able to propose schemes for Albanian partition and dismemberment, with the aim of securing the desired Balkan alliance. By the end of 1915, this scheme had failed, the Serbs were fleeing south over Albania's northern mountains, admittedly towards the Adriatic, but not under the victorious circumstances of which they had dreamed for so long, and the future of an independent Albanian state was once more in doubt.

Conclusions

The discussions surrounding entry into World War One are illuminating for the question of Albanian independence. From the start, 'Albania' or Albanian territory was a significant feature of proposals to create a Balkan confederation. It was to provide compensation to Greece and Serbia for concessions elsewhere. Admittedly, Austrian considerations were no longer relevant, but the Allies went further in abandoning the Albanians, especially in light of their pledges to other small states such as Belgium. Entente diplomacy with Greece and the other Balkan states in 1914-15 was short-sighted, misguided and ultimately unsuccessful, because Greek fears, especially of the Bulgarians, were consistently underestimated.[381] Most Balkan states preferred to adopt a wait-and-see attitude in order to determine correctly what their neighbours would do, and also to judge accurately who the potential victor would be. No state was prepared to sacrifice itself for a losing cause and, except for some Serbian victories in late 1914 in repelling the Austrian offensive, the Allies were not winning. Diplomacy was closely linked to military developments. But it was a vicious circle. The ever-worsening Serbian position required the Allies to obtain the support of the Balkan states to help Belgrade; in order to gain that help the Allies needed military success. This was clearly far from the predictions about small and neutral states seeking to balance the international system by siding with the weaker coalition. Instead it clearly fits with Paul Schroeder's views on 'bandwagonning'.[382] Such a strategy is particularly important for small states because of the greater risks associated with choosing the wrong side. As the British General, Sir William Robertson, later wrote, 'since the war began, diplomacy had seriously failed to assist us'. However, as Grey so rightly replied, 'diplomacy in war is futile without military success to back it'.[383]

The policies and actions of all the Allied great powers were clearly indicative of wider strategic trends. From the British perspective, the question of Albania was related to concerns about Russian pre-eminence in eastern Europe. In Poland, British negotiators favoured the creation of a semi-autonomous Poland as a counterweight to Russian ambitions.[384] In Albania they preferred a small semi-autonomous and Italian-controlled Albania for much the same reasons in the Adriatic, and as a means of protecting British sea power. For the Italians, although their gains did not correspond to their maximum irredentist claims, they secured much more than their initial demands. Their policy regarding Albanian territory had protected their three core objectives in the war effort: protection against Austria and Russia, control of the Adriatic and potential for expansion and dominance in the Balkans. For the Russians, under the agreement, Serbia had been enlarged and had finally gained ports on the Adriatic and an extended boundary with Greece. Both of these should have fostered Serbia's future stability and growth, and provided a good base for Russian expansion in the Balkans as a result. For the French, their Greek protégé and their Russian ally had both benefited. There were glimpses of hope for the Albanians too—at least some form of state would survive, albeit in the central region where the conservative Muslim peasants had shown themselves the least receptive to the nationalist programme. Whilst Russian and French policies on the Albanian question remained largely constant, the war had caused a revision of British and Italian interests in Albania and the Adriatic. The policies pursued and decisions arrived at in London in 1913 were unable to meet their geo-political interests in the region, or their wider war aims.

The change in British attitudes, especially considering the staunch defence of Belgium, was perhaps the most surprising. British ministers would face numerous questions in parliament on this dichotomy. They would persistently maintain that the questions of Belgium and Albania could not be compared. Regarding Albania, as Grey maintained, the situation was different: five out of the six powers who were signatories to the international guarantee for Albania were now at war, the machinery set up there to ensure that guarantee no longer existed, the government had disintegrated, and the new ruler, Prince Wilhelm, had left the country.[385] Conversely, it is possible to view the confederation discussions, and especially the Pact with Italy, as a continuation of the British policy of 1913. Grey saw both agreements as an application of the balance of power. In 1915, nobody expected, or even called for, the complete dismemberment of Austria-Hungary, the withdrawal of Russia or the creation of a Serb-Croat-Slovene state. In this sense, the 1915 Pact can be seen as an Anglo-French attempt to arrive at a new balance. For if the Russian government was to increase its position in the Balkans, particularly through the acquisition of Constantinople and Serbian access to the Adriatic, it was considered necessary to make concessions to the Italians as a counterbalance.[386] British policy makers were aware of the deficiencies of their agreement, but wartime expediency overrode any moral objections. Of the Pact more generally, Grey stated: 'In war you will have secret treaties. Many things regarded as criminal are regarded as inevitable in war.'[387] Clerk wrote, in what Cedric Lowe has aptly described as an unusual dose of *realpolitik*, 'the answer, if one ever has to be given, is that we cannot strain the principle of nationalities to the point of risking success in the war.'[388]

Chapter 5

Albanians at War: anarchy, occupations and renewed independence?

'The Albanian problem, though not the most important, is one of the most difficult of the war, and unfortunately one that under any practical solution involves a considerable measure of hardship to the Albanians.' [389]

In 'Albania' at the start of the war, traditional rivalries had resurfaced, and the new state had fragmented into separate zones, each controlled by a traditional local chieftain. Albania was not in a stable enough position to sustain a long-term single administration, and most 'Albanians' do not appear to have wanted this. For almost all of the war, counter-revolutionary forces were in the ascendancy with religion a major motivation, in line with Hastings's views on the conservatism of Islam, and its inability to be a force in favour of nationalism. [390] Only in the later stages, when other (non-national) courses and options had failed or been discredited, did an Albanian nationalism re-appear, based largely on the Orthodox south and its enlightened diaspora, although many local motives were also involved. All the powers, perhaps with the exception of Austria, had already decided that the future of the fledgling independent state should be revisited (either by great power negotiations or a subsequent peace conference), and that the guarantees agreed at London in 1913 were no longer viable. By 1918, Albanians living in Albania or abroad were once more leading the movement for an independent state of

Albania, on the lines of President Woodrow Wilson's principles.

Meanwhile, for the first sixteen months of the war, great power concerns about Albania related to any possible diplomatic lever or advantage. From January 1916, fighting between the powers took place on Albanian territory. This territory in turn took on more immediate significance, as both sides sought to consolidate and strengthen their possession and control of the areas they occupied, and to extend their authority. In pursuing these policies, the powers would come into conflict with both enemies and allies. For example, the Italians would find opposition to their policies in southern Albania, not only from the Greeks but also from the French. Each of the great power armies used propaganda, incentives and bribes to win over the Albanian nationalists and non-nationalists in the zones they controlled, and to disrupt activities in those of their rivals. Great power political objectives continued to be at the heart of all policies, especially the 1915 Pact of London, in spite of prior agreements, offers to Albanians of autonomy or independence, and the wider declarations in 1917 and 1918 in favour of self-determination and nationalism.

It is possible to identify three distinct stages. During the first, the Albanians were primarily left to their own devices and counter-revolutionary forces predominated. In the second, various foreign armies invaded territory previously determined as Albanian, each with differing impacts on the Albanians they came into contact with and on the question of Albanian independence, and some vying for the leadership of the Albanian national movement. In the third period, 'Albanians' became tired of their reliance on foreign states, and resolved once more to satisfy their national ambitions according to their own aspirations, and in opposition to realist rhetoric about weak states.

Albanian Activities (1914-15)

With the outbreak of World War One, most great power states had withdrawn their diplomatic representation from Albania, and had taken little interest in domestic affairs in Albania. Following Wied's departure, many 'Albanians', especially those who had played a role in the nationalist programme, also left Albania: some returned to their former homes in places such as Switzerland and the United

States; many southerners went into voluntary exile, as a result of the complications arising from the administration in Autonomous Northern Epirus. Outside Albania, pro-Albanian organisations continued to exist and function, but their national programmes seem to have been shelved temporarily. These 'Albanians' tended to be loyal and patriotic to their host government and its war efforts, and perhaps this is indicative of the variable allegiances of many Albanians.[391]

The response of those who remained in Albania was mixed. Local and regional considerations dominated, as had also happened before 1912. One important British report at the end of the war detailed the divisions as follows: in the north, Scutari and its neighbourhood under a local commission of Muslims and Christians; the Malissori under their local chieftains; Mirdita under Bib Doda; in the centre, the region of Durazzo and its neighbourhood district under Essad Pasha, although with various other opposition groupings; and the south, divided between Valona and its neighbourhood under the control commission; and the southernmost district occupied by the Greeks. After the war, this led some foreign observers to argue in favour of a system of administration similar to that in Switzerland, because they believed that each region was desirous of some form of federal or cantonal self-government.[392] It seems that, during much of the war, national identity was of little significance and that Albanian divisions, of the type that had proliferated under the Young Turks, were far more important.[393] The division of 'Albania' into smaller and smaller units, with few links between the different areas, was nevertheless a step back from the former nationalist movement. Local autonomy options were able to thrive because the differences and rivalry between the various Albanian groups resurfaced, and disrupted the uneasy coalition. The small number of international forces remained in a few select locations, such as Durazzo and Scutari. In any case, they did not consider it their duty to deal with internal Albanian problems. Many influential Muslims, *beys* and *agas* had signed up for the southern nationalistic package, in 1912, only because of the external threats, and as a means of protecting their traditional privileges and customs. There was never any intention or desire for Albania to become a modern, democratic, independent state of the type envisaged by (some) southern intellectuals. The war made it clear that most still looked east to Constantinople. This was to a large extent understandable because, as rich Muslims, they had often been educated there, and many had served in the Ottoman court. In addition, the attempt at independence had failed, or at least had not met the needs of the majority of the people in the short period in which it had existed. This had discredited the national ideal. Thus a range of groups and individuals who had opposed it, had not supported it, had used the nationalistic problem only for short-term purposes, or had been apathetic to it, sought to use the situation created by the war to further their own local or individual interests. The development of these various factions and rivalries was promoted by intervention and intrigue by representatives of great power states and small Balkan states. They hoped to secure willing clients that they could use to secure their ambitions in Albania after the war.[394] This in turn fostered and deepened Albanian divisions. Without stability and security, the problems of trying to forge an Albanian 'nation' after independence thus proved too difficult for the small nationalist elite.

The development of four factions was particularly important, especially as these groupings appeared to compete for the leadership of the Albanian 'national' movement, albeit usually to safeguard their own local interests, as opposed to national ones, and because of their dealings with the representatives of other states. They were the Senate of Central Albania, Essad Pasha, the Union of Kruja and an Albanian Committee under Bib Doda. The divisions between these groups were largely tribal and geographical, with religion of secondary importance. The first three were primarily Muslim, the fourth Catholic.

In the first months of the war, the most notable developments occurred in central Albania and involved the Senate of Central Albania (despite a similar name, this was a new initiative, distinct from that formed by Essad in 1913). Swire offers the most detailed account of this period, but even it remains muddled and confusing. Three days after Wilhelm's departure, members of the groups who had been involved in the Shiak insurgency entered Durazzo and hoisted the Ottoman flag. When they had achieved this initial objective, many involved in the rebellion to remove Wilhelm proceeded to fall out amongst themselves. This was perhaps the inevitable result of such a disparate group. Like the Albanians involved in the rebellions against the Porte, they all had very different objectives and they lacked consensus on what to do next and, most importantly, on what sort of Albanian regime they wanted—other than one not involving Wilhelm. The major dispute centred on who should be offered the Albanian throne. Numerous alternative candidates were proposed, even though Wilhelm had not officially abdicated. Muslim Albanians continually looked for Muslim alternatives, and the possibilities included Achmed Fuad, an Egyptian prince, who was supposedly very enthusiastic about the prospect. Some of the foreign powers tried to push Christian alternatives. The Germans were keen to have another German prince established: Prince Burann-Eudin and Prince Victor Napoleon were mentioned.[395] Others wanted a return to Ottoman rule, as they were concerned about the loss of traditional privileges following independence; and many viewed the Ottoman Empire as their natural protector against the Slavs. There were also some who had previously supported Essad Pasha, and amongst them were alleged Italian, Serbian and Ottoman agents. Despite these differences, the insurgents managed to form a 'Senate for Central Albania', consisting of twenty-nine people. Its formation was notified to the powers. The French, Austrian and Italian members of the control commission, who had remained in Durazzo, were informed that their services were no longer necessary, and they left at the end of September 1914. This ended diplomatic representation to Albania. The Senate dispatched a delegation to Constantinople to offer the Sultan the crown, or, as an alternative, to ask him to nominate a suitable prince. It also constituted a national assembly at Elbasan. Failing to procure the Sultan, they turned their attention to acquiring a Muslim prince, a German non-Muslim one or even the return of Wilhelm.[396] This episode is an interesting one. In itself it was relatively minor but it offers an unusual twist on Albanian nationalism. The protagonists recognised themselves as Albanians and purported to have national objectives. Unlike most developments, especially those in 1912, in which religion is not seen as important in Albanian nationalism, or else is a counter-revolutionary and conservative force, for these Albanians their religion was an integral part of their Albanian identity.

Meanwhile, the war gave Essad Pasha another opportunity to attempt to seize power. He was prepared to make arrangements with anyone, including Albania's staunchest enemies, as long as they promoted his personal position. According to Swire and Dušan Bataković, as early as September 1914, he met Serbian Prime Minister Nikola Pašic in Nish and was liberally supplied with funds and equipment.[397] In Dibra, Essad gained additional recruits for his 'army', and many signed up in the belief that this would free Dibra from Serbian control. At the same time, the Essadists in Durazzo had persuaded the Senate to send men against the Epirotes. In their absence, Essad crossed the frontier with over 5,000 men and marched quickly towards Durazzo, entering it on 2 October 1914. Within three days, he had forced the Senate to make him President, reportedly having threatened to shoot every member who opposed him. It is distinctly likely that there was Italian, and even French, involvement in this successful *coup*. On the day when Essad was declared President, and almost a month before the official Italian occupation of Saseno, the Italian and French representatives of the control commission returned to Durazzo and publicly embraced him. *L'Independence Albanaise*, a publication, based in Sofia, that promoted an independent Albania, asserted that the Italian government had advanced five million francs for this operation.[398]

The third grouping, the Union of Kruja, consisted largely of Essad Pasha's former allies, who now opposed him. It was not particularly nationalistic, and favoured union with the Ottoman Empire. On 20 December 1914, a meeting, which became known as the 'Union of Kruja', began at a farm near the town of Kruja, with delegates from all the districts opposed to Essad. They passed several resolutions: to be reincorporated in the Ottoman Empire; to invite an Ottoman prince to be their king; to drive Essad from the country; to elect an administrative council 'under no single leader' to protect the rights of the people; and to initiate compulsory military service. They also resolved to prevent anyone from the rival districts (especially Dibra and Mati) from passing into Union-controlled territory.[399] Essad's and the Union's actions largely offset one another. Few initiatives of substance resulted. Eventually, Essad obtained the upper hand, following the Serbian and Montenegrin occupation of much of northern and central Albania, in June 1915. This act was motivated more by fear of Italian intentions than of Albanian rivals. With the arrival of Austrian and Bulgarian forces, Essad too retired into exile.

He went first to Italy and then France, where, in his self-proclaimed capacity of Albanian President-in-exile, he was assigned two French diplomatic representatives (Krajewsky and Captain de Fontenay, who had previously been the French representative on the northern boundary commission), although the Italians no longer recognised his position.[400]

The Albanian Committee, under Bib Doda's presidency, which presided over Scutari, San Giovanni di Medua and Alessio, was the most nationalistic of the four groupings, in spite of Bib Doda's circumspect allegiance before the war. The Albanian Committee had successfully managed to suppress the spread of Essad's propaganda, despite his support by the Italians, and had forbidden him from entering the towns under its control. It found it more difficult to control the propaganda of the Union, especially as many Muslims agreed that only the Porte could protect them. They consequently called for the Ottoman flag to be flown over Scutari. Bib Doda managed to secure a compromise, by replacing the national Albanian flag with one of red and black stripes. The most nationalistic initiative of the Committee occurred in May 1915, when the Italian Consul suggested that a National Government be formed. This never took place because of Muslim opposition.[401]

Great Power Occupations
THE AUSTRIAN ZONE
The policy of the Central Powers towards Albania had evolved, but it included the maintenance of an independent Albania, although again purely for reasons of geo-politics. With the Allied retreat, Austro-Hungarian and Bulgarian troops occupied northern, eastern and central Albania, including Durazzo and Tirana. The Bulgarian government wished to retain considerable portions of Albanian territory for itself, in accordance with the rescinded treaty of San Stefano. The Austrians aimed at (re-)establishing a viable autonomous Albania under Austrian control, although the extent of this autonomy varied from proposal to proposal. The Porte appears to have supported the Austrian position, whereas Berlin wanted to adopt a wait-and-see attitude, and persistently opposed any unilateral Austrian action. Most disagreements occurred between the two most directly interested states, Austria and Bulgaria. In particular, a dispute

raged about the right to occupy the two important Kosovan (Serbian) towns of Prizrend and Prishtina, which both states claimed.[402] As Austria was the great power, and because its troops occupied far greater portions of the disputed territory, the Ballhausplatz's policy proved more effective.

From January 1916, the start of the Austrian occupation, the Austrians declared that they had entered Albania only to expel the Serbs and Italians, and they called upon the Albanians (both Christians and Muslims) to help them do so. Many Albanians, including the important Mirdite leader Bib Doda, welcomed the Austrians and invited their fellow Albanians to receive them as 'liberators'. An Albanian civil committee was established (29 April 1916) at Scutari, under Austrian control. The initial enthusiasm for the Austrian arrival soon waned. A significant number of Albanians began to view the Austrians with suspicion. Many remembered the part the Ballhausplatz had played in bringing down the Wied government. It was reported that the Austrian troops treated their Albanian hosts poorly. They forcefully requisitioned all sorts of commodities and supplies at very low prices, or on credit. On 23 January 1917, the Ballhausplatz reiterated its public proclamation that Austria-Hungary was endeavouring to preserve the integrity of Albania, and had only entered the country in pursuit of a common foe. This failed to reassure the Albanians. Very few joined the Austrian military or became its informal allies, despite considerable financial inducements and propaganda to do so. The most significant group that sided with the Austrians was a force under Ahmet bey Zogu, the future King Zog and nephew of Essad Pasha, who, despite being only 21 years old, had emerged for the first time as a notable force in Albanian affairs. Swire wrote that even those Albanians who did join 'lacked a definite national cause'. He added that they 'fought without the same ardour as in previous struggles against the Turks'. There were also concerns about what the Ballhausplatz planned for Albania after the war. A delegation, including Zogu, went to Vienna to demand immediate autonomy from the new Austrian Emperor. Despite speaking well of the civil administration, they apparently feared becoming only another province of the Habsburg Empire after the war.[403]

The most noticeable developments in the Austrian-occupied

zone had occurred in central Albania, especially in Elbasan, where the central powers hoped to gain Zogu's support for their proposals. In February 1916, Zogu used the vacuum created by the retreat of Serbian and Essadist forces, in the winter of 1915-16, to seize Elbasan and establish a national assembly. This elected a 'commission of initiative' under Zogu's presidency, which in turn convened a National Congress under Akif Pasha Elbasani, who had been the Minister of the Interior in Prince Wilhelm's government, and had never resigned from that post. The main programme of the National Congress was the restoration and return of Prince Wilhelm—a policy that several other nationalists and colonies abroad were also advocating, including even those who had previously rebelled against him. Zogu wrote to Auguste Kral, formerly Austrian representative on the international control commission, who had been appointed Civil Administrator in Albania, to express his confidence that the Congress would meet with his approval, and that Austria would in turn assure Albania 'the expansion of the frontier line in accordance with the principle of nationality'.[404] This meant reuniting the Albanians with their co-ethnics in Kosovo, Chameria (the area of Albanian-speakers allotted to Greece) and other areas.

This was far from the policy the Ballhausplatz intended. It had no intention of the Albanians leading their autonomy or independence movement themselves; rather it was to be strictly controlled. The Ballhausplatz had probably not yet definitely decided its policy, or obtained agreement for such a policy from its alliance partners. Under the pretext of a cholera epidemic, Austrian troops occupied Elbasan and established a military cordon around the town. The next day it was announced that assemblies for political purposes were prohibited in districts occupied by the imperial army. Subject to far superior forces, the Albanians were obliged to submit to this decision. On 14 February 1916, Akif Pasha resigned his position and declared that Albania would be governed temporarily by Austria-Hungary. Despite Zogu's initial co-operation with Austrian forces, he was interned for the rest of the war when he went to Vienna to congratulate the new Emperor. Swire alleges that this was because Zogu was conspiring with the Bulgarians for the re-establishment of Albanian administrative independence. Eventually, on 10 March 1917, the Austrian government granted immediate autonomy to the

Albanians, under Austrian protection. This caused a storm of protest from influential Albanians who claimed it was pointless, because Albania was already legally independent. Austrian actions at Elbasan had in any event revealed Austria's true intentions. Albania's rivals would persistently use this co-operation against them in future discussions on the state's future.[405] Zogu, however, does not seem to have been personally hindered by his involvement.

ALLIED RIVALRY AND INDEPENDENCE IN SOUTHERN ALBANIA

In southern Albania, in the territories occupied by the Allies, there was also controversy over Albanian territory, and competition for it. In the light of the Allied victory, these initiatives were to prove more important. To counter Bulgarian activities, and because the Allies had little faith in Greek forces, French troops had occupied territory near Koritza and, by November 1916, had advanced as far north as Monastir and Lake Prespa. Meanwhile, Italian troops had occupied northern Epirus, including territory south of the Florence Protocol line. This close proximity of Greek and Italian forces, especially the Italian occupation of Greek territory, produced considerable Greek resentment at the violation of its neutrality. There were numerous protests from Greeks in the occupied zones and from both Greek governments (that in Athens headed by King Constantine and the rival administration under Venizelos stationed at Salonika), all of which proved detrimental to the ongoing Allied efforts to induce Greece to enter the war.[406] The military developments had an impact upon the relationship between the Allies, and on their Albanian policies. These were based on three main considerations. Firstly, the Entente representatives were perturbed that the Italian intervention in northern Epirus had gone ahead without their prior knowledge or approval.[407] Secondly, French activities worried the Italians. They were concerned that the French might have designs on southern Albania and even on the island of Corfu, both of which the Consulta considered strategic interests.[408] Thirdly, the Italians were anxious about the Quai d'Orsay's continued support of Essad Pasha. On 23 August 1916, Essad arrived at Salonika with French recognition and considerable Serbian support, posing as President of the Albanian government-in-exile. His five to eight hundred *tabors* were to fight as part of the Allied Eastern Army.[409] All three sets of suspicions and antagonisms persisted and festered as the war continued, and in their own ways had an impact on the Allied war effort in the Balkans, and on policy towards Albania.

Surprisingly, the first significant developments took place in the French occupied zone. On 10 December 1916, fourteen Albanian representatives (seven Christians and seven Muslims) created an administrative council and proclaimed Koritza an autonomous republic. This regime was highly significant for the Albanian nationalist movement, and it was indicative of the resurgence of Albanian nationalism in one of the areas where it had been strongest before the war. According to Jan Karl Tanenbaum, this regime 'acted as if it were an independent state, for it minted its own coinage, printed its own stamps, and introduced its own flag'.[410] Stickney considered that the republic gave the Albanians the opportunity for self-government under the French, which she described as the 'tutelage of those well disposed toward and more experienced than themselves'. Overall, it was a successful experiment in which Muslims and Christians worked together in the administration, and, in particular, without all the complications of great power rivalry and intrigue that had so beset Wilhelm's regime.[411]

The great powers appeared far from uninterested. It has been suggested that the French became a new force in Albania, and showed new interest in it becoming an independent state.[412] In reality, as H. James Burgwyn in particular has shown, French activity was only at a local level, and for strategic as opposed to moral or national reasons. Colonel Henri Descoins, the French commander in Koritza, signed a proclamation stating that the regime was to be under French military protection. It was suspected that Descoins was even the author of the document. For the week prior to the proclamation, General Maurice Sarrail, Commander of the Eastern Army, and Descoins were in repeated communication about this project. On 8 December 1916, Sarrail had cabled that the Albanian nationalists should be supported. Tanenbaum contends that Sarrail instigated this action to protect Koritza from Venizelist forces, which had prompted guerrilla warfare by some Albanians. By expelling the Greeks and converting the Albanian nationalists to the Allied cause, Sarrail hoped to protect the left flank. A peaceful and stable Koritza under French control would reduce the number of French troops needed, discourage the Austrians from moving into southern Albania and enable the Eastern Army's left flank to join up with Italian troops in Valona.[413] Officials in Paris were far less duplicitous. Aristide Briand, the French Premier, was not well informed by Sarrail, even misinformed. Following an enquiry from Rome on 13 December 1916, Briand denied knowing anything about the new republic and had to cable Sarrail for details. In his reply, Sarrail asserted that the French military authorities had played no role whatsoever in the creation of the new state. Briand assured his Italian colleagues of this. Mehmed Konitza was a prominent Albanian who had previously been a representative of the provisional government to the London conferences. His assessment of the declaration was that French motives were not nearly so altruitsic. He argued that the fertile land in Koritza province, especially the copper and coal deposits which were near the surface, were sought by the French military in order to supply their troops.[414]

Irrespective of its cause, this move generated much tension with the Italians. Briand repeatedly assured Sonnino that the French had no designs on either Albania or Koritza. It appears that, even by March 1917 (when he resigned as Premier), Briand had not yet received full information. Sarrail's reports still insisted that the Albanians had proclaimed the republic, then asked for it to be put under French protection, and that Descoins had merely complied with the wishes of the local population. Sarrail wrote that he had 'always let the population do what it wanted; … it does not behove me to meddle in the Greek and Balkan internal political question. Koritza wanted to be independent: now it is.'[415] However, the ramifications of the Koritza declaration would continue to reverberate well into 1917 and beyond.[416] On 16 February 1918, Sarrail's successor eventually abrogated the proclamation. The Quai d'Orsay was far from keen to have the Albanian nationalist movement develop too far under French influence, in case it jeopardised their more important goals regarding Greece. Changes were only nominal: Greek schools re-opened and Essad was prevented from transferring his government to the town, as sops to the Italians and Greeks, following the latter's eventual entry into the war. But, Koritza retained essentially the same government, and the republic's flag continued to fly over the town. Inter-religious co-operation was maintained, and both faiths were thankful to the French for the opportunity of self-government without much interference. The Albanians were also assured that this action did not threaten their independence.[417]

Having achieved relatively little on the diplomatic front regarding French activities in Koritza, the Italians or, more precisely, Sonnino, took the initiative in order to secure Italian interests in southern Albania. From March 1917, the Albanian flag was hoisted throughout the Italian zone of occupation and a measure of autonomy was granted. On 3 June 1917, at Argyrocastro, Lieutenant-General Giacinto Ferrero, the commander of Italian forces there, proclaimed the unity and independence of the *whole* of Albania under the aegis and protection of Italy, although the Italians controlled only a small portion of Albania, and the Allies not much more.[418] By the terms of the proclamation, Albanians were promised full liberty in internal affairs, including free political institutions, law courts, schools and their own army. In foreign affairs, the state was to be supervised by Italy.[419] Although the Albanians enjoyed relatively little autonomy in the Italian occupied zone and the Austrians in practice controlled most of 'Albania', there were noticeable improvements in the affected areas. Swire wrote that 'the Italians assumed in Albania the attitude of a benevolent although somewhat autocratic guardian'. 200 miles of good roads and 50 miles of rail track were constructed, hospitals were opened, schools established, national newspapers circulated, model farms introduced and prices regulated. The Italians paid high prices for the produce they requisitioned, and this did much to improve the fortunes of the local populace. Relations between the resident 'Albanians' (no mention was made of the Greek- and Vlach-speaking populations) and the Italian military authorities appear to have remained good. This in turn helped improve relations between Albanian nationalists and the Consulta.[420] Despite some protests, including several from Essad, other Albanian leaders were not ill-disposed towards the new regime, and this helped its establishment. Durham was unhappy that the declaration had occurred without some form of referendum, but she hoped that the Albanians would try it for 'a while at least', until they had time to consolidate.[421] Her advice in turn influenced the attitudes and actions of some of the Albanian nationalists.

These provisions obviously ran counter to the 1915 Pact, whereby an independent Albania was to be limited to a small section in central

Albania, with the north going to Serbia and Montenegro, and the south (except Valona) to Greece. Sonnino had never whole-heartedly embraced the idea of Albanian partition, and he now returned to Italy's former policy of supporting Albanian independence. It appears that he hoped to gain Albanian sympathies and increase their confidence in Italy, in order to secure, before the peace conference, additional territory to that specified in the London Pact.[422] Sonnino was concerned by French activities in southern Albania, but even more so by the burgeoning idea of the union, after the war, of Serbia, Montenegro and the former Habsburg provinces with a substantial Serbian speaking population in Croatia and Slavonia. This idea was being promoted by Entente propaganda, to disrupt the Austrian war effort and to encourage the now stateless Serbs. In the London Pact, Sonnino had not taken account of the prospect of a united 'Yugoslavia' on the other side of the Adriatic, nor had any of the other Entente leaders. As a result of this prospect, Swire claimed, there was a change in Sonnino's policy, with Albania becoming far more important in Italian strategic interests. If the 'Yugoslavs' were to gain a large expanse of territory on the eastern Adriatic, that could endanger Italian strategic interests in the Adriatic, then Sonnino wanted an enlarged Albania as a counter-balance. In arguing for Albanian unity and independence, Sonnino was making arguments on the new basis of national self-determination (the principles upon which the United States would soon enter the war), but geo-politics were paramount. He did not want to relinquish other gains from the London Pact. For example, he intended to retain the claim to control Albanian foreign policy and also the port of Valona. Sonnino continued to emphasise the particular importance of Valona, especially regarding the Otranto straits, which continued to require Italian acquisition of the town. It would not be part of a renewed independent Albanian state. By contrast, Robert Woodall does not even mention the impact of the 'Yugoslav' threat. His discussion focuses solely on French and Greek antagonisms in southern Albania. This view seems far less convincing, as it would not necessitate a change in policy regarding northern Albania. Moreover, Italian complaints to Britain regarding the French declaration at Koritza only emerged in the summer of 1917 and after questions over the Italian declaration at Argyrocastro had been raised. Woodall has also argued that the Italian action was a response to Sonnino's fears that the Allies would renege on their promises in Asia Minor. He contends that Sonnino decided to 'tighten Italy's grip' on the territory already in Italian control, including reserving the occupation of Albania for Italy alone. This idea does not seem to be substantiated by later events; acquisitions in Asia Minor, and elsewhere in the Adriatic, proved far more attractive to the Consulta than those in Albania.[423]

This last move, along with the supervision of Albanian foreign policy, clearly revealed Sonnino's real intentions. His colleagues appear to have been less well informed: not even his fellow Cabinet ministers had prior knowledge of the Foreign Minister's plans. On 20 June 1917, Sonnino was forced to appear before the Chamber of Deputies in Rome to explain his actions. His statement backtracked from the 3 June 1917 proclamation. He declared that, when he spoke of the unity and independence of Albania under the protection of Italy, this meant protection against Albania's neighbours and not a protectorate in the colonial sense. He added that the future peace conference would have the task of determining the precise boundaries of the Albanian state. Italy claimed predominant influence over Albania on the grounds of strategic and national need only.[424]

Italy's allied partners were just as anxious about Italian activities in southern Albania, not least because of the impact on the Greek negotiations. Even before the proclamation, the British Foreign Office had considered sending Harry Lamb on a special mission to investigate Italian activities there.[425] Particularly concerning, from a British perspective, was the extension of the Italian zone of occupation into Greek territory: that is, south of the Florence line. Despite Italian assurances that this was only temporary, to protect Valona and the Corfu channel, Italian actions were treated with much suspicion. Whitehall and the Quai d'Orsay received repeated appeals and protests from the Greeks.[426] The Italian proclamation at Argyrocastro increased and confirmed these suspicions. Whitehall viewed the move as an 'implicit violation of the London declaration', in that it referred to these changes, foreshadowing that which would materialise in an eventual final peace treaty, and because they contravened the sections of the 1915 Pact relating to Greek and Serbian claims. The Italians had also acted without first gaining the consent of the other signatory powers to the London declaration.

Only token protests were communicated to the Italians, because the Foreign Office did not expect to receive much support from the Quai d'Orsay if it pursued the matter. For, as one clerk wrote, it looked as if the French had decided to allow a 'free hand for Italy in Albania', and that this was the '*quid pro quo* by which the French obtained their free hand in Greece'.[427] This French view appeared to be confirmed later in the year when Bertie, still British Ambassador in Paris, reported that the Quai D'Orsay considered Koritza to be 'part of Albania'.[428] This reflected a French u-turn from the London Pact and also Sarrail's policy in the Koritza republic. It hinted at French support for Italian claims in Albania. Moreover Rodd was anxious that it should not be leaked that Italy acted without Allied consent. He believed that this might precipitate a push in Rome for the resignation of the Foreign Minister, which he considered far from desirable for the war effort.[429] Albania's future had become closely tied with Italian geo-strategic interests and policy.

THE STRUGGLE FOR NORTHERN ALBANIA

French and Italian friction continued throughout 1917 and 1918, during the campaigns to push Austro-Bulgarian forces out of Albania and, in particular, in the rush to be the first state to occupy the town of Scutari. It was important for the Italians to occupy as much Albanian territory as possible, to facilitate their revised plans for a 'large Albania'. These Italian initiatives initially came in for much criticism. Georges Clemenceau, the French Prime Minister, claimed that the independent Italian activities and policies in Albania were endangering the security of the whole Allied Eastern Army. When, however, with the failure of the summer campaigns, the Italians again attempted to consolidate their position in southern Albania, including establishing a native administration under Italian control that would deter Serbian, Greek, French and Essadist forces from entering the Italian occupied area, the Quai d'Orsay raised no objections, in line with their new policy of allowing Italy a 'free hand' in Albania. Italian ambitions soon resurfaced because, after the defeat of Bulgaria (30 September 1918), the Austrians were forced to withdraw from their now exposed positions. Ferrero, however, informed Sonnino that, given the number of Italian troops available, he would be unable to occupy Durazzo or Elbasan before the French,

Serb or Essadist forces.[430] On 7 October 1918, at a conference at the Quai d'Orsay, Clemenceau, Lloyd George and Sonnino (but no American representative) made a crucial decision regarding the occupation of Albanian territory. Clemenceau agreed that the two French divisions occupying Albania should be withdrawn and be replaced by Italian ones. Sonnino interpreted this as meaning that his European partners had agreed to reserve all of Albania for Italy, and for the next eighteen months the Consulta justified the Italian occupation on the basis of this decision. The French took a different view. Michel Pichon, the Foreign Minister, insisted that although Italian troops had been allowed to occupy Albania, this did not preclude Serbian troops from occupying northern Albania, as stated in the Pact of London. He maintained that the agreement covered only territory up to the Mati river, in other words central Albania. North of the river would be within the jurisdiction of the French General Louis Franchet d'Esperey.[431] The Italians continued to object, and in effect attempted to argue that, on the Albanian question, the 7 October conference overrode the London Pact. Throughout these exchanges neither Whitehall nor Washington were kept informed. In July 1919, the Foreign Office complained of having no knowledge of any agreement relating to the occupation of Albania.[432]

This tenuous great power agreement was further complicated when it became clear that Serbian forces would be the first to reach Scutari. None of the powers relished this situation, especially the Italians. As a result, Sonnino revised his Albanian policy further. Discussions once more became bi-lateral between the Italians and the French. Sonnino, who still considered Albania reserved for Italian occupation, proposed that there should be no Serbian troops at Scutari, and that, if the Serbs arrived there first, they should be replaced by a mixed detachment of British, French and Italian troops (similar to the international regime which had operated before World War One). Despite giving Ferrero orders not to proceed past the Drin (Pichon having agreed to an Italian occupation to this point), Sonnino demanded talks with Clemenceau before that decision was made permanent. Clemenceau insisted that the rights of the powers to zones of occupation in Albania still rested on the London agreements of 1913 and 1915, and therefore also gave rights to the Greeks in the south, and to the Serbs in the north.

Despite having allowed an Italian occupation into the northern zone, he pointed out that this was due to military necessity, and did not reflect a change to or abandonment of the principles of the earlier treaties. Sonnino did not mollify his position. What mattered were not the negotiations, but actual possession of territory: the Italian troops would soon occupy territory north of the Drin, territory that was claimed by Serbia as part of 'Greater Serbia'. For wartime expediency, the French continued their conciliatory attitude to Italy in Albania. As part of this, but only after having failed to produce a rapprochement between Italy and Essad Pasha, the Quai d'Orsay eventually withdrew their *de facto* recognition of Essad, recalled his diplomatic representatives and informed Essad that he was not to attempt to return to Albania. When Serbian troops entered Scutari, on 5 November 1918, they were soon replaced by a French squadron under Colonel de Fourtou. This was later augmented by both Italian and British detachments, in accordance with Sonnino's ideas for an international regime (including once more for Britain, George Phillips, now a Brigadier General).[433] By the end of the war, the Italians had enjoyed much success in their plans for Albania: Italian forces were in possession of the bulk of Albanian territory; Sonnino had prevented the Serbs from occupying northern Albania, especially the key centres; and French conciliation had encouraged Sonnino to carry out his plans for a large independent Albania, under Italian control. In the ensuing years, these were all issues that would come up against considerable opposition. Sonnino found that his plans for Albania were not as easy to implement as he had hoped. Nevertheless the prospects for a revived, large, independent Albania looked more promising than they had in April 1915.

Entries and Exits

In 1917, three major political changes had an impact on the Albanian situation and the war effort generally. Firstly, following the overthrow of King Constantine and under immense Allied pressure, Venizelos finally brought Greece into the war on the Allied side (12 June 1917). This gave greater weight to Greek claims to northern Epirus, especially relative to any pledges to the Albanians.[434] Secondly, following the Bolshevik revolution, Russia withdrew from the war (November 1917). The true impact of the Russian withdrawal materialised only gradually. In 1916-17, the Russians had played only a minor role in discussions regarding Albania. After the Serbian capitulation, Russia was far less interested in the Balkans. On 23 November 1917, the new Soviet government published the details of the 1915 Pact. Many of its components had been suspected, but this was the first confirmation of its provisions. It had serious ramifications in all the Balkan states, especially Albania. The Austrians translated the Pact into Albanian and proceeded to distribute it throughout the country. This prompted tremendous protests, especially from Albanian nationalists abroad.[435] These revelations made many Albanian leaders and supporters realise that they could not depend on great power support, and that they needed to start reforming and organising ready for the end of the war. Nevertheless, many prominent Albanians believed that Russian absence would be helpful in the longer term, especially at the subsequent peace conference. One nationalist, Melida Frasheri, commented that, without Russia, the French would no longer have the same excuse to protect Greece and Serbia as they had before the war.[436]

Thirdly, and perhaps most significantly, on 7 December 1917 the United States entered the war on the Allied side, as an Associated Power. This would have a number of implications for Albania, even though the United States had never previously recognised an independent Albanian state, and at this point had no Albanian policy.[437] The Americans were not a signatory to the London Pact, and they entered the war on the basis of the rights of national self-determination, as later clarified in President Wilson's legendary fourteen points. This was in complete contradiction to the Pact, which had been based on strategic necessity and political ambition: the dichotomy that is central to this study. At the upcoming peace conference, the differences between the terms of American and Italian entry were to prove a major complication. However, the fourteen points were not entirely positive. No mention was made of Albania, in contrast to some of the other Balkan nationalities, and some provisions were counter to Albanian interests, above all those regarding Serbia, and perhaps Italy. American thinking influenced the policies of its Allies. This resulted in similar declarations and a revival of, for the British at least, their original objectives of helping and protecting small states.[438] These 'new' liberal nationalistic principles would form the basis on which the Allied and Associated Powers proclaimed they were now fighting the war. But the Albania question was viewed very differently to many of the other national questions under consideration. Albania's supporters considered the Albanian question equivalent to the Belgian question. The great power statesmen disagreed. Unlike the 'new' Slav nationalisms, there seemed to be nothing to gain from aiding the Albanian nationalists, or non-nationalists promoting Albanian nationalism.[439] On 18 February 1918, responding to questions in parliament, Arthur Balfour, Foreign Secretary, replied that

> the arrangements come to in 1913, to which Albania was not a party, have now ceased to have binding force, as all the signatory Powers are now engaged in war. As regards the future…His Majesty's Government would be glad to see the principle of nationality applied as far as possible to this as to the other difficult questions which will have to be settled at the Peace Conference.[440]

In drafting this response, one clerk noted that 'from a purely legal point of view, I should say that as four of the six signatories are at war with the other two the arrangement no longer possesses binding force'. This argument was dictated by 'policy rather than law'.[441] The London Pact would determine future British policy. In June 1918, Mehmed Konitza proposed an Albanian detachment under Herbert's leadership in return for independence after the war. The Foreign Office rejected this offer. As Harold Nicolson, at the time a junior Foreign Office clerk, wrote, 'we can scarcely in honour encourage the Albanians to fight for a dismembered country'.[442]

As Roger MacGinty has shown, for small-state European nationalisms in western Europe, the entry of the United States and Bolshevik activities had important impacts.[443] These ideas can also be applied to the Albanian case. American entry influenced the burgeoning Albanian nationalist movement. The most influential initiatives took place in the United States, especially within Vatra (the Pan Albanian-American Association). Vatra had initially supported Austria in the war, but the entry of the United States onto the Allied side necessitated a switch in allegiance. In particular,

Vatra understood and supported liberal American political ideals and institutions, and had confidence in Wilson's principles of self-determination. They thought these would be helpful in assisting the Albanian cause to regain those territories (Kosovo, Chameria, Hoti, Gruda, etc.) that they had been denied in 1913. Albanian-Americans started to expound their views to Albanian relatives and friends in Albania and elsewhere.[444]

Albanian Nationalist Revival (1916-18)

Albanian nationalist initiatives had started as early as April 1916, but there had been many problems. Durham alleged that the delays were the result of differences among the leadership of the Albanian-Americans, who had become important in the national revival because of their democratic inheritance and financial assistance. She contended that they squabbled amongst themselves and that, in particular, two rival factions (both originally from southern Albania) were competing for control of the Albanian-American nationalist movement. The result was a standstill in putting forward any united initiatives, thus repeating the problems experienced in the campaigns against the Young Turks.[445] British Foreign Office officials opposed any encouragement of an emerging Albanian national movement, in contrast to its support of, for instance, the Czech and Polish movements, because of Mehmed Konitza's perceived anti-Italian views. Mehmed's plans to visit Switzerland in April 1916, to meet Albanian-Americans there and discuss ways of gaining great power support, were consequently blocked.[446] According to Herbert, in 1917, on his recommendations and due to their close friendship, Mehmed came to support the idea of an Italian protectorate. These plans were postponed because Mehmed came under (unofficial) French influence, and temporarily came to support the unrealistic idea of a French protectorate.[447] Such a situation was by no means unique amongst the Albanian diaspora. Like other influential nationalists, Mehmed was inconsistent in his policy, and regularly shifted his allegiance between people and programmes that he saw as influential or useful. This weakened the position of the Albanians *vis-à-vis* their adversaries, because they were seen as unreliable or undependable, and sometimes even dishonest. It also meant that they persisted in pursuing a number of different, rival and often contradictory solutions, although their greatest successes had been achieved in periods of unity and consensus.

Vatra's first real impact was not felt until the summer of 1918, when a new President was elected to head the organisation, although the main driving force behind the new policy and tactics was Mehmed Konitza. Until then, the organisation had been under the influence of Bishop Fan Noli, who had been pro-Austrian. Since Italy's declaration at Argyrocastro, Mehmed had been anxious to work with the Italians for an independent Albania. He assured Sonnino that, if the Consulta made a formal declaration supporting an independent Albanian state, to include within its frontiers all territory with a predominantly Albanian population, then Italy would receive the full support of Vatra for a protectorate. Sonnino subsequently invited leading Albanian nationalists in exile, who called themselves the National Albanian Committee, to Rome in early December 1918. Sonnino was keen to harness the support of the Albanian nationalists for Italy, but he was not prepared to go so far as a formal declaration, for fear of the response it might produce from the Allies. In mid-October 1918, Pichon warned the Consulta to stop fermenting Albanian nationalism in the zones of Italian occupation, because the London Pact had reserved southern Albania for Greece. In early November 1918, the British Foreign Office and the American State Department, having heard reports that the Italians were preparing to establish a puppet government in Albania to present the peacemakers with a *fait accompli*, warned the Consulta against any unilateral action in Albania.[448] Sonnino was not so insensitive as to openly offend his partners. He did promise to help the Committee organise Albania as a modern state, and to assist it in gaining the territory it claimed as part of its *irredenta*, thus continuing his policy of trying to block Greek and especially Slav gains there. In return, the Albanians, except for, significantly, Dr Mihal Tourtoulis, an Orthodox Christian who had previously served as Minister of Public Instruction and Health under Wilhelm of Wied, agreed to recognise an Italian protectorate. Tourtoulis remained convinced that the Italians would not use their influence for the good of Albania, and that their presence would instead lead to continual discord and further conflict. He therefore never accepted the idea of an Italian protectorate and was a constant block to Italian aspirations.[449] It was only after enduring the occupation that other prominent nationalists came to support his views.

The Italians also worked with Albanian leaders inside Albania. As they moved northwards in 1918, Italian forces allowed the Albanians to continue with their local administrations, but simultaneously helped to organise meetings throughout Albania to draft petitions and demand independence under Italian protection. This policy had two objectives: in the short term, to make the areas easier to govern; in the longer term, to overturn the London Pact by creating organisations and manifestoes that could be used as propaganda, at the peace conference, in favour of an Italian protectorate.[450] The Consulta had no intention of relinquishing its authority, or of establishing one central regime or provisional government. French interference in the local administration at Scutari upset this scenario, and promoted amongst the Albanians the idea of the need for a central unified Albanian administration. On arrival in Scutari, the French forces had removed from power local Albanian leaders, including Bib Doda, who had collaborated with the Austrians during the war, and set up their own replacement government, which produced great discontent. Many of the leaders in Scutari thus came round to supporting the idea of an Italian protectorate, and the French insensitivity fostered further their desire to establish an Albanian provisional government under Italian protection.[451] Sonnino was less than optimistic about the project. He sent Colonel Ettore Lodi, considered an expert in Albanian affairs, to Albania in the capacity of Political Liaison Officer to the Albanian National Council. Lodi had instructions to prevent the formation of an Albanian provisional government, by manipulating any meetings which took place. General Piacentini, the Supreme Commander of Italian forces in the Balkans, likewise had orders to use troops and bribes, as necessary, to prevent its formation. About 100 Albanians met at Alessio on 9 December 1918, and Lodi was successful in his task of steering the meeting away from creating a provisional government.[452]

That was not the end of the matter. Throughout December 1918, Mehmed Konitza, now the central figure in the Albanian nationalist movement, travelled throughout Albania, with the object of organising a second meeting of Albanian leaders, *beys* and *agas*. This finally took place at Durazzo on 25 December 1918. Here Lodi was unable to control the meeting as he had done at Alessio. Over Lodi's objections, the Albanians proclaimed themselves a National Assembly, and then proceeded to form a provisional government with Turkhan Pasha recalled as Prime Minister, Bib Doda as Deputy Prime Minister and Mehmed Konitza as Foreign Minister. The Assembly issued a declaration protesting against the foreign intrigue that had led to the temporary withdrawal of Wilhelm, and asserted that this could not be used in favour of Albanian partition.[453] They expressed their desire for a restoration of the independent Albanian state of 1913-14, together with claims to their ethnic *irredenta*. Those attending the meeting consisted of delegates from across Albania, but there was no delegate from Koritza, which was still under French control, and Bib Doda was the only representative of the northern clans. The Albanians were once more acting independently. In these activities, they were making their own decisions and, for the first time, defying the great powers if their interests could not be reconciled with Albanian nationalist ones, and against the traditional realist rhetoric of the states system. Their abandonment of any hope of gaining great power support was a last resort. Only when efforts in this direction had been completely unsuccessful did the Albanians have the incentive to devise their own independent policy, given that there were no other alternatives. As late as October 1918, Mehmed was still advocating an Albanian regiment under Aubrey Herbert, and Albanian commitment to Britain, and even to Italy, in return for recognition of an independent Albania.[454]

The establishment of the provisional government was not welcomed in the Consulta. Although the meeting had been arranged with Italian support, Sonnino had misunderstood its purpose. Italian officials appear to have thought that the meeting in Durazzo was being called for the purpose of expressing the desires of the Albanian people to the expected peace conference, as earlier local meetings had done. Afterwards, Sonnino ordered that the Albanians be prevented from leaving Durazzo until they had explained their actions. Lodi therefore told the delegates that they must abrogate their decision. Mehmed went to Rome to explain why the government had been formed despite Italian objections.[455] Mehmed was fully aware that this move had taken the Italians by surprise, and had gone much further than they had anticipated, but he was anxious not to lose

Italian support. He ascribed the appointment of Turkhan Pasha as Prime Minister as an attempt to mollify Italian objections.[456] Meanwhile, Sonnino wanted to maintain Albanian support for Italy. Appreciating that it was too late to undo this move, he merely insisted that all reports and acts of the Albanian Assembly would have to be reviewed by the Italian military authorities, and that the Italian government would not recognise the Albanian government, pending the outcome of the peace conference. The French, British and American governments likewise refused to recognise it. Lodi cleverly explained to the Albanians that these decisions had been forced on Italy by their Allies, but that, in reality, the Consulta fully supported the Albanian nationalists. The Italians were attempting to play a double game: not to lose face with their Allies, but also to maintain support of the Albanian nationalists.[457] In reality, they had already lost control of the nationalists. The Albanians were attempting to take their future out of the hands of the great powers and rival neighbour states, and to have a role in determining the future of their state.

Conclusions

Throughout World War One, all the powers changed their positions and attitudes regarding Albania, whilst the Balkan states remained largely constant, but devised new methods and techniques for achieving their goals. As the war progressed, nationalism and nationalist interests played an increasing role. Following on from Wilson's fourteen points, the Allies pledged to uphold the interests of subject nationalities and small states. This was primarily for reasons of self-interest and position in the wider war effort. For the British, particularly, appeals to the Poles and Czechs were designed to upset Austrian war efforts. In south-eastern Europe, a similar agenda was pursued, despite the lack of direct British interests there. One War Cabinet memorandum stated that British general-European interests were too deeply rooted in the Balkans for Britain to be detached from Balkan politics. Although Britain had 'no material interests in south eastern Europe', it was 'indirectly almost as much affect[ed] as [the] other great powers'.[458]

The Foreign Office considered the Albanian question as different to many of the other small-state national questions under consideration during the war. Britain had no commitments to Albania because those signed before the war were 'void', as all the signatories were now at war.[459] MacGinty has shown how western European small states benefited from a 'seminal structure of empowerment' produced by the war.[460] Such ideas could also be applied to small states in eastern Europe. The war improved their position at the bargaining table, and the Greeks, especially, sought to capitalise upon the new opportunities and on their increased importance in the international (great power) system. By contrast, the Albanians were slow both to profit from and also to seek to benefit from the new international order. They still faced opposition to their national goals from the Greeks, Serbs and Italians, had the great powers opposed to their national aspirations, and for most of the war they were internally divided, and therefore weak, especially in comparison to their rivals. Only towards the end of the war, and with the new steps towards unity, did the Albanians make any progress in capitalising on the opportunities this crisis in the great power system provided for small states.

By the end of 1918, the Albanians had once more achieved a nominal administration over the whole country. In reality the French, Italians, Greeks and Serbs still occupied and controlled the vast majority of territory the Albanians would claim at the peace conference, and the government remained unrecognised, mirroring its predicament in 1912. However, the counter-revolution had been defeated. As with Albanian initiatives during the Balkan wars, it took greater external threats, and a realisation that they could not rely on the support of others, to create this unity and resolve. Significantly, the Albanian movement was again marked by an absence of religious differences, whereas in times of discord religious affiliations appear to have been more prominent. The great powers' mistrust of, and concern about, each other meant that they paid scant attention to Albanian actions or activities. In the last months of the conflict, and in those immediately after the armistice, rapid progress was made on the Albanian national front. This was similar to the experiences of other eastern European nationalities, but also different, because of the lack of great power support for these activities in Albania. Nevertheless, internationally, the Albanians viewed the situation at the end of the war with promise, as the most interested states would no longer be involved. Melida Frasheri wrote to Herbert that

I think that the new situation of the three states—Russia, Austria and Turkey—will cause a salutary change for Albania, as much for the morale of the Albanians as for the politics of the powers and the little states towards us.

He added that the three powers most interested in the Albanian issue before the war, Italy not withstanding, would no longer be a political factor at the peace conference. Therefore he considered that the Albanian question would be resolved by 'friendly and disinterested powers'[461] with less concern for power-politics, and would provide a fairer settlement, based on Wilsonian principles. This view was naïve and would not be realised: geo-political interests were at least as important after the war, if not more so, because larger prizes were at stake.

Chapter 6

The Peace Conference of Paris

'Is Albania to become the Poland of south-eastern Europe?'[462]

This chapter considers the respective roles and interactions of nationalism, especially when defined as language nationalism or self-determination, and geo-politics in the Albanian question during the Peace Conference of Paris (1919-20). For as Michael Dockrill and J. Douglas Goold have argued, in settling the many questions produced by the war in eastern Europe, the great power policy-makers faced the problem of reconciling conflicting wartime priorities and commitments with the supposedly new self-determination diplomacy.[463] The great powers sought to try and prevent the decomposition of eastern Europe and the Middle East into smaller and smaller sub-divisions, based on nationality, and to make the new states as rational as possible. Yet, as Alan Sharp has argued, the 'demand for nation-states, based on a single nationality, was not itself rational in the world of 1919'. It was not possible to place all Poles in Poland or all Germans in Germany, even if the peacemakers had desired to do so. The result was that, in Europe, over thirty million people were left in states in which they were an ethnic minority, an object of suspicion by the dominant nationality and a target for their co-nationals abroad.[464]

Such arguments only applied to those states whose independence fitted in with great power policy projections. Where independence was viewed as neither beneficial nor necessary for great power interests, or for the balance of power, it was, despite the new rhetoric, not supported. The Albanians were a small grouping, and this was not something that was viewed positively in 1919-20. Across central and eastern Europe, borders were unable to meet the Wilsonian principles because of the mixture of nationalities, outdated and unreliable population figures and also due to the tendency for the peacemakers to consider economic, historical and strategic factors in addition to ethnic ones, even when their own strategic interests were not at stake.[465] Such an eventuality was not new. The 1913 Ambassadors' Conference had already shown the effects that a narrow definition of nationality, an interlaced population, and alternative priorities, could have on the attempt to produce ethnic or national frontiers. Not only was self-determination not new, neither were the problems associated with establishing states and delimiting them on this basis.

Language Nationalism Revisited

The problem in 1919, as in 1913, was how to define a nation or a nationality, now under the supposedly new guise of Wilson's national self-determination. It appears that for Wilson this had two main components: the right of autonomy for national groups, and the democratic processes within states. Wilson tended to confuse these two elements. As Alfred Cobban pointed out, national self-determination was essentially a synonym for popular sovereignty. Sharp has argued that Wilson essentially followed the western civic tradition, which has tended not to distinguish between the concept of a person as a member of an ethnic group and as a citizen of a state. Such a view was understandable considering the ethnic mix of the United States and, in particular, Wilson's views, as a Southerner, on the right of secession.[466] Given the ethnic mix of eastern Europe in particular, such a conception was never going to be practical. As Sharp pointed out, the question that the American delegation asked themselves was, 'if national self-determination was to legitimise the new frontiers, what criteria would determine nationality?' The western tradition emphasised choice in establishing nationality, but the eastern or German one did not. Instead nationality was '*determined not self-determined*, and the determining factors included ethnicity, language, religion, culture, historical allegiance and geography.[467] For the Americans in 1919, as for the ambassadors in London in 1913, language came to be the favoured criterion. The evidence soon showed that it was inadequate, and could not be neatly delimited on maps, especially in eastern Europe, where many nationalities overlapped and were intermingled; and the various categories could also be subject to further subdivisions, by language or religion, or both.[468] This was a particularly pertinent point for the Albanians. Wilson therefore came to regret his commitment to national self-determination. As he admitted to the Senate, 'when I gave utterance to those words ["that all nations had a right to self-determination"] I said them without the knowledge that nationalities existed, which are coming to us day after day'.[469] In addition to the general ignorance of eastern Europe on the part of the leading members of all the main delegations, a further problem was created, as Sharp has maintained, by the innate contradiction between the right of self-determination and the right of a state to maintain its existence.[470] This proved particularly problematic in eastern Europe, because of the competing national claims. It therefore led Allied experts to believe in both *ethnic* (based on pseudo-linguistic foundations) and *historical* bases for small states in the region.

Even more importantly, none of the great power representatives, not even Wilson, was ever entirely committed to the principle of self-determination. The British Foreign Office wanted to see minority groups assimilated into newly created states or enlarged ones. If the right to appeal *de facto* was granted to, for example, the Macedonian Bulgarians, then it would be difficult to refuse it in the case of other nationalist movements, for example the southern Irish, Flemings, Catalans and French Canadians. These ideals were therefore limited to eastern Europe.[471] The fourteen points included many features that might be considered contrary to self-determination, and they allowed for other priorities in the drawing of frontiers, including international stability, historical development, economics, defensible frontiers, security and communication.[472] Above all, for the Albanian question, Point 11 provided for Serbian access to the sea and economic independence, and the restoration of Serbian, Montenegrin and Romanian frontiers. The most likely location for Serbian access to the sea was in northern Albania, especially before the dissolution of Austria-Hungary. Albania was also not listed as one of the Balkan states to be restored after the war. The Albanian question had a further complicating factor, in that it was covered by the Pact of London. Despite the supposedly new basis for negotiations, Georges Clemenceau and David Lloyd George, the French and British Prime Ministers, and the Italians, still adhered to this, at least when it suited their purposes to do so. As negotiations progressed, it became clear that Italian claims far exceeded the terms of the 1915 agreement. Thus the Albanian settlement would be a combination of national self-determination based on language, great and small power interests and previous agreements between the powers.

Preparations for Peace (1917-19)

GREAT-POWER POLICIES AND POSITIONING

The changed international climate had profound implications for the Albanian question. There were no representatives from Austria (previously the staunchest advocate) or Russia (formerly the strongest opponent). Of the five great powers represented in Paris (the United States, British Empire, France, Italy and Japan), Italy was the most directly interested in the Albanian question.[473] Since Italy had entered World War One, Italian policy had undergone considerable revisions. In 1915, Italian Adriatic policy had been motivated by a fear of Austria, and was designed to weaken Austrian power. With the break-up of the former Austro-Hungarian Empire into several small states, this issue was no longer relevant. But, the former Italian policy had not taken into account the prospect of a large, strong Yugoslavia as a replacement for Austria on the northern and eastern shores of the Adriatic. By January 1919, Italian policy had changed to reflect this. The Consulta sought to curb potential Yugoslav claims in Trentino, Dalmatia and Albania. At the start of the Conference, possession of Valona remained Italy's key objective in Albania, but elsewhere Sonnino, still Foreign Minister, no longer sought Albania's dismemberment, and pursued a policy in favour of Albanian nationalism. This policy change dated from the 1917 protectorate. For Sonnino, there were several advantages in supporting a 'large' Albania. Most importantly, he hoped it would act as a counterpoise to Yugoslavia on the eastern side of the Adriatic, especially if Albania could be established under Italian protection. This would give the Consulta its long-coveted footstep in the Balkans. A large Albania would be much better for this project than a small one. A large Albania would also better protect the Italian enclave at Valona from the potentially hostile Yugoslavs. Throughout 1919-20, Italian policy and priorities would be modified to adapt to international opposition, domestic pressures and Albanian activities. For the Consulta, as for the Greek government, more spectacular and grandiose gains elsewhere came to take precedence over less attractive ones in Albania.[474]

French policy was also similar to that in 1913 and, as then, did not favour the Albanians. For the Quai d'Orsay, as for the Foreign Office and State Department, there were no strategic or economic interests at stake in Albania, or in the larger Balkan peninsula. With the two main determinants of French Balkan policy (Russian interests and German encroachments into Greece) now removed, French officials used Balkan issues to improve France's alliance network throughout Europe, and therefore its own security. The French sought to use the Albanian question to foster relations with Italy, Yugoslavia and Greece. This effectively meant trying to contain Italian influence in Albania, and to secure gains for the Greeks and Serbs, but simultaneously maintaining good relations with the Consulta. This proved difficult to achieve in Paris because of the revised Italian claims in the Adriatic, and even more so in Albania, because of French support for the Greeks and Serbs. French officials were particularly perturbed that these Italo-Greek antagonisms might spill over into Asia Minor. Therefore, soon after the start of the Conference, the French delegates reverted to their Pact of London policy involving the tri-partition of Albania. As Clemenceau maintained, this policy was legally correct and offered something to all sides (strategically, economically and ethno-nationally). However, by maintaining French troops in Albania (Scutari, Koritza and Pogradec), despite appeals by the French military to recall them, the Quai d'Orsay kept open the possibility of allowing a non-partitioned Albania under an Italian mandate, in exchange for French gains elsewhere.[475]

Before 1918 there was no American strategy on Albania.[476] Albanian writers have often based Wilson's programme on his alleged statement 'I have one voice at the Peace Conference and I will use that voice in favour of Albania'. However, there is no mention of this in Wilson's correspondence.[477] The Inquiry, a body consisting mainly of academics, was established by Wilson to formulate plans for a lasting peace, based on scientific principles. An initial report on Albania (December 1917) recommended that, for primarily economic reasons, an 'independent Albania is almost certainly an undesirable political entity'.[478] The final report (21 January 1919) failed to make definite recommendations. It considered that the problems involved were 'so complicated in details, and the proposed settlements are so experimental in form', that 'definite recommendations' were 'unsafe'. Specific problems were identified with the 'highly artificial' 1913 boundaries, which cut off economic intercourses, national affiliations and tribal ties, the latter being considered the strongest bond amongst Albanians. A united Albania was considered impracticable, owing to the weakness of the national affiliation of the people, backward institutions, difficulties in communications and disruption by neighbouring states, based on a combination of ethnic, economic and strategic factors. The Inquiry, therefore, tentatively proposed a solution similar to the 1915 Pact: a small independent Albanian state should continue to exist, but with areas in the north ceded to Yugoslavia, in the south to Greece and Valona to Italy.[479] Central Albania was the most difficult question. It was suggested, with the utmost caution, that central Albania should be granted nominal independence under some disinterested power, as mandatory of the League of Nations, because the Albanians were considered incapable of governing themselves. The mandatory power was 'left open': the authors opposed Italy for a number of reasons (past interference in Albania, including in 1914, and hostility to Yugoslavia and Greece being the main ones). However, neither Britain nor the United States, the only two powers who, according to the report, would 'be willing to spend their efforts unselfishly', would accept the mandate. Therefore the Italians should be allowed a temporary mandate limited to Valona, but much less than the Consulta wanted.[480]

Unlike most Inquiry proposals, these recommendations did not become policy. By the start of the Peace Conference, the American position had become more sympathetic towards Albanian nationalism. The only original feature that remained was the belief that the Albanians were unprepared for full independence of the type proclaimed in 1912. The Americans, therefore, reluctantly came to support the idea of an Italian mandate. They insisted that the nature of the mandate, and therefore Italy's power and influence, must be strictly limited. The reasons for this shift remain unclear, for there were no special directives regarding Albanian policy. Although Wilson himself often went against the principle of self-determination, he insisted that any violation of it must be reported to him and justified. Neither Pietro Pastorelli nor Erik Goldstein's explanations, of the change that followed discussion with members of the British delegation, seem adequate.[481] The American records for the winter of 1918-19 are scant in references to such conversations between American policymakers and junior British officials, who in any case often had their ideas vetoed, and were themselves inconsistent in their support of Albanian nationalism.[482]

British policy was based on a series of complicated paradoxes: national sovereign states were necessary for order in Europe, but the application of national self-determination in itself might lead to international tension or internal anarchy. Maintenance of the balance of power, despite Wilson's views to the contrary, remained the main driver. The Foreign Office hoped to exploit national self-determination to strengthen the states system, by the creation of consciously sovereign states. Therefore, when the idea of a Balkan confederation failed, Britain sought to balance Italy in the Adriatic and the Balkans with a strong Greece and Yugoslavia. Whitehall wanted a strong Greece, to replace the Ottoman Empire and protect British interests in the eastern Mediterranean, including the India route and the Straits. Whatever the higher rationale, the first steps to supporting the selected regional proxy nationalisms were usually strategic. Greece was chosen for this role because Venizelos was clearly seen as the key to long-term friendly Anglo-Greek relations.[483] By contrast, the Albanians were not viewed as useful to maintaining the British interests in the region, and were therefore not supported. Despite its importance in Middle Eastern policy, religion (specifically the Muslim population) does not seem to have influenced British policy on Albania and the Balkans.[484]

Unlike the Inquiry, no central body co-ordinated British peace preparations, but the Political Intelligence Department (PID) soon became influential.[485] Overriding traditional interpretations, Goldstein and others have maintained that, in questions associated with eastern and central Europe, especially in the territorial committees, the Foreign Office retained considerable influence in the formulation of British policy. On the presumption that the balance of power would continue to be the major plank of British policy, the PID considered that, following the dissolution of Austria-Hungary, the formation of new, smaller, 'national' states would produce sovereign entities that would stabilise and reinforce the new international order produced by the war. Self-determination was therefore supported because 'there is every reason to hope that states based upon the conscious existence of a common nationality will be more durable and afford a firmer support against aggression than the older form of state'.[486] In south-eastern Europe, the PID contended that self-determination offered 'the best prospects of a permanent peace', and was therefore 'desirable and advantageous' for British interests. Recommendations were to be based 'on the principles of nationality, self-determination, security and free economic opportunity' in order to ensure future stability and remove possible friction. For these reasons, the PID advocated that Yugoslavia and Romania should obtain their ethnic *irredenta*.[487] However, in Albanian policy the PID does not seem to have been as influential as Goldstein and others have maintained, primarily because of the Albanian question's interconnectedness with Italian ambitions. Senior colleagues were not prepared to distance themselves from these plans, because issues that involved great power interests were to be dealt with by the Council of Ten, commonly called the Supreme Council, which was a meeting of the five chief representatives of the United States, France, British Empire, Italy and Japan, each accompanied by his foreign minister. Eventually, in December 1919, Lloyd George assumed personal control of British policy.

The policy for Albania advocated by Allen Leeper and Harold Nicolson, the two officials assigned to investigate the Albanian question, did not give such prominence to self-determination. Leeper and Nicolson considered the 1913 settlement obsolete, and they emphasised that the northern commission had never fully reported. Three ideas were proposed: a tri-partite scheme similar to that under the London Pact (north to Yugoslavia, south to Greece, and centre to Albania); leaving the frontiers as in 1913 but with increased rights for the Greeks and Yugoslavs in their respective spheres of interest; and, a third scheme favoured by Leeper and Nicolson. This third scheme left the north boundary unchanged, ceded Greece a large proportion of northern Epirus and the remainder to Italy under mandate, with the Albanian coast and the Corfu channel both neutralised. Various other government departments independently came up with similar proposals to the PID. British policy towards Albania was therefore determined by a combination of motives: although it employed the new self-determination rhetoric, geo-political and strategic concerns continued to be the prime determinants, especially the balance of power and position of Greece. Albanian territory was considered a bargaining chip that could be used to facilitate negotiations with the Italians in areas where British interests were more directly involved. For this reason, Leeper and Nicolson recommended co-operation between the South-eastern Europe and Middle Eastern sections, in order to co-ordinate policy relating to Tripoli, the Dodecanese, Anatolia, Abyssinia and Albania.[488]

REVIVED BALKAN NATIONAL AMBITIONS

Venizelos and the other Greek representatives had an accurate picture of their position in great-power policy projections. They appreciated the positive attitudes of both France and Britain and hoped to capitalise on this. On the other hand, they were acutely aware that the Italians were the main obstacle to their national ambitions. Woodall has alleged that the Greeks were not concerned with Italy, particularly the danger of Italian influence in the Balkans. As Woodall and N. Petsalis-Diomidis argue, the Greek policymakers became fixated on becoming a Mediterranean power, as opposed to a Balkan one. They became fanatical with the *Megali Idea* (Great Idea) of eastern Mediterranean acquisitions (eastern Thrace, the Dodecanese, Asia Minor, even Constantinople), and were prepared to compromise over Albania to achieve them. Greek officials were less concerned than the Yugoslavs (Serbs especially) by Italy being granted concessions in Albania, but there were several calculated reasons for this. During the war, the focus of Italian interests, except for Valona, had shifted further north, and had thus become less incompatible with the gains sought by Greece. Venizelos welcomed the prospect of an Albania under Italian influence, because he considered that it posed fewer risks than an independent state. Venizelos was shrewd enough to realise that it cost little to be magnanimous on issues such as an Albanian mandate, in which Greece had few interests, in the hope of greater gains elsewhere. Greek claims were therefore limited to the provinces of Argyrocastro, by the right of self-determination, and Koritza, for primarily economic and strategic reasons. They believed that these goals would be attainable, and would also help offset potential Italian gains elsewhere in Albania.[489] In the pursuit of its national ambitions in northern Epirus, Greece occupied a stronger position than the Albanians and their claims to southern Albania, because Venizelos had been able to align Greek ambitions more closely with the policies of the great powers.

At the opening of the Peace Conference, Yugoslavia (which until 1929 was known officially as the Kingdom of Serbs, Croats and Slovenes) had a much weaker position in the international system. Serbia and Montenegro were internationally recognised and had accredited representation at the Conference, but none of the great powers had recognised Yugoslavia as an independent state, although they had recognised Czechoslovakia and Poland. This made it difficult for the Yugoslav delegates to have their claims heard, which was particularly important now that there was no longer a Slav state (Russia) recognised as a great power, and able to protect their interests. As the Yugoslav delegation was involved in territorial disputes with six of their seven neighbours, including Italy and Albania, this proved problematic. The Italians in particular were in a much stronger position: they would be involved in the inner discussions of the Supreme Council; had the London Pact which bound Britain and France to support their claims in the northern Adriatic; and were in possession of many of the disputed areas, including much of northern Albania, although not the town of Scutari. As well as these external problems, internal divisions, especially the rivalry between the Catholic Croats, who considered themselves more highly cultured, and the Orthodox Serbs created problems in devising a policy that was acceptable to all sides. The Italians sought to exploit and promote these divisions and rivalries.[490]

The different linguistic groupings of the delegation had different priorities. The Serbian and Montenegrin delegates maintained that the territorial restoration of the medieval kingdoms, especially the

Drin frontier and Scutari, should be the main targets, and that concessions should be offered to Italy in the northern Adriatic. The Croat and Slovene members argued that Fiume (an Istrian port not provided for by the London Pact, but now sought by the Italians), the Dalmatian coast and islands, as the home to native Slav populations, should be the primary focus, at the expense of claims in northern Albania, where ethnic arguments and self-determination were more questionable. Initially the Serbian section held the upper hand, but eventually the Yugoslav delegation pronounced in favour of an independent Albania within the 1913 frontiers. Their main motive was strategic: to prevent Italian control over Albania and penetration into the Balkans. They sought to prevent the bizarre and dangerous situation of being bordered by Italy on both their northern and southern frontiers. This initially appears as a reversal of Serb policy in 1913 and a triumph for the Croatian delegates. Their back-up position, adopted because the former policy was unlikely to be successful as no great power supported it, was far more favourable to Serbian and Montenegrin ambitions in northern Albania. The Yugoslavs therefore asserted their right, in the event that Italy was granted a mandate over Albania, or a foothold in it, to acquisitions in northern Albania (as far south as the Drin river) as compensation, including Scutari. This would make the southern Yugoslav frontier more defensible, provide for the long-coveted Serbian Adriatic port and fulfil Serbian and Montenegrin ambitions in the region.[491] With Serbian forces occupying much of northern Albania, they were well placed to pursue this alternative, should the opportunity present itself.

THE ALBANIAN DELEGATIONS

The position of the Albanian delegations was even weaker than that of the Yugoslavs. At the opening of the Peace Conference, on 19 January 1919, 'Albania' was no longer recognised internationally as an independent state. This decision made Albanian status effectively equivalent to that of an enemy or previously non-existent state. As one Inquiry report stated,

> The attempt to establish a State of Albania in 1912-1914 met with such incomplete success that it seems not accurate to put Albania into ... [the] class of possible new States.

Whether it will exist in the future as a separate political entity, and whether it will be left by the Peace Conference free from such outside control as will make it an independent government, are too uncertain.[492]

In addition, Albania's chief defender in 1913, Austria, had been defeated and, as a consequence, had lost its great power status. The support of the Italian delegates for Albanian nationalism was counterproductive because of the hostility of the other (stronger) great powers and small states to Italian ambitions. This did not bode well for consideration of the Albanian question or for receptivity to Albanian claims, although initially the various Albanian delegations do not seem to have appreciated this.

There were many rivals for the title of leaders of 'Albania' and 'official delegation'. The most prominent proved to be that constituted by the Durazzo Congress (December 1918), and led by Turkhan Pasha (Sunni), Mehmed Konitza (Bektashi), Dr Mihal Tourtoulis (Orthodox) and Bishop Luigi Bumçi (Catholic), and which thus ensured that all four Albanian faiths were represented. The delegation was sent to argue Albanian claims, to prevent Albania's dismemberment and to nullify the claims of what the Durazzo Congress termed pretenders to the title of Albania's government, such as Essad Pasha or Wilhelm of Wied.[493] Wilhelm never attended the Conference but Essad Pasha presented himself in April 1919, proclaiming himself Albanian President, and referring to his recognition in this capacity by both the French and Italian governments. Other delegations included those from the Albanian colonies in Romania, Switzerland and the United States, most notably Vatra. There was also a range of 'special interest' groups who continued to press for the interests of a particular locality, region or town. One notable example was the provisional government of Autonomous Northern Epirus—a Greek-inspired venture designed to enhance Greek claims. The Albanian community in Kosovo was not represented directly. Although he was eager to attend the Conference, Hasan Prishtina was prevented from doing so by his inability to secure a passport. Prishtina blamed this on the opposition of many Tosk Albanian southerners, above all Turkhan Pasha, who, Prishtina claimed, desired to restrain Kosovan pretensions and ambitions. Hasan increasingly bemoaned the lack of an official 'Kosovan' delegate at Paris, especially within the Durazzo delegation, as the major reason why claims to reunite Kosovo with Albania were not considered in Paris.[494]

Gregory Pano has suggested that there was little difference between the ideas of the various Albanian groups and that, as none of the delegations were recognised, it was therefore of little significance who argued them.[495] In truth, the existence of so many competing delegations pursuing such a wide variety of tactics was in itself important, and proved detrimental to their national cause. Albanian differences could be exploited by Albania's rivals as evidence that the Albanians were not ready for self-government, because they could not even decide amongst themselves what constituted Albania, how it should be run and by whom. As the Conference progressed, there was a definite widening in the type and variety of policies pursued, and much disagreement emerged within delegations, most clearly in the split in the Durazzo delegation in April 1919.

This study concentrates primarily upon the role and policy of the Durazzo government delegation, because it was the closest the Albanians came to gaining 'official' status. As a result of its late formation, the delegates did not meet together before their arrival in Paris, although separately they had drawn up several proposals. The delegates believed that the great power statesmen would act in accordance with Wilsonian principles, and thus support the re-establishment of the independent Albanian state. Therefore, before the Supreme Council, Turkhan Pasha, as Prime Minister and leader of the Durazzo delegation, began by stating that

> The Albanians base all their hopes on the justice of [the] High Assembly, on whom they rely utterly. They trust that the principle of nationality so clearly and solemnly proclaimed by President Wilson and his great Associates will not have been proclaimed in vain, and that their rights— which have, up to now, been trampled underfoot—will be respected...[496]

In accordance with these principles, the Albanians made extensive claims. The primary goal of the Durazzo delegation was to prevent the dissolution of the 1913 Albanian state. They also advocated reconstituting Albanian frontiers on ethnographic lines, including that territory which the great power decisions in 1878 and 1913 had awarded to other states. Similar ideas were also promulgated by most other groups purporting to subscribe to an Albanian national programme.[497] There seems to have been little consideration given to how best to counter the arguments of the rival states, or how best to align Albanian aspirations with the expected policies of the great powers, not even with the Italians to any significant extent, which had proven so productive in 1912. The Durazzo delegation identified three pivotal international factors that would impact upon the successfulness of its programme (the international occupation, diplomatic agreements, especially the 1915 London Pact, and lack of international recognition of the government), but it did not devise ways to tackle these problems.[498] Although based on the new self-determination or ethnic rationale, the Durazzo delegation's aspirations had little likelihood of success because they were too extravagant and too remote from the plans of any of the great powers.

Southern Albania or Northern Epirus? (January–July 1919)

The southern Albanian question was considered in three stages. During January to March 1919 the small states had a formalised role in the international system but the great powers remained the key decision-makers and geo-political interests still predominated. From March to July 1919 the small states were not invited to take part and needed to resort to petitions and low level meetings to argue their cases. Finally in July 1919 the Italians made a bi-lateral agreement, outside the Peace Conference, with the Greeks. The Albanian position in the new international system was therefore little stronger than under the concert system in 1914.

The Durazzo delegation official presented its claims to southern Albania to the Supreme Council on 24 February 1919 and three days later to the Greek Committee. Before the Supreme Council, Turkhan Pasha detailed the losses in early settlements. He blamed this on Albania's advantageous geographical position and lack of great power protector. He disputed Greek statistics on southern Albania and claimed that there were, at most, 20,000 Greeks living there, most of whom were migrant farmers working on Albanian-owned land. Turkhan contested that all Orthodox Albanians should be considered Greek because the clergy, in collaboration with the

Ottomans, had prevented education in Albanian. Whilst admitting that a small number of Greeks would need to be incorporated into Albania, he bemoaned the far greater numbers of Albanians excluded and maintained that the Greeks were merely pursuing claims in northern Epirus to intimidate the Albanians into renouncing their claims to southern Epirus. Turkhan went further in the Greek Committee. He stated that of the 240,000 inhabitants, 212,000 were Albanian and only 16,500 Greek, again far in excess of even the most generous great power statistics. He then proceeded to claim there 'was not a single Greek' in the town or district of Koritza, and that, in Chameria, 54,000 out of 60,000 inhabitants were Albanians, despite this region not even being part of the Committee's remit, as territory ceded to Greece in 1913.[499]

These interviews were important because they were two rare occasions on which Albanians were allowed to present their views to the great powers, and given a formal role in the great power system. The weak position of the Albanians is clearly evident. In the Supreme Council no great power leader even showed up to listen. Both Albanian presentations generated a poor reception, and they seem to have hindered rather than helped the nationalist cause. Crowe minuted that the Albanian claims were 'hardly worth reading', and Nicolson added that their 'claims are fantastic and even the Italians do not propose that Albania should annex what is now Greek territory'.[500] The French delegates objected to hearing the claims because there were potentially 'persons of enemy nationality' amongst the Albanian delegates and as there was no official delegation it was questionable whether Turkhan could be considered to govern Albania. The Greek Committee agreed to hear the Durazzo delegation only on the condition that representatives of northern Epirus were also heard.[501] On being admitted, Turkhan proceeded to introduce the Durazzo delegation as 'a pure representation of the entire people of Albania'. This statement far exceeded the delegation's authority, received a hostile reception and differed significantly from the perceptions of the great power representatives in the room.[502]

These experiences were very different from that of the Greek representatives. Venizelos had been heard by the Supreme Council three weeks before the Albanians (3 and 4 February 1919), when the Greek Committee was first established. On the same day that Turkhan appeared before the Supreme Council, Venizelos presented his claims on northern Epirus to the Greek Committee. Somewhat ironically, Nicolson wrote of that speech that Venizelos 'is overwhelmingly frank, genial and subtle. His charm lights up the room.'[503] More generally Venizelos and the Greeks were better received. Venizelos, the astute and charismatic politician, was able to charm the Allied leaders in a way that others could not, and in a way that it seems most Albanians could not even envisage. Venizelos was well prepared and was adept at paying well-orchestrated compliments to all the leaders. For instance, Lloyd George 'beamed' at Venizelos' reference to the insignificance of the language test in northern Epirus, because many prominent Greeks spoke Albanian in their homes in the same way that 'Mr Lloyd George spoke Welsh to his children'.[504]

Venizelos was all too aware of his good reception,[505] but personality and charisma could only get him so far, in accordance with international relations theory and the weakness of small states. This was especially so because Greek ambitions conflicted with great power interests in many areas. The Greeks divided their territorial claims into four categories: northern Epirus, the Dodecanese, Thrace and Asia Minor. The claim to northern Epirus was a line passing through Chimara, north of Tepelena, west of Voskopoja, to Lake Prespa, to join the Greek frontier. Venizelos based his claim on the majority of the population being Greek (120,000 to 80,000 Albanians). He admitted that not all the 'Greeks' spoke Greek. Many spoke only Albanian, and hence the 1913 boundary commission, which had conducted its census solely on the basis of language as proof of nationality, recorded all the Albanian-speaking families as Albanian. He maintained that 'neither race, nor language, nor skull' could be taken as the basis for determining nationality, and that national conscience must be the overriding factor. This was determined by religion and national sentiment, not language. Venizelos claimed that all the Christians within the region had always been attached to Greece, not to Albania or the Ottoman Empire. To him, this explained why over 300,000 had already emigrated to Greece. Although they maintained their Albanian language, these Christians had nonetheless been Hellenised in manners and customs, and they played an important part in economic life. Venizelos listed key Greek officials of Albanian origin, such as the Vice-President of the Council of Ministers and

the Commander-in-Chief of the Greek Armies.[506] Interestingly,
and in spite of the numerous efforts since 1913 to portray the area
as Greek, Argyrocastro was not emphasised. Venizelos sought to
use claims in northern Epirus and the Dodecanese as bargaining
tools with Italy for his greater goals in Asia Minor. He wrote that
'the foremost virtue of a politician is to make the necessary partial
sacrifices in time to secure the big results.'[507] The representatives of
the 1914 provisional government of Autonomous Northern Epirus
appeared before the Greek Committee. They also contested the
Albanian claims and reinforced the Greek ones.[508]

Great-Power Interests in the Greek Committee

Following the presentation of Greek claims to the Supreme Council,
and in accordance with the pattern already decided for other
territorial questions, the Supreme Council referred Greek claims
to a territorial committee.[509] F.S. Marston, an authority on the
procedures of the Conference, claimed that there was an unwritten
understanding that the committees were to determine the frontiers
on the basis of nationality, and that the principle was not considered
to constitute an interference in political matters.[510] Yet geo-political
interests hindered the functioning of the Greek committee from the
outset. The representatives had clearly been instructed to protect
strategic interests, and further problems resulted from restrictions
on their remits, a lack of definite principles on which to base their
judgments, and a feeling by many members that they belonged to
merely advisory bodies.[511] On the Albanian question specifically, one
major problem was that the Greek committee was assigned to deal
only with issues pertaining to Greek ambitions, whereas it was later
determined that Yugoslav and Italian ambitions were to be dealt with
by other parts of the Conference. This made the Albanian claims
weaker still as it would not be possible for them to make trade-
offs for similar claims elsewhere, although such 'trading' would be
possible for Greek aspirations.

The Committee met from 12 February until 6 March 1919, and
once again in November 1919.[512] Each of the four powers had two
representatives, with technical experts also attending on occasion.
The Italian representatives (Giacomo de Martino , who had been the
personal representative to Wilhelm of Wied in 1914, and Castoldi)

were indicative of Italy's hostile attitude towards the Committee, and the importance of retaining Italian gains in Albania. French 'disinterestedness' was also questionable, as their technical expert was the controversial Leon Krajewsky. Jules Cambon, the French committee chairman, declared that the purpose of the Committee was to find 'the best means of satisfying the ancient claims of the Hellenic nation and of at last completing the work of independence begun by the liberal nations of Europe a century ago'.[513] It was clear that the Albanians would find themselves in a difficult predicament, and that the principle of self-determination would not be fully applied.

The southern Albanian issue[514] was discussed in the first three meetings (12, 18 and 19 February 1919) because it was considered the most simple. It soon became apparent that the French and Italian views diverged, with the British and Americans in between. Nicolson thought that nobody wanted to 'show their hand'.[515] When positions were finally presented, on 18 February, there was much consensus between the British, French and American delegations. All three delegations accepted the Greek proposal that the frontier should start about twenty-five kilometres north of Chimara, at Gramala Bay, because the area was essentially Greek in character and because the Voyussa river was an important defensive line.[516]

The main differences regarded territory north of the Voyussa. The Americans considered it impossible to divide the region into purely Albanian and Greek zones and also to ensure communication links in the region (Valona for the Albanians, Janina for the Greeks). They proposed a line denying Greece about two-thirds of the area it claimed.[517] Contrary to British and French views, and also to Inquiry reports, Clive Day, one of the American representatives, argued that economic and trade patterns tied Koritza with Valona not Santa Quaranta, and that strategic considerations were not relevant as another road linking Greece and Yugoslavia could be built.[518] The British and French proposals ran only a few kilometres north of the American line until it reached the Voyussa, but north of the river showed variations.[519] As Goldstein argued, considering that Venizelos' aims were to achieve the maximum possible gains, they 'received a remarkable degree of support from within the FO'. This was especially true of northern Epirus where they were accepted on strategic grounds.[520] The important factor in British thinking continued to be the long-term position of Anglo-Greek relations. In the short term, this meant ensuring that Greece achieved tangible gains to maintain Venizelos in power. Harold Nicolson noted that 'I need not elaborate the disastrous effects which any weakening of M. Venizelos' position would have upon Greece itself and general Entente interests in the eastern Mediterranean'.[521]

The Italians proposed a very different frontier that was largely based on the 1913 Florence Protocol (and contrary to the 1915 Pact). De Martino and Castoldi argued that their proposal represented the 'best approach' to a just division between the two nationalities, based on both ethnical and other considerations. De Martino criticised the significance of both the religious and language tests. Castoldi meanwhile cited economic factors in support of the Italian scheme. He argued that the regions north and south of the Voyussa could not be separated, as both were dependent upon Santa Quaranta as their natural sea outlet and line of communication.[522] He considered that the question of southern Albania was inseparable from Italian interests in the Adriatic, and above all the necessity of maintaining the neutralisation of the Corfu straits.[523] The Italian representatives compromised little in the ensuing debates, and this clearly showed the importance of Albania in the Consulta's general Adriatic policy. In particular, the Italians opposed any starting point of the southern boundary north of Cape Stylos (approximately sixty kilometres further south than the other three proposed and being the point agreed by the ambassadors in London in 1913). De Martino repeatedly insisted on the military and strategic importance of southern Albania to Italy. If the coast from Valona to Corfu passed into the same hands as those that held Corfu, namely Greece, this would constitute a threat to Italy. They argued that geography (sea, mountains, and the Prespa and Ochrida lakes) favoured the 1913 frontier, whereas to its north there was no natural obstacle, which would make the rest of Albania (Italian-controlled) vulnerable to Greek assaults.[524] The Italian arguments proved very unpopular and their information was often questioned.[525] Nicolson wrote of one exchange that de Martino

then turns on old Castoldi to tell us all about the delimitation of 1913. Luckily I have brought with me the *Procès Verbal* of that commission. Castoldi says they had unanimously decided that the district, ... of Argyrocastro, should go to Albania. I quickly looked up the reference. It said that the Italian Delegate (i.e. Castoldi himself) had expressed this view, but that all his other colleagues had dissented. Crowe reads this out. Castoldi turns purple. He tries to bluster. '*Lascia stare*', snarls Martino to him. It is all very embarrassing. But Castoldi, who is a good fellow, took it well: '*vous êtes un terrible diable*', he said to me afterwards.'[526]

The Albanian question next came up for discussion on 24, 26 and 27 February 1919, when the committee heard the Greek, Albanian and northern Epirote representatives. It has already been shown how the great power audience in the Greek committee seemed biased towards the Greek representatives, and that Venizelos was much more adept at currying favour with the great power statesmen. But Venizelos was concerned by Italian hostility to Greek claims, and his inability to prevent the Chimara coast being considered part of the Adriatic question. He therefore reduced Greek claims by 1300 square kilometres to 5138 square kilometres and 195,000 people, which made the Greek claims only marginally different from the French proposal. He hoped that such a 'generous' offer, which in reality affected only 28,516 'Albanians' and 1,157 'Greeks', would show Greek goodwill and help offset Italian opposition, by making Greek ambitions appear moderate and realistic to the other powers.[527] It appears that none of the Albanian delegates envisaged using such tactics. The Albanians believed passionately in their cause, the merits of their argument and the honesty and integrity of the great power representatives, and their determination to base the southern Albanian question on ethnic principles. This naivety was indicative of the inexperience of the Albanian representatives and their understanding of the international system. It placed them in an even weaker position in the states system than their weak or non-state status implied, because they were not able to capitalise upon the tactics available to small states to increase the receptivity of their claims.

Before the Greek Committee next discussed the Albanian question (4 March), Nicolson worked with representatives from the French delegation to prepare a joint Franco-British proposal. The major problem remained Koritza. Nicolson remained unconvinced by French arguments of its necessity as a road connection, but Laroche refused to allow it to become Albanian. He argued that the establishment of Italy as the mandatory power in Albania, and therefore across the only line of communication between Monastir and Santa Quaranta, would drive a permanent wedge between Serbia and Greece. It is clear from his diary that Nicolson was torn between his moral inclinations over the 'Albanianness' of Koritza, the strategic necessities of maintaining Greco-Serbian communication, and British mistrust of Italian intentions. Nicolson wrote 'it is terribly bad luck on Albania, who has Italy imposed upon her as a mandatory power, and then gets her frontiers cut down merely because none of us trust Italy in the Balkans'.[528] As in 1913, great power rivalry and interests persistently predominated and were decisive. In the end, Harold Nicolson's moral concerns were overruled by Crowe's desire to bolster Greece with a settlement based on economic and strategic necessity. Of this decision, Nicolson recorded 'I feel heart-heavy about Koritza. I am convinced that it ought to go to Albania, Italians or no Italians'.[529]

When they met on 4 March 1919, the positions of the American, French and British delegations had changed and all to Greek advantage, with opposition to Italy the major motivation, but they still lacked consensus. The Americans were prepared to grant Greece the Voyussa frontier, but nothing further north. The British now proposed a line that closely resembled the French suggestion. The French also advocated further Greek gains, above all the town of Premeti because it connected Santa Quaranta and Janina. The discussion again failed to decide upon a definite recommendation. There were two votes: one on the 'up to the Voyussa' proposal, and the second on that north of it, in effect the American and the Franco-British proposals. The first was accepted by three votes to one, with the Italians objecting. The second produced a two-two deadlock, with the Americans this time siding with the Italians. No progress was made, and so the final report (8 March 1919) contained three recommendations: the Franco-British, the American with the variant over Koritza and the Italian, which Crowe managed to relegate to a separate annex.[530] The Central Territorial Committee, whose responsibility it was to collate the reports of the various territorial committees, also failed to agree and so confined itself to reiterating the views of their respective representatives on the Greek Committee.[531] During the Greek Committee, geo-politics superseded self-determination with the result that there was little movement from the original great-power positions.

Anglo-American Co-Operation and Initiatives

Between March and June 1919, a series of Anglo-American negotiations took place outside the official Conference proceedings, in an attempt to satisfy the Supreme Council's request for a single recommendation on southern Albania. It was hoped that if these two powers could agree, then the other two, especially Italy, would be inclined to compromise. Geo-politics remained central to these discussions. Throughout, neither the Albanians nor the Greeks were consulted or informed: it was traditional old-style diplomacy, despite the new international rhetoric, with the small states as mere supplicants. The British appointed Harold Nicolson and Captain Jim Barnes, a junior member of the PID who had travelled extensively in Albania. The Americans appointed Dr Sidney Mezes, the Senior American Delegate on the Co-ordinating Committee and former Head of the Inquiry. Although all three were sympathetic to Albanian claims and the principle of self-determination, their superiors often vetoed their ideas because of wider strategic interests and priorities. They quickly became out of touch with the general trend in Albanian and in wider Adriatic and Balkan policies. This made their proposals neither realistic nor practical, given the changing international climate.

On the British side, Nicolson and Barnes both produced a range of schemes, driven by a variety of motives. Barnes, whom Nicolson once described as 'far more Albanophile even than I am myself',[532] made a number of naive suggestions based on ethnic principles, but not ones that either his superiors or the other powers' representatives would accept. It appears that Barnes held the misguided conception that the Conference 'seriously desired to constitute an Albania capable of surviving as an independent self-respecting State'.[533] For instance, on 25 April he proposed that Valona be given to Italy under a twenty-one year mandate, and that the rest of Albania be given as a personal mandate to the Italian Duke of Abruzzi, under the League of Nations, with Abruzzi as High Commissioner and the title *mpret*!

Barnes contended that this arrangement satisfied the competing geographical, economic, cultural and ethnographic interests. It would maintain a non-partitioned Albania, including Koritza and eventually Valona, which the Americans would support. It would preserve Italian interests by means of the prince, and also benefit Greece and Serbia because there would be no outright Italian mandate.[534]

Nicolson was more mindful of the wider British interests at stake. He proposed, however, a number of curious schemes designed to fulfil different priorities. In one (27 March), he devised an agreement based on the 1914 Corfu protocol: the disputed areas would become a League mandate with Greece as mandatory power. He admitted that the scheme was far from perfect, as there was the prospect of the Greeks obtaining the upper hand and voting for union with Greece, but at least it maintained Greek strategic control of Koritza, and partially offset Italian objections to annexation.[535] Another, equally implausible scheme (28 May 1919), but for different reasons, involved a tri-partitioned Albania: northern Albania would become an autonomous state under Yugoslav mandate; central Albania would go to Italy; southern Albania would go to Greece; and Koritza would be neutralised as a centre of Albanian culture and learning, including a central Albanian university under American protection. The Yugoslav and American mandates would last for twenty years, and a unified and independent area (including Ipek and Djakova in the north, which had gone to Serbia in 1913), would be created.[536] As Goldstein quipped, it is difficult to know whether Nicolson was completely serious or whether having 'seen all serious solutions fail he decided to try a silly one'.[537]

All these ideas met with little success because the British delegation remained divided over its priorities and commitments, although it was obvious that Nicolson and Barnes' superiors (especially Balfour, Crowe and Baron Hardinge) were less sympathetic to Albanian nationalist claims and an un-partitioned independent state. It was appreciated that Koritza had been a significant factor in Albanian nationalism, but it was considered necessary for 'strategic security' for it to go to Greece.[538] Nicolson was himself concerned about his ideas, especially those of 28 May, which would have provided a territorial connection between the Italian zone and the 'Bulgarian' (Macedonian) part of Serbia.[539] Generally, the British delegation persisted in supporting ethnic self-determination as long as it also promoted their wider strategic goals.

Disagreements within the American delegation were even more problematic. The Americans were also holding their own internal debate on the importance and practicability of applying ethnic rationales to the various peace settlements. Although Mezes was willing to negotiate with Nicolson and Barnes, these internal conversations seriously hindered his ability to do so. Thus by 21 April 1919, Mezes was forced to return Nicolson's initial draft (27 March) because the Americans were 'too pre-occupied' to consider it.[540] The Americans were still debating on what to base their policies but an anti-Italian stance was developing, which would impact on the Albanian questions because Albanian gains were viewed as synonymous with Italian ones. Dr Douglas Johnson, whose views Wilson considered 'authoritative' on the Albanian problem, had become particularly hostile to Italian gains in the Adriatic, including Albania. On 17 March, Johnson had circulated a memorandum seeking to use Albania as a bargaining chip against other Italian claims in the Adriatic and Mediterranean. At the same time, Mezes was still contemplating giving Greece gains in northern Epirus at Albanian (Italian) expense.[541]

Developments within the wider Conference complicated these Anglo-American initiatives further, by making Lloyd George, Clemenceau and, in particular, Wilson even more hostile to Italian ambitions, including Albania. From 24 April to 6 May 1919, the Italian Prime and Foreign Ministers left Paris, protesting at the reluctance of the Conference to consider Italy's claims and Wilson's direct appeal to the Italian people to accept his fourteen points as the basis of the settlement.[542] Wilson's mounting opposition to the Italians, especially Sonnino, whom he held personally responsible for blocking resolution of the outstanding issues, had profound implications on his attitudes towards Albania, and above all his doubts as to whether Italy should receive the mandate. In a meeting with Clemenceau and Lloyd George on 6 May 1919, and in what constitutes one of Wilson's few direct references to the Albanian question, Wilson remained adamant that the Albanians should become independent and argued against Lloyd George's concerns about their unity.[543]

The rest of the American delegation was less convinced. According to Woodall, Day expressed support for the Italian mandate plan to his American colleagues, but reiterated Wilson's refusal to partition Albania due to Wilsonian ideology and opposition to Italian imperialism, as eulogised in the London Pact, to the European delegations. He considered an Italian mandate within the 1913 frontiers as the most feasible plan to gain consensus from all the powers, although personally he preferred giving the Argyrocastro district to Greece for 'national reasons'.[544] For Day and other American delegates, political questions about small states were generally more important than rationale. They therefore became more sympathetic to Italian designs in Albania, to help facilitate Italian concessions on Fiume, Trentino and Dalmatia (the opposite of the scheme envisaged by Mezes).[545] In essence, in spite of Wilson's pledges to remove such trade bargaining from international politics, his own officials were equally willing to play the bartering game that had been such a typical feature of old diplomacy.

Although his advisers, including House and Johnson, emphasised the need to be conciliatory on the Albanian question, because of the wider Adriatic and Balkan concerns, Wilson remained adamant that Albania should not be used as a pawn and that, possibly, even at this early stage, self-determination should be applied. During his return voyage to the United States, he cabled Robert Lansing, Secretary of State, who now headed the American delegation:

> I meant before leaving to express to you and my other colleagues my very profound interest in the fortunes of Albania. I am fearful lest midst the multitude of other things that might seem more pressing and important, due consideration of those rights should be overlooked. I beg that you will be very watchful concerning them.[546]

Woodall suggested that Wilson's concern came too late,[547] but it proved significant. Admittedly, in the second half of the Conference, the Albanian question was not considered independently but as part of the wider Adriatic question, given the ascendancy of political and strategic issues, but nevertheless Wilson's attitudes had profound implications. In delaying a decision on the question of Albanian independence and its borders, Wilson inadvertently ensured that by the time that a sufficiently stable, organised and anti-Italian national government was formed in Albania (by the Congress of Lushnje), there was still a viable Albanian entity to preserve.

Bi-Lateral Italo-Greek Negotiations

Surprisingly, it was the Italians who secured an agreement over southern Albania, which had so flummoxed the other great power delegations. This was the result of direct bi-lateral negotiations with the Greek delegation, of the type that all governments had pledged to abandon in favour of the new open variety, but which the other great powers seemed willing to accept.[548] This was indicative of the continued weakness and difficulties of the Albanians. The new Italian Prime Minister, Francesco Nitti, and Foreign Minister, Tommaso Tittoni, pursued a markedly different Albanian policy to their predecessors. Nitti, who had substantial experience in the finance ministry, was appalled at the expense of the Italian occupation of Albania (40,000 men and over 300 million *lire* annually). He was especially concerned because the occupation did not seem to be having the desired result, of making the Albanian population more receptive to nominal independence under Italian control, which could be utilised in Paris. Instead, there were daily reports of growing unrest in the Italian occupied zone, and resistance to the idea of an Italian protectorate, with the Italian troops needing to use coercive measures to control the local population. Harry Lamb put these complaints into three categories: restriction of liberty, disregard of property rights, and attempts at denationalisation.[549]

In this climate, Nitti was eager to come to a direct arrangement with the Greeks, which could in turn be presented to the Allies as a *fait accompli* on southern Albania. Such an idea had been mooted by Venizelos before the Conference (December 1918), but Sonnino had ruled it out. In any event, Venizelos had been encouraged to play a waiting game, because pro-Greeks persuaded him that he would gain more of northern Epirus at the bargaining tables because of British and French support.[550] By the resulting secret Tittoni-Venizelos agreement (19 July 1919), the Consulta agreed to support Greek claims, as defined by the Franco-British line in the Greek committee, to northern Epirus (Clause 2), including Argyrocastro and Koritza, and the Greek government agreed to an Italian mandate over Albania, Italian sovereignty of Valona, neutralisation of the Corfu straits, and demilitarisation of northern Epirus to twenty-five kilometres inland (Clause 3). On the surface, the agreement appeared to involve the abandonment of all but the most basic of Italian interests (Valona) in southern Albania. It was a pragmatic policy. By securing neutralisation of the Corfu straits, Italian strategic interests were safeguarded but without the costs of occupation. In private, it was much easier to abandon the new supposed ethnic rationale in favour of *realpolitik*. More importantly, Tittoni gained Greek support for Italian ambitions in Asia Minor, but Italy also secured full freedom of action in Asia Minor if Italian ambitions there were not fully satisfied, with the Consulta left free to determine whether or not this was so (Clause 7). This was a major Greek diplomatic blunder, although none of the Greek delegates, including the usually astute Venizelos, realised it. It undid most of the settlement, especially as Italian designs in Asia Minor came up against extensive Allied opposition.[551] Nevertheless, Tittoni felt sufficiently confident to be able to focus his attention on northern Albania and the northern Adriatic, without the distraction of questions in southern Albania. It also gave the Consulta time to court the Albanians, and to work out an agreement with their Allies on northern Albania and the Adriatic, and possibly even Asia Minor. Tittoni soon reduced his support for Greek gains in northern Epirus, in an attempt to offset American objections to Italy gaining the port of Fiume. As early as 3 September 1919, Tittoni would argue that the Greeks should not be allowed to occupy Koritza following the French evacuation, because the Albanians would not accept it, and that its status should be determined by plebiscite.[552] In the second half of 1919, the question of southern Albania was considered only sporadically, when it encroached on the larger Adriatic problem.

The Problem of Northern Albania and the Adriatic

On 4 July 1919, Harold Nicolson wrote to the Foreign Secretary that Albanian territory should no longer be used 'as an item in the general give-and-take of an Adriatic settlement'.[553] His wishes were not to be realised. As in 1913, the northern Albanian question proved even more controversial than the southern problem. The dilemma of what to do with northern Albania was closely tied up with the balances of power in the Balkans and the Adriatic, especially Italian ambitions and rivalry with the Yugoslavs, as diplomacy both inside and outside the formal Conference became much less Wilsonian and more *realpolitik*. In these discussions, two distinct phases were evident. From March 1919 to January 1920, the question of northern Albania was considered as a subsidiary part of the Adriatic question - there was no place for the small states or ethnic nationalism. From January to March 1920, ethnic and national considerations became more important, and the Yugoslavs were invited to contribute to the deliberations, but the Albanians were neither consulted nor allowed to present their claims. Yet, by March 1920, Wilson had managed to secure the removal of the Albanian problem from the Adriatic question, and the revival of an Albanian-centred one.

The Italian Mandate And Strategic Interests: the defeat of the 'Albanian problem'

During the first half of the Paris Peace Conference there was little progress on the related northern Albanian, Albanian mandate or Adriatic questions. For the Albanian questions, these problems centred on the important but divisive question: *Would Albania become independent or be given as a mandate to Italy?* Difficulties emerged due to opposition to Italian claims and problems in determining who had jurisdiction to consider these issues. Whilst being unfruitful, these exchanges were illuminating because they illustrated the particular weakness of the Albanian small state during the Peace Conference. In being considered suitable for mandate status Albania had been deemed equivalent to a colony or previously none existent state. These deliberations also reflect the changing balance of power in the Adriatic. They illustrate that the primary Italian interests in Albania had moved northwards (to the former Austrian zone) from their traditional base in southern Albania.

When the Yugoslav delegation presented their claims to the Supreme Council (18 February 1919), this generated a series of Italian objections, starting with northern Albania, that such issues could not be dealt with by a territorial committee and should be reserved for the Supreme Council. This was in accordance with the decision that territorial committees were excluded from considering questions relating to geo-political interests. It was also a reaction to the opposition that had materialised to Italian ambitions on other questions, such as those allocated to the Greek Committee. The question of northern Albania was important, Sonnino maintained, because it was politically and strategically linked to Italian claims in the Adriatic.[554] By March 1919, and the time when the territorial committees were due to start finalising their recommendations, these matters had still not been resolved and were causing problems for the territorial committees. As some members of the territorial committees appreciated, there was the possibility of a three way paradox: the Greek Committee was to consider Greek claims to Albania, the Romanian Committee Yugoslav ones and the Supreme Council Italian ones.[555] On 4 March 1919, a particularly heated debate took place in the Greek Committee, after the Italian delegates had raised a question about the size of an 'independent Albania' and the extent of the Italian mandate. One of the Italian delegates, de Martino, explained that the Consulta now sought a large 'independent' Albania, instead of the small protectorate allowed for under the London Pact, or the larger 'unauthorised' one proclaimed in 1917. He maintained that the enlargement of Yugoslavia and Greece, and the continuation of their common frontier in Macedonia, meant that it was no longer necessary, or advisable, for these states to make gains in Albania. These arguments were very poorly received by the French and British delegates. Sir Eyre Crowe, one of the British delegates, indignantly suggested that the Italians only used the Pact when it suited their purposes but otherwise ignored it. He went further proposing, that in light of these 'changed circumstances', there should be a thorough re-evaluation of the whole of the 1915 Pact of London, which he knew the Italians could not accept, for fear of losing their other promised acquisitions.[556] The Supreme Council's decision on this matter was a strange one: questions that were explicitly vital to Italy were reserved to the Supreme Council, including consideration of the northern Albanian boundary and whether Albania should become independent; the southern boundary did not fall into this category and was suitable for consideration by the Greek committee.[557] The decisions regarding Albanian independence and the northern boundary issue had been deferred, but they were considered inextricably linked to the wider Adriatic problem.

Between March and July 1919 a number of proposals were put

forward which incorporated the problem of northern Albania.[558] One of the most significant was known as the Tardieu Plan (28 May 1919), named after its author. It was one of the few schemes covering the Albanian question to be put before the Council of Four, a meeting of David Lloyd George, Vittorio Orlando, Georges Clemenceau and Woodrow Wilson. Its central feature was the creation of a 'Free State' including Fiume, which would act as a buffer between Italy and Yugoslavia. The Albanian clauses were more specific than previous ones had been: a mandate would be given to Italy, stretching from the present northern frontier to a southern boundary to be determined by the Conference; a railroad was to be constructed in northern Albania (with forty percent Italian capital, forty percent Yugoslav, and twenty percent from other sources) for use by the Yugoslavs. Interestingly, there was no mention of Valona going to Italy in full sovereignty, indicating that it was believed Italian interests there would be sufficiently served by possession of the mandate.[559]

As with other proposals, American objections proved problematic. The American delegation, Wilson especially, seem to have been concerned that the Albanians were not ready for self-government. However, the State Department were also concerned about the alternative idea of a mandate scheme. Wilson was suspicious of Italian intentions regarding Albania, but saw no practical alternative because none of the other three great powers desired the mandate themselves. It was also unlikely that the Consulta would agree to another great power having the mandate. Unsure what to do, Wilson played for time and declined to comment on the Albanian clauses.[560] Appreciating that American objections were the prime reason for the delay in settling the Adriatic question, Frank Polk, the Under Secretary of State and Head of the American Delegation following Wilson and Lansing's departure, advocated a more flexible position on Albania. He proposed that the Americans should be more sympathetic to Italian claims. Nevertheless his stance was persistently compromised by Wilson.[561] These difficulties would become even more pronounced in the second half of the Conference.

Submerged in the Adriatic Question: excluding the small states

As with the problem of southern Albania, the change in the Italian delegation (July 1919) sparked a new phase in consideration of the

Adriatic question, including northern Albania.[562] The Italians were not the only ones to have revised their Albanian policy, as geopolitical interests (especially a desire for a quick settlement) overrode moralistic rhetoric.[563] Nevertheless, as with the southern Albanian question, most initiatives came from the new Italian delegation. Unlike the southern problem, these initiatives took place at great power level, excluded the Yugoslavs and failed to reach an agreement. In two months, Tittoni proposed three different schemes (12 August, 15 September, 8 October), each with different implications for Albania.[564] These three proposals were indicative of the changing priorities of the Italian government, its domestic problems, the opposition of the other great powers and, in part, the resistance to an Italian occupation in Albania and other places.[565] The largest difficulties stemmed from the activities of Italian nationalist poet Gabriel D'Annunzio, who had led a successful raid on Fiume on 12 September 1919, and now governed the town. Designed to help Italian nationalist claims and well received in the Italian press, who became very vocal in its demands that the Italian government must keep the town, it complicated the position of the Italian negotiators. As the *coup* took place only three days after presentation of the second Adriatic plan, it appeared that the Italian government supported the move and had not been genuine in their earlier conciliatory overtures.[566] The impact on the American delegation was particularly significant. On 14 September, Wilson had finally accepted the idea of an Italian mandate for Albania, albeit with strict controls. However, the *coup* revived his suspicions of Italian intentions, and made it more difficult for the American delegation and other great powers to get his support for their ideas to settle the Adriatic question on this basis. Admittedly, however, Wilson's major concession of the Italian mandate for Albania was conditional upon Italian acceptance of the Fiume Free State, which the Consulta could not accept, especially following 12 September.[567] As a result, settlement of the Albanian question on these grounds was not possible, despite Wilson finally, albeit reluctantly, accepting the idea of an Italian mandate for Albania.

Most of the American delegation, including for the first time Douglas Johnson, although still not Wilson, seem to have agreed that the Albanians were not ready for self-government, but that they were a distinct nationality who were worthy of it at some point in the future. In order to foster that eventually, a single Albania was preferable to a partitioned one, and Italy was the only power prepared to take the mandate, and by implication the responsibility. Therefore, rather than oppose it, the Americans sought to use their influence to tighten the mandate's terms, to prevent Italian exploitation of the fledgling state. They were still undecided as to what the boundaries should be.[568]

Whilst Wilson's reservations could not be ignored, it appears that Polk harboured the misconception that the European powers could persuade Wilson to concede over the Albanian question. Consequently, Polk encouraged European endeavours to come up with a joint memorandum about Albanian boundaries. He merely suggested that the mandate question should be considered at a later date.[569] The British and French representatives therefore attempted to facilitate a compromise between the Italian and American positions. The idea that was most favoured by the European great powers seems to have been a scheme whereby Italy would gain Valona in full sovereignty and the Albanian mandate. The southern frontier would be as proposed by the American delegate on the Greek Committee (Argyrocastro to Greece, Koritza to Albania), which incidentally went against new Italian policy in the Tittoni-Venizelos agreement. Yugoslavia would not be given any territory, only the right to build and operate a railroad in the Drin Valley—a concession to both Yugoslavia and France. After consultation with Johnson, the European proposal was modified to eliminate the suggestions that Fiume city should go unequivocally to Italy, and that northern Epirus should go to Greece. The latter clause was agreed to by the Italians, even though it contradicted the Tittoni-Venizelos agreement.[570] The Italian representatives were willing to renege on their pledge to the small state, in pursuit of its wider interests; having the support of at least two great powers made this all the easier.

Throughout September and October 1919, negotiations remained tense and little progress materialised. The Franco-British belief that a united front would mollify Wilson's position proved unrealistic. The American hope that the Consulta would accept the Albanian mandate as a substitute for Fiume was equally implausible. Although it was not included in the 1915 Pact, the retention of Fiume, which had become a nationalistic symbol of Italian aspirations, in what had been an unpopular war, had become essential for Italian policymakers because of the precarious domestic situation in Italy. Nitti and Tittoni (like all Italian politicians of the period) faced immense public and political pressure, and needed a speedy resolution in Italy's favour for their personal survival. This was not something any of the other delegations were prepared to give them. In addition, there was growing unrest in Albania and mounting opposition to an Italian mandate amongst the Albanian delegations, which resulted in two official protests (9 and 12 October 1919). This made the mandate less desirable for the Consulta, even though the other powers had all now agreed to it.[571]

The position of Eyre Crowe, Assistant Under-Secretary of State for Foreign Affairs, who had succeeded Balfour as Head of the British Delegation, was also complicated by the differing views of the Foreign Office and Prime Minister.[572] For Lloyd George, the crucial strategy was to achieve a solution as quickly as possible. As with other areas of the settlement, as long as British interests were not affected, he did not concern himself with the details or the (in)justice of the case. For the Prime Minister, the Albanian problem was part of the much larger dispute over the division of Ottoman territory. He was motivated by a desire to gain Italian goodwill over British policy in the Adriatic, in order to gain what he considered much-needed Italian support for British interests in Asia Minor. Thus the marginal issue of Albania, and other issues in the Adriatic, where British interests were minimal (other than naval and Mediterranean ones), were expendable in order to foster goodwill on issues where British interests were greater. The Foreign Office pursued a different agenda. It persisted in seeking a permanent peace based on the balance of power. Leeper was instructed to work for an arrangement with the Americans. He determined that Wilson was prepared to accept the Italian mandate over Albania, but that only a very small area around Valona would be able to go to Italy directly, sufficient for the economic needs of the town and its security.[573]

The American delegation left Paris (10 December 1919) understanding that they had reached an agreement with Britain and France on the Adriatic, including Albania (the 9 December memorandum). Generally considered Wilson's 'absolutely final conditions' or 'last word' on the Adriatic the agreement largely resembled an earlier proposal by Wilson (18 November), but with significant modifications on Albania. American support for Albanian nationalism had started to wane. The initial (18 November) proposal made no mention of Greek claims in southern Albania and had retracted from the position of allowing Italy increased territory around Valona.[574] By 9 December Italy was to be granted Valona and the Albanian mandate, the northern and eastern frontiers were to be as determined in 1913 and the southern frontier was to be decided separately. Until Italy and Greece agreed a settlement on the southern frontier, and in order to not delay the general Adriatic settlement, Greek troops would be allowed to occupy Argyrocastro but not Koritza. For the first time, a draft of the mandate was included. The clauses relating to northern Albania were not changed. Under these clauses the Yugoslavs would have the right to construct and operate railways in northern Albania (defined specifically and arbitrarily as north of parallel 41° 15'), and full privileges of international transport. The right to control the development of the Boyana River was to be vested in the League of Nations, with power to delegate it to either Yugoslavia or Italy.[575]

However, the British and French leaders, Lloyd George and Clemenceau, who had both taken personal control of the negotiations, used the departure of the Americans and Wilson's deteriorating position, following the November mid-terms, to attempt to modify these arrangements further. They sought to satisfy both Italian and Greek claims at the expense of Albanian and Yugoslav ones, but also to impress Wilson.[576] The results of these discussions are more important than the details for the Albanian question. Nitti's initial proposal (6 January 1920) made no reference to Albania, but the revised one (10 January 1920), formulated with Franco-British assistance, and formalised by a memorandum on 14 January 1920, made slight modifications of the proposals on the southern Albanian frontier. It proposed that a Greek and Albanian representative be allowed to argue the case before representatives of the great powers, who could then make an award or resort to a plebiscite. Any Albanian territory and coast ceded to Greece should be neutralised.[577] Therefore there appeared to be agreement about resurrecting a unified Albania, but the Italians were not being entirely honest. They hoped to use Albanian partition as a means of forcing compromise on the

Yugoslavs in the wider Adriatic question. To assert pressure on the Americans and Yugoslavs, the Italians asked for fulfilment of the London Pact if these new proposals were not accepted. In so doing, they had also distanced themselves from their support of Greece in southern Albania. Nevertheless, by 14 January 1920, there had been a dramatic shift in the Adriatic question. The British and French governments were at last prepared to work directly for a settlement of the Adriatic, particularly the heavily debated point of the territorial continuity of Italy with the *corpus separatum* (the name given to the semi-autonomous status of Fiume, modern day Rijeka, in the Austro-Hungarian Empire 1776-1918), and to champion it in Belgrade. In a joint note, after pointing out the magnitude of concessions the Yugoslavs were being asked to make, they concluded that they were being asked 'for the sake of an amicable and prompt settlement of a question which now threatens the peace and progress of southern Europe'.[578]

Reviving The Albanian Question: involving a small state

As René Albrecht-Carrié wrote the prospects of an agreement seemed promising, but Yugoslav, and especially American, opinion had not been taken into account.[579] Neither would accept the scheme. Despite Franco-British initiatives for a resolution of the Adriatic question being once more unsuccessful, this section of the Peace Conference deliberations will be considered in some depth because of its importance to the Albanian problem and the insights it provides for the role of small states in the great power system.

Nitti's position had become increasingly difficult, in part because of delays in settling the Adriatic question in accordance with Italian designs and leaks of the 9 December memorandum. On Albania, whilst conceding that the southern frontier could be redrawn, he insisted that the northern and eastern frontier must remain that of 1913.[580] This prompted a change in the negotiations. For the first time since their representations to the Supreme Council and territorial committees, the interested small states (in practice only the Yugoslavs) were invited to present their case. Before the great powers, the Croat Foreign Minister and former leader of the Yugoslav Committee, Ante Trumbić, argued that the Yugoslavs were convinced that the best solution was to trace the Albania state as it was when created [in 1913], with an autonomous administration … From all that we know of the Albanians, they have adequate elements for the establishment of an administration capable of governing the country.

He disputed Italy's judicial right to a mandate, since the League covenant envisaged mandates for states that had previously only been territories or colonies, not those that had enjoyed independence. On the other hand, if the great powers determined that Albania was not to be independent then Yugoslavia must claim northern Albania, especially the Drin Valley and Scutari.[581] Both alternatives were aimed at protecting Yugoslavian strategic interests against Italy.

Trumbić's ideas were not popular with any of the great powers and unlikely to be successful, but the Yugoslavs thought they would be more acceptable to the great powers than claiming this territory directly themselves. According to Ivo Lederer, Lloyd George, 'flanked by his expert Leeper and armed with maps', kept interrupting Trumbić with pointed questions about the Slovenes, Zara and Albania.[582] The Italians insisted that Albania was incapable of independence, and that Yugoslavia should give up its London Pact claims. If Italy *first* received the city of Fiume and a mandate over central Albania, then Nitti would agree to 'discuss' northern Albanian boundaries further. Lloyd George and Clemenceau were satisfied by this idea, having apparently agreed that northern Albania should be used as a bargaining tool to induce the Yugoslavs to accept the wider Adriatic settlement. For if the Yugoslavs did not receive Scutari, then they would feel cut off from the Adriatic, in both the north and the south. The purpose was to obtain Yugoslav acceptance of the Adriatic settlement devised by the European leaders, in order to exert pressure on Wilson to agree to it. They believed that Yugoslav (Croat) disappointment regarding Fiume could be offset by Yugoslav (Serbian) contentment over northern Albania, including the important town of Scutari.[583]

Nevertheless, Nitti refused to give up Scutari in order to gain Fiume, just as Imperiali and Mensdorff had refused to give up Scutari to gain towns in Kosovo in 1913. His reasons were, similarly, based on ethnic and geo-political foundations. Nitti claimed that Scutari was so important to the Albanians that if denied the town they would revolt, and it would then prove impossible for Italy, as the mandatory power, to maintain order. Eventually, however, he was forced to give up Scutari as he, unlike the Austrians in 1913, had no great power ally. The European proposal for settlement of the Adriatic question therefore included the partition of Albania, and the allocation of the three important towns of Scutari, Koritza and Argyrocastro to other states. Italy would receive Valona and the mandate; northern Albania would be an autonomous province of Yugoslavia; southern Albania would be delimited at the Franco-British line on the Greek Committee.[584] Geo-political strategic interests were far more significant than ethnic or national ones. This was even more evident in the discussions with the Yugoslav delegation on the precise frontier. Lederer wrote that Lloyd George 'handed Trumbić a pencil and a map, suggesting the latter mark the extent of Yugoslav desires in northern Albania'. Trumbić declined to do so, claiming that he could not improvise on the 'national frontier'.[585]

According to Clemenceau, there was a split in the Yugoslav delegation: the Serbs, who were 'reasonable', and wanted to accept the Allied offer in order to gain Scutari, as opposed to the Croats, the 'intransigent' ones, who refused to moderate on Fiume, in order to secure Scutari.[586] It would have been expected that such disunity would weaken the position of the small Yugoslav state in its negotiations with the three European great powers. However, the Yugoslav delegation managed to outmanoeuvre the three great powers by securing opposition to the scheme from the American great power, which the European great power leaders had been trying to prevent. Their actions would also benefit the Albanians. As Woodall asserts, Trumbić seemed to be fully aware that the Americans, despite their apparent lack of interest, would not allow the European powers to follow through with their bluff to enact the London Pact if the Yugoslav delegation did not accept the new scheme. Trumbić therefore kept Hugh Campbell Wallace, the American Ambassador in Paris, well informed and sought to use their regular contact to obtain American support to defy the ultimatum.[587]

American support for the Yugoslav position came swiftly, but it was not yet decisive. Wallace devised a scheme that gave a prominent position to Albanian national interests. Rather than Italy, Yugoslavia and Greece gaining Albanian territory outright, this should be awarded as mandates, except for Argyrocastro, which would go to Greece in full sovereignty. The Foreign Office was also toying once more with the idea of a triple mandate.[588] Although most of the State Department agreed that the new European plan was unacceptable, they placed a far higher priority on a satisfactory strategic settlement of Yugoslav-Italian disputes. They had therefore distanced themselves from ethnic arguments pertaining to Albanian interests. Polk, for instance, proposed two alternatives: withdraw from discussion of the Adriatic question after one final effort to settle upon the principles of 9 December; or insist that the Italians accept on the lines of 9 December, whilst hinting that American aid would otherwise be withdrawn. He warned that the State Department was no longer in a position to bring effective economic pressure to bear against Italy because there was no loan pending, an interruption of American coal shipments was unlikely to be effective and a full economic blockade would most likely have unfortunate results.[589] The most valuable assistance came from Robert Lansing, the Secretary of State, who expressed his dismay at the way 'Italian questions' were proceeding, including whether the British and French representatives were trying to solve the Adriatic question without first consulting with the Americans. In response, the British and French Prime Ministers stressed that the scheme had not lost sight of the American viewpoint, and that the only changes to Wilson's 'last word' were the partition of Albania and substitution of the Free State.[590] Even this was not sufficient to guarantee the Yugoslavs the much-needed American support, because President Wilson had still not commented and therefore no objections could be officially communicated. On 27 January 1920, Edith Wilson, the First Lady, replied that there would be no further changes to her husband's position regarding the Adriatic. A week later, Polk was directed to follow his second course of 'moral persuasion' and the Yugoslavs were advised to accept no Franco-British compromises.[591] The small Yugoslav power had effectively stymied its European great power counterparts by using another great power to block their designs.

Wilson's long awaited reply was eventually received on 9 February 1920. Using ethnic arguments, he brutally attacked the 14 January proposal. His main objection was that the proposal violated the principle of national self-determination in Albania: 'the memorandum of 14 January partitions the Albanian people against their vehement protests, among three alien powers'. In comparison, he maintained that his 'last word' memorandum prevented these injustices and maintained a degree of unity amongst the Albanian people. This intervention was highly significant, and can probably be considered Wilson's strongest support for Albanian nationalism and independence. Clemenceau and Lloyd George may have been bluffing about their threat to invoke the London Pact, but Wilson had a far more powerful threat to use. As Woodall so accurately put it, 'instead of threatening Italy with economic sanctions, Wilson … aimed his bolt at France and England'.[592] The manifesto closed with the warning that if the Adriatic Settlement was not settled in accordance with the principles of 9 December:

> the President desires to say that he must take under serious consideration the withdrawal of the treaty with Germany and the agreement between the United States and France of 28th June, 1919, [the military guarantee treaty] which are now before the Senate.[593]

Wilson's reply transcended much more than the Albanian or Adriatic questions. The Senate failed to ratify either treaty, but to the British and French representatives at the time the threat endangered their core objectives in the Peace Conference. It is remarkable that Wilson was prepared to go to such lengths, over such a small issue as self-determination in Istria and Albania.[594] He used geo-political interests against the British and French representatives, and in an area where their direct interests were at best marginal, to secure an ethnic basis for the settlement of the Albanian national question. According to Woodall this harsh response was suggested by Johnson. Woodall wrote that on 7 February Lansing received a memorandum which stated that the President 'approves the telegram prepared by Dr. Johnson, including the paragraph threatening the withdrawal of the Treaties in the event that the American view is not accepted.'[595] It has not proven possible to verify these assertions.

The controversy thus centred on American and Franco-British divisions, the very situation that Clemenceau and Lloyd George had been trying to avoid. There was only a limited role for the representatives of the other states, including the Italians. The British and French Prime Ministers tried to be conciliatory: they contended that the 14 January proposal was preferable to the 9 December one, insisting that it included only minor changes, and that these were to the Yugoslav advantage rather than the Italian in respect of Fiume. Regarding Albania they pointed out that

> the details of the administration of this country by Jugo-Slavia, Italy and Greece, have not yet been elaborated and in working to this end sight will not be lost of the feelings and future interest of the Albanian people and every endeavour will be made to carry out the arrangements in full consultation with them.

They maintained therefore that the arrangements were made in the interests of Yugoslavia, in order to give the southern part of Yugoslavia a natural maritime outlet. The northern part of the population in Albania north of the Skumbi was predominantly Christian, whilst the southern part was Muslim (by which they presumably meant the central plains). Therefore, they thought it best to separate the administration between Yugoslavia and Italy respectively. They did concede that the whole of Albania should be brought under the mandatory system to make it possible to eventually satisfy the aspirations of the Albanian people for unity and self-government.[596] This tri-partite mandate was a late attempt to overcome Wilson's scruples on Albanian nationalism.

Wilson was not so easily convinced. He objected to the idea that the proposals were being made in Yugoslav interests and that the tri-partite mandate would help Albanian aspirations for unity and independence.[597] Although he was more conciliatory in other areas of the settlement, Wilson reinforced his objections regarding Albania. Above all, he

> would of course make no objection to a settlement mutually agreeable to Italy and Yugoslavia regarding their common frontier in the Fiume region, provided that such an agreement is not made on the basis of compensation elsewhere at the expense of nationals of a third power.[598]

His willingness to accept such a scheme was on the basis that the proposed joint Italo-Yugoslav agreement affected only the nationals involved. This third 'power' was obviously Albania. Although Wilson understood that a three-fold division of Albania might be acceptable to the Yugoslav government, the American government was 'just as vigorously opposed to injuring the Albanian people for the benefit of Yugoslavia as it is opposed to injuring the Jugo-Slav people for the benefit of Italy'. Wilson insisted that the differences between the Christian and Muslim populations would be increased by putting the two sections under the control of nationals of unlike language, government and economic strength, especially if one mandatory power (Italy) was represented in the Council of the League of Nations and the other (Yugoslavia) was not. Therefore he considered that to withdraw the mandate/s at some future point would be 'well nigh impossible'. Although he was willing to accept a joint Italo-Yugoslav proposal, as long as that proposal only had an impact on their interests and was compatible with self-determination, but Albanian questions were outside the scope of such bi-lateral talks.[599]

The European great powers failed to move Wilson from this position.[600] Wilson insisted that the 9 December memorandum must be the basis for future negotiations on Fiume, but that the Albanian question was extraneous to the issue as his 'last word' made adequate provisions for a Yugoslav economic outlet in northern Albania.[601] To ensure that the Allied leaders did not attempt to circumvent his proposals, Wilson published a series of documents, in what has been termed 'open diplomacy', relating to the Adriatic discussions. The European governments backed down. They needed American support and financial assistance. They were not prepared to risk the Americans withdrawing from the remaining negotiations or rescinding former promises to them.[602]

It is difficult to understand Wilson's reasons for holding out on the Albanian issue, when in so many other areas of eastern Europe the principle of self-determination had been disregarded in favour of other priorities. All explanations to date (pledge to Albanian cause; tiredness with deliberations; desire to make a stand on one issue of self-determination) seem unsatisfactory. Whatever his motives, the result ended the idea of Albanian partition or the Albanian problem being considered a part of the Adriatic question. Direct Italo-Yugoslav relations finally culminated in the 1920 Treaty of Rapallo, which settled Italo-Yugoslav disputes in the northern Adriatic, Dalmatia and Istria, but Albania was specified outside its remit.[603] The deliberations during the Peace Conference of Paris had therefore not resolved the Albanian question, but Wilson's insistence on an ethnic settlement had ensured that it had been removed from the power bargaining over the wider Adriatic problems. The question of Albanian independence had been revived and there was some level of great power understanding that, once more, it would be considered holistically, not as part of several other questions.

Albanian Initiatives and Responses

In spite of the supposed 'new diplomacy' and espousals in favour of self-determination, it was typical for the representatives of the small(er) states to have only a limited role in determining their own future during the peace deliberations in Paris. This was particularly so for the Albanians. Although an Albanian state had existed in 1914, in considering Albania suitable for mandate status, the great powers did not initially deem the Albanian question to be a national question at all, but instead equivalent to a colonial problem, in areas not yet ready for independence. The Albanian absence from the Peace Conference deliberations (except for the two brief audiences for Turkhan Pasha) is one of the most striking features of the previous discussions. It illustrates very clearly the importance of 'international' as opposed to 'national' factors, and the periodic inability of Albanian nationalism to influence either the international system or their own fate. A variety of tactics were used by the various Albanian nationalist organisations and their international spokesmen, as they attempted to raise the importance of the Albanian question, and to gain great power support for their national ambitions. Prishtina and his friends in the Committee for the National Defence of Kosovo, for instance, worked tirelessly publishing newspapers, leaflets and other propaganda aimed at highlighting the Kosovan issue.[604] Most Albanian involvement in the Conference was therefore localised, marginalised and often revolved around competition between themselves; what influence they had also tended to be negative.[605]

The Durazzo delegation, and many of the others, had been initially anxious to work with the Italians, as the policies of the Consulta seemed to coincide with Albanian national aspirations, and it was believed that such a policy would therefore be beneficial. Opposition to such a policy soon mounted, as a result of the Italian policies pursued in Paris, and of Italian actions in Albania, which were not compatible with Albanian national interests. It also became increasingly obvious to the Albanian leaders that the Italians had limited influence with the other three powers, and even with the small states. This seems to have been responsible for many members of the delegation asking how effective a protector Italy would be against Yugoslav and Greek aggression and intrigue. Turkhan Pasha remained loyal to Italy, but Mehmed Konitza and Tourtoulis sought a non-Italian option. These views were reinforced by reports of Italian activities from within Albania, and a realisation of what an Italian mandate might mean. The trigger for this 'revolt' was the arrival of Essad Pasha in Paris on 1 April 1919. On the one hand, this exacerbated animosities because he was a traditional rival but, on the other, it intensified the resolve amongst the previously competing factions that something needed to be done to prevent Essad from taking control of the Albanian movement in Paris. This was particularly important as Essad seemed instantly to be better received, especially by the American delegation, than many other Albanian representatives had been.[606] Their united front was illustrated most obviously in the presentation of identical memorandums by several of the delegations (4 and 7 April 1919). The Albanians resolved to prevent partition, re-take control of their national movement on the international front and to prevent themselves being subject to domination or interference by outside forces (a less than veiled reference to the Italian, Serbian, Greek and also French and British troops in Albania, as discussed in chapters 5 and 7). The first petition was signed by the Albanian government, and the second by Vatra, the Albanian delegation from Constantinople and the Albanian colony in Romania. They also informed the Supreme Council (14 April 1919) that they no longer accepted the Italian mandate, and cited five reasons for this: the London Pact; fears of Italian aspirations; the harshness of the occupation, especially relative to that in Koritza; the work by Italian forces to divide the Christian and Muslims populations; and Italian designs on Valona, which they considered jeopardised long-term security in the Balkans. They requested an independent Albania under an American or

British mandate.[607] This represented the complete failure of Sonnino's Albanian policy.

This revised Albanian policy had little impact on proceedings. Although MacGinty and Handel have maintained that the 'new diplomacy' of 1919, the Peace Conference and League of Nations represented a hiatus for small states in which their power and influence in the states system increased,[608] this was far from the experience of the Albanians. Their presence in Paris, like that of many other factions, lobbies and pressure groups interested in a particular question, was at best tolerated or else deferred, ignored or ridiculed. In his useful but limited article, Gregory Pano investigated the work of Albanian-Americans, especially Vatra, and their influence on the American negotiators. Although his study is based on limited source material and applies only to the American situation, it includes many useful ideas that can be applied to the various Albanian delegations and support organisations. Pano argued that Albanian proposals had so little impact that it was immaterial who argued them. Their fallback position was an apparent 'blind belief' in Wilson's support for them and their cause, based on his alleged pledge to them. Pano is correct that it was hardly a formal commitment, and that Wilson most likely made many similar casual promises in his innumerable meetings with various groups, including those with irreconcilable and contradictory claims. However, Wilson, if indeed he did make such a promise, cannot have failed to understand the raising of aspirations that such a positive avowal of support would entail. Until the latter stages of negotiations, especially those associated with his 'final word', there is no indication of such support. In the preliminary discussions, Wilson had even commented that Italy could 'probably have Valona'.[609]

The influence of Albanian support organisations appears as minimal as that of the diaspora groups. The records of the United States delegation clearly indicate that the American delegates respected the opinions of British pro-Albanians, especially Aubrey Herbert.[610] Rothwell, meanwhile, has shown that Herbert had close personal ties with many influential members of the British delegation, but this does not necessarily seem to have translated into influence on policy. There is much criticism of him, especially by senior British officials such as Crowe. Other pro-Albanians experienced an even more hostile reception. Of one Crowe minuted, 'Captain Spencer is notoriously an adventurer of the shadiest character and of the most unsavoury antecedents. He ought to be in the dock.'[611]

This experience seems typical of the limited effectiveness of diaspora organisations. Joseph O'Grady's study of the impact of other immigrant groups argues that such organisations were typically less influential on American policy than has generally been assumed. O'Grady sees sponsors in the American Senate (for the Czechs and Poles especially), rather than immigrant groups, as more important in policymaking.[612] For the Albanians, it is also difficult to find any tangible influence in the American Congress or the British Houses of Parliament. By contrast, the change in Albanian attitudes did impact on Italian policy makers. Sonnino was anxious about the anti-Italian turn, lest their sentiments disrupted his plans. He instructed that any Albanians in Paris be prevented from returning to Albania and that their mail, which usually went on ships from Italy, be intercepted, to avoid their frosty attitudes having an impact upon the already turbulent domestic Albanian situation, and the restless Italian troops there.[613] His successors were even more receptive to Albanian initiatives and responses.

In the short term, the anti-Italian turn by most Albanian representatives was more detrimental to Albanian causes than any other. It 'proved' what the Greeks and Serbs had been arguing about Albanian duplicity and inconsistency, and reinforced great power concerns about Albanian readiness for independence. It also meant that Mehmed Konitza and others needed to formulate a new policy quickly, but significantly after their *only* opportunity to present their claims (February 1919) had passed. They now found themselves arguing ideas supported by none of the great powers (except perhaps, in part, Wilson), and against ones they had earlier presented to the Conference. Their inability to impact on great power policy became self-evident as the Conference progressed. For instance, in October 1919, having received news of the leaked Tittoni-Venizelos arrangements, the Albanians called daily upon the American and British negotiators with protests, but they were merely advised to accept the Italian mandate scheme.[614] When the Yugoslavs were invited to participate in the discussion on the northern Albanian problem, no great power representative, not even Wilson, thought such an opportunity should likewise be afforded to the Albanian representatives. Finally, the changed policy generated irreconcilable differences between the leading Albanians. Turkhan Pasha never signed any petition against Italy, and as a result the other three leading members of the Durazzo delegation implemented a form of *coup* to oust him. Turkhan Pasha was not officially replaced until January 1920, but he left Paris and Mehmed became the nominal leader, but with no greater success. Albanian initiatives and activities were mostly low-key and unsuccessful. Neither their support for an Italian mandate, nor, from April 1919, their ambition of an American mandate were much of a counterweight to the ambitions of other states. This lack of influence and resistance to an Italian-dominated and controlled 'independence' meant that the Albanians were unable to gain a great power supporter; or, more correctly, they were unable to obtain one that they wanted, once Italian intentions had become clear to them. As such, neither dependency on a great power, by aligning policy with that of the great power, or the 'going-it-alone' approach produced anything significant. The great power interests at stake in the issues being determined were too significant.[615]

Conclusions

Perceptions of nationalism in Britain, the United States and France in 1919-20 were based on the civic model, but problems materialised in eastern Europe, where this model was not practicable. For the Americans, language became the main determination of nationality, irrespective of the problems of bi-lingualism of some people, or of other affiliations or markers of identity. In eastern Europe, it was a matter of which groups would be sovereign, and which would not form part of the dominant group. As Margaret MacMillan wrote,

> "self-determination" was the watchword but this was not a help in choosing among (often many) competing nationalisms. The peacemakers had to act as policemen and they had to feed the hungry. If they could, they had to create an international order that would make another Great War impossible. Wilson promised new ways of protecting the weak and of settling disputes.[616]

However, she failed to point out that the powers also had their own interests at stake. They were not disinterested policemen, but rather like loan sharks: the beneficiaries of their own decisions and actions. As Lansing later maintained, the self-determination principle was 'loaded with dynamite, raising hopes which can never be realised'.[617] The answer turned out to lie in those groups that organised themselves and had established their position before the start of the Conference, such as the Poles, the Czechs and the Yugoslavs.[618] Despite expectations to the contrary, the small or weak states, especially the smallest and weakest, remained just as weak as before under the new diplomacy. The great powers did not feel able to undo some pre-conference decisions, such as Yugoslav or Czechoslovak independence, yet it was deemed possible to overrule the similar Albanian resolutions in 1912 and 1918, and the great-power one in 1913. The Albanians were even weaker than their rivals. In 1919, their influence was limited because they had formed several different delegations, each with contradictory objectives and agenda. Their rivals could use this against them, and it made the great powers take them less seriously. Thus, whenever the self-determination principle conflicted with great power interests, self-determination was usually ignored or marginalised, even by the Americans. In practical terms, the powers were not prepared to make any great efforts to ensure that the new boundaries would be respected, unless there was an impact on their own interests or on the balance of power.

The Albanians also suffered from the problem of being small in size. For many of the diplomats in Paris, size was a key consideration in terms of self-determination, especially as it linked to their other interests. For the British representatives, this meant the balance of power, and for the Italian and French a desire for grateful client states. Britain aimed to establish national states in central and eastern Europe to replace the old multinational empires, and they intended these states to be strong and stable. There was much to suggest that small states were weak, volatile and likely to be subject to aggression from their neighbours, regardless of the numerous examples that indicated otherwise. As one Whitehall official commented, he did not agree with small states becoming independent, and instead liked to see 'a small state as part of a great empire'.[619] In general, Whitehall did not want to protect the weak. It wanted states to be strong enough to protect themselves. Yugoslavia and Greece were far more likely than Albania to provide a counter-balance to Italy in the Balkans and the Adriatic. Thus, they could argue that a large(r) independent Albania, especially an Italian dominated one, would not provide for stability and the maintenance of the *status quo*. Such a view clearly influenced the Albanian question, and was common to many of the arguments used against the Albanians in 1913. By 1919, their rivals had a stronger argument, based on evidence from the collapse of the Wied regime and Albanian divisions during World War One and the Paris Peace Conference.

To Arnold J. Toynbee, the PID member and historian, the principles of nationality, democracy and self-determination were 'the essential aim and expression of their cause'.[620] The gap in Toynbee's argument, and it was one common to most British and other great power officials, was the assumption that the mandatory power the local peoples themselves would choose would be the correct one and in line with their own great power policy projections. None of the great powers wanted the Albanian mandate, except Italy, and the Durazzo delegation eventually resolved that it did not want the Italians. The support and protection of a great power was considered indispensable for the 'new' states. British Cabinet discussions regarding Mesopotamia (that would become Iraq) recommended that, should the inhabitants of the region express a desire for Britain to act as mandatory power, then this should be taken up.[621] The Albanian desire for an American or British mandate, as the only two powers they trusted to act in Albanian interests, was refused. The powers had a very strange interpretation of self-determination, especially for south-eastern Europe, where it is questionable whether any of the powers were really interested in or committed to the principle of self-determination. Plebiscites were used only sparingly, and in the Balkans not at all, in case people *chose* the wrong nationality! Instead, as Sir James Headlam-Morley maintained, 'self-determination is quite démodé. Leeper and Nicolson *determine* for them what they *ought* to wish, but they do it *very* well'.[622]

Chapter 7

Post-war Albania: allied occupations and nationalist resurgence

'The Albanian people… are not minded to submit to being sold like cattle in the European markets as the spoils of Italy, Serbia and Greece.'[623]

Despite the intense and protracted deliberation in Paris, the substantial developments in post-war 'Albania' would ultimately prove more important to the emergence of Albanian independence. This chapter examines the character and work of the various Albanian governments, especially their realisation, by the beginning of 1920 (at the latest), that they could no longer depend upon the great powers, especially Italy, for protection or support. Therefore, as in 1912, the Albanians resolved to take matters into their own hands and not leave the outcome of Albania's future to others, including this time the great powers. In so doing the Albanian case conforms only partially to traditional theories about weak states in the great power system and structural realism, on the one hand, and to the experiences of other resurgent eastern European nationalisms in the post-war era, on the other.

A Plethora of Regimes and Albanian Reactions

The formation of the Durazzo government (December 1918) was not a progression that the Italians had expected or planned for, but Sonnino realised that it could not be reversed. There were a number of promising developments under this new regime, not least the experience of Christians and Muslims working together, and the agreement regarding the delegation to send to Paris.[624] There were clear problems. To the nationalists, international recognition was more important than domestic concerns. The policy of the provisional government was therefore to await the decisions from Paris. This left a vacuum. The most influential, able and well-known leaders in the government, including both the prime and foreign minister, were at the Peace Conference in Paris. Those ministers left in Albania worked to preserve the status quo, and considered it their responsibility not to make any changes until Albania's future had been settled. Additionally, none of the great powers (including Italy), or any other state, had recognised the new Albanian government. Although the Durazzo government had claimed jurisdiction over the whole of Albania as constituted in 1913-14, in practice it had authority over about one-fifth of the pre-war state, and much of this only with Italian endorsement or co-operation. The other four-fifths of pre-war Albanian territory was occupied by the French (Koritza and Pogradec), the Serbs (northern and eastern Albania), and the rest by the Italians. There was also the inter-Allied regime in Scutari (British, French and Italian). The Allied occupation of Albania proved a major obstacle to the formation of a genuinely independent post-war Albanian government. It also affected Allied relations with one another, producing much discord and friction. The deteriorating relations and intensification of inter-power rivalry helped promote the Albanian policy of independent action. Gradually, it became clear to a broad section of national and tribal leaders, although not to all, that the powers were not interested in 'genuine' independence, but at best in a token one under Italian 'protection'. Italian control would be used to further Italian interests in the Balkans, rather than to benefit Albania.[625] This rivalry mirrored events taking place within the Peace Conference, but for most ordinary Albanians events at home were more compelling.

The first half of 1919 was stable in southern Albania, especially in the French zone. In the Italian zone, British reports described some Albanian disenchantment, although much of this was attributed to the pro-Greek elements. Still awaiting the decisions from the Peace

Conference in Paris, neither the Italians nor the Greeks wished to be seen using force in the region.[626] By contrast, in northern Albania, especially in and around Scutari, there was much animosity, although these disagreements rarely turned violent. With negotiations still proceeding in Paris, nobody wanted to be accused of being aggressive or of breaking the peace. The Italians had agreed to an international regime only to prevent the Serbs from occupying Scutari town. The French Colonel (later General) de Fourtou, who led the international force in Scutari, found himself frequently clashing with the Italian Commander, Major Perricone, who controlled the Italian-occupied territory surrounding the town. As early as 1 January 1919, de Fourtou wrote of his inability to work with the Italians, and Phillips, now a Brigadier-General, of the incompatibility of the two men.[627] In particular, there proved to be disagreement over the jurisdiction and the nature of the regime. This escalated to such an extent that D'Esperey was forced to spend two days in Scutari inspecting the situation and speaking to Piacentini, the Italian Supreme Commander in the Balkans, directly. This initiative failed, and the French, with British support, responded by requesting that the Italians withdraw to beyond a zone ten kilometres around Scutari.[628] This was just one of many incidents indicative of the deteriorating Franco-Italian relationship in Albania. The situation was complicated because the French at Scutari did not follow exactly the same policy as their representatives in Paris. Military leaders appeared eager to support Serbian aims, regardless of the impact on Franco-Italian relations. According to Woodall, Pichon repeatedly refused to agree to their requests to withdraw troops from Scutari. He explained that their presence was symbolic rather than effective because of the pivotal role of Scutari in the larger Adriatic question. Pichon sought to use Scutari as a possible trade-off in the Adriatic dispute, and even observed that there was a 'southern Adriatic question', centred on Scutari.[629] There were also numerous Franco-Italian complaints about Phillips, including his pro-Albanian tendencies. Nevertheless, Whitehall resolved to keep him in post, to maintain the international character of the regime and to restrain their Allies.[630] Relations between the Italians and Yugoslavs were particularly tense. It appeared that the Italians were using their base in northern Albania to attempt to destabilise the new Yugoslav regime.[631] The Serbs sought to take advantage of the

Italians' loss of support in Paris in the spring of 1919, by refusing to recognise Italy's right to occupy all of Albania within the 1913 frontiers. In particular, the Serbs refused to demilitarise the disputed zone north and east of the Drin.[632]

Albanian responses once more varied. Some joined forces with the occupiers and intriguers, but others were more resistant. Essadists sided with the Serbs and many northern tribes, including the Mirdites, colluded with the Italians. These alliances were based on local requirements and included the supply of weaponry to Albanian fighters in exchange for assistance, rather than for any national purposes. In one incident, on 1 March 1919, seven Italians were killed and 12 taken prisoner by Essadist forces and turned over to the Serbian forces at Dibra. In another, Italian forces and Albanian *comitadji* (irregular armed bands) were accused of attacking a Yugoslav post. There were also reports of numerous atrocities being committed, including villages being occupied and burned, and hostages taken. Meanwhile, Albanians in Plava and Gusinje appealed to Britain for protection against the Yugoslavs, of whose state they were now part.[633] The situation appears to have been particularly difficult in Kosovo. Due to its inaccessibility, no great power had occupied the area during the war. With the Austro-Bulgarian retreat, the Serbs sought to re-occupy it. This prompted a revolt by the Kosovo-Albanians, especially the Sunni Muslims, which was heavily crushed by the Serbian forces, as an example to other minorities. This in turn produced an influx of Kosovan refugees into Albania.[634] One observer went so far as to claim that the Yugoslavs were deliberately expelling Albanians in order to change the ethnic character of the region, and to prevent the Durazzo government from claiming the region as part of 'ethnic Albania'.[635] This flood of refugees added to the tensions. They formed the base of a large Albanian nationalist movement, the Committee for the National Defence of Kosovo, which claimed to represent 15,000 Albanians and called for the return of Kosovo and other Albanian-inhabited areas. Most importantly, it was a movement the Italian authorities had no control over. Italian reluctance to help this group contributed greatly to their unpopularity amongst the Albanians. Although the British forwarded repeated reports of Yugoslav-Albanian fighting to their Allies, there was no action to prevent the hostilities, because the French and Americans refused to participate in the proposed ultimatum to Belgrade.[636]

Most Albanians focused on local, tribal or family problems and concerns. As in earlier complaints, they generally failed to see beyond their immediate environs and could not relate their grievances to wider issues. The traditional problems of geography, climate, poor transportation links and low literacy (rather than religious differences) all hindered communications between the various groups, and joint action.[637] The military presence and the assorted Allied regimes added further complications, because movement between zones was restricted by internal barriers (similar to state boundaries), with official crossing points. This was something many Albanians were not accustomed to, especially in the north. These various regimes also blocked the Durazzo government's ability to extend its authority. This may be one of the reasons why the impetus came from abroad, including Kosovo, where, despite it being under Serbian rule, freedom of movement (if not freedom of speech and political thought) was easier. The most significant actions, although admittedly even these still had little impact on the national picture, took place within the diaspora and support groups. The Anglo-Albanian Society repeatedly asked questions in the Houses of Parliament, wrote numerous press articles and held a variety of campaigning events. There were similar initiatives in the United States.[638] Hasan Prishtina tried to launch a press campaign for Kosovo's inclusion in a reconstituted Albania, but as he was 'in prison' in Vienna it was difficult for this to be very effective.[639] Nationalism still remained irrelevant to the needs of most ordinary Albanians. After at least eight years of war, they wanted stability and the opportunity to rebuild their lives and livelihoods, although others profited from the occupations by selling produce and materials. Only as opposition grew to the foreign occupiers could the small narrow band of nationalists seek to draw supporters from these disparate groups. In 1913-14, the 'people' had put their faith in Wilhelm to bring them prosperity. When it became obvious that he could not, they turned against him, and against the ideology of an independent Albania. When the occupations in 1918-19 likewise failed to deliver what Albanians demanded, in much the same way as the British and Americans have in Iraq (and elsewhere) more recently, the people turned against them and sought other alternatives, both home-grown and imported. Nevertheless, as late as August 1919, the nationalists were still unsure of what to do, and were seeking advice from their foreign supporters.[640]

Italian officials, forces and actions proved unpopular for several reasons. The Italian administration persistently tried to undermine, overrule or circumvent Albanian intentions, or else it attempted to control Albanian nationalism by asserting that all decisions of the Durazzo government must be ratified by the Italian High Commissioner. The provisional government did not want a small, central, Muslim-dominated Albania as described in the London Pact. This was shown most obviously in the protests of 3 June 1919, the second anniversary of the Italian proclamation. The Consulta had decided it no longer needed this policy either, but Italian actions and policy in Albania consistently had the opposite effect to that intended. Above all, they continued to offend the Albanians. One such incident, which provoked immense uproar, involved taking down all Albanian flags on 28 November 1919, which had been put up to celebrate the seventh anniversary of 'independence'. Italy's opponents (Essadists, Serbs and Greeks) all used this to their advantage.[641] By contrast, the French zone of occupation in southern Albania was marked by comparative order and tranquillity, as a result of the tact and ability of the French officers. Pastorelli contends that Piacentini persistently failed to understand the Albanians or their ambitions, and underestimated their strength and resolve. Piacentini's reports remained optimistic, and he failed to convey accurately to his superiors the growing discontent, or his inability to quell the escalating dissatisfaction. By contrast, other great power representatives were reporting considerable anti-Italian antagonism and that, as far as they could ascertain, the Italian press knew little of it. The Italian representatives in Albania emphatically denied that there was any truth in these suggestions, although they did acknowledge a few skirmishes between Italian and Serbian outposts. In addition, news of Italian problems in Paris began to emerge in Albania. Many Albanian leaders were disturbed by the Italian resolve to maintain Valona, which, as the town where independence had been proclaimed in 1912, was considered integral to an independent Albania. Italian failings also indicated that Italy would be an insufficient protector of Albanian integrity. The incursions on the northern frontier reinforced this view. Relations between the Italians, on the one hand, and the

Serbs and French, on the other, also continued to deteriorate. Italian troops initially attempted to use force to push the Serbs further back. As this policy backfired, and as the Albanians became even more resistive to Italian occupation, the Consulta was persuaded to use diplomacy to expel the Serbs from Albania. The Consulta had previously argued that a strong military presence was needed to strengthen Italy's bargaining position. As the costs soared, and the talks in Paris floundered, the Italian people became disillusioned with the occupation, and the policy became increasingly untenable.[642]

Nevertheless, in the short term, the Consulta sought to consolidate its position in northern Albania vis-à-vis Serbian forces. In June 1919, Sonnino attempted to secure British and American support for the removal of Serbian troops from central Albania, after failing to secure French support, on the basis of the November 1918 agreement. Although it was not a party to that agreement, Whitehall decided that the Italians, rather than the Serbs, could best preserve peace in Albania. With the larger Adriatic settlement still unresolved, British officials thought that their support on this issue might placate the Italians. The Foreign Office sent an official warning to the Yugoslav government, but Serbian activities continued and even intensified. The Yugoslav government proclaimed that Serbian troops were under the control of the Interior Department, not the War Department, as the area represented territory occupied by Serbia before August 1914, and was thus not subject to the control of D'Esperey. They declared that the boundary of northern Albania was the Drin, and accused the Italians of violating it.[643] This move was too much for even the Quai d'Orsay, but the great powers were unable to prevent the advance of Serbian and Essadist forces in northern Albania. Once more, Italian ambitions were detrimentally affected. This demonstrated to the Albanians the inability of the Italians, especially, and the great powers more generally, to protect 'Albanian' borders. This in turn convinced many that independence, free from the interference of all outside forces, even great power ones, was the best option for Albania's future stability and integrity. Events in Scutari echoed those in Paris, and further illustrated Italian weakness relative to the other powers, and even the small Yugoslav state. The most damaging event was French success in defeating Italian efforts to launch a gunboat on Lake Scutari. It was particularly humiliating for the Italians that a Serbian gunboat was stationed there instead, and that they were forced to withdraw their commander.[644]

Events in southern Albania confirmed these views. Piacentini was particularly disliked because he did not conform to the Albanian image of a 'strong man'. In August 1919, rumours emerged of the projected French withdrawal and a Franco-Greek plan to replace French troops with Greek ones—an eventuality which the Albanian nationalists and the Italians feared greatly. It appeared that the Allies were colluding against the Albanians. Despite Italian efforts to prevent this move, especially the Greek occupation of Koritza, in contravention of the Tittoni-Venizelos agreement, the Italians were again portrayed as weak and undependable protectors. The Italians ultimately secured French agreement that their occupation would continue, but once more Italy proved to be the loser.[645]

The Albanian resolve to determine their own future was mounting. By August 1919, Phillips had concluded that the Albanians were resolutely opposed to the idea of an Italian protectorate, and were talking of proclaiming a *besa* against all foreigners. These initiatives escalated in the ensuing months. Following Nitti's public proclamation of Tittoni's Adriatic plans, including the partition proposal for Albania in the Italian parliament (27 September 1919), the Albanians became all too acutely aware of great-power designs. These fears were reconfirmed when news of the Tittoni-Venizelos agreement leaked out, but Phillips continued to advocate a strictly limited Italian mandate as the best option for the Albanians, following Sonnino's old policy of entente with them.[646] He correctly maintained that the alternatives, and those currently being proposed by Tittoni in Paris, all involved partition. Although he argued that Argyrocastro should go to Greece, Phillips maintained that Kosovo should become part of Albania—a policy which was never likely to get much support. This increased his prestige amongst the Albanians, but his promotion of these ideas did much to distance Phillips from the Serbs, Italians and French, the very people he was supposed to be working with and encouraging to compromise. His position was further weakened when five of the northern Albanian tribes proclaimed a *besa* and resolved to prevent Serbian seizure of Albanian territory. De Fourtou alleged that Phillips had helped orchestrate this. In response, Crowe ordered Phillips not to support the *besa*, for it was quite likely that Britain might sponsor the partition of Albania and give northern Albania to the Serbs. As one official wrote, 'General Phillips seems to think Albania is the centre of the universe', and his independent actions, contrary to Crowe's instructions, continued to work against British official policy. Until his recall, and despite Whitehall directives, Phillips proved to be a strong promoter of Albanian nationalism.[647]

To counter the tide of Albanian nationalism, the Consulta requested the Durazzo government to send negotiators to Rome. Under an agreement signed on 20 August 1919, it was agreed that all of Albania would come under the control of the provisional government at Durazzo, except for Valona, where the Italian army was to maintain its *presidia*, and a few frontier regions. The Albanian negotiators agreed that their government was to be subordinate to a civil Italian High Commissioner, and that the Albanian militia would be under Italian military command. There were special provisions for Argyrocastro where the Italian Officer, Colonel Lodi, was made Prefect in order to overcome Christian fears about Muslim rule and presumably, therefore, Greek objections to the agreement. The Italian government failed to ratify the agreement—by this point Nitti had decided to partition Albania. Military rule continued but it did little to support the provisional government.[648] By October 1919, Morton Eden, Phillips' secretary, was writing that the popularity of the provisional government depended upon it being anti-Italian.[649] Support for the regime had already been dwindling because of its lack of progress, and its inability to achieve recognition or to secure Albania's objectives in Paris. The real turning point came in November 1919, when news of the proposed agreement between Italy and the Durazzo government emerged, including the acceptance of the Italian High Commissioner. Protests sprang up throughout Albania, demanding an explanation as to why *their* government had agreed to such an outrage.[650] As with governments in other states, especially Italy, public opinion left little room for compromise on national ambitions and integrity, and demanded quick success in achieving these goals. The representatives of other (stronger) states were opposed to granting them.

Congress of Lushnje and the Tirana Government

The growth of anti-Italian hostility and a deterioration of the provisional government's popularity went hand-in-hand. Fears about the future of the country seemed justified when it became known that Bumçi and the Italian delegation in Paris had worked out a further compromise agreement, whereby Albanian integrity and independence were preserved, but under Italian control. In protest, a meeting of all 'true nationalists' in the country was called, and it eventually turned into a National Congress held at Lushnje, a small town in central Albania, between Durazzo and Berat, from 28-31 January 1920.[651] By then, it included not only opponents of the Durazzo regime but also defectors from it. The Congress would prove to be one of the most important developments in the emergence of Albanian independence. Its root causes lay in the delay in settling the Albanian question in Paris to Albanian satisfaction, and the declining influence of the great powers, especially Italy. Albanian nationalists were exasperated by Italy's apparent intention to remain in occupation, and felt betrayed by the news that it appeared that the London Pact would be enacted. The Albanian delegation in Paris was isolated, and the Durazzo government had lost popular support due to its ineffectiveness and its inability to obtain recognition. Throughout December 1919, Albanians from across the country, but especially from districts in central Albania, elected delegates to represent them.[652] During these preparations the Italians did not hinder the Albanians. Members of the Durazzo government were far more concerned. On 13 January 1920, the Durazzo government ordered their prefect in Lushnje to prevent the meeting, but the two companies of militia sent to disperse it refused to do so.[653]

Fifty-six delegates from across the country met, including representatives from Valona, Koritza and Pogradec, and some regions outside the 1913 state. The meeting began by expressing the dismay of those assembled at the prospect of Valona being given to Italy. The delegates considered that they had been misled, by the great powers, into believing that the principles of justice and self-determination would be applied to Albania. They argued that to trust the great powers was to believe in a 'broken reed', and that the Albanians must rely on themselves alone to secure their complete independence and territorial integrity. They determined that a 'Sacred Union' must be formed to reject the great-power plans for the partition of Albania. To accomplish this, they resolved to replace the provisional government, which was criticised as nothing more than a 'puppet Italian regime', with a new administration 'composed of honest men trusted by the people', and to hold a general election to elect a national legislative assembly, which would draw up a new constitution. They also agreed that the peace delegation in Paris would be reconstituted, and would be charged with the mission of requesting the complete independence of Albania within its ethnographical frontiers. Mehmed Konitza and Midhat Frashëri remained as members of the Peace Delegation, but Turkhan Pasha, whom the Congress was 'especially disappointed with', Bumçi and Tourtoulis were replaced by Pandeli Evangjeli and Dr Charles Telford Erickson.[654] The delegates in Lushnje drafted an emotive protest, addressed to the Italian Parliament and the Paris Peace Conference, against the partitioning of Albania on the lines of the London Pact. Invoking President Wilson's principles of self-determination, the protest declared that Albania was an independent state and that the Albanian people were not prepared to accept an Italian mandate on any part of its territory, any form of foreign protectorate, or limitation of its sovereignty, without the explicit consent of the Albanian people. The delegates reaffirmed the *besa* covering the whole country and pledged to die in defence of Albania's political and territorial integrity. Other resolutions determined that the new government should be located at Tirana, then a small town in central Albania. The choice of capital proved to be one of the most contentious points, as different delegates proposed their respective spheres of influence. They settled on Tirana because, although situated in a Muslim-dominated area, it was inland and away from any of Albania's borders, to prevent interference, intrigue or attack from Albania's rivals. It also had good transport links with the port at Durazzo. Piacentini declared that he would not recognise the actions of the Congress, but the Italians faced a double whammy: they had lost control of the Albanian national movement, yet the momentum of Albanian nationalism was increasing. The Italian Commander decided that he would not bother the new government unless it interfered with his activities or disturbed public order.[655]

The Congress also addressed the issue of what type of state Albania should be. It reaffirmed the Organic Constitution of 1914, which had created the monarchy under Wilhelm, and had never been abrogated or suspended. It resolved that the war had not altered these conditions. As Wilhelm had never formally abdicated, the Congress attributed limited executive powers to a Supreme Council of Regency (High Council). This was to consist of four persons, one representing each of the four religions: Sunni and Bektashi Muslims, Orthodox and Catholic Christians. They were appointed in place of the absent sovereign, and were to act on his behalf. To complement this Council, a new government was created by electing a cabinet of nine members under the presidency of Suleiman bey Delvina, with Mehmed Konitza as Foreign Minister and Ahmet Zogu as Interior Minister.[656] The Congress also established a thirty-seven member National Council or Senate, which was to be entrusted with the parliamentary powers until a general election could be held. On 20 February 1920, all those members of the Durazzo government who had remained there under the protection of the Italian navy deserted the town and brought the archives and treasury to Tirana. It was a peaceful and bloodless handover, largely because of hesitancy by the Italian military and the popularity of the new government.[657]

For the time being, events in Albania appeared relatively stable. The delegation in Paris continued its efforts unsuccessfully; in Albania, the new government in Tirana, under Ahmet Zogu's leadership, was making preparations for direct action. Like Essad Pasha under Wilhelm, Zogu gained control of the most important office in the government, which would be responsible for carrying out many much-needed reforms, and through which he would control the all-important armed forces. He became Commander-in-Chief of the Albanian army, the core of which included his own men because tribal affiliations continued to be important. In the coming months, it proved to be the young Zogu who came to take the lead in the Albanian nationalist movement. He was successful in winning the support of the gendarmerie and in inviting all Albanian prefects to join the new regime.[658]

Great Power Withdrawals and the Extension of Tirana's Control

Allied actions provided the impetus for the next developments. On 11 March 1920, the inter-allied occupation of Scutari ended, although the Italians under Perricone were authorised to remain. With Wilson's prevention of the Albanian problem being included in the general Adriatic question (February-March 1920), the main reason for British and French involvement in Albania was removed. More generally, there was increasing public pressure to reduce costs and bring the troops home. The justification given in the House of Parliament was that the War Office had decided that political missions could no longer be financed from army funds. If British involvement was needed for political purposes, then the Foreign Office would need to finance it, but it had decided that this was unnecessary.[659] The Franco-British withdrawal removed the buffer between the Serbs and Italians. When de Fourtou and his troops evacuated the city, they apparently expected their place to be taken by the Serbs. They handed over the defence of Mount Tarabosh and the Boyana line to them, and gave them weapons and ammunition. However, the Tirana government managed to secure control of the town. Phillips wrote that de Fourtou handed Scutari over to the municipality of Scutari, which in turn passed control to two members of the new government (Zogu and Hoxhë Kadriu). Owen Pearson, in his detailed study of 20th century Albania, alleges that Zogu's involvement had begun much earlier. Anticipating a Serbian response, Zogu had managed to forestall them by secretly occupying Scutari with a force of Mati clansman, before the French left.[660] Despite Serbian annoyance, and plans for an immediate assault, Phillips argued in March 1920 that there was no real advantage to be gained from such an initiative, especially with the San Remo (April 1920) talks opening, and Perricone's detachment still stationed there. (The San Remo talks were held to determine the allocation of League of Nations mandates for former Ottoman-ruled territories in the Middle East.) Zogu was appointed governor of Scutari by the Albanian government, which had been impressed by his initiative and speedy action. Meantime, Phillips was recalled to Britain, as the Foreign Office became increasingly receptive to the Consulta's requests. This would ultimately complicate Britain's policy towards Albania. Although Phillips was undoubtedly sympathetic to the Albanian cause, from this point on Britain no longer retained any personnel in Albania, and had to rely on Italian information about what was happening.[661]

As the primary task of the Tirana government was the expulsion of all foreign forces from Albanian soil, the events at Scutari were exceedingly popular, especially in contrast to the hesitancy and apparent feebleness of the Durazzo regime. This impression was reinforced by the withdrawal of French forces from Koritza on 21 June 1920, with the French handing over control to the Albanian Committee there. By the Protocol of Kapishtica (15 May 1920) between the Tirana government and Greece (the first agreement between it and another government), the Albanians managed to ensure that Albanian rather than Greek forces would occupy Koritza following the French withdrawal. Both sides agreed to observe the *status quo* until the Peace Conference had concluded. The Albanians agreed to protect Greek nationals and guaranteed the right to Greek schools, churches and language, and allowed Greek troops to occupy twenty-six villages in Albania, southeast of Koritza and north of the Florence line.[662] The Albanian achievement regarding Koritza should not be undervalued. It enhanced the prestige of the Albanian government both at home and abroad, secured a temporary understanding regarding Koritza, and avoided the anticipated atrocities, which would have hindered the Albanian cause on the international front.[663] For the Greeks too there were advantages: the expected bloodshed did not take place, and the Italian occupation was prevented. However, Tirana had agreed to a form of Greek occupation, and the frontier issue remained unresolved. The role of outside forces was once more significant. Lloyd George had ensured that the French withdrawal did not take place until completion of the San Remo Conference because he hoped to use Albania as a bargaining tool. As Woodall maintains, once more the great power leaders' overestimated the importance of Albania in Greek thinking. In comparison to potential gains in Asia Minor, Koritza was not highly prized.[664] Moreover, the main objections to an Albanian occupation of Koritza had been removed. Whitehall had previously believed that Albanian control would *ipso facto* mean Italian control—either directly or indirectly. The independence of the new Tirana regime, combined with Whitehall's new conviction that Italy did not have enough troops (less than 25,000) in Albania to occupy Koritza, meant that the Albanians could not be viewed as Italian puppets. These arguments also seem to have satisfied Venizelos. Crowe maintained that the problems that had previously necessitated the maintenance of French control, to provide a buffer between the Greeks and Italians, were now removed.[665]

The new government also made progress in central Albania.

When Essadist forces attempted to seize control, the Tirana regime acted swiftly and decisively. They issued a manifesto to the population, warning against participation in the propaganda meetings being held by Essadist agents. They sent delegates to Paris to attempt to negotiate directly with Essad. There was little anticipation of success, but Zogu thought that the initiative would gain the Tirana government valuable time. It did. An agreement was signed with some of the rebels, and by mid-April 1920 Zogu's forces had managed to defeat those that remained.[666] With Essad's threat removed, the Albanian government was able to send an armed force further south and to take a number of key settlements, including Argyrocastro, by 24 April 1920. On 13 June 1920, Essad was murdered in Paris by Avni Rystemi, an Albanian revolutionary student and Kosovo Committee member.[667]

By contrast, the Tirana government had not proven very successful in securing an Italian withdrawal, but prospects were good with the Greek agreement and a change in attitude in Rome as to the benefits of an Italian occupation. The need for action against Italy was crucial, because the lack of this had been the main reason why the Durazzo government had lost popular support. It was also the basis of the new Tirana government's ascendancy. Another interesting aspect of the Essadist revolt was the role of Castoldi, who had been appointed Italian Commissioner in Albania, and was suspected of being heavily involved in the planned Essadist conspiracy. This did nothing to improve the Italian position in Albania.[668] Meanwhile, by June 1920 the Italians had resolved to vacate Albania, except for Valona and key frontier zones. Woodall cites two reasons for this policy. Firstly, there was the deteriorating position of the Italian military relative to the growing strength of Albanian nationalism, especially the Islamic elements, and the Consulta's failure to gain support for the protectorate. Secondly, the Tirana government insisted that the Italian troops be withdrawn and that the control of Albania be handed over to them.[669] There were other factors. In May 1920, the Consulta agreed to reduce Italian troop strength in Albania to 10,000, to save money: in effect to withdraw all detachments from the interior, and concentrate on the major coastal ports. It was finally becoming obvious to the Consulta that relations between it and the Tirana government were deteriorating. The British reported that there appeared to have been no co-ordinated policy, and a considerable divergence of views, between the authorities in Rome and Italian officials in Albania. The latter did little beyond constructing roads and, in particular, failed to suppress brigandage. Their attempts to enforce the teaching of Italian in schools were particularly unpopular.[670] One Italian Deputy commented that Italian policy 'alternated between the mailed fist and the stricken glove'. It was reported that the Italian-trained gendarmerie refused to take orders from their Italian officers, and that many had joined forces with the insurgents. There were also Italian moves towards a return to a policy of an independent Albania on the 1913 model, and away from Nitti's ideas of partition. Pragmatic reasons appear to have motivated these changes. If Yugoslavia obtained Scutari and territory as far south as the Drin, then as many as one million more 'Albanians' would be incorporated into Yugoslavia. These Albanians would naturally gravitate towards central Albania, the area that was to be Italian-controlled, and leave this area exposed to disruption and instability.[671]

The Italians did not give up hope of retaining influence in Albania, especially Valona. Having secured the occupation of Koritza, the Delvina-led government decided to concentrate on negotiations with the Italians. Castoldi received instructions to drag out discussions as long as possible, and to support the Essadist elements. The Consulta hoped that by attempting to play off one group of Albanians against another, it might still be able to achieve Nitti's policy of partition, and without the costs of a formal occupation.[672] The Tirana government resolved to concentrate its forces, correctly surmising that they were too weak to defeat both Italians and Serbs. They came up with the ambitious scheme of offering an entente to Italy. By this, they hoped to secure an Italian withdrawal and to obtain Italian aid to prevent a Serbian invasion in the north. Playing for time, the Italians rejected this proposal in the hope that the more pliable Essadists might gain the upper hand. Castoldi held negotiations with Albanian leaders in Durazzo and Tirana. He made little progress, because Delvina seems to have decided that Italy, not the Yugoslavs, was the greater threat.[673] Delvina sent negotiators to both Belgrade and Athens in an attempt to gain allies. As a result, Castoldi informed his superiors that the Consulta should work for control of Albania through economic rather than military means.[674] The Consulta returned to a policy of a united

Albania, along the lines proposed by Sonnino, but out of strategic expediency. On 24 June 1920, the new Premier, Giovanni Giolitti, declared in the Italian parliament that the Government was 'not in favour of a protectorate in Albania, but wishes the independence of that country'. On 27 June 1920, he enlarged upon his speech, stating that Italy could not abandon Valona until Albania was strong enough to ensure that the port did not fall to another power. This was an acceptable position, but the Italian government was under considerable pressure. The press insisted on the necessity of keeping Valona but the socialists, who had made considerable gains in the elections in November 1919, openly objected to the policy.[675]

The small weak (non-state) had humbled a great power, but the revised Italian position was completely irreconcilable with the Tirana government's intentions. Delvina had also already secured an agreement in Athens. A variety of incidents had brought Albanian indignation about the Italian occupation to a head and prompted Giolitti's pronouncements. With the start of the withdrawal, it was clear that the Italians were not prepared to pull out completely, and incidents between Albanians and Italian troops increased. The Italian military authorities continued to make a number of significant blunders. For instance, they arrested the newly appointed Albanian prefect of Tepelena, allegedly because he had refused to sign a declaration in favour of an Italian protectorate. Such incidents convinced the Albanians that the Italians would be removed only through force, and that diplomacy was futile.[676] In a report he sent to Herbert, Delvina detailed the events. Despite his obvious partiality, his description differs only marginally from those of other contemporaries. He portrayed the decision to use force against Italy as being taken only following numerous petitions about the future of Valona—to which his government received very evasive replies. The spur for the revolt came from the inhabitants of the town. At a meeting of the Committee of National Defence (29 May 1920), the men involved pledged to drive the Italians out of Valona. An ultimatum sent to Piacentini demanded the withdrawal of Italian troops from Valona and the handing over of Valona, Telepena and Chimara within twenty-four hours.[677] Instead of replying to the Albanian ultimatum, Piacentini replied with gunfire. The impasse was only lifted when Giolitti announced the immediate withdrawal of Italian troops (16 June 1920). Giolitti would have liked to maintain control of Valona but he saw the situation as pointless, for, as Swire argued, there was 'no alternative but to withdraw'. Giolitti feared that sending more Italian troops might provoke general strikes and popular demonstrations that would gravely injure the solidarity of the army. The sordid conditions of the Italian army in Albania had become notorious (disease, especially malaria, death, demoralisation, possible conflict with Greeks, Serbs and Albanians) and lacked any attraction for soldiers. The Italian troops declined to take orders, and some units had refused to embark on ships stationed at Bari and Brindisi and destined for Albania.[678]

The Italians sought, by diplomatic means, to try and retrieve their Albanian adventure, their long-coveted foothold in the Balkans and security in the Adriatic. Giolitti sent Aliotti and Castoldi to Tirana to negotiate an agreement. By 16 July 1920, talks had broken down, resulting in a resumption of hostilities. The Consulta had expected its mission to be successful because of the two men's involvement in Albania 1913-14. However, once more, the Italians had misunderstood the Albanians. Both men were unpopular in Albania because of their connection with the Italian conspiracy against Wilhelm, and Aliotti for his perceived role in the Pact of London. The Italians were no longer in a position to prolong the negotiations. On 22 July 1920, Count Carlo Sforza, whom Giolitti had chosen as his Foreign Minister, rescinded the Tittoni-Venizelos agreement on the grounds that Greece had violated its secrecy. Sforza declared that the

> nationalistic affirmations of the Albanian people have obliged the Italian government to modify the ends which they proposed to attain, and to establish a new policy...to safeguard...Italian interests in that region.[679]

Sforza later wrote, in an attempt to justify his actions in forgoing Italian national ambitions, that he did not see how the agreement reached in the London Pact benefited Italy on any essential points of Italian interests in Albania. To him it appeared a contradiction. If the object of Italy was the maintenance of a viable and stable independent Albania on the lines of the principle of self-determination, then it did not seem understandable to deprive it of one of its 'lungs' in the port of Valona. He concluded that Albania should enter the Italian sphere of influence, but not as the result of some international agreement to which the Albanian people were opposed, for that would be costly and probably unsustainable.[680]

An armistice was concluded on 2 August 1920, followed by a secret protocol. The Italians acknowledged the complete independence and sovereignty of Albania within the integrity of the frontiers defined in 1913, relinquished their claims to the protectorate declared in 1917, the occupation and administration of Valona and a mandate over the country, or interference in Albania's internal affairs. The Italian government agreed to withdraw all war materials from Valona and to evacuate its holdings on the Albanian mainland. The Consulta was allowed to retain possession of Saseno and the garrison on it until the great powers determined what to do with the island. By 2 September 1920, all remaining Italian troops had left Valona. The agreement had numerous results. On the Albanian side, it bolstered the prestige of the Tirana government amongst Albanians, both at home and abroad. It was hailed as the first diplomatic pact between Albania and a foreign power, albeit an Albania that excluded the *irredenta*. For the Consulta, it represented a dramatic shift in approach if not policy. By acquiring Saseno (until its status was finally determined), Italy had obtained its major objective in Albania—protection of the Otranto Straits and the Adriatic. By holding the island, they would also be well positioned should an unfriendly regime come to power, or another state try to gain influence in Albania. The major drawback for the Consulta was the nature of the withdrawal. Although the Italian government had agreed to use all its influence to obtain the full and unreserved recognition by the powers of the independence of Albania within its 1913 frontiers, these were not promises that the Consulta could definitely fulfil. A certain element of luck was also involved. The breakdown in Italo-Yugoslav talks because of the Italian cabinet crisis gave the Tirana government breathing space in which to secure the Italian withdrawal. If the Italians and Yugoslavs had managed to come to an agreement, this would have been much more difficult.[681]

Conclusions

By August 1920, the prospect of an independent Albania had considerably improved: only the Serbs remained as foreign occupiers in any large numbers. The work and initiatives of the Tirana government towards this purpose was impressive, especially its ability to remove the Italian great power through a combination of diplomacy and force. In these experiences, the Albanian example contradicts traditional theories about weak states in the great power system at the time, a system still largely based on multi-polarity and the balance of power.[682] Handel's arguments that weak states are not always 'helpless', or mere pawns of the great powers, rests on the contention that the small state is able to gain external help from other weak states or other great powers.[683] The Poles, Czechs and Greeks were all able to foster French support and increase their relative post-conflict strength, but this was clearly not the case for the Albanians. Rothstein's interpretation, meanwhile, gives more weight to Albanian initiatives: he contends that a small power can 'affect its chances of survival, primarily by altering the expectations which the Great Powers held about its position and its likely response to external pressures'.[684] The experience of the war and occupation strengthened and enhanced Albanian national solidarity, and Albanian activities simultaneously weakened Italian aspirations regarding Albania. This theory also has its limitations, for none of the nationalist leaders or either government ever had such a well-thought out plan. There was a distinct lack of consistent and coherent policies and, more often than not, they were merely responding to situations or the actions of individuals, rather than pursuing a set agenda. Moreover, as Holtsmark's 'asymmetry of expectations' theory illustrates, the small power assigns far greater priority to its relationship with the great power than does the great power.[685] Only when the Consulta, and the other great powers, proved to be uncommitted to the Albanian project, did some Albanians, but not all, move to a policy of expulsion, and of independence from them. Furthermore, such ideas do not take account of the remarkable situation produced as a result of World War One, or of what Stanley Page has described as 'the historically unusual juxtaposition of forces in the post-war, revolutionary and interventionist vortex'. In this, Handel's explanation for the nationalistic success of the Baltic and Danubian states can equally be applied to the Balkans.[686] In the post-war period, a power vacuum emerged because the great powers that had previously dominated—in the Balkans, Russia and Austria—were temporarily (in Austria's case permanently) defeated and weakened internally. Italian policy makers, and to a lesser extent French, were attempting to take on the great power role in the region but, due to the opposition both faced in Paris and on the ground in Albania, neither had been able to secure this by late 1920. In the interim, this increased the strength of the Balkan nationalists, including the Albanians. When British, French and American pressure was withdrawn and Italy under Benito Mussolini regained its strength, this position could not endure. In the 1930s, Zogu became increasingly dependent upon the Italians, and the Germans began to penetrate economically in the Balkans more widely.

Chapter 8

The Emergence of Independence: the Ambassadors' Conference of Paris and League of Nations (1920-1926)

'To refuse recognition to a Balkan Government is like tying down a man outside an ant heap.'[687]

On 5 May 1920, Mehmed Konitza wrote to President Wilson thanking him for his efforts to prevent Albania from being dismembered and calling attention to Wilson's suggestion that Albania be recognised as an independent state by the newly formed League of Nations. He added that

> the Albanian nation, leaders and people alike, have no confidence in the declaration of Italy's Premier that 'She is ready to aid Albania in its national insurrections,...desiring only her independence and the development of the Albanian race'.[688]

The experiences of the Peace Conference, epitomised in the open diplomacy of the publication of documents pertaining to the Adriatic question and leaks of the secret diplomacy Tittoni-Venizelos agreement, had revealed the true intentions of the great powers. It illustrated to the new Albanian government that they could not depend on any of the great powers, least of all Italy. With the advent of the new Tirana government, the idea of pursuing the

League of Nations proposals took shape. This chapter illustrates how the Albanians, although still anxious to secure the support of the British and Americans, worked to secure their independence in the new diplomacy of the League, the old diplomacy having seemingly failed them. They sought to use the League, as an impartial body, to ensure their recognition as an independent and sovereign state.

There were limits to the extent to which the League could fulfil this function. League supporters refused to admit that, although the League would play a valuable role in international politics, the foreign offices and chancelleries, especially those of the great powers, would still be of paramount importance. They convinced themselves that international relations had now substantially changed, with the establishment of the League. But, in foreign policy, the primary goal of most states remained advancement of their own position rather than the moralistic international rationale of the League. Geoffrey Roberts maintained that states systems often have multiple and overlapping power networks, each competing for power and influence in international relations.[689] After World War One this was definitely the case. The League sat contemporaneously with the Ambassadors' Conference in Paris, which was a continuation of traditional old great-power diplomacy, and had been set up to resolve outstanding issues from the Paris Peace Conference. In this role, the Ambassadors' Conference had been given, and still retained, responsibility for the final decisions regarding Albania's independence and frontiers. As James Barros commented, the Conference of Ambassadors ensured 'the preponderance of the Great Powers'. Despite its wider remit, it was remarkably similar in composition and procedure to ambassadorial conferences before the war.[690] In 1920-21, the Albanians and other groups challenged this authority. They deployed similar initiatives to those used in 1912, in terms of securing the support of other states, but significantly not the great powers, and by the end of 1921 Albania was recognised, once more, as an independent state. By 1926 the boundaries of the new state were also agreed, and have remained largely unchanged until the present day.

Admittance to the League: ascendancy of the small states?

The pursuit of League of Nations support was to prove the most pertinent and ultimately important aspect of Delvina's new policy.

Letters regarding the Albanian issue had been sent to the League throughout 1919, but the main impetus was the drive by the Tirana government. It maintained that

> we are anxious for the assistance of the League of Nations. We have confidence in the League of Nations and believe that it will assist us to our independence and the territorial integrity which is essential if Albania is to exist.

The reasoning included both ethnic and strategic arguments. Considering Serb, Greek and Italian claims to Albanian territory to be unjust, it outlined the privileges and concessions that it was prepared to grant the ethnic and religious minorities, especially the Orthodox Christians in the south, in an attempt to overcome its neighbours' objections to this territory becoming Albanian. The Tirana Government thought that the disappearance of Austria as a great power removed the main reason to offer Italy the concessions outlined in the London Pact. The position of the new government appeared fairly moderate throughout, and not too different from its predecessor.[691] It also sought the support of pro-Albanian parties in both Britain and the United States, to put pressure on their respective governments. In May 1920, a memorandum signed by over twenty British MPs and other influential persons argued in favour of the British government's recognition of the Tirana government, and advocated the League as a satisfactory means of settling the Albanian question. There were also numerous parliamentary questions, especially by Aubrey Herbert and other members of the Anglo-Albanian Society. As late as November 1920, Herbert was sending memoranda to the Foreign Office, although he did not expect any action to be taken. He hoped that this situation might change if Albania was recognised by the League of Nations, but was worried that, 'if it is refused admission into the League, its only chance of life is through fighting' because, he added, Albania is a 'small, weak, defenceless state' open to aggression from all sides.[692] As in 1919, these activities did little to influence British policy.

The changes in Italian approach during 1920 have already been introduced. It was not what the Albanians had anticipated or expected. The Italian government decided to adopt a policy aimed at both circumventing the agreement with the Tirana government and securing its interests in Albania, but, at the same time, saving the costs of a formal occupation (having been unable to secure this through force or diplomacy). It sought to use the Ambassadors' Conference, which, as the successor of the Peace Conference, had been invested with the task of the final determination of the Albanian question. The Italian government advocated an independent Albania. They did not seek a mandate, but to be granted 'special interests' in Albania, which would allow Italy to intervene diplomatically and militarily, should Albania need it. Significantly, that 'need' would be determined by the great powers, not the Albanians.[693]

There is little to suggest that the Ambassadors' Conference made much progress on the Albanian question in its first six months. Only following the Tirana agreement (2 August 1920) between Italy and the Tirana government did conversations appear to resume, focusing on what could be done to secure a withdrawal of Yugoslav forces.[694] Debate settled on two traditional questions: the futures of Scutari and northern Epirus. These issues had become directly related to one another, because the Yugoslavs had expressed their intention to press their Scutari claim if Greece made gains in northern Epirus.[695] This complicated relations between the great powers because, under Italian influence, the ambassadors were opposing the allocation of Scutari to the Yugoslavs, although the British favoured Greek gains, including Koritza. The next major developments took place within the League.

The most critical development began on 12 October 1920 when Pandeli Evangjeli, chief member of the new Albanian peace delegation, addressed a formal request for Albania's admission to the League of Nations. Due to the importance of this development to the question of Albanian independence, and the minimal attention it has received elsewhere, it is necessary to consider it in some depth. In asking for the League to recognise Albanian independence, permit Albania to manage its own affairs and guarantee its integrity under the sanctity of the League, the Albanians were thus attempting to determine their own future and to take it out of control of the great powers and the Ambassadors' Conference specifically. However, as members in both the League's Council and Assembly, great power policy would still be of paramount importance. The petition was in accordance with Article One of the League's Covenant which allowed for a 'fully self-governing State, Dominion or Colony not named in the Annex' to become a member if agreed to by two-thirds of the Assembly and providing that the applicant gave effective guarantees to observe its international obligations, and accepted any regulations prescribed by the League regarding its military, naval and air forces and armaments. The Albanian government maintained that Albania's independence was based upon the constitution of the Albanian state, as drawn up by the Ambassadors' Conference (1913) and Florence Protocol (17 December 1913 and ratified 1914). They maintained that Albania's international status was recognised by the six European powers, plus Romania, Serbia, Greece and Bulgaria, who had accredited diplomatic representation to its 1914 government in Durazzo. Information was also given regarding the gendarmerie and the present and future armed forces.[696]

Sir Eric Drummond, League Secretary-General and former British diplomat, has often been criticised for merely being a puppet of the British government, and for subordinating the League to Whitehall. Indeed in the case of Albania, it appears his oratory masked his complicity.[697] In the memorandum he drew up on Albania's application, it is clear that British interests were protected, because the conditions applied to Albania were far more extensive than those applied to other states. Drummond maintained that Albania appeared to meet the 'necessary conditions' because the 1913 Ambassadorial Conference and subsequent acts by the powers had constituted Albania as a fully self-governing state, and it had not been deprived of that status. However, the Secretary-General suggested that the Assembly might consider that the attempt by the powers to establish Albania in 1913-14 had not been successful. In particular, the outbreak of the war had interrupted the establishment of Albania as an organised and self-governing political community. Albania had undergone several serious internal disturbances in the course of the war, and, since its conclusion, the position of Albania had been rendered precarious by the difficulties that had arisen during the Adriatic question discussions. In particular, he drew attention to the 1915 Pact of London that, whilst not denying Albanian national claims, decreed that the international status of the country was a matter to be decided after the war. He concluded that it needed to be decided

> whether in 1913-14 Albania in fact acquired the political
> organisation and the character of a State in so definitive
> a manner that she cannot be considered to have lost such
> character by reason of events which have since occurred,
> or whether, on the contrary, the international status of the
> country is at present doubtful.[698]

On 17 December 1920, exactly eight years after the opening of the
Ambassadorial Conference in London, and seven years after the
signing of the Florence Protocol, the General Assembly considered
Albania's submission. Lord Robert Cecil, as South African delegate,
argued vehemently in favour of Albania's admission. In an impassioned
speech, he declared that once a state was first recognised it remained
in existence, even though its government might not be sanctioned.
(In reality it was not unusual for states to disappear, as the examples
of Poland in the late eighteenth century and German and Italian
unification had shown.) Cecil countered the objections that Albania
could not be admitted, as it was not a Christian state, by arguing
that 'religion was outside the question, and there was "no reason for
impugning the good faith of Albania, or her desire and power to
fulfil her international obligations"'.[699] This 'spirited championship'[700]
appears to have influenced the Assembly delegates considerably.
Cecil's 'plea for justice' on behalf of the Albanians resulted in
Albanian membership being unanimously accepted (thirty-five votes
to nil).[701]

The results of this achievement were profound. By being admitted
into the League, the Albanian state was finally recognised *de jure*
as a sovereign and independent state, albeit with its frontiers with
Yugoslavia and Greece still undefined.[702] Thus 17 December 1920
should, as such, be considered the true date when Albania achieved
independence. Following its admission, Albania established normal
diplomatic channels with all the powers, including Greece, Yugoslavia
and Italy; but, significantly, its government was still not recognised.
Admittance also required Albania to subscribe to a declaration to
protect its minorities, and conferred specific international obligations,
including full protection without distinction for birth, nationality,

language, 'race' or religion; use of any language to be permitted; equal rights for minorities to maintain charitable, religious and educational institutions.[703] Albania, with its multi-faith and bi- and multi-lingual population, with a nationalistic tradition that tended to respect and promote difference, was perhaps better prepared for this than other European, especially Balkan, states at the time. More importantly, in the short term, in securing admission to the League, the Tirana government had ensured that Albania would continue to exist in some form, albeit with its frontiers undecided and doubts still existing about the stability and viability of the regime. Crucially, Yugoslav forces still occupied large tracts of the north. Nevertheless, the Albanian admission was remarkable, especially when one considers other applications before the same meeting. Countries as diverse as Azerbaijan, Ukraine and Liechtenstein were rejected, on the grounds either that they did not have stable enough governments for acceptance, or that they were too small.[704] Countries that are today considered well established and with a long history and tradition, certainly more so than the Albanians, were rejected. Albania was also the only country to obtain a unanimous vote in favour of admission.

The admittance of Albania had not been expected. It is doubtful whether this would have occurred without the determination and actions of Cecil, or the British Delegate, Herbert A.L. Fisher, the President of the Board of Education, who went against British policy. The fifth committee, which had been established to consider applications, including Albania, had recommended against Albania's entry. The committee had divided into two camps: smaller, disinterested states who favoured membership versus the representatives of the great powers and smaller, interested states who opposed it, but not because of any balancing tendencies on the part of the smaller states. Those in favour of admission argued that Albania constituted a nation by virtue of the unanimous desire of its inhabitants. The country possessed frontiers that had been fixed by an international convention, and neither the London Pact nor the occupation of Albanian territory had been able to deprive it of its position as an independent state. The main opposition was led by the French delegate, René Vivani. Rather than opposing directly, he maintained that, as the chief Allied Powers had not yet decided on the status of Albania, the League Assembly would risk running counter to the will of the great powers if they came to a quick decision. It was also argued that Albania could not constitute a state due to its large Muslim population. On 6 December 1920, the committee voted by 13 votes to 8 in favour of Vivani's proposal to adjourn until Albania's international status and frontiers had been established by the Ambassadors' Conference in Paris.[705] It appeared that the French and British delegates had succeeded in keeping control of the Albanian question within the Ambassadors' Conference, and that the Albanian attempt to remove its settlement from the control of the great powers had failed.

In the Assembly, this arrangement was upset by Cecil and Fisher. Cecil has been described as, amongst other things, the 'most sincere' founder of the League and, at this point, 'the principal advocate of the Albanian case'.[706] In various questions, above all in south-eastern Europe, on Albania (successfully) and on Macedonia (less so), he used his influence and position to try and produce a moral or ethnic settlement based on League principles. He was in regular contact with Albanian activists, especially those associated with the Anglo-Albanian Society, and he encouraged them to keep up their pressure and activities. It is not clear how this relationship developed or why.[707] Cecil had not expected much success: he had proceeded in the hope of securing some kind of pledge that the issue would eventually be settled.[708]

Fisher's actions were also hugely important in influencing the attitudes of other delegates, despite being in opposition to British policy. The Foreign Office was anxious not to admit states whose boundaries had not been definitely fixed, and the governments of which had not been recognised *de jure*. In this category, it listed Albania, Armenia, Estonia, Georgia, Latvia, Lithuania and Ukraine as not being sufficiently established independent entities to warrant admission. The Foreign Office was chiefly concerned about the prospect of what it called 'running the risk' of defending these states against external aggression. Of all the countries under consideration, the Foreign Office favoured admitting only Finland and Costa Rica, and possibly also Luxembourg and Iceland, but opposed the admission of the previous seven and also Lichtenstein, Monaco and San Marino. Moreover Earl Curzon of Kedleston, the new British Foreign Secretary, was against the admittance of any of the smaller states, and he believed that a minimum population limit should be fixed. He did not mention Albania specifically, but its application would probably not succeed if population size was taken into account. Curzon was particularly opposed to admitting Albania and Ukraine because of their political instability.[709] Despite having supported the French proposal in committee, and in line with official British policy, in the Assembly Fisher declared that the British delegation 'is now prepared to accept the motion of Lord Robert Cecil and to vote for the admission of Albania to the League'.[710] On hearing this, Crowe minuted,

> this is perhaps the most astounding of the many curious acts of the Assembly. Apparently the British delegate voted for the admission of Albania, a country obeying no one recognised government, racially and religious divided into warring tribes, and having no defined frontiers. This is in spite of Cabinet instructions to the contrary. Presumably Balfour will explain to the Cabinet how this came about.[711]

Crowe was never particularly sympathetic to the Albanian case, but he was correct that Fisher appeared to have deliberately contravened official British policy. Some Foreign Office officials only became aware of Britain's vote through a report in *The Times*.[712] Whitehall proved at a loss to explain or justify it, and Arthur Balfour, now Lord President of the Council and *rappateour* to the League Assembly, came in for some tricky questions in the Cabinet. This is not to say that Albanian acceptance would not have been agreed, but it is unlikely that it would have been unanimous. When it came to the vote, even the Greek, Yugoslav, and French delegates voted in favour, in spite of their arguments against in the fifth committee. To save face, the Greek and Yugoslav representatives claimed that the past fortnight had seen a 'great consolidation' in Albania's situation, and that they could now 'regard the situation as sufficiently normal' to vote in favour of admission. In line with Schroeder's ideas about 'bandwagonning', they probably did not want to have a (new) hostile neighbour, however small, on their immediate borders.[713] Britain's apparent support, believed to be so important in the vote because it encouraged others to vote in favour, was largely due to the solitary actions of the British delegate

rather than the design of British policymakers. The great powers were
unable to control their own delegates, and the small states were not as
powerless as had been suspected.

British Revisionism

The British government continued to refuse to recognise Albania for
nearly a year. It maintained that admission to the League did not
imply the recognition of Albania by all its members, and that the
Ambassadors' Conference must establish an agreement on Albanian
frontiers before according formal recognition. Although it appointed
a representative (Consul without exequatus), Sir Harry Eyres, it
stipulated that this implied no endorsement of the Tirana government
or the state of Albania.[714] The British attitude was still determined
largely by that of the Italians and Yugoslavs. The Italians had, by the
Tirana Protocol, conceded some form of *de facto* recognition of the
Tirana government, but the Yugoslavs remained decidedly hostile to
even this. Whitehall appears to have found the Yugoslav view quite
convincing. It was not considered possible to adequately predict the
likelihood of the stability of the Tirana regime. Additionally, Britain
was still officially bound by the London Pact. There were also some
vague references to a settlement based on the old chestnut of the
'merits of the case', which presumably meant 'ethnic' or 'national'
frontiers.[715] This non-recognition of Albania was common across
the European powers and neighbouring states. Although diplomatic
representation was sent to Albania, it remained unrecognised, as
did the Tirana government. This put the Albanians in an unusual,
even dangerous, position in the great power system: on the one hand
their independence in some form had been assured by admittance to
the League, but as yet no government had officially approved that
independence or the government, despite votes in the League to the
contrary. With no fixed borders, the state was particularly vulnerable
to assault.

Nevertheless, in 1921, there was a change in British strategy. As
early as 20 April 1921, Curzon had communicated to de Martino,
who had become Italian Ambassador in London, that Britain
fully shared the Italian government's desire to co-operate in the
creation of an autonomous and independent state of Albania. This
was the first British reference to such a commitment after World

War One.[716] What prompted this remarkable u-turn is trickier to determine. Inevitably, Albania's admission to the League must have played a part, but it does not explain what prompted the change at this point. One plausible explanation and one which William Bland and Ian Price advanced, was linked with proposed oil concessions for the Anglo-Persian Oil Company (later British Petroleum), following the discovery of oil in Albania, during the war, by Italian and Austrian geologists. On 25 March 1921, Eyres signed an agreement between the Albanian government and Anglo-Persian giving the latter sole right to prospect for oil on Albanian territory, and, after exploitation, to select a portion of territory for use for the next fifty years.[717] As with the discovery of oil in other parts of the world, especially the Middle East, both then and subsequently, it appears economic considerations provided far more attractive and lucrative incentives for the promotion of an independent and democratic state than any moral or ethnic arguments. These developments were also a result of political changes in Greece. With the defeat of Venizelos in the Greek elections (14 November 1920) and the return of King Constantine (19 December 1920), the Foreign Office became more supportive of Albanian nationalism, because a strong pro-British Greek state was no longer a realistic possibility.[718] So long as Albania was not dominated by Italy it was no longer necessary to offer Greece substantial portions of Albanian territory. An independent Albania might even strengthen the international system by contributing to the balance of power, as the Foreign Office had hoped in 1913.

An important memorandum for the Albanian question, drawn up on 10 June 1921, detailed the possible lines that Curzon would accept for settlement of Albanian frontiers. It was essentially the policy the British would adopt throughout the subsequent negotiations: the war had put the 1913 settlement of Albanian frontiers once more into the 'melting pot'; but the Pact of London, in turn, 'went to pieces under the pressure of events'. The powers were therefore responsible for substituting territorial arrangements acceptable to all parties concerned. On the southern boundary, it contended that Koritza and the surrounding mining area should go to Albania, primarily due to Italo-American opposition to it becoming Greek, but they still hoped that there might be the possibility of a Greek road connecting Macedonia and Epirus. There were some sops to the ethnicity principle: the memorandum argued that it was not defensible to give Koritza to Greece, because of its importance in Albanian history and to the Albanian people. On the northern boundary, the report contended that ethnic considerations 'scarcely affect[ed] the question, if they did the boundary would have to be considerably extended'. Instead a 'strong geographic frontier' was needed, to correct the local economic and administrative defects revealed in the frontiers drawn in 1913, and to improve the possibilities of defence without conferring offensive advantages to either side. It listed five possible changes: the Serbs to retreat from Mount Tarabosh; the Dibra road to become entirely either Albanian or Serb; Lin to become Albanian (all designed to provide freedom of economic access); Yugoslavia to retreat to the 1913 boundaries but to receive about ten kilometres of territory east of Scutari lake to protect Podgorica, and a strip of territory near Prizrend (both for strategic protection and to make tribal limits conform more closely to the political territorial boundaries); and Scutari to remain in Albania. Curzon did not expect the Serbs to oppose this, although his reasons were not mentioned.[719]

Further Albanian Initiatives in the League

Meanwhile, the Tirana government had been attempting to deal with other urgent problems, resulting from the Yugoslav and Greek occupation, especially the aggressive actions of the Yugoslavs.[720] Albanians and their supporters stressed the importance of removing the Yugoslav forces, and securing the recognition of Albania and establishing its frontiers, as a means of deterring foreign aggressors.[721] By June 1921, there were even some reports of renewed Italian intrigue.[722] Between February and May 1921 the Tirana government appealed repeatedly to the League.[723] They asked for protection of Albanian borders in the north, and called attention to the difficulties with Greece on the 'southern border', where the Greeks still occupied twenty-six villages, pending their final determination by the great powers. These memoranda requested confirmation of Albanian frontiers as drawn in 1913, thereby excluding Kosovo, Plava, Gusinje, Hoti, Gruda, Chameria and the other areas of Albanian-speakers previously claimed.[724] These areas appear to have been dropped, because Albanian officials had finally admitted how unrealistic and unattainable these were, especially within the international system in which they had to operate. This was in spite of objections from prominent nationalists like Hasan Prishtina. Moreover, the pledges made to secure League membership meant that the government could not covet this territory, and certainly could not use force to acquire it. Instead, it would focus purely on the 1913 frontiers. Strategic and pragmatic motives superseded ethnic nationalism, even for the Albanian leaders. On 21 June 1921, the Albanians renewed their appeal to the League. The new Albanian Prime Minister, Iljas bey Vrioni, described in detail the 'abnormal' conditions of Albania. He appealed for the evacuation of Yugoslav and Greek forces from those parts of Albania's 1913 boundaries under Yugoslavia and Greek occupation, under Article 2 of the Covenant (which dealt with acts of aggression or war by member states).[725] These events illustrated most clearly the precarious nature of the Albanian position, and the necessity of resolving the boundary issue. Despite much success in its other initiatives, as a small weak state Albania still needed the international system to guarantee its security.

On 25 June 1921, Albanian, Greek and Yugoslav delegates were invited to express their views on the question of Albanian boundaries in a public session of the League Council. All parties used well-established arguments, already presented to the Peace Conference.[726] Despite Fan Noli's, the Albanian delegate, impassioned appeal, it was decided that the question of Albania's petition was outside the jurisdiction of the League. Noli had asserted that the League of Nations should have authority over these questions, as it was the successor of the European concert that had originally fixed the Albanian frontiers, rather than the Ambassadors' Conference, which was to deal with issues pertaining to relations between the victors and the defeated. As Albania had remained neutral, it was outside its scope. As the Conference of Ambassadors' had already started discussing the Albanian question (as a result of the timely initiative of the Italians regarding recognition), the League merely recommended that the Ambassadorial Conference come to a decision as soon as possible.[727] Various Albanian nationalist and diaspora groups had also petitioned the League, considering it the only 'competent tribunal to pass judgment' upon their case. They continued to petition the great-power governments, and urged Herbert and other supporters to apply pressure on their respective governments.[728] These appeals do not seem to have generated any noticeable results, once again illustrating the limited effectiveness of such lobbying.

Within a few days of the League hearing, Vrioni declared that Albania did not recognise the competence of the Ambassadors' Conference to re-open discussion regarding the settlement of Albanian frontiers. In particular, he maintained that the 'Albanian people will vigorously oppose any decision involving dismemberment' of the 1913 frontiers. In their appeal against the decision of the Council, the Tirana government attacked the established international order and moved further from their former tactics of attempting to gain great-power support for their claims. Eventually, on 2 September 1921, it was agreed that both Albanian issues under consideration by the League of Nations (determination of Albanian frontiers, and the purported violation of Albanian territory by Yugoslav bands), should be dealt with by the Assembly. This was because the two issues appeared inherently interlinked; it seemed strange that the Assembly should deal with one and the Council with the other. This resolution seemed completely incompatible with the earlier decision (25 June 1921), whereby it had been decided that the League was not competent to deal with the issue of Albanian boundaries. The Assembly appointed a sixth committee to investigate the whole subject, and a commission of inquiry was agreed to investigate the conditions in Albania. Once more, the League was to potentially have a key role in determining Albania's future, and there was the possibility for conflict with the great powers in the Ambassadors' Conference. The committee determined that the Albanians should merely await the decision of ambassadors, as to the delimitation of its frontiers.[729] The great powers had managed, once again, to maintain control of the question of Albanian boundaries. However, as the Foreign Office was by now anxious for a quick resolution of the remaining Albanian questions, it seemed probable that progress would be made. As Barros argued, British policy in the Ambassadors' Conference was not consistent, 'twisting and turning like a pirouetting ballerina'.[730] This was particularly true of discussions pertaining to the Albanian question. As it was not a matter of direct strategic interest, British policy makers had the flexibility to shift their allegiances in response to changing circumstances and priorities. The Greek situation had necessitated such a change.

*Ambassadors' Conference: international recognition and Albanian
boundaries*

As the result of an Italian initiative to resume Albanian discussions,
there had been important developments on the Albanian question
within the Ambassadors' Conference in Paris. Throughout 1920
and the first part of 1921, Albania was rarely discussed within the
Conference, despite French and British representatives arguing in
the League for the importance of the Conference as the mechanism
for settling the Albanian question. The Albanian question had
meanwhile been designated outside the Rapallo agreement. The other
powers did not want to endanger that settlement by considering the
Albanian one simultaneously. As Allen Leeper wrote, it 'was clever of
the Italians to have adopted a conciliatory attitude to the Yugoslavs
on this point [Albanian question] and to put the onus of refusing
Scutari on the British and French governments'.[731] In June 1921,
the Italian representative re-opened three issues: Albanian frontiers,
recognition of Albania by the powers and Italy's 'special interests' in
Albania. Under this third category, the Italians asked that should
Albanian independence prove unattainable in practice, the privileged
position of Italy in Albania should be recognised. The Italians were
still determined to preserve their strategic and economic interests
in Albania.[732] De Martino claimed that 'Italy has continuously
adopted a line of favouring Albanian independence' which was a
policy the Consulta would 'continue whole-heartedly to propound
and support'.[733] Like the Greeks in the Corfu Protocol, the Italians
sought to circumvent a former agreement regarding Albania, one
that still preserved Albanian sovereignty and independence, but
which also ensured that Italian cultural links, economic investments
and, in particular, strategic interests would be retained. Curzon had
agreed in advance to the first two points but was far less inclined to
accept the third. He persistently refrained from answering the notes
he received.[734]

Negotiations proceeded regarding the nature of Albania's
recognition and, in particular, whether Italy should have any 'special
interests'. The Italians sought two main gains: the island of Saseno,
and the right to bring aggression against Albania to the attention
of the League, should the Albanians not do this themselves. The
Consulta had initially sought to have the determination of Albania's

frontiers also entrusted to Italy, but this had met with considerable opposition, and was eventually dropped.[735] By mid-August 1921, it had become apparent that the British were the main obstacles to Italian 'special interests'. The Consulta consistently protested that the British, unlike the French, would not give assurances that they recognised Italian interests in Albania.[736] On the northern frontier, there was much consensus: disagreement persisted over the southern boundary. The Italian and French representatives insisted that Chimara and Argyrocastro be allocated to Albania, but the British delegate still argued that these should go to Greece. The British delegate also remained hostile to Italian claims to Saseno, which resulted in a committee being established to investigate its future.[737] Eventually, on 29 September 1921, the Conference of Ambassadors agreed to maintain the political independence and territorial integrity of Albania, and to recognise Italy's so-called 'special interests'.[738] On 16 November, but backdated to 9 November 1921, the day it was formally agreed, the great powers then involved in the Conference (British Empire, France, Italy and Japan, but not the United States) formally recognised an independent and sovereign state of Albania, and committed to protect its integrity. The Greek and Yugoslav governments' request to present their views to the Conference of Ambassadors was refused. On 7 November 1921, the British had informed Eyres that they recognised the existing Albanian government as the *de jure* government for the whole of Albania.[739]

This declaration was obviously of immense importance in the development of an independent Albanian state. It committed the great powers not only to recognise Albania, but also to protect it against foreign aggressors. The powers agreed that the maintenance of Albanian independence was of international concern, primarily because of Italian interests pertaining to the Albanian coastline. As any violation of Albanian independence or frontiers might constitute a menace to Italian strategic security, it was agreed that, if Albania found itself unable to maintain its territorial integrity, it had the right of recourse to the League for international assistance. A second clause stated that, in the event of a threat being made to Albania's independence or integrity (due to foreign aggression or any other cause), and if Albania did not 'within reasonable time' make an application for foreign assistance, then the great powers would bring the issue to the notice of the League Council. If the Council decided foreign assistance was necessary, the great powers would entrust this task to Italy. There was a fourth, and secret, clause. This was not communicated to anyone but the signatories, presumably to avoid opposition in the League. It stated that, if the League decided by majority vote that they could not usefully intervene, the governments represented in the Conference of Ambassadors would reconsider the question.[740] Nothing to this effect was specifically mentioned, but the inference was that, if the powers thought it necessary, such a task would be entrusted to Italy. This was potentially the most important part of the agreement. It undermined the sanctity of the League, as the new arbiter of international disputes, and it meant that the Italians had finally managed to secure international recognition of their Albanian interests by the other great powers, and a legal means of protecting them. The opportunity for intrigue to facilitate this was obvious, for the agreement gave great scope for possible Italian intervention, based on either territorial or economic threats to Albanian integrity and independence. It could be described as representing at best a 'conditional independence', similar to that which was suggested for Kosova more recently. Italy's claim to be the protector attained reality by the signing of two treaties with Zogu, especially the Treaty of Tirana (27 November 1926).[741]

The 9 November declaration also announced that the great powers had decided to essentially reconfirm the Albanian frontiers as traced in 1913-14. The southern boundary was to be delimited on the basis of the lines of the Florence Protocol, with the important towns of Koritza, Argyrocastro and Chimara, together with all surrounding territory, becoming Albanian. This meant that the Greeks were obliged to return the twenty-six villages that they had occupied since 1918. The northern and eastern boundary line agreed (provisionally) in 1914 was to be rectified in four sectors, three to the advantage of the Yugoslavs and one to the Albanians: north-east of Scutari to Yugoslavia would guarantee the approaches to Podgorica; a slight rectification in favour of Yugoslavia, in the neighbourhood of Prizrend, would protect the town from Albanian assault (Albania would thus lose Gora and approximately 50,000 inhabitants, including a number of non-Serb Slavonic speakers); the road from Dibra to Struga would pass entirely through Yugoslav territory; the district of Lin would go to Albania to ensure economic communications between Elbasan and Koritza along the shores of Lake Ochrida. Hoti and Gruda were both confirmed as belonging to Montenegro (Yugoslavia) and Scutari as part of Albania. The powers also demanded that the Yugoslav troops be withdrawn from northern Albania, under threat of economic sanctions under Article 16 of the Covenant.[742]

The declaration also acknowledged that the 1913-14 northern commission had been interrupted by the war and had not completed its operations. It therefore established a further boundary commission to determine the boundary in those areas not yet investigated, and to delimit the northern, eastern and southern boundaries in loco. This lasted for four years (1922-26). As with all post World War One boundary commissions (and in contrast to those in Albania before the war), it received detailed instructions regarding protocol, procedure and membership.[743] The delimitation commission, consisting of members of the three European great powers, began its work in March 1922, the decision having been taken to delay its start until the conclusion of the Albanian winter. Like the 1913-14 commissions, it had an ethnic or national remit, but great power interests were again protected. All its protocols were to be submitted to the great (Principal Allied) powers for their approval. Unlike the pre-war commissions, the 1922-26 delimitation commission was empowered to take advisers from the states on either side of the frontiers, and to consider requests from the Albanian, Greek and Yugoslav governments.[744]

The commission arrived in Albania after holding preliminary meetings in Paris and Florence. Once in Albania, the Italian delegate, General Enricou Tellini, proposed, and the ambassadors in Paris agreed, that he and the Italian topographers would delimit the southern boundary with Greece, whilst the British and French delegates would supervise the northern one with Yugoslavia.[745] With the Italians having secured an agreement about the northern Adriatic with the Yugoslavs, their interest turned again to focus upon southern Albania. This was clearly to protect Italian interests in southern Albania, but, in light of the far tighter directives and the different nature of the commission, this in itself should not have produced many problems. The representatives considering the northern sections of the frontier proceeded slowly and cautiously. They encountered no real problems because most Yugoslav troops had grudgingly retreated from their advanced positions. By contrast, the difficulties faced by the representatives considering the southern boundary were greater then those faced by either of the two pre-war commissions. The Greeks felt that Tellini was prejudiced against them and partial to the Albanian viewpoint. A crisis was provoked when Tellini and four other members of the Italian commission were murdered at a border town situated in Greek territory. The Italian fleet responded by occupying Corfu island. As Barros has shown, this episode illustrated the inherent weakness of the League. Despite pressure from the smaller powers, the French sought to find a diplomatic solution in the Conference of Ambassadors (which continued until 1931), and outside the League.[746] Although it delayed the workings of the commission and made the Italians, especially, hostile to the Greeks, this incident does not appear to have altered the final settlement.[747]

Conclusions

This chapter has shown a further tactic deployed by the Albanian nationalists in their activities within the great power system. It illustrated how they used an international organisation (the League of Nations) in their attempt to elude or defeat the policies of the great power states when the policies of the latter ran contrary to the national ambitions of the smaller 'state'. In so doing, the Albanians used one of the most effective techniques available to small states: they appealed to the rights of justice and international law. The Albanians also improved the chances of the survival of their state by pursuing a moderate and non-provocative policy. To secure acceptance of Albania as an independent and sovereign state, the Tirana government modified its objectives. It resolved to compromise on the ethnic ideal of a majority Albanian-speaking population defined state, in order to secure others goals, namely internal stability, defensive or strategic frontiers and international recognition. Rather than hold out for the ultimate, ethnic, but unachievable goal, they made the realistic decision to opt for a more limited but possible version of the Albanian state, within the constraints of the international system in which they operated. In so doing, and, as Rothstein argues regarding other questions, they were able to appear stronger and more unified. They appeared to represent a coherent national state without substantial dissident minorities, and they were attempting to secure non-irredentist neighbours.[748] They were also pursuing more pragmatic policies, and were functioning in a similar manner to other states within the system.

However, the Albanians still placed too much faith in the importance of the League in international affairs, as they had likewise placed too much trust in the intentions of great power statesmen. In practice, the 'new diplomacy' of the League operated only marginally differently to the 'old diplomacy' of the concert. Such a view was typical of many small states. Throughout the Paris peace negotiations, the underlying assumption was that states would henceforth follow disinterested foreign policies, motivated only by community interests, and that, as a result, the settlements would represent a 'final and permanent solution' to national questions in eastern Europe.[749] The rejection of the League by the Senate in the United States led the European great powers to re-examine their policies towards the League. In the end, the League Council could be no more effective than the great powers allowed it to be, and in any case they continued to sit simultaneously in the Ambassadorial Conference in Paris. As Barros has argued, British representatives patronised the League only in so far as it could supplement their more established modes of negotiation. Geo-political interests therefore remained central to international decision-making.[750] The principle of self-determination was never going to be applied fairly to the Albanian question, because the territory the Albanians claimed was of strategic importance to a variety of victorious states. Likewise, self-determination was completely disregarded for the defeated Bulgarians. As one commentator recorded, using Philip Noel-Baker's famous categorisation of British policy-makers, 'on the international plain and vis-à-vis small states all British diplomats were hawks'.[751]

In 1921, British policy towards Albania became more sympathetic. This decision was the product of a reassessment of British strategic interests in the Adriatic and the Balkans. Albanian activities, such as their anti-Italian stance, which made a 'large independent Albania' less threatening to British naval interests, the increased political stability inside Albania and the revised boundary claims, all contributed to this. But events extraneous to Albanian activities were more important, most notably changes resulting from domestic developments in Greece. It now helped British policy, and also Italian, to bolster the fledgling Albanian state. Admittedly the great powers pursued a two-pronged approach: by the secret annex to the 9 November 1921 memorandum, they somewhat curtailed the independence and sovereignty of the new state that the memorandum had supposedly endorsed publicly. In so doing, they ensured that geo-political, above all Italian, interests in Albania were protected in the event that the Albanian state proved too weak and fragile for existence, or susceptible to foreign (Greek or Yugoslav) hostility, aggression or intrigue.

Therefore, by 1921 the great powers had acquiesced in the re-establishment of an independent Albania within the borders of 1913, thereby excluding many Albanian speakers. The Albanian problem had not been solved. With the exception of a period during the Second World War (1939-44), Albania has remained independent ever since and its boundaries, except in that same period, have remained unchanged. On the other hand, Albania has remained one of the weakest and most isolated states in the European international system. In the short term, it was already possible to identify problems. Albania in 1926 was very different from the Albania of 1921, when its final boundary commission was formed. There had been numerous changes of government. The Regency had been replaced and Ahmet Zogu had instituted a successful *coup d'etat*, with himself proclaimed first President (1925) and later King Zog (1928)— Albania's, and Europe's, first and only Muslim king. The great power delay in recognising Albania, and in determining its boundaries, had contributed to the political instability and rivalry that once again resurfaced, in a manner similar to 1914, but this time with even more profound implications. It aided the fall of the Delvina-led cabinet and destabilised the Regency, helped the rise of Zogu and, thus, in the longer term, jeopardised Albanian democracy. External factors were also once more divisive, with the traditional Italo-Yugoslav rivalry a particularly negative force against the consolidation of the Albanian state. The Yugoslavs were dissatisfied with the 9 November 1921 declaration, by which they had been forced to remove their military forces, and the Italians had acquired a privileged position. Both the Italian and Yugoslav governments continued to pursue policies of penetration into Albania, and their leaders tried to create clients in political, economic and scientific circles. Despite its success in utilising the League to support it in 1920 and 1921, the Albanian small state, like the other small states in central and eastern Europe, proved less effective during the period of peace that followed. When the Italians, under Mussolini, finally invaded Albania, on 7 April 1939, no assistance was offered to it by the British or French governments, despite the guarantees made in 1921. In the end these guarantees, like those to Czechoslovakia, were practically worthless.

Conclusions

'A house divided against itself cannot stand. A dismembered nation cannot live, it must fight for unification or die.'[752]

The Emergence of Albanian Independence

Sir Edward Grey asserted that, in the settlement of the Albanian question in 1913, 'the primary thing was to preserve agreement between the powers'.[753] His comment could equally be applied to the discussions during and after World War One. As IR theory predicts, geo-political interests and international or external influences certainly pre-dominated in the question of Albanian independence. Nevertheless, national or domestic factors were also influential, and on occasion made timely and decisive contributions. The relative importance of these various national and international factors in the emergence of independence depended to a large extent upon the point in the cycle of the great power system at which these developments occurred. As the cycle changed, the priorities and interests of the great powers shifted, and this in turn altered the relative strength and importance of the contribution made by the small-state actors of the Albanian national process. Thus, following points of crisis at which the power-relativities of the international system were shifting, the Albanians, like the other small states, although not always able to play off one power against another, were able to make considerable advances in their national programme. By contrast, when the international system was relatively stable, and the great powers could use the Albanian question for their own purposes, then home-grown

Albanian factors were less productive, and international ones were more significant.

It has been illustrated that the role of small states, including newly aspiring ones, in the international system is greater than the theoretical literature on international relations allows for, and therefore indicates that further study on this question is required. Despite being an example of small-state nationalism, Albania was not a mere supplicant. At particular points, the Albanians themselves made significant and decisive contributions to the settlement of the Albanian question. They were able successfully to make use of the unusual political climates (1912 in the Balkans, post-1918 in Europe) that destabilised the respective balances of power and strengthened the position of small states, including themselves, relative to other more powerful states. After World War One, it took the Albanians longer than some other small states to capitalise on this opportunity, because they were weaker and smaller than those other small states with which they were in competition, and were themselves as yet far from united. Nevertheless, it is important to note that, although a small state may be more effective in the great power system than its size and position would initially suggest, in the Albanian case this happy situation was usually of limited duration, and came about only because it was in the interest of one or other of the great powers to exploit it. The initiatives of the Tirana government in 1920 only proved so successful because of Italian domestic issues and the Italian pre-occupation with Yugoslav questions, which the Consulta had determined as being, for the moment, strategically more important. It is also necessary to note that, at certain points, such as the radicalism of their presentations at the Paris Peace Conference, Albanian national efforts could actually be detrimental to the national cause, the success of which would depend on the attitude of the great-power representatives. This consideration also points to the need for further study of the interplay of the various roles and influences of small states in the great-power system and national questions especially.

In the international arena, five supplementary processes were identified, four of which were diplomatic, and the fifth military. On the diplomatic side, there was the 'old' or closed diplomacy of the Conference of Ambassadors of 1912-13; the secret diplomacy that resulted in the Pact of London; the Paris Peace Conference and the subsequent Conference of Ambassadors in Paris, supposedly the 'new diplomacy' of the Wilsonian era, but with a marked tendency to the continuation of old-diplomacy tendencies; and the activities within the League of Nations, which were closer to the ideals of the new diplomacy. These international processes were of course influenced by national considerations, such as the decision to convene the Ambassadors' Conference in London; they also had an impact upon national forces, such as the resurgence of Albanian nationalism that resulted in the Congress of Lushnje. There was, as we have seen, a complicated interaction and interplay between these various forces. The powers, even in the supposedly 'international' decisions of the League, were generally able to maintain their hegemony: this is well illustrated by their separate, and secret, resolution giving Italy the right to intervene in Albania, which undid much of the value of Albania's admission into the League and international great power guarantee. Therefore, rather than ignoring these 'international' influences, theorists of nationalism, and especially of the nationalism of small states, would be well advised to incorporate the contribution made by such influences, if their theories are to be applicable to the real world.

The motives of the great-power representatives were, naturally enough, both varied and variable. Generally speaking, it is possible to argue that they were less concerned with the Albanian question *per se*, except for certain relatively junior individuals such as Brigadier-General Phillips—that is, with the desire to create a practical, viable, and ethnographically distinct and independent Albania—than with protecting their own direct and indirect interests. Their policies may also have indirectly served the interest of the small state, but this was not their primary concern in determining their chosen course. Great power representatives were realistic not idealistic. They determined policy according to their own interests, and anticipated advantages rather than morality or sentiment. For example, British policy on the Albanian question seems to fit well the theory of defensive realism.[754] The British intended to maintain what they saw as the balance of power in Europe, and to maintain British naval supremacy. Albania's strategic location on the Adriatic and in the Balkans was, although perhaps only of indirect interest to Britain, still a matter for concern, because it had the potential to impact on these important direct interests. British policy thus set out to ensure that the declining Ottoman and Hapsburg empires would not be replaced by a dominant Russia, and, after 1918, by a dominant Italy, in the Balkans, the Adriatic and the eastern Mediterranean. British policy-makers thus sought to bolster those states, whether great powers or small states, that they viewed as the best instruments for achieving these objectives at any particular point. To achieve these goals, they were prepared to work with other states and compromise other lesser objectives. When an independent Albania would help achieve these goals, as in 1912-13 and again in 1921, British policy was generally supportive; whereas when an independent Albania was perceived as compromising these goals, as in 1919, it was opposed. In 1919, Foreign Office support shifted to the Yugoslav and Greek small-state nationalisms, as it was then considered that these states would provide a better counterbalance to the Italians. By comparison, the Italians persistently, and most notably in the London Pact, pursued offensive-realist practices in pursuit of their goals. At the 1912-13 conferences, they were prepared to work with the Austrians and other powers, but this soon gave way to more aggressive tendencies. They returned to a theoretically less aggressive stance only in 1919, when the high degree of opposition to their ambitions from stronger great powers became manifest. For the Consulta, Italian policy goals were naturally always paramount. They had clearly resurfaced by 1921, although to be accomplished by different means, when they managed to secure approval for their plan to circumvent the idea of a fully sovereign Albanian state, and thereby safeguard their interests.

The Balkan small states, as R.W. Seton-Watson and Farrar have pointed out also operated within a Balkan small-states system, which functioned in a similar manner to the larger European great- power system. Their ambitions, rivalries and actions were not so much about national or ethnic goals, as about their strength and security in their relations with one another, and also with the great powers.[755] Again, realist tendencies can be seen to have predominated throughout— most obviously in their various decisions about entry into World War One. By 1920, the Tirana government appears to have been acting in a similar manner to these other small states, in seeking to secure its position in the Balkan states system.

Explaining Albania's Geographical Limits

Lord Curzon once said that 'as a branch of the science of government, frontier policy is of the first practical importance and has a more profound effect upon the peace and warfare of nations than any other factor, political or economic'.[756] The decisions made regarding the delimitation of Albanian boundaries in 1912-14, and again in 1919-21, and applied by 1926, were supposed to be based on ethnic principles: it was, in short, deemed that those areas where Albanian was the majority spoken language should become part of the newly independent Albanian state. This was in line with the contemporary view that equated nationality with ethnicity, and ethnicity with language. In practice, however, the great powers, the small Christian Balkan states, and, by 1920, even the Tirana government itself, had alternative priorities and interests (strategic, geographic, economic and even historical) that needed protection in the boundary settlement. For all the great powers, even those supposedly disinterested, geo-political interests overrode sentiments about nationality or the rhetoric of morality. Albanian claims for a truly 'ethnic' or 'national' settlement proved far too radical and ambitious for the great power representatives, especially in the light of their own interests, the rival claims of other small Balkan states and the potential instability within the international system that such a change would have produced.

For the great power representatives, in particular the British, the boundaries represented a reasonable compromise between considerations of nationality, geography, economic expediency and strategic security. In the Kosovo and Monastir *vilayets*, the boundaries undoubtedly fell far short of nationalistic hopes on both sides, but in practice this does not seem to have been a particular liability for Albanians within the new state at least. The introduction of a wider set of factors in addition to ethnicity (such as a larger consideration of the factors determining nationality, geographical features, strategic concerns and economic interests), rather than limiting Albanian nationality and the extent of its independence, can be seen instead as promoting Albanian self-determination and a realistic application of the nationality principle. The Albania created was much more homogeneous, without significant dissident minorities or other ethnic groups, as would have been incorporated (at least without a population exchange) had the borders been extended in the north, south and east. There is every reason to suppose therefore that, if, after 1914 and again after 1926, the independent Albanian state so defined had been sufficiently supported by the great powers (with adequate funding, military backing and without the internal and foreign intrigue) the new Albanian 'nation' could have solidified, unified and strengthened itself, and developed into a modern and fully functioning small state in the international system. This conclusion supports Thomas Hylland Eriksen's finding that the introduction of other factors (a wider consideration of nationality, geographic features, strategic concerns, economic interests), which seem at first sight to compromise the concepts of ethnicity and self-determination, can in fact be a 'healthy corrective'. They can supplement the understanding of ethnicity when it becomes a 'straitjacket' too narrowly defined, as in the case of a definition based solely on language. Admittedly, these theoretical ideas were far from the thoughts of international statesmen at the time, but the practical outcomes studied here do suggest that there is much plausibility to Hylland Eriksen's theorizing.[757] For the excluded 'Albanians' the experience would be somewhat different.

In 1920, the Tirana government resolved to accept the 1913-14 'partition' in order to secure international recognition, promote stability in Albania and foster goodwill with its neighbours. Its decision had a fourth advantage, albeit one that none of the great powers or Albanian representatives at the time, or the Albanians since, appear to have appreciated. In the unlikely event of its having secured the Kosovan plain, Albania would have been placed in a much weaker position militarily, and would have been more vulnerable to a Yugoslav invasion, and vice versa. As the logistical difficulties of the Serbian retreat in the winter of 1915-16 had illustrated, the mountains of northern Albania formed a more effective barrier to the passage of troops, and thus a more defensible frontier for both sides, than any possible line further to the north and east in Kosovo.[758]

Early 20th Century Criteria for Statehood and the Role of Language

For great-power policy makers in early twentieth century Europe, nationality would appear to have been synonymous with language and ethnicity. It has generally been supposed that these ideas were at their pinnacle in the period after World War One, and were most cogently articulated by President Wilson. In reality, as this study has demonstrated, European great-power representatives had already adopted 1919 Wilsonian-style self-determination in their discussions regarding the establishment of an 'ethnographic' and 'mother-tongue' Albanian state well before 1914. The phraseology may have differed but the rhetoric was very similar: the idea being for all Albanian speakers to live in an independent Albanian state. Thus we see that the consideration of the Albanian question before World War One produced major developments in how great powers thought about small states, and in having what was, in effect, the German 'primordial' model applied to such nationalisms. During World War One, these ideas were canvassed more widely (though of course not applied in practice to Albania), and the Paris Peace Conference accepted language as the major indicator of nationality. However, in the case of Albania, and for the reasons already given, in the initial discussions of 1919, the connection was not made with those earlier considerations of the Albanian question, which had been based on similar principles of nationality, or with the problems that had been posed by using a language-based definition of nationality.

Briefly stated, the theory was that each linguistically-distinct group had the right to self-determination and, if it so desired, its own state, with its political boundaries corresponding to its linguistic ones. In practice, however, there were many difficulties in applying such theories, in particular in an area like south-eastern Europe. By 1913, the southern Albanian boundary commission had already recognised the inadequacy of using language to determine nationality and, in turn, national boundaries. In reality, in the Balkans and other areas, nationalities often overlapped and intermingled, and many people spoke more than one language, contrary to the simplistic assumption of the time that each nationality was a coterminous bounded entity which could be neatly delimited in linguistic maps.[759] Nevertheless, throughout this period (and when it suited their purposes), great-power policy makers persisted in advocating an 'ethnic' settlement of statehood and boundaries, based on the language principle. This was in spite of it having been recognised as an inadequate criterion for this purpose during consideration of the Albanian and other questions. In addition, self-determination was deemed to apply only to a select group of small-state nationalities, most of which were located in eastern Europe, and all of which were *pre-determined* by the great powers as suitable for inclusion. Chapters Six and Eight showed how the great powers resisted (even theoretically) applying these ideas to the Albanian question in 1919 because it was not in their own interests to do so.

Meanwhile, policy makers in small states and interested great powers took a more diverse approach to the ethnic basis of states. Some of the Albanian ideas appear similar to the theories articulated by great power statesmen and officials, especially their insistence on oral as opposed to written language. The policy makers in other small states took an alternative view that was largely dependent upon their own interests. For the Greeks, for instance, religion remained the prime indicator of nationality. At Paris in 1919, they refused to consider the language test, and instead pointed to the large number of prominent Greeks who were 'Albanian' by 'descent', but regarded as 'Greek' by 'religion'.[760] In short, there remained much confusion and inconsistency over the criteria for determining nationality, and this left politicians in both great and small states free to shape their attitudes according to what was most expedient.

Concluding Remarks: ethnicity and national frontier-making

There has been considerable debate on what role ethnicity should play in defining national boundaries (particularly where ethnicity is defined in narrow linguistic terms), and how far the 'primordial' model of national identity can be applied. Gellner and Hylland Eriksen, for instance, have been particularly critical of the viability of using ethnicity as a basis for nationality and statehood, considering it too vague and ambiguous. They argue that, not only should a wider range of ethnic factors be used (for instance religion, beliefs, customs and kinship), but that other factors (such as historical, economic and strategic ones) all contribute to national self-identification. The consideration of only one or a limited number of factors, therefore, tends to produce only a limited and artificial definition of nationality.[761] Rogers Brubaker and Oliver Zimmer have gone further, contending that even the civic-ethnic division in definitions of nationhood is too constricting and that it too needs refining.[762] Elsewhere, Ger Duijzings has argued that 'identity' is a much better indication of identification and self-determination, because it is more fluid than the narrow concept of ethnicity. In his study on Kosova, he contends that Balkan peoples often have more than one identity and that allegiances change over time, and he points particularly to the past religious conversions and re-conversions of large sections of the population.[763] Others go further, asserting that the very process of making boundaries itself reinforces or creates differences, especially in areas of ethnically mixed populations. Brubaker calls this process 'ethnic unmixing'.[764] This is what seems to have occurred in the case of Kosova.

In practical terms too, there were genuine problems in producing national or ethnographic frontiers in the early twentieth century. Besides the problems in applying the criteria of language decided upon, there were other difficulties, often of a severely practical nature. The great-power representatives, in particular the boundary commissioners (1912-14), often had only rudimentary knowledge and expertise, and they lacked resources. The ethnographic information and the maps available to them showed huge variations, largely determined by political or national preconceptions, and they rarely indicated either the distribution or the density of the population.[765] The mountainous terrain, coupled with the time of year, made it difficult to produce new maps. It was therefore difficult in practice to refine the broad determinations of the 1913 Ambassadorial Conference into more sophisticated ethnographic findings; and it is also clear that not all of the great-power representatives were fully committed to their task.[766] Taken together, these problems made a sincere, dispassionate and non-political determination of the Albanian frontiers unattainable. The attempts more generally after 1918 to produce ethnographic frontiers elsewhere, especially using boundary commissions, also came up against similar problems to those that arose in Albania before and after World War One. The idea that there were tidy ethnographic frontiers just waiting to be determined by boundary commissioners from the great powers hardly survived these practical experiences on the ground.

Nevertheless, whatever the practical problems of frontier-making in detail may have been, it remains clear that they were minor in comparison to the alternative priorities and criteria (strategic, political, economic and indeed cultural) which *all* the decision-makers had to consider. None of the great-power representatives were entirely committed to the ethnic or national objectives that they proclaimed, especially when these came into conflict with their own geo-political interests. To be critical of their actions is to be critical of the system in which they operated, and of the real world of international politics, and that is not the business of the historian. If policy-makers in the past were to be effective, then they had to be realistic and pragmatic, or cease to be policy-makers. In the practical world of power politics, great-power representatives have always acted to preserve the perceived and paramount interests of their state, regardless of ideology, rhetoric, idealism or the latest fashionable remedy for the wrongs of the world (whether ethnic solutions, concern for the rights of small nations, support for supra-national organisations, or even action on climate change). As we have seen, ethnicity as the basis for state-building was used, and would be used, only in so far as it coincided with, supported and reinforced the larger policy objectives of the interested great powers. In these transactions, there were many competing influences and priorities, and ethnicity or the national principle was not the only one that was compromised. All such decisions were the outcome of a balancing process in which a wide range of priorities had to be considered. To give just one instance from the period under review: when the Russian government agreed to the establishment of an independent Albania in 1912, it thereby accepted Austria's scheme of denying Serbia an outlet to the sea on the Adriatic coast; this was widely perceived to be contrary to long-term Russian strategic interests, but it was nevertheless accepted for overriding considerations of short-term expediency. Russian officials could not, in 1912-13, support the interests of their Serbian client-state without risking a war for which Russia was as yet unprepared, and without alienating the support of its power-political partners, France and especially Britain. These great-power calculations, wholly extraneous to the merits of the Albanian case, were largely instrumental in securing the initial creation of an independent state of Albania. In November 1919, at the Peace Conference of Paris, Sir Eyre Crowe responded to the suggestion that ethnic considerations should always take precedence over strategic ones, and his comment will stand as a fitting epitaph for this study. He stated that 'in preparing the treaties, they had to make compromises on all points', and enquired: 'Why maintain that in this question particularly principles were sacred?'[767] Whatever Wilsonian rhetoric and the principle of the self-determination of peoples might propose, expediency dictated otherwise.

A Selective Who's Who[768]

Albanian Committee of London (1912-14)

Established in London to advocate the Albanian national cause during the London conferences and to act as a pressure group to raise funds and draw attention to the appalling situation in Albania. Aubrey Herbert was its President and Lord Lamington its Vice President, former Conservative MP (1886-90) and Governor in Queensland (1896-1901) and Bombay (1903-7). The Committee included a number of politicians, academics, lawyers and journalists amongst its membership.

Baron Carlo Aliotti (1866-1924)

Aliotti was Italian Envoy Extraordinaire and Minister Plenipotentiary to Albania in 1914, having previously been Consul General in Corsica and a Military Attaché in embassies across Europe. He helped draft the Albanian clauses of the 1915 Pact, and in 1920 was one of the Italian negotiators who failed to secure an agreement for Italian retention of Valona. After World War One he served as Ambassador in China and the United States.

Anglo-Albanian Association (1943-45 and 1963-present)

In 1943, during World War Two, when the future of an independent Albania was once more in doubt, Mary Herbert, Aubrey's widow, helped set up the Anglo-Albanian Association, as a successor to both the Albanian Committee and the Anglo-Albanian Society. The Association has continued intermittently since and its current President is the historian Noel Malcolm.

Anglo-Albanian Society (1918-23)

In 1918, Aubrey Herbert reconstituted the Albanian Committee as the Anglo-Albanian Society,, with the aim of gaining support for the Albanian national cause after World War One. Herbert became the first President and Edith Durham Joint Secretary-Treasurer.

Count Alexander Benckendorff (1849-1917)

He was Russian Ambassador to Britain from 1903-1917, having succeeded his father in the post, and proved influential in establishing the Anglo-Russian Entente (1907). Benckendorff died in office before the outbreak of the February revolution.

Constantine Bilinski (d.1913)

Senior Austrian delegate on the 1913 southern Albanian boundary commission, and previously Consul in Janina, where he had been subject to much criticism for his anti-Greek views. His death in November 1913, whilst delaying the commission, eventually made a compromise on the southern Albanian boundary easier to facilitate.

Isa bey Boletin (Boletini) (1864-1916)

Boletin was a great Kosovan freedom fighter. He was Captain of the Sultan's bodyguard 1902-6. Although initially supporting the Young Turks, Boletin participated in various resistance activities during the first Balkan war, being the joint commander of the Albanian national militia 1912-13. He was a member of Ismaïl Kemal's provisional government, and his troops defended Wilhelm of Wied in 1914. He fought with the Serbs in World War One and was later interned in Podgorica, where he is said to have been killed in a shootout.

Bishop Luigj (Luigi) Bumçi (1872 -1945)

Nephew of the Albanian writer Pashko Vasa and an important political and Catholic leader, being Bishop of Alessio 1911-1943. He was the Catholic representative of the Albanian delegation to the Paris Peace Conference and in the High Regency 1920-21. He participated in the December 1921 coup d'etat and was dismissed for his involvement. He then withdrew from politics and retired into ecclesiastical life.

Vice-Admiral Sir Cecil Burney (1858-1929)

Burney was President of the International Administration of Scutari (May-November 1913) and Second-in-Command of the Grand Fleet (1914-16) and Second Sea Lord (1916-17).

(Pierre) Paul Cambon (1843-1924)

Cambon was French Ambassador to Britain from 1898-1920, having previously served in Tunis, Madrid and Constantinople. As Ambassador in London, he most notably helped negotiate the Entente Cordiale in 1904 and helped secure British entry into World War One on the French side. His brother, Jules Cambon, was also active in French diplomatic affairs, including serving as Foreign Ambassador to Berlin (1907-14).

Captain (later Colonel) Fortunato Castoldi

Castoldi was an Italian diplomat, being junior Italian delegate on the 1912 Southern Albanian Boundary Commission, political advisor to Wilhelm of Wied in 1914 and representative on the Greek Committee during the Paris Peace Conference. In 1920, he became Italian High Commissioner to Albania. He tended to be both anti-Austrian and anti-Greek, but this did not prove popular with the Albanians. He also served as Italian Minister at Santiago (1922-24) and La Paz (1924-26).

Lord Robert Cecil MP (1864-1958)

Cecil was a Conservative MP 1906-10 and 1911-23. He was Parliamentary Under-Secretary of State for Foreign Affairs (1915-16) and Minister for the Blockade (1916-18) in David Lloyd George's war cabinet. In July 1918, he became Assistant Secretary of State for Foreign Affairs, but resigned in January 1919 to become a South African delegate to the Paris Peace Conference and later the League of Nations. As South African delegate to the League of Nations, he championed the Albanian national cause and managed to secure Albanian admission to the League.

George Russell Clerk, from 1917 Sir (1874-1951)

A British diplomat serving as Acting First Secretary in Constantinople (1910-12), a senior clerk in the Foreign Office (1912-14) and Head of the War Department (1914-19). In 1919 he became Private Secretary to Earl Curzon, when the later was Acting Foreign Secretary. He continued to have an illustrious diplomatic career after World War One, becoming an important figure in the building of the 'New Europe', including strengthening British ties with Hungary, Czechoslovakia and Turkey.

Committee for the National Defence of Kosovo (*Komiteti Mbrojta Kombëtare e Kosovës*)

Illegally founded on 1 May 1918 with the aim of promoting Kosovan interests and campaigning against the Albanian borders established in London in 1913-14. The Committee's leaders included Hoxhë Kadriu, Hasan Prishtina, Bajram Curri and Avni Rystemi. On 6 March 1919, the Committee called for a general uprising in Kosovo. This led to a large-scale revolt at Drenica, involving some 10,000 rebels. The uprising was brutally crushed by Yugoslav forces as an example to other ethnic minorities.

Sir Eyre Crowe (1864-1925)

Crowe was a career civil servant. He held a variety of positions in the British Foreign Office, including Assistant Under-Secretary of State for Foreign Affairs (1912-20) and Permanent Under-Secretary of State for Foreign Affairs (1920-25). At the Paris Peace Conference, he was a Minister Plenipotentiary and became the head of the British delegation after the departure of Lloyd George and Balfour (10 September 1919). He sat on the Greek Committee, and was one of the British representatives most resistant to Albania's demands for self-determination.

Bajram Curri (1862-1925)

Curri was an Albanian guerrilla leader. Originally from Djakova, Curri was a founder of the second League of Prizrend (1899-1900), was actively involved in the insurgency against the Balkan states and Young Turks (1912-13) and helped found the Kosovan Committee in 1918. Following the Congress of Lushnje (January 1920), he became Minister without Portfolio and assisted in the Congress's activities in suppressing the Essadists. His opposition to Zogu resulted in him committing suicide to avoid capture during a siege in March 1925.

Christo Anastas Dako (1878 –1941)

Dako was an Albanian-American journalist. He vied with Fan Noli for leadership of *Vatra*, becoming its President in 1913 and editor of its publications, including the weekly *Dielli (The Sun)*. In 1919, he wrote a history of Albania, *Albania: The Master Key to the Near East*, which detailed Albanian origins as far back as the Illyrians.

Clive Day (1875-1951)
> Day was a college professor and writer of economic history. He was head of the Balkan Division in the American Commission to Negotiate Peace in Paris (1918-19), in which capacity he sat on the Greek Committee.

Prenk Bib Doda (Bibë Doda) (1858-1919)
> In 1876 Bib Doda inherited the hereditary title of *Kapidan* (captain) of Mirdita, a predominantly Catholic area in north-western Albania. As the largest Catholic tribe, the chieftain of the Mirdites was a figurehead for all Albanian Catholics. Having played an active role in the League of Prizrend (1878-81), he was exiled to Anatolia, only to return to Mirdita in 1908, after the Young Turk revolution. Although he never left Mirdita, he served as Vice-President in Ismail Kemal's provisional government (1913-14), and despite having some hope of acceding to the Albanian throne, he remained loyal to Wilhelm, whom he served as Minister of Public Works and for a short time as Foreign Minister. After World War One, he served as Deputy Prime Minister in the government of Turkhan Pasha (1918-19). Whilst serving as Deputy Prime Minister he was assassinated as part of a blood-feud.

Lieutenant-Colonel Charles Doughty-Wylie (1868-1915)
> Doughty-Wylie was British representative and chairman of the southern Albanian boundary commission. Before that he was Consul at Addis Ababa (1909-12), and Director of the British Red Cross in the Ottoman Empire during the Balkan Wars. After the commission he became a passionate advocate of the Albanian cause, although his reports seem to indicate that he took his role in the commission seriously. He died on 26 April 1915, the same day as the London Pact was signed, while leading a charge at Gallipoli, for which he was awarded the Victoria Cross.

Sir Eric Drummond (1876-1951)
> Drummond was private secretary to the British Foreign Secretary (1915-18) and then the first Secretary-General of the League of Nations (1919-33). He then served as British Ambassador in Rome (1933-39).

(Mary) Edith Durham (1863–1944)
> Durham was a traveller, writer and journalist who specialised in Balkan affairs and wrote a number of important works including *Twenty Years of Balkan Tangle* (1920), *High Albania* (1909), and *The Struggle for Scutari* (1914). Initially a supporter of Slav nationalism, her sympathies turned towards the Albanians following her first visit there in 1909. In 1918, Durham founded the Anglo-Albanian Society with Aubrey Herbert and became its Joint Honorary Secretary-Treasurer. Despite being unable to visit Albania after 1921, for health reasons, she continued to campaign on Albanian issues until her death. She is believed to have written over eight hundred letters on Albanian issues.

Pandeli Evangjeli (Vangjeli) (1859-1949)

Born in Koritza to an Orthodox family, Evangjeli spent most of his early years amongst the Albanian community in Bucharest. In 1907, he formed the Committee for the Freedom of Albania. He returned to Albania after 1914 and became Prefect for Koritza. In 1920 he took part in the delegation to the Peace Conference. He served as an Albanian parliamentary deputy (1921-25 and 1928-39) and a senator (1925-28), being Foreign Minister twice (1921 and 1922-24), and Prime Minister at the head of a short-lived liberal government in 1921. In 1925, he was made President of the Senate and Zogu's deputy. He served as Prime Minister again from 1930 to 1935, and as Parliamentary President during the last years of Zogu's reign.

Sir Harry Eyres KCMG (1856-1944)

Eyres served for the British Foreign Office in Constantinople, Beirut and Damascus. After his retirement in December 1914, he was employed in special service at Corfu and Janina, and in 1920 in Albania. In January 1921 he became British Consul without exequatus in Albania, residing at Durazzo. He then served as the Envoy Extraordinary and Minister Plenipotentiary in Albania (1922-26).

Lieutenant-General Giacinto Ferrero (1862-1922)

Ferrero was a Commander of the XVIII Army Corps of the Italian Army and Italian Commander in Albania (1917-19), having previously led an Italian expeditionary force to Durazzo (February 1916). As Commander of the Italian forces, Ferrero proclaimed the unity and independence of the whole of Albania, on 3 June 1917, at Argyrocastro.

Midhat Frashëri (1880-1949)

Midhat served as the Minister for Public Works (1912-13, 1914), Governor of Koritza (1914) and the Minister without Portfolio (1918-19).

Naim Frashëri (1846-1900)

The Albanian romantic poet who, along with his brothers Sami and Abdyl, was a prominent figure in the Albanian national renaissance (*Rilindja Kombëtare*). He came from a notable Bektashi family in the Permeti district, and served as an Ottoman official in Santa Quaranta, Berat and Janina. He wrote 22 major works (15 in Albanian, four in Turkish, two in Greek, and one in Persian) and translated the works of other writers. He was especially well known for his patriotic and lyrical poems, including the epic poem 'The History of Skanderbeg' (Bucharest, 1898), which retold a dramatised and embellished life of Skanderbeg.

Colonel Edward J. Granet (b.1858)

Granet was British delegate on the northern Albanian boundary commission (1913-14). He served (1911-15) as the British Military Attaché to the embassy in Rome, and the legation in Berne.

Captain Duncan Heaton-Armstrong (1886-1969)
>   An adventurous Irishman, who became Wilhelm of Wied's private
>   secretary in 1913, having taken part in a European-wide competition
>   for the position. In August 1914, he escorted Wilhelm's children back
>   to Neuwied and became the first British prisoner of war. He was
>   interred for the rest of the war. A book based on his memoirs of his
>   time in Albania was published as *The Six Month Kingdom: Albania
>   1914* in 2005.

Colonel Aubrey Herbert MP (1880-1923)
>   Herbert is believed to be the inspiration for the legendary John
>   Buchan character Greenmantle. He was half-brother of the fifth Earl
>   of Caernarvon, who would later fund the opening of Tutankhamen's
>   tomb, and served as Conservative MP for Somerset South (1911-
>   23). He was the founder and first president of both the Albanian
>   Committee (1912-14) and the Anglo-Albanian Society (1918-23)
>   and twice offered the Albanian throne. He died in 1923 aged only 43.
>   In 1929 his mother, Lady Carnarvon, funded the Herbert Library in
>   Tirana, which became the Albanian National Library, and donated
>   his extensive book collection (in excess of 10,000 volumes) to it. A
>   book, *Albania's Greatest Friend*, including selected correspondence,
>   papers and memoirs detailing Herbert's considerable support for the
>   Albanian national cause was published in 2011.

Count Guglielmo Imperiali (1858-1944)
>   Imperiali was Italian Ambassador in Constantinople from 1904 to
>   1910, and then in London from 1910 to 1920. In London, he played
>   a significant role in bringing Italy into the First World War and
>   negotiating the Pact of London (1915).

Hoxhë Kadriu (1878-1925) (Also known as Kadri Lutfulla Prishtina and Kadri
Hodj Effendi')
>   Having spent some years in prison for his 'political activities' in the
>   Ottoman Empire, Kadriu worked as a lawyer, professor of law and,
>   finally, as a banker. Following Albanian independence, he moved to
>   Scutari (1914), where he continued to work as a lawyer. In 1918, he
>   helped establish the Kosovo Committee and, after the Congress of
>   Lushnje, became Minister of Justice and then Deputy Speaker in the
>   Albanian parliament.

Ismail Kemal bey Vlora (1844-1919)
>   Ismail was an important character in the Albanian national movement
>   before World War One. Following an established career in Ottoman
>   politics, most notably being President of the Danube Commission
>   (1870-3) and serving as a parliamentary deputy for Berat (1908-12),
>   Ismail led the initiatives to gain international recognition of Albanian
>   claims in 1912. On 28 November 1912, at the national congress in
>   Valona, he proclaimed Albania independent. He became President
>   of the provisional government, which transferred its authority to

the international control commission in January 1914. He then left Albania, never to return.

Faik bey Konitza (Konica) (1876-1942)
An influential Albanian-American whose literary review *Albania*, became a focal point for Albanian writers living abroad, especially in the United States. Although he wrote little himself, he had a major impact on the development of Albanian culture and writing. He stressed the need for a more 'western' culture in Albania, and the need to create a unified literary language. It is believed that his version of written Tosk was adopted at the 1908 Monastir Congress. He co-founded Vatra in 1912 and served as an Albanian parliamentary deputy (1924-25) and the Albanian Minister in Washington DC (1926-39).

Mehmed (Mehmet) bey Konitza (1881-1946)
Mehmed was a member of the Ottoman Consular Service (1908-12) and then a member of the Albanian delegation to the St. James Conference (1912-13), and afterwards Albanian representative to Britain (1914 and again 1922-24). He was a member of the Durazzo delegation to the Paris Peace Conference, and was Foreign Minister in both the Durazzo and Tirana governments (1914, 1918-19 and 1920). During World War One, he was one of the Albanian nationalists most active in bringing Albanian issues to the notice of the great powers.

Léon Alphonse Thadée Krajewsky (b. 1863)
Krajewsky, of Polish descent, was persistently pro-Slav, including as the French representative on the international commission of control (1913-14), personal representative to Essad Pasha, and French technical expert on the Greek Committee in 1919.

Auguste (August) Ritter von Kral (1869-1953)
Kral entered the Austrian diplomatic service in 1894, serving in both the Ottoman Empire and Persia. In 1914, he became Austrian Consul at Scutari and representative on the international control commission in Albania, during which he was involved in much intrigue and rivalry with the Italian representatives. Following the Austrian occupation of Albania, he was appointed Austrian Civil Administrator (1916-18) and from April 1917 Chairman of the Administrative Council. After World War One he served in Hamburg, Sofia and Ankara.

Harry Harling Lamb, from 1919 Sir (1857-1948)
He served as Chief Dragoman at the British Embassy in Constantinople 1903-07 and Consul-General at Salonika (1907-13), when he was appointed British representative on the international control commission in Albania (1913-14). He worked at the Foreign Office from October 1914 until November 1915, when he was placed in charge of the British Adriatic Mission. In January 1920, he was appointed Chief Political Officer attached to the British High Commissioner in Constantinople, and soon became Assistant High Commissioner.

A. W. Allen Leeper (1887-1935)
Leeper entered the British Foreign Office in 1918 and was attached

to the South-eastern European section of the Political Intelligence Department (1918-20), where he helped draft policy on Albania. Amongst other accomplishments, he served as First Secretary to Vienna (1924-28), and Counsellor in the Foreign Office (1933).

Ahmet Mufid bey Libohova (Libhova) (1876-1927)

Libohova was a member of the Albanian cabinet nine times between 1912 and 1927, holding positions including Justice Minister (1914, 1924), Minister of the Interior (1912-13, 1919-20), Foreign Minister (1913, 1925) and Finance Minister (1925). He was Foreign Minister when he resigned to become the Albanian delegate on the international control commission. He was one of the representatives of the Durazzo government who agreed in 1919 to the unpopular decision that the government would be subordinate to a civil Italian Commissioner, that helped facilitate the Lushnje Congress.

Prince Karl Max Lichnowsky (1860-1922)

Lichnowsky was Political Division Counsellor in the Wilhelmstrasse responsible for appointments, but was forced into retirement after accusations of acting too independently of official policy. He was later recalled, and served as German Ambassador to London from 1912-14. During and after World War One, Lichnowsky received much criticism within Germany for not keeping Britain out of the conflict.

Giacomo de Martino III (1868-1957)

As Secretary-General in the Italian Foreign Ministry (1913-20), de Martino was influential in Albanian affairs. He served as personal Italian representative to Wilhelm of Wied in 1914. He led the Italian negotiators in the Greek Committee at the Paris Peace Conference, and in 1920 became Italian Ambassador to London. He later served as Italian Ambassador in Berlin (1920-21), London (1921-22), Tokyo (1922-25) and Washington DC (1925-33).

Count Albert von Mensdorff (1861-1945)

Mensdorff entered the Austro-Hungarian diplomatic service in 1886. In 1889 he was transferred to London, where from 1904 to 1914 he served intermittently as Ambassador. He made use of his personal friendship with the British sovereigns, and family relations in the British court, to develop friendly relationships between the British and Austrian governments. During World War One, he was involved in several unsuccessful initiatives to bring about peace.

Dr. Sidney Mezes (1863-1931)

Mezes was an American academic chosen by President Wilson to head the Inquiry. He had previously been President of the University of Texas (1908-14) and in 1917 was the President of the College of the City of New York (1914-27). During the Paris Peace Conference, he also served as the senior American delegate on the Co-ordinating Committee.

Sir Harold Nicolson (1886 -1968)

    The son of Arthur Nicolson, the British Permanent Under-Secretary of State for Foreign Affairs (1910-16), Harold initially followed in his father's footsteps and entered the diplomatic service in 1909. In 1918 he was attached to the British peace delegation in the South-eastern European section of the Political Intelligence Department, where he was one of the officials responsible for drafting British policy regarding Greece, including Albania, and he served as technical expert on the Greek Committee. He also served as Private Secretary to the Secretary-General of the League of Nations (1919-20), and in the Central Europe and Eastern Departments in the Foreign Office (1920-25). He later decided that diplomatic life was not for him. Having left the service, he wrote a number of informative and interesting books, including *Peacemaking 1919* (1933) and served as a National Labour MP (1935-45).

Bishop Fan (Theofan) S. Noli (1882-1965)

    Noli was an Albanian Orthodox bishop and politician from Adrianople. Whilst living in Boston, Massachusettes, he co-founded Vatra, becoming their representative to the Albanian parliament. In 1913 he lobbied the London conferences on behalf of the Albanians in the United States. He served as Albanian representative to the League of Nations, an Albanian parliamentary deputy (1921-24), Foreign Minsiter (1921-22) and briefly as Prime Minister and Regent of Albania in 1924. He was responsible for establishing the independent Orthodox Albanian Church (1923) and served as Bishop of Koritza (1923-24).

Nikola Pašic (Pasitch, Pachitch, Pašić) (1845-1926)

    Pašic was an influential Serbian, and later Yugoslav, politician whose career spanned almost forty years. He was Mayor of Belgrade twice, Prime Minister of Serbia five times (1891-92, 1904-05, 1906-08, 1909-11 and 1912-18) and Prime Minister of the Kingdom of the Serbs, Croats and Slovenes three times (1918, 1921-24 and 1924-26). He headed up the Yugoslav delegation to the Peace Conference (1919-20).

Colonel George Fraser Phillips (later Brigadier-General) (1863-1921)

    Phillips was the British governor of Scutari 1913-14 and head of the international squadron stationed there from April 1913 until September 1914, Military Attaché to Belgrade and Head of the British Military Mission to Albania and Montenegro (1918-20). His pronounced pro-Albanian sympathies, including becoming a member of the Anglo-Albanian Society in 1918, led to much criticism of him by members of the British Foreign Office and other governments.

Hasan bey Prishtina (1873-1933)

    Prishtina was a tribal chieftain from Kosovo, who initially supported the Young Turks and was elected parliamentary deputy for Prishtina to the Ottoman Parliament (1908-12), when along with all other Albanian delegates he lost his seat. Subsequently, he was a persistent proponent of the Albanian cause, especially Kosovo, including formulating the autonomy demands known as 'The Fourteen Points of Hasan Prishtina' (1912). He served as Minister of Education under Ismail Kemal, and as Minister for Posts and Telegraphs under Wilhelm, and later helped set up the Kosovo Committee. He became a member of the Albanian parliament for Dibra region (the town itself being part of Serbia), took part in a coup d'etat and served as Prime Minister for five days (7-12 December 1921). He continued to oppose Zogu and was assassinated in 1933.

Sir Rennell Rodd, from 1933 Baron Rennell (1858-1941)
Rodd was British Ambassador in Rome (1908-1919), having previously served in Paris, Berlin, Oslo and Stockholm. He was influential in getting the Italians to sign the Pact of London in 1915. He left the Diplomatic Service in 1919 but nonetheless served on a British mission to Egypt (1920) and as British Delegate to the League of Nations (1921-23). He later served as a Conservative MP in the British House of Commons (1928-32).

Avni Rystemi (Rustemi) (1895-1924)
Rystemi was a member of the Committee for the Defence of the Nation and, whilst a student in Paris, he murdered Essad Pasha. He served only six months imprisonment for his 'political crime' due to his acclaimed 'nationalist' intentions. He then returned to Albania as an associate of Zogu, but he soon became a vocal opponent of his former colleague.

Skanderbeg (Skenderbeg, Skenderbeu, İskender Bey) or Georgi Castrioti (Gjergj Kastrioti) (1405-68)
Skanderbeg was the medieval Albanian national hero, who was the effective ruler of 'Albania' in the successful revolt against the Ottoman Empire (1443-68). His efforts are often considered responsible for stopping the spread of Islam into western and central Europe. Although a Christian, he was known to all Albanians by his Muslim name of Skanderbeg. His family flag (a double black-headed eagle on a red background) became the Albanian national flag.

Sidney Sonnino (1847-1922)
Sonnino had a long and illustrious career in Italian politics. He was the Italian Prime Minister (1906 and 1909-10) and Foreign Minister (1914-19). His ambitious, yet oscillating, policy in Albania throughout the war and Peace Conference in Paris was instrumental in fostering the resurgence of Albanian nationalism, on the one hand, and opposition from other great power states to Italian designs on the territory, on the other.

Essad Pasha Toptani (1853-1920)
Essad was an unscrupulous but influential pasha who dominated much of central Albania from his base around Durazzo and Tirana.

He served as a parliamentary deputy for Durazzo in the Ottoman Parliament (1908-12), before embarking on a controversial career in Albanian affairs. This stemmed from his surrender to the Montenegrins (allegedly for a bribe) of the garrison he was controlling at Scutari (April 1913). In October 1913, he established the Senate for Central Albania and in 1914 became the Interior Minister under Prince Wilhelm. During World War One and the Paris Peace Conference he promulgated himself as the self-styled 'President of Albania in exile'. He was assassinated in Paris by Avni Rystemi.

Dr Mihal Tourtoulis (Turtullis, Turtulli) (1847-1935)
Tourtoulis had a long and extensive involvement in the Albanian national movement. In 1914, he was selected as Minister of Public Instruction and Health in Wilhelm of Wied's cabinet. He played an active role in the Durazzo and Tirana governments, represented both at the Paris Peace Conference and was selected as the Orthodox representative on the Albanian High Council of Regency. He was renowned for his anti-Italian views, and was one of the few Albanians never to accept the idea of an Italian mandate for Albania.

Ante Trumbić (1864-1938)
Trumbić was the Croatian national leader and a moderate reformer in the Austrian lower house. After the July Crisis, he fled to exile in Italy and tried unsuccessfully to build Allied support for South Slav unity. He established the so-called 'Yugoslav committee' in 1915, and worked from London to persuade Pašic of his scheme. He became Foreign Minister of the Kingdom of Serbs, Croats and Slovenes in 1918, and a representative to the Paris Peace Conference. He resigned from that post on 22 November 1920 having agreed the Rapallo Treaty, which settled the Yugoslav-Italian boundary. He thereafter worked to protect minority rights, especially Croat ones, in the new state.

Turkhan (Turhan) Pasha Përmeti (1846-1927)
Turkhan was Prime Minister in Wied's government (1914), and then Prime Minister and leader of the Durazzo government's delegation to the Peace Conference in Paris (1918-20). He does not seem to have been particularly nationalistic and was criticised for being pro-Italian. Turkhan had previously enjoyed an illustrious career in the Ottoman diplomatic corps, and was Ambassador to St. Petersburg (1908-13).

Vatra (literally trans. 'Hearth') (1912-present)
The Pan Albanian Federation of America that originally operated out of Boston, Massachusetts and now New York City. It was founded by Faik Konitza and Fan Noli, when following a meeting in December 1911 they succeeded in bringing together all the Albanian-American groups into one organisation. It continues to produce the Albanian newspaper *Dielli* (*The Sun*) to promote the Albanian national cause and other pro-Albanian purposes.

Eleftherios Venizelos (1864-1935)
Venizelos was a long serving, charismatic and astute Greek politician,

who served as Greek Prime Minister five times (1910-15, 1917-20, 1924, 1928-32 and 1933). His persuasive arguments and tactics were influential in the Albanians having difficulty in securing recognition from great power statesmen during the Paris Peace Conference for Greek claims in southern Albania.

Iljas bey Vrioni (1882-1932)

Vrioni served as Prime Minister and Foreign Minister (1920-21, 1924, and 1924-25), Foreign Minister (1927-29) and Minister in Paris (1929-32). In 1921, he was responsible for planning the significant Albanian appeal to the League of Nations for a settlement of Albanian boundaries and securing the removal of Yugoslav forces.

Wilhelm of Wied (Wilhelm zu Wied) (1876-1945)

Wilhelm was the German Lutheran prince who was chosen by the great powers to lead the short-lived Albanian kingdom (March-September 1914). He was the third son of the Prince of Neuwied, had previously been a captain in the German army and his aunt, who was the Queen of Romania, had pressed his candidature for the throne. In 1914, he decided to fight for Germany in World War One, despite being under no obligation to do so, as head of state of a neutral country. This decision was unpopular with many Albanians, and one of the reasons they resolved that he should not return as head of state.

Ahmet bey Zogu (King Zog, Zogou, Ahmed Zogolli) (1895-1961)

After the death of his father, Zogu became head of the Muslim Mati clan in 1911, when he was only 16. During World War One, he initially supported the Austrians and spent much time in Vienna, only returning to Albania in 1919. In 1920, he became Interior Minister in the Tirana government and played a key role in ridding Albania of its foreign occupiers. He was Prime Minister of Albania (1922-24) and President of Albania (1925-28). In 1928, following a coup d'etat, in which he proclaimed himself King Zog, he became Europe's first and only Muslim king. Although receiving support from Benito Mussolini throughout his career, Zogu was deposed on 7 April 1939, following the Italian invasion. He went into exile, first in Egypt, then Britain, then the United States and finally settled in France, where he eventually died.

Georgios Christakis Zographos (1863-1920)

Zographos had a controversial career in Greek politics, serving as Foreign Minister (1909 and again 1915-16). He also served as President of the Provisional Government of Autonomous Northern Epirus (1914-16).

Appendix A

*The Ottoman vilayets, including Kosovo, and the
newly independent state of Kosova*[769]

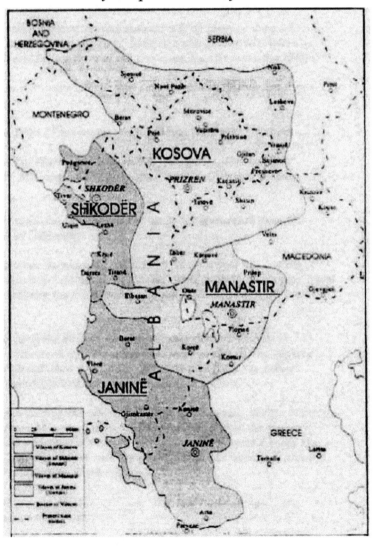

Appendix B

Austro-Italian and Russian proposals, Albanian claims and the agreed boundaries (1912-13)[770]

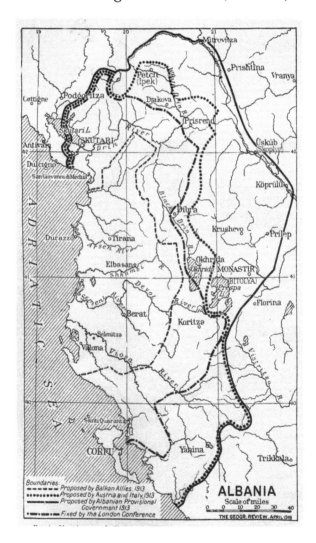

Appendix C

The Florence Protocol (17 Dec. 1913)[771]

Description of the frontier line:
The frontier starts from point C (on the Austrian map, hill 1738 north-east of MANDRA NIKOLICA) where the southern frontier of *kaza* KORITZA joins the summit of GRAMMOS. It goes towards the south following the summit of GRAMMOS as far as MAVRI PÉTRA, from there it passes the hills 2536 and 2019 and reaches GOLO. From there, after following the river alongside hill 1740, it passes between the villages of RADATI and KURSAKA, it goes towards the hill found to the north-east of KUKESI from where it goes downhill in order to reach the SARANDAPOROS.

It follows the river until it reaches its mouth in the VOJUSSA from where it continues to the top of mount TUMBA, passing between the villages of ZIPALIÇA and MESSARIA and over hills 956 and 2000.

From the top of mount TUMBA the frontier goes towards the west over hill 1621 passing to the north of ZIRMAZES.

From there it follows the river to the hilltop which is found to the north-east of the village of EPISKOPI (previously annexed according to the information on the map) from there it goes towards the south keeping to the ridge between RADATI, which is in Albania, and GAIDOHOR, which is in Greece. It falls into the ZRINOS valley, crosses the river and climbs the hill above KAKAVIA, a village which is in Albania. It follows this new river, leaving VALTISTA and KASTANIANI in Greece and KOSSOVIÇA in Albania and reaches MURGANA, hill 2124.

From there it reaches STUGARA, and then VERTOP and hill 750, leaving JANIARI and VERVA in Albania. It passes over hills 1014, 675 and 839 and goes towards the north-east, leaving KONISPOLI in Albania. It follows the summit of hills STILO, ORBA and finally reaches hill 254 before turning south and reaching PHTÉLIA bay.

Appendix D

The Northern Epirote revolt (1914) [772]

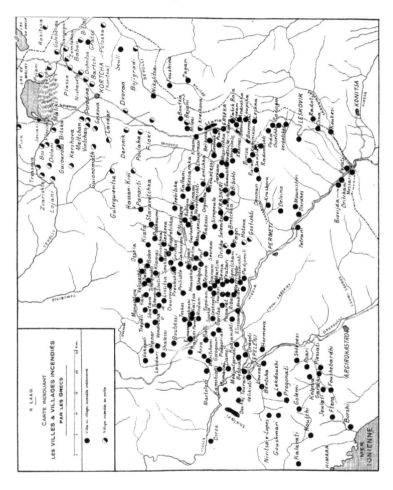

Appendix E

The Albanian speakers excluded (1912–26)[773]

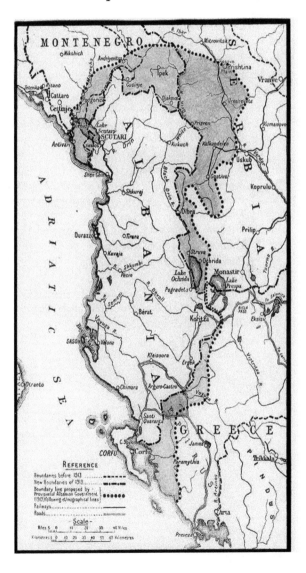

Abbreviations

DBFP	*Documents on British Foreign Policy 1919-1939*
DDF	*Documents Diplomatiques Français*
DDI	*I Documenti Diplomatici Italiani*
DMI	British Department of Military Intelligence
DOS	United States Department of State
EDW	*Entente Diplomacy and the World*
FRUS PPC	*Papers Relating to the Foreign Relations of the United States of America 1919: The Paris Peace Conference*
KA	*Krasnyi Arkhiv (Red Archive)*
FO	British Foreign Office
MOEI	*International Affairs in the period of imperialism: Documents from the Archive of the Tsar and Provisional Government 1878-1917*
NACP	National Archives at College Park, Maryland, USA
PID	Political Intelligence Department
PRO	Public Record Office, Kew, London
RG	Record Group
SAC	Procès-verbaux de la Commission Internationale pour la delimitation de la Frontière Méridionale Albanaise
TNA	The National Archives, Kew, London

Notes

1   For further details see N. Malcolm, *Kosovo: A Short History* (London, 1998), pp.xxii, xlix, 3-4.

Introduction

2   Thucydides, *History of the Peloponnesian War*, V, 17.

3   *The Times*, London, 27/3/2007 and 18/2/2008.

4   T.U. Raun, 'Nineteenth and early twentieth-century Estonian nationalism revisited', *Nations and Nationalism*, 9 (2003), pp.129-47, at pp.129-30.

5   J. Swire, *Albania, the Rise of a Kingdom* (London, 1929); E. P. Stickney, *Southern Albania or Northern Epirus in European International Affairs, 1912-1923* (Stanford, 1926): the latter only focusing on issues affecting the southern half of Albania.

6   O. Pearson, *Albania in the Twentieth Century*, 3 vols. (London, 2003), I, pp.23-184 *passim*.

7   H.N. Brailsford, *Macedonia, its Races and their Future* (London, 1906), p.280; T. Winnifrith, *Badlands-Borderlands: A History of Southern Albania/ Northern Epirus* (London, 2002), p.11; B. Kondis, *Greece and Albania, 1908-1914* (Thessaloniki, 1976), p.12.

8   K. Verdery, 'Introduction' to I. Banac and K. Verdery (eds.) *National Character and National Ideology in Interwar Eastern Europe* (New Haven, Connecticut, 1995), p.xiv.

9   F. Barth (ed.), *Ethnic Groups and Boundaries: the Social Organization of Cultural Difference* (Prospect Heights, Illinois, 1969), p.11.

10   E. Gellner, *Encounters with Nationalism* (Oxford, 1994); M. Glenny, *The Balkans 1804-1999: Nationalism, War and the Great Powers* (London, 1999); F.H. Hinsley, *Nationalism and the International System* (London, 1973), pp.139-72: Hinsley leaves it until his conclusion to compare the two directly.

11   E.C. Hobsbawm, *Nations and Nationalism since 1780: programme, myth and reality* (Cambridge, 1992), pp.165, 171; Raun, 'Estonian nationalism revisited', p.131.

12   M. Hroch, *Social Preconditions for National Revival in Europe* (New York, 2000), pp.22-3; See also M. Hroch, 'National Self-Determination from a Historical Perspective', *Canadian Slavonic Papers*, 37 (1995), pp.283-99.

13   See for example Z. Steiner, *The Lights that Failed: European International History, 1919-1933* (New York, 2005).

14   A.D. Smith, *Nationalism and Modernism: a critical survey of recent theories of nations and nationalism* (London, 1998), pp.42, 120, 122, 132-3; E.J.

Hobsbawm and D.J. Kertzer, 'Ethnicity and Nationalism in Europe Today', *Anthropology Today*, 8 (1992), pp.3-8, at p.3; B. Arnold, 'The Contested Past', *Anthropology Today*, 15 (1999), pp.1-4, at p.1; E.J. Hobsbawm, 'Introduction' in E.J. Hobsbawm and T. Ranger, *The Invention of Tradition* (Cambridge, 1990), p.1; A.D. Smith, *The Nation in History: Historiographical Debates about Ethnicity and Nationalism* (Hanover, New Hampshire, 2000), p.32; Hobsbawm, *Nations and Nationalism*, esp. chps. 4 and 6; B. Anderson, *Imagined Communities: Reflections on the origin and the spread of nationalism* (London, 1983), pp.11-2.

15   A.D. Smith, *The Nation in History: Historiographical Debates about Ethnicity and Nationalism* (Hanover, New Hampshire, 2000), p.37; A. Hastings, *The Construction of Nationhood: Ethnicity, Religion and Nationalism* (Cambridge, 1997), esp. pp.173-77, and on the South Slavs, pp.125-46.

16   Smith, *Nation in History*, pp.34-5; A.D. Smith *Myths and Memories of the Nation* (Oxford, 1999), pp.39-40.

17   E. Gellner, *Nations and Nationalism: New Perspectives on the Past* (Oxford, 1983), p.56.

18   Smith, *Modernism and Nationalism*, p.127.

19   A.D. Smith, *The Ethnic Origins of Nations* (Oxford, 1986), p.200; E. Kedourie, *Nationalism* (London, 1993), p.112; M. Rady, 'Encounters with Nationalism Review', *Slovo*, 8 (1995), pp.109-15, at p.110.

20   Smith, *Ethnic Origins*, p. 191; Smith, *Modernism and Nationalism*, p.137.

21   Hastings, *Construction of Nationhood*, pp.11, 185-206; Smith, *Nation in History*, pp.37-9.

22   See for example: A.B. Sula, *Albania's Struggle for Independence* (New York, 1967); S. Pollo, and A. Puto, (Wiseman, C. and Hole, G. (trans.)), *The History of Albania: From its Origins to the Present Day* (London, Boston and Henley, 1981); M. Çami, *Fundamental Aspects of the Albanian National and Democratic Movement in the Years 1913-1920: National Conference Dedicated to the 70ᵗʰ Anniversary of the Proclamation of Independence November 19, 1982* (Tirana, 1983).

23   N. Malcolm, 'Myths of Albanian National Identity: Some Key Elements, as Expressed in the Works of Albanian Writers in the Early Twentieth Century', in S. Schwander-Sievers and B.J. Fischer (eds.), *Albanian Identities: Myth and History* (London, 2002), pp. 70-90, at p.73; For a good study of Albanian ethnic origins see E.E. Jacques, *The Albanians: An Ethnic History from Prehistoric Times to the Present* (Jefferson, North Carolina, 1995).

24   See for example G.W. Gawrych, *The Crescent and the Eagle: Ottoman Rule, Islam and the Albanians, 1874-1913* (London and New York, 2006), p.21.

25   See for example G.W. Gawrych, 'Tolerant Dimensions of Cultural Pluralism in the Ottoman Empire: The Albanian Community, 1800-1912', *International Journal of Middle East Studies*, 15 (1983), pp.519-36; B. Fischer, 'Albanian highland tribal society and family structure in the process of twentieth-century transformation', *East European Quarterly*, 33 (1999), pp.281-301.

26   J.C. Hobhouse cited by Turkhan Pasha in *FRUS PPC*, IV, p.114.

27 Malcolm, *Kosovo*, pp.xxii, xlix, 3-4.
28 G. Duijzings, *Religion and Politics in the Identity of Kosovo* (London, 2000), pp.7-8, 27-8; Malcolm, *Kosovo*, p.xxix.
29 Smith, *Nations and Nationalism*, pp.25-6; Hastings, *Construction of Nationhood*, pp.165-6, 184-6.
30 For alternative interpretations see for example A. Doya, 'Confraternal religion: From liberation theology to political reversal', *History and Anthropology*, 14 (2003), pp.349-81; A. Doya, 'The Politics of Religion in the Reconstruction of Identities: The Albanian situation', *Critique of Anthropology*, 20 (2000), pp.421-38; and N. Clayer, 'Bektachisme et nationalisme albanais', *Revue des Études Islamiques*, 60 (1992), pp.271-300.
31 Smith, *Nations and Nationalism*, p.26; Tilly quoted in Smith, *Nation in History*, p.35.
32 L.L. Farrar Jr., 'Aggression versus Apathy: The Limits of Nationalism during the Balkan Wars, 1912-1913', *East European Quarterly*, 37 (2003), pp.257-80, at pp.259, 262; M. Todorova (ed.), *Balkan Identities: Nation and Memory* (London, 2000), p.291.
33 See for example M. Rendell, 'Defensive Realism and the Concert of Europe', *Review of International Studies*, 32 (2006), pp.523-40, at p.525.
34 P. Salmon, *Scandinavia and the great powers 1890-1940* (Cambridge, 1997), pp.xv, 8; D. Vital, *The Inequality of States: A Study of the Small Power in International Relations* (Oxford, 1967), pp.7-9; D. Vital, *The Survival of Small States: Studies in Small Power/Great* Power Conflict (London, 1971), pp.2-10
35 See for example: R. MacGinty, 'War Cause and Peace Aim? Small States and the First World War', *European History Quarterly*, 27 (1997), pp.41-56, at p.41; and P. Schroeder, 'Historical Reality vs. Neo-Realist Theory', *International Security*, 19 (1994), pp.108-48, esp. pp.115-6, 129-31, 147-8.
36 M. Handel, *Weak States in the International System* (London, 1981), p.257; Salmon, *Scandinavia*, p.4.
37 Handel, *Weak States*, pp.257-8; R.L. Rothstein, *Alliances and the Small States* (New York, 1968), pp.194-5; Salmon, *Scandinavia*, p.14; Vital, *Inequality of States*, pp.183-4.
38 For further details see: A. Baker Fox, *The Power of Small States: Diplomacy in World War II* (London, 1959), pp.183-5; and Vital, *Survival of Small States*, p.129.
39 Vital, *Inequality of States*, pp.3-4; Salmon, *Scandinavia*, pp.12-4; Handel, *Weak States*, p.3.
40 Vital, *Inequality of States*, p.5; Salmon, *Scandinavia*, p.2.
41 Holtsmark cited in Salmon, *Scandinavia*, pp.15-6; Vital, *Survival of Small States*, pp.127-8.
42 Rothstein, *Alliances and Small States*, pp.191-212 *passim*; Salmon, *Scandinavia*, p.15.
43 See for example: P. Schroeder, 'Historical Reality', pp.108-48; G. Roberts, 'History, theory and the narrative turn in IR', *Review of International Studies*, 32 (2006), pp. 703-14; and J. Levy, 'The Theoretical Foundations of Paul W. Schroeder's International System', *International History Review*, 16

(1994), pp.715-44, at pp. 715, 742-3.

Chapter 1

44   *BD*, IX.i, nos.614, 659.
45   Brailsford, *Macedonia*, p.273.
46   *FRUS PPC*, IV, pp.111-16; S. Skendi, 'Albanian political thought and revolutionary activity, 1881-1912' *Südost-Forschungen*, 13 (1954), pp.159-99, at pp.159-61; S. Skendi, *The Albanian National Awakening, 1878-1912* (Princeton, New Jersey, 1967), pp.31-110 *passim*; On the Congress of Berlin, see in general W.N. Medlicott, *The Congress of Berlin and After: a diplomatic history of the Near East settlement, 1878-1880* (London, 1938); on the ethnographic considerations see particularly W.L. Langer, *European Alliances and Alignments, 1871-1890* (2nd edn., New York, 1960), pp.59-166 *passim*.
47   Brailsford, *Macedonia*, p.229.
48   I. Blumi, 'Contesting the edges of the Ottoman Empire: Rethinking Ethnic and Sectarian boundaries in the Malësore, 1878-1912', *Middle East Studies*, 35 (2003), pp.237-56; Gawrych, *Crescent and Eagle*, esp. pp.22-3.
49   Skendi, *Albanian National Awakening*, pp.300-405.
50   Smith, *Ethnic Origins*, p.199.
51   G. Maksutovici, 'L'Albanie' in V. Moisuc and I. Calafeteanu (eds.), *Assertion of Unitary, Independent National States in Central and Southeast Europe (1821-1923)* (Bucharest, 1980), pp.170-89, at pp.170-1.
52   I. Blumi, 'The Role of Education in the Formation of Albanian Identity and Myths', in Schwander-Sievers and Fischer, *Albanian Identities*, pp.49-59, at p.52.
53   Anderson, *Imagined Communities*, p.66.
54   Blumi, 'Role of Education', pp.51-2; T. Hocevar, 'The Albanian Economy, 1912-1944', *Journal of European Economic History*, 16 (1987), pp.561-8, at p.565.
55   D. Heaton-Armstrong, *The Six Month Kingdom: Albania 1914* (London, 2005), p.27.
56   I. Blumi, 'Thwarting the Ottoman Empire: Smuggling Through the Empire's New Frontiers in Yemen and Albania, 1878-1920', *International Journal of Turkish Studies*, 9 (2003), pp.251-70.
57   *BD*, IX.i, nos.181, 498, 517, 513, 504, 500, 524; Lamb to Lowther, 28/12/1911, TNA:PRO, FO421/279, no.38; Skendi, *Albanian National Awakening*, pp.411-52; Gawrych, *Crescent and Eagle*, pp.140-69.
58   Skendi, *Albanian National Awakening*, pp.430-6; E.C. Helmreich, *The Diplomacy of the Balkan Wars 1912-1913* (Cambridge, Massachusetts, 1938), p.45.
59   Lowther to Grey, 29/4/1912, FO421/281, no.26; Lowther to Grey, 27/5/1912, FO421/281, no.129; R.J. Crampton, *The Hollow Detente: Anglo-German Relations in the Balkans 1911-1914* (London, 1979), p.50; Skendi, *Albanian National Awakening*, pp.438-44.
60   *BD*, IX.i, no.591; State University of Tirana, *Historia e Shqipërisë II: 1909-*

1919 (*The History of Albania II: 1909-1919*) (Tirana, 1965), pp.43-5.
61 Skendi, *Albanian National Awakening*, pp.433-4.
62 Marling to Grey, 27/7/1912, FO421/282, no.173; Marling to Grey, 8/8/1912, FO421/282, no.203; Skendi, *Albanian National Awakening*, pp.434-5; Gawrych, *Crescent and Eagle*, pp.194-5, 211.
63 *BD*, IX.i, nos.613, 646; Skendi, *Albanian National Awakening*, p.437.
64 Ibid.
65 See for example M. Konitza, *The Albanian Question* (London, 1918), FO371/3570/4540.
66 *BD*, IX.i, no.658.
67 See treaties in I.E. Gueshov, *The Balkan League* (London, 1915), pp.19, 112, 115-6.
68 See for example: Helmreich, *Diplomacy*; E.C. Thaden, *Russia and the Balkan Alliance of 1912* (University Park, Pennsylvania, 1965); R.C. Hall, *The Balkan Wars 1912-1913: Prelude to the First World War* (London, 2000).
69 *KA*, VIII, no.1; *BD*, IX.i, nos.614, 643; De Salis to Grey, 27/12/1911, FO421/279, no.35; O'Beirne to Grey, 27/6/1912, FO421/282, no.9.
70 *KA*, VIII, no.3; *BD*, IX.i, nos.614, 659.
71 *MOEI*, Series 2, XX.i, nos.456-457; *MOEI*, Series 2, XX.ii, no.502; F.R. Bridge, (ed.), *Austro-Hungarian Documents Relating to the Macedonian Struggle, 1896-1912* (Thessaloniki, 1976), no.450 [trans A. Guy].
72 *EDW*, no.421.
73 Farrar, 'Aggression versus Apathy', pp.257-80, esp. pp.257, 266; G. Young, *Nationalism and War in the Near East* (Oxford, 1915), p.151.
74 Ed. Note, *EDW*, p.226 and no.415; *BD*, IX.i, no. 142.
75 King Peter quoted in L. Freundlich, 'Albania's Golgotha: Indictment of the Exterminators of the Albanian People' (Vienna, 1913), in R. Elsie (ed.) Kosovo in the Heart of the Powder Keg (Boulder, 1997), pp.332-60, at p. 333.
76 For further details see B. Kondis, 'The Role of the Albanian Factor upon Greek-Bulgarian Understanding of 1912', *Balkan Studies*, 25 (1984), pp.377-87.
77 *BD*, IX.ii, pp. 1007, 1018; *BD*, IX.i, no.755; Helmreich, *Diplomacy*, p.45.
78 For example see *KA*, XV, no.1; *BD*, IX.ii, pp.1015-18; *EDW*, nos.400, 405; Popov quoted in L. S. Rubinchek (compiled, translated and annotated), *A Digest of the Krasnyi Arkhiv: A Historical Journal of the Central Archive Department of the U.S.S.R*, Vols. 1-30 (Cleveland, 1947), p.153; Thaden, *Russia and the Balkan Alliance*, p.101; Helmreich, *Diplomacy*, pp.76-7.
79 *KA*, XV, no.12; *BD*, IX.ii, p.1018; M.E. Durham, *Twenty Years of the Balkan Tangle* (London, 1920), p.221; M.B. Petrovich, *A History of Modern Serbia, 1804-1918*, 2 vols. (New York and London, 1976), II, p.596; Thaden, *Russia and the Balkan Alliance*, pp.106-7.
80 *KA*, XV, no.12; *EDW*, no. 531; E.C. Helmreich, 'Montenegro and the Foundations of the Balkan League', *Slavonic and Eastern European Review*, 15 (1937), pp.426-34; Helmreich, *Diplomacy*, pp.85, 89.
81 Gueshov, *Balkan League*, pp.9; Kondis, 'Role of the Albanian Factor', pp.377-87.

82 *BD*, IX.ii, pp.1015-18.

83 *BD*, IX.ii, no.70.

84 *Historia e Shqipërisë*, II, p.352.

85 Brailsford, *Macedonia*, p.279; Swire, *Albania*, p.135, Skendi, *Albanian National Awakening*, pp.451-2; *Historia e Shqipërisë*, II, pp.353-4.

86 Lamb to Lowther, 28/12/1911, FO421/279, no.38; D. Mikich, 'The Albanians and Serbia during the Balkan Wars' in B. Kiraly and D. Djurdjevich (eds.), *East Central European Society and the Balkan Wars* (Boulder, 1987), pp.165-96; Helmreich, *Diplomacy*, p.45; Swire, *Albania*, pp.128, 133.

87 Durham, *Balkan Tangle*, pp.244-5; Skendi, *Albanian National Awakening*, p.452; *Historia e Shqipërisë*, II, p.350; Kondis, *Greece and Albania*, p.84.

88 A.F. Pribram, *The Secret Treaties of Austria-Hungary*, 2 vols. (Cambridge, Mass., 1920-1), I, p.167; B. Jelavich and C. Jelavich, *The Establishment of the Balkan National States 1804-1920* (Seattle and London, 1977), pp.218-9.

89 *BD*, IX.ii, no.165.

90 *Historia e Shqipërisë*, II, p.357; Kondis, *Greece and Albania*, p.53.

91 P. Milo, '*Albania and the Balkan Entente*', Association International d'études du Sud-Est Européen Bulletin, 30 (2001), pp.39-66, esp. pp.41-2.

92 *BD*, IX.ii, no.173; S. Story (ed.), *The Memoirs of Ismail Kemal Bey Vlora and his Work for the Independence of Albania* (London, 1920), p.372; Durham, *Balkan Tangle*, p.231.

93 *Historia e Shqipërisë*, II, p.360; Kondis, *Greece and Albania*, p.91; Story, *Memoirs of Ismail*, p.372; Durham, *Balkan Tangle*, p.231.

94 Swire, *Albania*, p.134; Crampton, *Hollow Détente*, pp.60-2.

95 *BD*, IX.ii, no.165; *KA*, XVI, no.36; Also at *EDW*, no.438.

96 Ed Note, *BD*, IX.i, p.618.

97 *DDF*, IV, no.170; Lady E. Grogan, *The Life of J. D. Bourchier* (London, 1926), pp.136, 209-17; Helmreich, *Diplomacy*, p.79; Durham, *Balkan Tangle*, pp.222-3; Thaden, *Russia and Balkan Alliance*, p.107; Schroeder, 'Historical Reality', pp.118-24.

98 *BD*, IX.i, nos.569, 572, 611; *KA*, VIII, no.9: *EDW*, no.371; L.S. Stavrianos, 'The Balkan Committee', *Queen's Quarterly*, 31 (1941), pp.258-67, at p.262.

99 *KA*, IX, no.45; S.B. Fay, *The Origins of the World War, Before Sarajevo: Underlying Causes of the War* 3 vols. (New York, 1929), I, p.430.

100 See for example *KA*, VIII, no.18; Ed. Note, *EDW*, p.23; S. Sazonov (trans N.A. Duddington), *Fateful Years, 1909-1916: Reminiscences of Sergei Sazonov Russian Minister for Foreign Affairs* (New York, 1928), p.80; Durham, *Balkan Tangle*, p.225.

101 See for example *KA*, XVI, no.45; Helmreich, *Diplomacy*, pp.163-4.

102 *BD*, IX.i, no.737; Ed. Note, *EDW*, no.404.

103 Ed Note, *BD*, IX.ii, p.183.

104 *BD*, IX.ii, no.173.

105 *BD*, IX.ii, nos. 583, 408, 749; Carnegie Endowment for International Peace, *Report of the International Commission to Inquire into the Causes and Conduct of the Balkan Wars* (Washington D.C., republ. 1993, of original of 1914),

p.418; M.B. Petrovich, *A History of Modern Serbia, 1804-1918*, 2 vols. (New York and London, 1976), II, p.603.

106 Swire, *Albania*, p.126.

107 Cartwright to Grey, 26/6/1912, FO421/281, no.241.

Chapter 2

108 *BD*, IX.ii, no.1226.

109 See for example H. Wilkinson, *Maps and Politics: A Review of the Ethnographic Cartography of Macedonia* (Liverpool, 1951), pp.316-7.

110 Barth, *Ethnic Groups and Boundaries*; K. Verdery, 'Ethnicity, Nationalism and State-making', in H. Vermeulen and C. Glovers (eds.), *The Anthropology of Ethnicity: Beyond 'Ethnic groups and Boundaries'* (Amsterdam, 1994).

111 A. Sharp, 'The genie that would not go back in the bottle: National self-determination and the legacy of the First World War and the Peace Settlement', in S. Dunn and G. Fraser (eds.), *Europe and Ethnicity: the First World War and contemporary ethnic conflict* (London, 1996), pp.10-29, at p.12.

112 Sharp, 'Genie', p. 13; A. Sharp, 'Britain and the Minorities at the Paris Peace Conference', in A.C. Hepburn (ed.), *Minorities in History* (London, 1978), pp.170-88, at p. 178.

113 G. Schöpflin, *Nations, Identity, Power: the new politics of Europe* (London, 2000), pp.121-2, 254; Barth, *Ethnic Groups*, p.11.

114 *EDW*, nos.504, 507; *BD*, IX.ii, no.165; R.J. Crampton, *The Hollow Détente: Anglo-German Relations in the Balkans, 1911-1914* (London, 1979), pp.67-76; R.J. Crampton, 'The Balkans, 1909-1914', in F.H. Hinsley (ed.), *British Foreign Policy under Sir Edward Grey* (Cambridge, 1977), pp.256-70, at p.261.

115 Brailsford, *Macedonia*, p.282.

116 *Albania*, Foreign Office Handbook, Historical Section No.17 (London, 1920), FO373/2/1, p.105.

117 Jelavich, *Establishment of Balkan National States*, p.235; A.F. Pribram, *Austrian Foreign Policy*, 1908-1918 (London, 1923), pp.38-9; Z. Zeman, *A Diplomatic History of the First World War* (London, 1971), p.14.

118 A.F. Pribram (trans. F.D. Morrow), *Austria-Hungary and Great Britain 1908-1914* (London, 1951), p.164; A.F. Pribram, *Austrian Foreign Policy, 1908-1918* (London, 1923), pp.18, 46-7.

119 Crampton, *Hollow Détente*, p.76.

120 *Albania*, FO Handbook, FO373/2/1, pp.91, 93-94, 105-6; Brailsford, *Macedonia*, p.283; J. Pettifer, *Albania and Kosovo* (London, 2001), p.106.

121 Crampton, *Hollow Détente*, p.76.

122 Brailsford, *Macedonia*, pp.282-4.

123 Author of maxim probably Count Constantino Nigra. See A.F. Pribram, *Secret Treaties*, II, p.136.

124 Ibid, I, pp.249, 257.

125 Rodd to Grey, 9/11/1912, FO371/1513/47771; R.J.B. Bosworth, *Italy, the Least of the Great Powers: Italian Foreign Policy before the First World War*

(Cambridge, 1979), p.253; Pribram, *Secret Treaties*, II, p.178.

126 Goschen to Grey, 9/11/1912, FO371/1513/47772; Pribram, *Secret Treaties*, I, pp.158, 178.

127 K.M. Wilson, *Empire and Continent: Studies in British Foreign Policy from the 1880s to the First World War* (London, 1987), p. 147; C.M. Lichnowsky, *My Mission to London* (London, 1918), pp.5-7: Lichnowsky later wrote that German policy-makers should have insisted on a fairer Albanian settlement and not been so prepared to back Austria-Hungary.

128 *KA*, VIII, no.44.

129 *EDW*, no.500; Sazonov, *Fateful Years*, p.71.

130 Pribram, *Austrian Foreign Policy*, p.42.

131 Grey, *Twenty-five Years*, I, p.274.

132 *KA*, X, no.51.

133 Ed. Note, *EDW*, p.214; Grey, *Twenty-five Years*, I, pp.267, 274.

134 *BD*, X.i, no.100; Grey, *Twenty-five Years*, I, pp.272-3.

135 Wilson, *Empire and Continent*, pp.145-7.

136 Sazonov, *Fateful Years*, p.62.

137 Grey, *Twenty-five Years*, I, pp.272-3.

138 *BD*, IX.ii, no.387; Grey, *Twenty-five Years*, I, pp.271-2.

139 Crampton, *Hollow Détente*, p.75.

140 *EDW*, no.473; Pipinelis, *Europe and Albanian Question*, p.15.

141 *EDW*, no.488; *DDF*, IV, no.586; Sazonov, *Fateful Years*, p.74; Crampton, *Hollow Détente*, p.77.

142 *BD*, IX.ii, nos.391, 1091.

143 Grey to Goschen, 21/12/1912, Grey MSS, FO800/62; Pribram, *Austria-Hungary and Britain*, pp.169-70.

144 *BD*, IX.ii, no.391.

145 Pribram, *Austria-Hungary and Britain*, p.182.

146 *BD*, IX.ii, no.391.

147 *BD*, IX.ii, no.403; *DDF*, IV, no.597.

148 *EDW*, no.510.

149 *BD*, IX.ii, no.428; Pribram, *Austria-Hungary and Great Britain*, p.178.

150 *BD*, IX.ii, no.538.

151 Pribram, *Austria-Hungary and Great Britain*, p.184.

152 *BD*, IX.ii, nos.543, 613, 663; Grey, *Twenty-five years*, I, p.268; Pribram, *Austria-Hungary and Great Britain*, pp.184-5; Crampton, *Hollow Détente*, p.85.

153 Duijzings, *Religion and Politics*, pp.13-9.

154 Crampton, *Hollow Détente*, p.84.

155 Sazonov, *Fateful Years*, p.74; Crampton, *Hollow Détente*, p.88.

156 Pribram, *Austria-Hungary and Great Britain*, pp.173-9.

157 Crampton, *Hollow Détente*, p.115.

158 *BD*, X.i, no.6; Malcolm, *Kosovo*, p.257; Durham, *Balkan Tangle*, p.249.

159 *BD*, X.i, no.45.

160 *BD*, X.i, no.64; B.D. Destani (ed.), *Albania and Kosovo: Political and Ethnic Boundaries 1867-1946*, 2 vols. (London, 1999), I, no.77.

161 Greek documents cited in Stickney, *Southern Albania*, p.1.

162 Crampton, *Hollow Détente*, pp.125-6.
163 War Staff memo., 15/4/1913, FO371/1801/17496.
164 Wilkinson, *Maps and Politics*, pp.238-9.
165 *BD*, IX.ii, nos.1036, 1038, 1027; Stickney, *Southern Albania*, pp.35-6; Wilkinson, *Maps and Politics*, pp.238-9.
166 Pribram, *Austria-Hungary and Great Britain*, p.198.
167 *BD*, IX.ii, no.1027; Stickney, *Southern Albania*, pp.35-6.
168 Buchanan to Grey, 21/6/1913, FO371/1801/28493; Grey to Buchanan, 3/7/1913, FO371/1801/31232; Crampton, *Hollow Détente*, pp.125-6.
169 *BD*, IX.ii, no.1104.
170 Grey to Cartwright, 8/8/1913, FO371/1802/37169.
171 Elliot to Grey, 8/9/1913 and Grey minute, 9/9/1913, FO371/1802/41432.
172 *BD*, IX.ii, no.1226.
173 Attachment in Doughty-Wylie to Grey, 5/10/1913, FO421/287/46428.
174 Doughty-Wylie to Grey, 6/10/1913, FO371/1803/45565; Granet to Grey, 23/9/1913, FO371/1822/43551; Crowe minute, 24/9/1913, FO371/1822/43551: 'It seems to me extraordinary that the British delegate on the frontier commission should have neither description nor map of the frontier laid down.'
175 Crowe minute, 6/10/1913, FO371/1822/45864.
176 Granet to Grey, 23/12/1913, FO371/1823/57915.
177 Granet to Grey, 1/10/1913, FO881/10492, no.4.
178 Grey to Granet, 7/11/1913, FO421/287/50160; Granet to Grey, 23/10/1913, FO371/1823/49925; *Albania and Kosovo*, I, no.80.
179 Granet to Grey, 4/12/1913, FO371/1823/54900; O'Beirne to Grey, 8/12/1913, FO371/1823/55409.
180 Attachment in Granet to Grey, 23/12/1913, FO421/287/57994; *Albania and Kosovo*, I, no.80; Malcolm, *Kosovo*, pp.256-7.
181 Granet to Grey, 12/12/1913, FO371/1823/56104.
182 *Albania and Kosovo*, I, no.90.
183 Enclosure in Granet to Grey, 2/5/1914, FO421/293, no.78; Granet to Grey, 6/6/1914, FO421/293, no.166; Granet to Grey, 10/6/1914, FO421/293, no.183; H.M.V. Temperley, *A History of the Peace Conference of Paris* 6 vols. (London, 1921), IV, pp.337-9.
184 Crowe to Granet, 2/6/1914, FO421/293, no.149.
185 Doughty-Wylie to Grey, 26/10/1913, FO421/287, no.193; Doughty-Wylie to Grey, 30/10/1913, FO421/287, no.202; Doughty-Wylie to Grey, 26/10/1913, FO421/287, no.162; Kondis, *Greece and Albania*, p.118.
186 Swire, Albania, pp.170-1; Pribram, Austria-Hungary and Great Britain, p.209.
187 *BD*, X.i, no.75; Doughty-Wylie to Grey, 26/10/1913, FO421/287 no.202; Doughty-Wylie to Grey, 1/11/1913, FO421/287, no.245; Grey to Doughty-Wylie, 6/11/1913, FO421/287, no.242.
188 Ed. Note, *BD*, X.i, p.62; Stickney, *Southern Albania*, pp.36-7.
189 A. Nicolson to O'Beirne, 4/11/1913, A. Nicolson MSS, FO800/371; *BD*, X.i, nos.72, 73, 77; O'Beirne to Grey, 4/11/1913, FO421/287 no.210; Grey to Dering, 3/11/1913, FO421/287, no.222; Grey to Dering, 4/11/1913,

FO421/287, no.229.

190 'Procès-verbaux de la Commission Internationale pour la delimitation de la Frontière Méridionale Albanaise' [hereafter cited as SAC minutes], 13/11/1913, FO93/1/36; Also at FO881/10355X, pp.49-50.

191 *DDF*, VIII, no.497.

192 SAC Minutes, 5/12/1913, FO93/1/36.

193 SAC Minutes, 10/12/1913, FO93/1/36.

194 *BD*, X.i, no. 84.

195 It was clear by this point that Greece would not gain northern Epirus but Grey wanted to keep Venizelos in power.

196 A. Nicolson to Grey, 2/10/1913, Grey MSS, FO800/94; *BD*, X.i, nos.90, 91 and IX.ii, no.1202.

197 *BD*, X.i, no.103; Swire, *Albania*, p.184; Stickney, *Southern Albania*, pp.38-9; Grey to Bertie, 26/11/1913, FO421/287, no.373.

198 Erskine to Grey, 23/6/1914, FO421/293, no.239; Erskine to Grey, 25/6/1914, FO421/293, no.263.

199 Carnegie Endowment, *Causes and Conduct*, p.418.

200 Grey quoted in G.M. Trevelyan, *Grey of Fallodon: Being the Life of Sir Edward Grey Afterwards Viscount Grey of Fallodon* (London, 1937), p.233; Grey, *Twenty-five Years*, I, p.271.

201 Grey, *Twenty-five Years*, I, p.271.

202 Ibid, pp.273, 276.

203 Vansittart minute, 5/12/1913, FO371/1823/54900.

Chapter 3

204 Story, *Memoirs of Ismail*, p.372; Swire, *Albania*, p.137.

205 Jacques, *Albanians*, pp.343-44; Swire, *Albania*, pp.180-1.

206 Lamb to Grey, 22/1/1913, FO421/287, no.375; Swire, *Albania*, p.181.

207 Koti cited in Jacques, *Albanians*, p.344.

208 Lamb to Grey, 30/12/1913, FO421/292, no.7.

209 Lamb to Grey, 22/11/1913, FO421/287, no.375; Swire, *Albania*, p.181.

210 Lamb to Grey, 30/12/1913, FO421/292, no.7.

211 Swire, *Albania*, pp.179-80.

212 *BD*, IX.ii, no.1091.

213 Ibid, no.1186.

214 Ibid, no.1226.

215 Lamb to Grey, 22/10/1913, FO421/287, no.158.

216 Lamb to Grey, 16/10/1913, FO421/287, no.135.

217 Lamb to Grey, 21/10/1913, FO421/287, no.157; O'Beirne to Grey, 26/10/1913, FO421/287, no.163; Lamb to Grey, 18/10/1913, FO421/287, no.142; Lamb to Grey, 30/10/1913, FO421/287, no.184; Lamb to Grey, 27/10/1913, FO421/287, no.164.

218 Lamb to Grey, 15/10/1913, FO421/287, no.111; Lamb to Grey, 22/10/1913, FO421/287, no.158; Lamb to Grey, 14/10/1913, FO421/287, no.72; Goschen to Grey, 20/10/1913, FO421/287, no.123; Lamb to Grey, 30/10/1913, FO421/287, no.214; Story, *Memoirs of Ismail*, p.378.

219 See for example: Lamb to Grey, 22/10/1913, FO421/287, no.158; Doughty-Wylie, 23/10/1913, FO421/287, no.146.

220 Herbert to Grey, 18/9/1913, Grey MSS, FO800/108.

221 Herbert to Grey, 31/5/1913, Grey MSS, FO800/108; Heaton-Armstrong, *Six Month Kingdom*, p. 20: Heaton-Armstrong reiterated this view when he noted the good impression that the 'height', 'soldierly bearing' and 'blonde' hair of Prince Wilhelm had following his arrival.

222 *BD*, X.i, no.71.

223 *BD*, IX.ii, no.1113.

224 Swire, *Albania*, pp.182-3; Durham, *Balkan Tangle*, p.257.

225 Russell to Grey, 7/11/1913, FO881/10492, no.273.

226 *BD*, X.i, no.76.

227 For the Dutch experience see G.T.A. Goslinga, *The Dutch in Albania* (Rome, 1972).

228 Durham, *Balkan Tangle*, p.259.

229 Enclosure 2, Wilhelm to Jagow, 31/12/1913, in Goschen to Grey, 3/1/1914, FO421/292/480; Lamb to Grey, 19/11/1913, FO421/287, no.374.

230 *BD*, X.i, no.95.

231 Lamb to Grey, 2/1/1914, FO421/292, no.24; Kondis, *Greece and Albania*, p.121.

232 Lamb to Grey, 19/1/1914, FO371/1890/2437; Lamb to Grey, 10/1/1914, FO421/292, no.57.

233 Russell minute, 1/1/1914, FO371/1890/1974

234 Lamb to Grey, 12/1/1914, FO371/1890/1446; *BD*, X.i, no.111; Swire, *Albania*, p.186.

235 Lamb to Grey, 31/1/1914, and Essad Pasha, Lamb and Nadolny memo., 13/1/1914, FO421/292, no.137.

236 Goschen to Grey, 8/1/1914, FO421/292, no.25; Goschen to Grey, 10/1/1914, FO421/292, no.40.

237 B.D. Destani (ed.), *Faik Konitza: Selected Correspondence 1896-1942* (London, 2000), no.29.

238 Lamb to Grey, 20/12/1913, FO421/287, no.515.

239 Swire, *Albania*, p.198.

240 Story, *Memoirs of Ismail*, pp.385-6; Durham, *Balkan Tangle*, p.261; Swire, *Albania*, p.201.

241 Lamb to Grey, 1/1/914, FO421/292, no.39; Lamb to Grey, 17/3/1914, FO421/292, no.225; Swire, *Albania*, pp.200-1; Durham, *Balkan Tangle*, p.261; D. Heaton-Armstrong (G. Belfield and B. Destani (eds.)), *The Six Month Kingdom: Albania 1914* (London, 2005), pp.26-7; D. Bataković, 'Српска влада и Есад-паша Топтани' ('Serbian government and Essad-Pasha Toptani'), in A. Mitrović (ed.), *Срби и Албанци у XX веку* (*Serbs and Albanians in the 20ᵗʰ Century*) (Belgrade, 1991), pp.25-78, at pp.37, 59: Ismail Kemal's proclamation of Albanian independence was written in Turkish because the nationalist leaders present were not sufficiently literate in Albanian written in the Latin script adopted in 1908.

242 Durham, *Balkan Tangle*, p.265.

243 *BD*, X.i, no. 141.

244 Ibid, no. 132.
245 Elliot to Grey, 5/3/1914, FO421/292, no.218; *BD*, X.i, no.119.
246 *BD*, X.i, no.119; Kondis, *Greece and Albania*, pp.130-2.
247 Elliot to Grey, 23/5/1914, FO421/292, no.228, Elliot to Grey, 8/3/1914, FO421/292, no.213; Grey to de Bunsen, 5/3/1914, FO421/292, no.208; Sazonov to Benckendorff, 4/3/1914 in Grey to Buchanan, 6/3/1914, FO421/292, no.212; Kondis, *Greece and Albania*, pp.127-30.
248 Appendix 1 'The Corfu Protocol', FO608/37/92/1/1/4392; Lamb to Grey, 1/5/1914, FO421/293, no.59, Lamb to Grey, 2/5/1914, FO421/293, no.60; Lamb to Grey, 6/4/1914, FO421/293, no.12; Elliot to Grey, 30/3/1914, FO421/293, no.9; Elliot to Grey, 30/3/1914, FO421/293, no.10; Lamb to Grey, 9/4/1914, FO421/293, no.19; Lamb to Grey, 24/4/1914, FO421/293, no.50; Lamb to Grey, 10/4/1914, FO421/293, no.20; Lamb to Grey, 5/5/1914, FO421/293, no.71; Lamb to Grey, 5/5/1914, FO421/293, no.72; Swire, *Albania*, pp.202-5.
249 Lamb to Grey, 17/5/1914, FO421/293, no.108; Grey to Erskine, 17/6/1914, FO421/293, no.210; Kondis, *Greece and Albania*, pp.130-2.
250 Ed. Note, *Austro-Hungarian Documents*, pp.33-4.
251 Lamb to Grey, 3/6/1914, FO421/293, no.151.
252 *BD*, X.i, no.141; Swire, *Albania*, pp.186-7.
253 Durham, *Balkan Tangle*, pp.258, 269.
254 Lamb to Grey, 29/11/1913, FO421/287/54708; *BD*, X.i, no.114; Crampton, *Hollow Détente*, p.156.
255 *BD*, X.i, nos.134, 137: The British Foreign Office conceded troops might be necessary to protect Prince Wilhelm, but such a pretext was never deemed to materialise.
256 Bosworth, *Italy*, pp.377-417; Rodd to Grey, 23/6/1914, FO421/293, no.259.
257 *BD*, X.i, no.139.
258 Crackanthorpe to Grey, 21/10/1913, FO421/287, no.171; Swire, *Albania*, pp.194-6.
259 Rodd to Grey, 21/5/1914, FO421/293, no.103; Lamb, Various Reports, FO421/293, nos.95-170 *passim*; Heaton Armstrong, *Six Month Kingdom*, pp.46-150; Swire, *Albania*, p.207.
260 Heaton-Armstrong, *Six Month Kingdom* pp. 66-7.
261 Ibid; Swire, *Albania*, p.210; Jacques, *Albanians*, p.357; Lamb to Grey, 22/5/1914; FO421/293, no.129; Lamb to Grey, 27/5/1914, FO421/293, no.131; Lamb to Grey, 4/6/1914, FO421/293, no. 185.
262 Swire, *Albania*, pp.208-9; Heaton-Armstrong, *Six Month Kingdom*, pp.84-9.
263 Jacques, *Albanians*, p.357.
264 Rodd to Grey, 15/6/1914, FO421/293, no.217; Jacques, *Albanians*, p.357; Durham to Herbert, 28/7/n.d., Herbert MSS, Somerset Record Office, DD/HER/54 [hereafter cited as DD], pp.1-2, 8-12.
265 Lamb to Grey, 20/5/1914, FO421/293, no.126; Swire, *Albania*, p.207; Jacques, *Albanians*, p. 56; Durham to Herbert, 28/7/n.d., Herbert MSS, DD/HER/54.

266 Heaton-Armstrong, *Six Month Kingdom*, pp.66-9.
267 Lamb to Grey, 31/5/1914, FO421/293, no.158; Rodd to Grey, 21/5/1914, FO421/293, no.103.
268 Lamb to Grey, 24/5/1914, FO421/293, no.116.
269 Rodd to Grey, 15/6/1914, FO 421/293, no.217.
270 Durham to Herbert, 28/7/n.d., Herbert MSS, DD/HER/54, p.7; Heaton-Armstrong, *Six Month Kingdom*, pp.90-5.
271 Heaton-Armstrong, *Six Month Kingdom*, for example pp.69, 76.
272 Ibid, pp.84-6.
273 Lamb to Grey, 31/5/1914, FO421/293, no.158.
274 Enclosure in Lamb to Grey, 11/7/1914, FO421/294, no.42.
275 Crowe to Lamb, 17/6/1914, FO421/293, no.11: The international troops stationed at Scutari were not considered to conflict with these principles.
276 Swire, *Albania*, p.237.
277 Rodd to Grey, 3/8/1914, FO421/294, no.86; Grey to Rodd, 12/8/1914, FO421/294, no.90; Grey to Lamb, 12/8/1914, FO421/294, no.91; Rodd to Grey, 31/8/1914, FO421/294, no.93.
278 Durham 'Albanian Letter', 14/8/1914, in B.D. Destani (ed.), *Edith Durham -Albania and the Albanians: Selected Articles and Letters, 1903-1944* (London, 2001), pp.62-3.
279 Durham 'Notes from Albania', 3/9/1914, in Ibid, p.65; Swire, *Albania*, pp.230-2
280 Wilhelm to Swire, 5/8/1928 quoted in Swire, *Albania*, p.232.
281 Durham, *Balkan Tangle*, p.258.
282 Hroch, *Social Preconditions*, pp.22-3.
283 Hastings, *Construction of Nationhood*, pp.165-6, 200-2.
284 Wilhelm quoted in Swire *Albania*, pp.199-200.
285 *Faik Konitza*, no.31.

Chapter 4

286 Durham, *Balkan Tangle*, p.289.
287 Grey minute, 16/8/1914, FO371/2171/39796.
288 Grey minute, 13/8/1914, FO371/1900/38875.
289 Buchanan to Grey, 14/8/1914, FO371/1900/39186.
290 D. Lloyd George, *The Truth about the Peace Treaties*, 2 vols. (London, 1938), II, pp.1208-9.
291 Bax-Ironside to Grey, 15/8/1914, FO371/1900/39571; Erskine to Grey, 15/8/1914, FO371/1900/39564.
292 Grey to Buchanan and Bertie, 22/3/1915 in Trevelyan, *Grey of Fallodon*, pp.296-7.
293 Grey to Erskine, 20/8/1914, FO371/1900/42267.
294 C. Howard, 'The Treaty of London, 1915', *History*, 25 (1940-41), pp.347-55, at p.348.
295 W.A. Renzi, 'Italy's Neutrality and Entrance into the Great War: A Re-examination', *American Historical Review*, 73 (1968), pp.1414-32, at p.1426; C.J. Lowe, 'Britain and the Italian Intervention, 1914-1915', *The Historical*

Journal, 12 (1969), pp. 533-48, at p.539

296 *MOEI*, Series 3, V, nos.411, 453.

297 *MOEI*, Series 3, V, nos.521, 529; Petrovich, 'Italo-Yugoslav Boundary', pp.164-5.

298 P. du Quenoy, 'With Allies Like These, Who Needs Enemies?': Russia and the Problem of Italian Entry into World War I', *Canadian Slavonic Papers*, 45 (2003), pp. 409-40, at p.415.

299 Lowe, 'Britain and Italian Intervention', p.534; R. Albrecht-Carrié, *Italy at the Paris Peace Conference* (New York, 1938), pp.14-5; W.W. Gottlieb, *Studies in Secret Diplomacy during the First World War* (London, 1957), pp.198-9.

300 *Albania*, FO373/2/1, pp.91, 93-4, 105-6.

301 Grey to Rodd, 12/8/1914, FO371/2171/38844; Rodd to Grey, 15/8/1914, FO371/2171/39538.

302 Rodd to Grey, 17/8/1914, Clerk minute and Grey reply, 18/8/1914, FO371/2171/40193; Bertie to Grey, 19/8/1914, FO371/2171/41000; Buchanan to Grey, 19/8/1914, FO371/2171/41123; Rodd to Grey, 13/8/1913, FO371/2008/38816; Rodd to Grey, 13/8/1913, FO371/2008/38817.

303 Crowe minute, 16/8/1914, FO371/2171/39796.

304 Rodd to Grey, 27/9/1914, FO371/2171/53584.

305 Clerk minute, 12/9/1914, FO371/1901/48596.

306 Rodd to Grey, 19/9/1914, and Grey to Bertie, 20/9/1914, FO371/2008/51128; Bertie to Grey, 21/9/1914, FO371/2008/51576; Bertie to Grey draft, 28/10/1914, Bertie MSS, FO800/173.

307 Elliot to Grey, 12/10/1914, FO421/294, no.94; *MOEI*, Series 3, VII.i, no.355.

308 *DDI*, Series 5, I, no.880; B. Kondis, 'The Northern Epirus Question during the First World War', *Balkan Studies*, 30 (1989), pp.333-49, at p.333.

309 Elliot to Grey, 14/10/1914, FO421/294, no.95.

310 Rodd to Grey, 17/10/1914, FO421/294, no.98; Grey to Rodd, 6/10/1914, FO371/2009/55875; Rodd to Grey, 7/10/1914, FO371/2009/57096; *DDI*, Series 5, I, no.886.

311 Rodd to Grey, 19/10/1914, FO421/294, no.99; Rodd to Grey, 20/10/1914, FO421/294, no.101.

312 Elliott to Grey, 20/10/1914, FO421/294, no.102.

313 Grey to Rodd, 6/10/1914, FO371/2009/55845; Rodd to Grey, 7/10/1914, FO371/2009/57096; *DDI*, Series 5, I, no.886; Bosworth, *Italy*, p.405.

314 Clerk and Crowe minutes, 8/8/1914, FO371/1896/36827; Lamb to Grey, 11/8/1914, FO421/294, no.89; Clerk minute, 15/9/1914, and Grey to Buchanan, 16/9/1914, FO371/1903/49463; des Graz to Grey, 18/9/1914, FO371/1903/66981; de Salis to Grey, 21/9/1914, and Clerk minute, 22/9/1914, FO371/1903/51613; Swire, *Albania*, p.247.

315 Grey to Bertie, 21/10/1914, FO421/294, no.103.

316 Buchanan to Grey, 22 Oct. 1914, FO421/294, no.104.

317 Sonnino quoted in Albrecht-Carrié, *Italy*, p.18.

318 Lowe, 'Britain and Italian Intervention', p.538.

319 *DDI*, Series 5, I, no.823
320 Elliot to Grey, 4/11/1914, FO371/1902/67231; Buchanan to Grey, 6/11/1914 and Olliphant minute, 7/11/1914, FO371/1902/68116.
321 Bertie to Grey, 7/11/1914, and Clerk minute, 9/11/1914, FO371/1902/68556.
322 Grey to Bax-Ironside, 13/11/1914, FO371/1902/71355; Bax-Ironside to Grey, 16/11/1914, FO371/1902/71816.
323 Bertie to Grey, 17/11/1914, FO371/1902/72036.
324 Bertie to Grey, 7/11/1914, FO371/1902/68557.
325 Bertie to Grey, 28 /11/1914, FO371/1902/76590; Bertie to Grey, 29/11/1914 and Clerk minute, 30/11/1914, FO371/1902/76686; des Graz to Grey, 2/12/1914, FO371/1902/78118.
326 Buchanan to Grey, 29/11/1914 and Clerk minute, 30/11/1914, FO371/1902/76689.
327 Buchanan to Grey, 27/11/1914 and Olliphant and Clerk minutes, 28/11/1914, FO371/1902/76211.
328 Buchanan to Grey, 29/11/1914 and Clerk minute, 30/11/1914, FO371/1902/76689.
329 Grey to Buchanan, 2/12/1914, FO371/1902/77504; Elliot to Grey, 1/12/1914, FO371/1902/77623; Buchanan to Grey, 2/12/1914, FO371/1902/78111.
330 Elliot to Grey, 7/12/1914, FO371/2241/249; L.H. Curtright, *Muddle, Indecision and Setback: British Policy and the Balkan States, August 1914 to the Inception of the Dardanelles Campaign* (Thessaloniki, 1986), p.61.
331 Elliot to Grey, 28/12/1914, FO371/2503/2625.
332 Bax-Ironside to Grey, 9/12/1914, FO371/1902/81073; Bax-Ironside to Grey, 9/12/1914, FO371/1902/80984; Bax-Ironside to Grey, 9/12/1914, FO371/1902/81174.
333 Swire, *Albania*, p.246; T.N. Page, *Italy and the World War* (New York, 1920), pp.175-6.
334 Rodd to Grey, 26/12/1914, FO421/294, no.107; Page, *Italy and World War*, p.174.
335 *DDI*, Series 5, II, no.377; du Quenoy, 'With Allies Like These', p.423.
336 Elliot to Grey, 8/1/1915, FO371/2241/2970.
337 Percy memo., 9/7/1915, FO371/2264/102672, p.12.
338 Clerk minute, 11/1/1915, FO371/2241/3601; Buchanan to Grey, 3/2/1915, FO371/2242/13210.
339 Buchanan to Grey, 5/3/1915, FO371/2243/25532; Bertie to Grey, 4/3/1915, FO371/2243/25532; Percy memo., 9/7/1915, FO371/2264/102672, pp. 24-6.
340 Elliot to Grey, 22/3/1915, FO371/2243/33524; Buchanan to Grey, 4/4/1915, FO371/2243/39315; N. Petsalis-Diomidis, *Greece at the Paris Peace Conference 1919* (Thessaloniki, 1978), p.39.
341 See for example: Renzi, 'Italy's Neutrality and Entrance into the Great War', p.1426; or Lowe, 'Britain and the Italian Intervention', p.539.
342 Rodd to Grey, 16/2/1915, Grey MSS, FO800/65.
343 Rodd to Grey, 28/2/1915 and Clerk minute, 1/3/1915, FO371/2375/23560.

344 Grey minute on Imperiali verbal, 4/3/1915, FO371/2507/28275; *MOEI*, Series 3, VII.i, pp.446-8.

345 *MOEI*, Series 3, VII.i, nos.276, 331; M.B. Petrovich, 'The Italo-Yugoslav Boundary Question, 1914-1915' in A. Dallin et al, *Russian Diplomacy and Eastern Europe, 1914-1917* (New York, 1963), pp. 162-93, at p.179.

346 *DDI*, Series 5, II, no.39; du Quenoy, 'With Allies Like These', p.426.

347 Lowe, 'Britain and the Italian Intervention', p.542.

348 Untitled memo. cited in K. Neilson, *Britain and the Last Tsar: British Policy and Russia, 1894-1917* (Oxford, 1996), pp.358-9.

349 Buchanan to Grey, 12/3/1914, FO371/2507/29374.

350 du Quenoy, 'With Allies Like These', p.427.

351 Delcassé to de Fleurian, 13/3/1915, FO371/2507/30052; Petrovich, 'Italo-Yugoslav Boundary', pp.181-2.

352 Grey to Rodd, 16/3/1915, FO371/2507/30931.

353 Clerk minute, 13/3/1915, FO371/2507/29374.

354 Bertie to Grey, 18/3/1915, FO371/2507/31946.

355 A. Nicolson minute, 22/3/1915, FO371/2507/34055; Grey to Rodd, 25/3/1915, FO371/2507/35461; Buchanan to Grey, 25/3/1915, FO371/2507/34568; Sazonov to Benckendorff, 17/3/1915, FO371/2507/31554; Buchanan to Grey, 19/3/1915, FO371/2507/32449; Buchanan to Grey, 19/3/1915, FO371/2507/32075.

356 A. Nicolson minute, 22/3/1915, FO371/2507/34055; Grey to Rodd, 25/3/1915, FO371/2507/35461; Buchanan to Grey, 25/3/1915, FO371/2507/34568; Sazonov to Benckendorff, 17/3/1915, FO371/2507/31554; Buchanan to Grey, 19/3/1915, FO371/2507/32449; Buchanan to Grey, 19/3/1915, FO371/2507/32075.

357 Rodd to Grey, 2/4/1915 and Clerk minute, 3/4/1915, FO371/2507/38809.

358 *DDI*, Series 5, III, no. 121.

359 Gottlieb, *Studies in Secret Diplomacy*, p.343.

360 Grey to Buchanan and Bertie, 14/4/1915, FO371/2508/44480.

361 A. Nicolson memo., 15/4/1915, FO 371/2508/45066.

362 Buchanan to Grey, 16/4/1915 and Grey reply, 17/4/1915, FO371/2508/45196; Buchanan to Grey, 20/4/1915, FO371/2508/46987.

363 Grey to Bertie, 21/4/1915, FO371/2508/47656.

364 Rodd to Grey, 23/4/1915, FO371/2508/48886.

365 Rodd to Grey, 24/4/1915, FO371/2508/49188; Grey to Rodd, 24/4/1915, FO371/2508/49773.

366 'The Treaty of London, 26 April 1915' in Temperley, *History of the Peace Conferences of Paris*, V, pp.388-9.

367 Salandra quoted in Renzi, 'Italy's Neutrality and Entrance into the Great War', p.1432.

368 *MOEI*, Series 3, VII.ii, no.564.

369 Percy memo., 9/7/1915, FO371/2264/102672, pp.41-2.

370 Buchanan to Grey, 12/3/1915, FO371/2507/29374; Grey to Buchanan and Bertie, 14/4/1915, FO371/2508/44480; A. Nicolson minute, 15/4/1915, FO371/2508/45066.

371 Rodd to Grey, 9/8/1915, FO371/2265/109491; Rodd to Grey, 11/8/1915, and Grey to Bertie, 12/8/1915, FO371/2265/111103; DMO memo., 10/8/1915, FO371/2265/110393.

372 Grey to des Graz, 27/8/1915, FO371/2265/120224.

373 des Graz to Grey, 28/8/1915, FO371/2265/121477; des Graz to Grey, 1/9/1915, FO371/2265/123654; Grey to Bertie, 3/9/1915, and Clerk minute, 3/9/1915, FO371/2265/124331.

374 Stavrianos, *Balkans since 1483*, pp.561-3.

375 O'Beirne to Grey, 17/9/1915 and Clerk minute, 18/9/1915, FO371/2269/133735.

376 Percy memo., 22/10/1915, FO371/2278/174823; Elliot to Grey, 9/11/1915, FO371/2278/167911; Zaimis quoted in CAB42/2/31, par.214; C.J. Lowe, 'The Failure of British Diplomacy in the Balkans, 1914-1916', *Canadian Journal of History*, 4 (1969), pp. 73-101, at p.93; Petsalis-Diomidis, *Greece*, p.41.

377 Stickney, *Southern Albania*, pp.61-3; Swire, *Albania*, p.245.

378 Buchanan to Grey, 21/11/1915, Percy minute, 22/11/1915 and Grey to Buchanan, 23/11/1915, FO371/2279/175469; Grey to Rodd, 21/11/1915, FO371/2279/177332; Durham, *Balkan Tangle*, pp.284-5.

379 Buchanan to Grey, 24/11/1915, FO371/2279/177902; Buchanan to Grey, 22/11/1915 and Percy minute, 23/11/1915, FO371/2279/17657.

380 Memo., 10/11/1916, Herbert MSS, DD/DRU/35/1; Troubridge to Admiralty, 9/1/1916, ADM137/1141.

381 Curtwright, *Muddle, Indecision and Setback*, p.64.

382 Schroeder, 'Historical Reality', pp.108-48, esp. pp.117-23; For similar views see Baker Fox, *Power of Small States*, esp. pp.182-3, 187.

383 Trevelyan, *Grey of Fallodon*, p.330.

384 For further details see Neilson, *Britain and the Last Tsar*, pp.363-4.

385 Grey to Rodd, 17/12/1914, FO371/1902/85201.

386 Albrecht-Carrié, *Italy*, pp.30-1.

387 Grey cited in D. Lloyd George, *Memoirs of the Peace Conference* 2 vols. (New Haven, 1939), II, p.502.

388 Clerk minute, n.d, FO 371/2376/37639; Lowe, 'Britain and the Italian Intervention', p. 544.

Chapter 5

389 Clerk minute, 17/8/1916, FO371/2623/161285

390 Hastings, *Construction of Nationhood*, esp. pp.200-2.

391 *Edith Durham*, pp.67-8, at p.68.

392 *Albania*, FO Handbook, FO373/2/1, pp.85-6.

393 However as Duijzings and others have shown Albanian local identities were not necessarily incompatible with their national identity. See for example Duijzings, *Religion and Politics*, p.24.

394 A. Mitrović, 'Албанци у политици Аустро-Угарске према Србији 1914-1918' ('Albanians in the policy of Austria-Hungary towards Serbia 1914-1918'), in Mitrović, *Serbs and Albanians*, pp.79-136, at pp.81-8, 109-16;

H.J. Burgwyn, *The Legend of the Mutilated Victory: Italy, the Great War, and the Paris Peace Conference, 1915-1919* (London and Westport, Connecticut, 1993), pp.55-64.

395 Rodd to Grey, 27/10/1914 and H. Nicolson minute, 9/11/1914, FO371/1896/68866; *Edith Durham*, pp.67-8; Rodd to Grey, 29/9/1914, FO371/1896/54150; H. Nicolson minute, 25/9/1914, FO371/1896/53190; Swire, *Albania*, pp.236-41.

396 Swire, *Albania*, pp.236-41.

397 Swire, *Albania*, p.237; Bataković, '*Српска влада*', pp.41-3 and 63-5; des Graz to Grey, 19/9/1914, FO421/294, no.53.

398 Page to Lansing, 1/5/1915, 875.00/4 (National Archives Microfilm Publication M1211 [hereafter M1211], roll 1 [hereafter r.]), Relating to the Internal Affairs of Albania 1910-1944, Political Affairs 1910-29, Records of the Department of State [hereafter DOS], Record Group 59 [hereafter RG59], National Archives at College Park, Maryland, USA; Swire, *Albania*, pp.237-8; Pearson, *Albania*, I, pp.81-4; *L'Independence Albanaise* cited in Jacques, *Albanians*, p.359; Bataković, '*Српска влада*', pp.43, 65.

399 Jacques, *Albanians*, p.359; Swire, *Albania*, pp.238-9.

400 Pearson, Albania, I, pp.100-3.

401 Swire, *Albania*, pp.240-1; Pearson, *Albania*, I, pp.90-1.

402 GFM33/2201/5004, E285612-E285748, TNA:PRO; Mitrović, '*Албанци у политици*', pp.88-90, 116-8.

403 War Trade Intelligence Department memo., 20/10/1916, FO371/2619/210652; Swire, *Albania*, pp.259, 265; Pearson, *Albania*, I, pp.95-6, 105; Mitrović, '*Албанци у политици*', pp.128-13; Fischer, *King Zog*, p.12.

404 Spiers to War Office, 13/3/1918, FO371/3155/49228; Spiers to War Office, 14/3/1918, FO371/3155/49231; Swire, *Albania*, pp.260-2.

405 Pearson, *Albania*, I, pp.99, 106; Fischer, *King Zog*, pp.12-14; Swire, *Albania*, p.260-62.

406 Elliot to Grey, 22/7/1916, FO371/2617/143317; Rodd to Grey, 6/10/1916, FO371/2623/199687; Elliot to Grey, 23/10/1916, FO371/2623/211740; Italian embassy memo., 26/10/1916, FO371/2623/219357; Elliot to Grey, 1/11/1916, FO371/2623/219594; Pearson, *Albania*, I, pp.100-2.

407 Rodd to Grey, 12/10/1916, FO371/2623/204081; H. Nicolson minute and Clerk minutes, 2/11/1916, FO371/2623/219594.

408 Rodd to Grey, Rome, 12/10/1916, FO371/2623/204081.

409 Serbian memo., 31/1/1916, FO371/2615/20162; Elliot to Grey, 28/9/1916, FO371/2615/203979.

410 J.K. Tanenbaum, *General Maurice Sarrail, 1856-1929: The French Army and Left Wing Politics* (Chapel Hill, North Carolina, 1974), pp.163, 165.

411 Burgwyn, *Mutilated Victory*, pp.77-9; Stickney, *Southern Albania*, pp.69-70.

412 Pollo and Puto, *History of Albania*, p.163.

413 Tanenbaum, *Sarrail*, p.164; J.H. Burgwyn, *The Legend of the Mutilated Victory: Italy, the Great War, and the Paris Peace Conference, 1915-1919* (London and Westport, Connecticut, 1993), pp.77-9.

414 Tanenbaum, *Sarrail*, p.164; M. Konitza to Page, 24/9/1918, 875.00/33 (M1211, r. 1), DOS, RG59.

415 Sarrail quoted in Tanenbaum, *Sarrail*, p.164.
416 See for example Clerk and Campbell minutes, 21/8/1917, FO371/2879/163402.
417 Stickney, *Southern Albania*, p.70; Pearson, *Albania*, I, p.111; Swire, *Albania*, p.272: although Swire indicates there were more fundamental changes.
418 Nabokoff to Campbell, 25/3/1917, FO371/2878/63552; Swire, *Albania*, p.272; Pearson, *Albania*, I, p.106.
419 Pearson, *Albania*, I, pp.106-7; C.A. Chekrezi, *Albania Past and Present* (New York, 1919), pp.161-2; C.A. Dako, *Albania: The Master Key to the Near East* (Boston, Mass., 1919), pp.145-6; Stickney, *Southern Albania*, p.65.
420 Swire, *Albania*, p.276.
421 Essad Pasha to Lansing, 5/6/1917, 875.00/7 (M1211, r.1), DOS, RG59; Durham to Herbert, 28/6/1917, Herbert DD/DRU/47: Unfortunately, within Herbert's papers there is no record of Herbert's own opinions on the subject.
422 R. Woodall, 'The Albanian Problem during the Peacemaking, 1919-20' (PhD Thesis, Memphis State University, 1978), p.18; Pearson, *Albania*, I, pp.106-7.
423 Rodd to Balfour, 20/8/1917, H. Nicolson, Cecil and Campbell minutes, 21/8/1917, FO371/2879/163402; Swire, *Albania*, pp.274-6; Burgwyn, *Mutilated Victory*, pp.81-4; Woodall, 'Albanian Problem', pp.18-20.
424 *DDI*, Series V, VII, nos. 174, 208; Burgwyn, *Mutilated Victory*, pp.80-1; Pearson, *Albania*, I, p.107; Stickney, *Southern Albania*, p.72; Swire, *Albania*, p.273, Albrecht-Carrié, *Italy*, p.239.
425 Graham minute, 23/5/1917, FO371/2878//112639.
426 Rodd to Balfour, 8/6/1917, FO371/2881/113449; Elliot to Balfour and Granville, 25/3/1917, FO371/2883/63110; Granville to Balfour, 9/4/1917, FO371/2878/92555; Gennadius commn., 23/5/1917, FO371/2878/103707; Granville to Balfour, 23/5/1917 and H. Nicolson and Olliphant minutes, 24/5/1917, FO371/2878/103957; Elliot to Balfour, 28/5/1917, FO371/2878/113282; Elliot to Balfour, 6/6/1917, FO371/2878/113747; Rodd to Balfour, 9/6/1917, FO371/2878/115250; Graham to Balfour, 9/6/1917, FO371/2878/115251; Rodd to Balfour, 12/6/1917, FO371/2878/117015: Eventually Sonnino was forced to forbid Italian forces moving any further south.
427 H. Nicolson minute, 6/6/1917, FO371/2881/112035.
428 Bertie to Balfour, 21/9/1917, FO371/2879/183833.
429 Rodd to Balfour, 7/6/1917, FO371/2881/113449; Cecil minute, n.d., FO371/2881/113449: Robert Cecil disagreed seeing no reason to conceal the fact that the Italians acted without consulting Britain.
430 Swire, *Albania*, pp.278-80; Woodall, 'Albanian Problem', pp.22-4.
431 *DDI*, Series 6, I, nos.75, 250; Pastorelli, *L'Albania*, pp.68-9; Woodall, 'Albanian Problem', pp. 25-6.
432 *DBFP*, IV, no.15.
433 Pearson, *Albania*, I, pp.114-6; Pollo and Puto, *History of Albania*, p.170; Swire, *Albania*, p. 333; 'Memorandum on the Occupation of Albania', 3/7/1919, cited in Woodall, 'Albanian Problem', pp.26-9.

434 Stavrianos, *Balkans since 1453*, pp.566-8.

435 Pearson, *Albania*, I, pp.110, 112; Swire, *Albania*, p.265.

436 M. Frasheri to Herbert, 15/11/1918, Herbert MSS, DD/DRU/33/1.

437 Lansing to Barnard, 5/10/1914, 875.00/2 (M1211, r.1), DOS, RG59.

438 Stickney, *Southern* Albania, pp.70-1; Pearson, *Albania*, I, pp.110-11, 114.

439 Durham to Herbert, 19/3/1918, Herbert MSS, DD/DRU/47; Army Council to Grey, 13/2/1916, FO371/2615/28547.

440 Lambert minute, 18/1/1918, FO371/3154/34264; Durham to Herbert, 19/3/1918, Herbert MSS, DD/DRU/47.

441 Lambert minute 18/1/1918, FO371/3154/34264; WED minute, 16/2/1918, FO371/3154/34264.

442 H. Nicolson minute, 22/7/1918, FO371/3157/127525.

443 MacGinty, 'Small States', pp.45-8.

444 Woodall, 'Albanian Problem', p.29; Swire, *Albania*, p.266.

445 Durham to Herbert, 28/6/1917, Herbert MSS, DD/DRU/47; Elliot to Grey, 30/4/1916, FO371/2619/94755.

446 Elliot to Grey, 30/4/1916, Lamb minute, 24/5/1916, Clerk and A. Nicolson minutes, 25/5/1916, FO371/2619/94755.

447 Durham to Amery, 23/10/1917, Herbert MSS, DD/DRU/47.

448 *DDI*, Series 6, I, no.694; *FRUS PPC*, II, pp.374-5; Pastorelli, *L'Albania*, pp.64-6; Woodall, 'Albanian Problem', pp.30-1.

449 Tourtoulis to Herbert, 12/1/1919, Herbert MSS, DD/DRU/33/1; Phillips to Clerk, 28/12/1918, FO371/3570/9031; Rumbold to Balfour, 7/1/1919, FO371/3570/6937.

450 *DDI*, Series 6, I, nos.32, 243, 305; Woodall, 'Albanian Problem', pp.32-3; Swire, *Albania*, p.284.

451 *DDI*, Series 6, I, no.492; Sonnino to Imperiali, n.d./12/1918, and LC minute, 17/12/1918, FO371/3148/206726: The Consulta promoted the idea of French culpability in the movement to (re-)establish an Albanian provisional government but Whitehall did not agree.

452 Woodall, 'Albanian Problem', pp.35-6; Pearson, *Albania*, I, p.112.

453 'Constitutive Act of the [Durazzo] Provisional Government', 25/1/1919, 875.00/29 (M820, r.555), General Records of the American Commission to Negotiate Peace, 1918-1931, Albania, DOS, RG59; Phillips to DMI, 28/12/1918, FO371/3570/9031; *DDI*, Series 6, I, nos. 402, 492, 536: Woodall, 'Albanian Problem', pp.35-6; Pearson, *Albania*, I, p.112.

454 M. Konitza to Graham, 23/6/1918, FO371/3157/118015; M. Konitza to Balfour, 20/7/1918, FO371/3157/127525; M. Konitza to Herbert, 8/10/1918, FO371/3157/169046.

455 *DDI*, Series 6, I, nos. 660, 661, 694, 732; Woodall, 'Albanian Problem', pp.36-7.

456 Lybyer minute, 16 Feb. 1919, 875.00/59 (M820, r. 556), DOS, RG59.

457 Sonnino to Piacentini, 29 Dec. 1918, *DDI*, Series 6, I, no. 694; Piacentini to Sonnino, 1 Jan. 1919, *DDI*, Series 6, I, no. 732; *FRUS PPC*, II, p. 375.

458 War Cabinet memo., 6 Feb. 1917, Herbert MSS, DD/DRU/35/1.

459 Lambert and H. Nicolson minutes, 18/1/1918, WED minute, 16/2/1918, FO371/3154/34264.

460 MacGinty, 'Small States', pp.42-3.
461 M. Frashëri to Herbert, 15/11/1918, Herbert MSS, DD/DRU/33/1.

Chapter 6

462 Herbert memo., n.d., Herbert MSS, DD/DRU/33.
463 M.L. Dockrill and J.D. Gould, *Peace Without Promise: Britain and the Peace Conferences, 1919-23* (London, 1981), pp.87, 254.
464 Sharp, 'Genie', p. 25; Also at M. MacMillan, *Peacemakers: The Paris Conference of 1919 and Its Attempt to End the War* (London, 2001), p.496.
465 Dockrill and Goold, *Peace without Promise*, p.91.
466 Cobban, *The National State*, p.63; Sharp, 'Genie', pp.12-3; Sharp, 'Minorities', p.178.
467 Sharp, 'Genie', pp.13-4 *emphasis added.*
468 Ibid, pp.14, 20, 23; Sharp, 'Minorities', pp.170, 178.
469 Quoted in Temperley, *History of the Peace Conference*, IV, p.429.
470 Sharp, 'Minorities', p.172.
471 League of Nations, *The Complaints of Macedonia: memoranda, petitions, resolutions, minutes, letters and documents, addressed to the League of Nations, 1919-1939* (Geneva, 1979), pp.20-1, 36-7.
472 Sharp, 'Minorities', pp.177-8; Sharp, 'Genie', p.13; Temperley, *History of Peace Conference*, I, pp.399, 434.
473 As the Japanese Delegation took no active part in European discussion their views will not be considered.
474 *DDI*, Series 6, I, no.590; I.J. Lederer, *Yugoslavia at the Paris Peace Conference. A Study in Frontiermaking* (New Haven and London, 1963), p.76; Woodall, 'Albanian Problem', pp.43-4; Burgwyn, *Mutilated Victory*, pp.135, 313-7.
475 P.S. Wandycz, *France and her Eastern Allies 1919-1925: French-Czechoslovak-Polish Relations from the Paris Peace conference to Locarno* (Minneapolis, 1962), esp. pp.4–7, 21; J. Jacobson, 'Strategies of French Foreign Policy after World War I', *Journal of Modern History*, 55 (1983), pp.78-95; Woodall, 'Albanian Problem', pp.44-5.
476 Lansing to Barnard, 5/10/1914, 875.00/2 (M1211, r.1), DOS, RG59.
477 For example Fiftieth Anniversary Book cited in G. Pano, 'The Albanian-American Effort to influence Wilson's policy toward Albania, 1918-1920', *South East European Monitor* 1 (1995), pp.1-8, at p. 5.
478 *FRUS PPC*, I, p.51.
479 'Outline of Tentative Report and Recommendations Prepared by the Intelligence Section in accordance with instructions, for the President and Plenipotentiaries', 21/1/1919, 185.112/1, pp.56-60 and maps 17 and 18 of item 648 (M820, r.323), DOS, RG256; D. H. Miller, *My Diary at the Conference of Peace*, 21 vols. (New York, 1928), IV, pp.209-81.
480 Ibid, pp. 49-50, 56-8 of item 648.
481 Pastorelli, *L'Albania*, p.90; E.D. Goldstein, 'Britain Prepares for Peace: British Preparations for the Paris Peace Conference (1916-1919)' (PhD Thesis, Cambridge University, 1984), p.339.
482 N. Nicolson, *Peacemaking 1919* (London, 1933), p.52.

483 H. Nicolson to Crowe, 15/3/1919, FO608/37/92/1/1/4392; Memo. on Europe, PID paper 3, FO371/4353/f23/pc55; Sharp, 'Minorities', p.177; Dockrill and Goold, *Peace without Promise*, pp.24, 128; Goldstein, 'Eastern Question', pp.150-1; E.D. Goldstein, 'Great Britain and Greater Greece, 1917-1920', *The Historical Journal*, 32 (1989), pp.339-56, at pp.339, 345; Curzon cited in B. McKercher, 'Old Diplomacy and New: the Foreign Office and foreign policy, 1919–1939', in M. Dockrill and McKercher (eds.), *Diplomacy and World Power: Studies in British Foreign Policy 1890-1950* (Cambridge, 1996), pp.79-114, at p.94.

484 On the importance of religion in other questions see *FRUS PPC*, V, p.756.

485 V.H. Rothwell, *British War Aims and Peace Diplomacy 1914-1918* (Oxford, 1971), pp.221-8; Calder cited in A. Sharp, 'Some Relevant Historians – the Political Intelligence Department of the Foreign Office, 1918-1920', *Australian Journal of Politics and History*, 34 (1988), pp.359-68, at p.365.

486 Memo. on Europe, PID paper 3, FO371/4353/f23/pc55; H. Nicolson to A. Nicolson, 25/2/1919, *Peacemaking*, pp.270-1; Goldstein, 'Britain and Greater Greece', p.341; Sharp, 'Some Relevant Historians', p.363; Sharp, 'Minorities', p.177; Dockrill and Goold, *Peace Without Promise*, p.93; McKercher, 'Old Diplomacy and New', p.90.

487 PID, 'South-eastern Europe and the Balkans' minute, n.d./12/1918, FO371/4355/f68/pc68; Goldstein, 'Britain Prepares', pp.103, 174-6, 179.

488 Toynbee to Headlam-Morley, 15/11/1918, FO371/4352/f18/pc18; DMI, 'Proposed Settlement of Albania', 17/9/1918, FO371/3148/209559; Goldstein, 'Britain Prepares', pp.103, 107-8, 121, 178-9;Petsalis-Diomidis, *Greece*, pp.60-3.

489 Petsalis-Diomidis, *Greece*, pp.135, 137-8; Goldstein, 'Britain and Greater Greece', p.344; Woodall, 'Albanian Problem', pp.42-3.

490 Lederer, *Yugoslavia*, p.82; Woodall, 'Albanian Problem', p.40; A. Mitrović, 'Југославија, Албанско Питање и Италија 1919-1939' ('Yugoslavia, the Albanian Question and Italy 1919-1939'), in Mitrović, *Serbs and Albanians*, pp.231-73.

491 Lederer, *Yugoslavia*, p.96; Woodall, 'Albanian Problem', p.41; Swire, *Albania*, pp.292-3; The deficiencies of the 1913 frontier in defensible terms had been illustrated due to raiding parties and perpetual fighting.

492 *FRUS PPC*, I, p.311.

493 Pollo and Puto, *History of Albania*, pp.171-5.

494 K. Nuro and N. Bato (eds.), *Hasan Prishtina: përmbledhje dokumentesh, 1908 - 1934 (Hasan Prishtina: published documents, 1908-1934)* (Tirana, 1982), nos.61,65 [trans J. Azemi]; Woodall, 'Albanian Problem', pp.129-30; Swire, *Albania*, pp.285-316 *passim*; Pearson, *Albania*, I, pp.119-44 *passim*.

495 Pano, 'Albanian-American Effort', pp.3-4.

496 *FRUS PPC*, IV, pp. 111.

497 See for example *FRUS PPC*, II, pp.374-5 and Municipal Authorities of Tirana memo., 2/1/1919, FO371/3150/4259.

498 Pearson, *Albania*, I, pp.116-24 *passim*.

499 *FRUS PPC*, pp.111-16; 'Minutes of the Committee for the Study of Territorial Questions Relating to Greece', 27/2/1919, FO608/37/92/1/4/3983

[hereafter referred to as Greek Committee minutes]; Petsalis-Diomidis, *Greece*, pp.142-3.

500 H. Nicolson and Crowe minutes, 18/2/1919, FO608/29/1/2193; Petsalis-Diomidis, *Greece*, p.143.

501 Greek Committee minutes, 12/2/1919, FO371/3593/27947; Greek Committee minutes, 26/2/1919, CAB29/8/WCP192.

502 Greek Committee minutes, 12/2/1919, FO371/3593/27947; Nicolson, *Peacemaking*, pp.268, 273.

503 Nicolson, *Peacemaking*, p.268; *FRUS PPC*, III, pp.859-61.

504 Nicolson, *Peacemaking*, pp.255-6; *FRUS PPC*, III, pp.859-61, 875.

505 See for example Venizelos to Repoulis, 4/2/1919, cited in Petsalis-Diomidis, *Greece*, pp.137-8.

506 *FRUS PPC*, III, pp. 859-61.

507 Venizelos to Repoulis, 4/2/1919, cited in Petsalis-Diomidis, *Greece*, pp.137-8.

508 Carapanos memo., 29/1/1919, FO371/3585/33955.

509 *FRUS PPC*, III, p. 875.

510 F.S. Marston, *The Peace Conference of 1919: Organisation and Procedure* (London, 1944), pp.111, 117; Petsalis-Diomidis, *Greece*, p.138.

511 Petsalis-Diomidis, *Greece*, pp.138-9.

512 For a record of these meetings in the official English translation see FO371/3593, FO608/37, and CAB 29/8, 9 and 11 (the latter set being incomplete).

513 Greek Committee minutes, 12/2/1919, FO371/3593/27947.

514 I will refer to the question of southern Albania, contrary to the terminology used by the representatives in the Committee who used northern Epirus.

515 *Ibid*; Nicolson, *Peacemaking*, p.260.

516 Appendices A, B and C, Greek Committee minutes, 18/2/1919, FO371/3593/34810

517 *Ibid*; Petsalis-Diomidis, *Greece*, p. 140: Admitting the deficiencies of language statistics in the northern section, the Americans estimated 5,000 Greek-speaking inhabitants to 115,000 speaking Albanian and in the southern section 35,000 Greek-speakers to 50,000 Albanian-speakers.

518 Lederer, *Yugoslavia*, p.172; Woodall, *Albanian Problem*, pp.55-6.

519 Appendices B and C, Greek Committee minutes, 18/2/1919, FO371/3593/34810; Petsalis-Diomidis, *Greece*, p.140.

520 Thwaites memo., 7/2/1919, FO608/37/92/1/1/1575; Goldstein, 'Britain and Greater Greece', p.346.

521 H. Nicolson to Crowe, 15/3/1919, FO608/37/92/1/1/4392.

522 'Italian Proposal', Greek Committee minutes, 18/2/1919, FO371/3593/34810.

523 Fuller minute, 20/2/1919, FO608/29/1657; Laroche memo., 18/2/1919, cited in Petsalis-Diomidis, *Greece*, p. 141.

524 Greek Committee minutes, 19/2/1919, FO371/3593/32612.

525 Ibid.

526 Nicolson, *Peacemaking*, p.265.

527 Ibid, p.268; L. Maccas, *La Question Gréco-Albanaise* (Paris, 1921), p.8;

Petsalis-Diomidis, *Greece*, p.142.

528 Nicolson, *Peacemaking*, p.276.

529 Petsalis-Diomidis, *Greece*, p.145; Nicolson, *Peacemaking*, pp.259, 277.

530 Greek Committee minutes, 6/3/1919, FO608/37/92/1/4/3931; Greek Committee report, 8/3/1919, CAB29/11/WCP401; Nicolson, *Peacemaking*, p.280; Petsalis-Diomidis, *Greece*, pp.146-7: Petsalis-Diomidis includes an interesting account of the differences in the French and English versions of the Greek Committee's recommendations and why the Italian proposal did not appear in the final version.

531 Central Committee on Territorial Questions minutes, 17/3/1919, FO371/3593/4244; Also at CAB29/10/WCP370; 'Central Committee report on Greece', n.d., CAB29/13/WCP630; Central Committee report, 31/3/1919 and 22/4/1919, FO608/92/1/4/5868; P.C. Helmreich, *From Paris to Sèvres: The partition of the Ottoman Empire at the Peace Conference of 1919-20* (Columbus, Ohio, 1974), pp.86-7.

532 Nicolson, *Peacemaking*, p.313.

533 Barnes, 'Proposed Settlement of Albania', 25/4/1919, FO608/29/1/8333.

534 H. Nicolson minute, 25/4/1919, FO608/29/1/8333; Also at Petsalis-Diomidis, *Greece*, pp.150-51 and Goldstein, 'Britain and Greater Greece, p.348.

535 Nicolson minute, 'Settlement on South Eastern Europe', 27/3/1919, FO608/37/4392; Also at FO608/46/8/5605; Nicolson, *Peacemaking*, pp.290, 314; Helmreich, *Paris to Sèvres*, p.88; Woodall, 'Albanian Problem', pp.62-3; Goldstein, 'Britain and Greater Greece', pp.347-8.

536 Nicolson, *Peacemaking*, pp.348-50; H. Nicolson memo. 'Albania', 28/5/1919, and minutes by Crowe, Hardinge and Balfour, 29/5/1919, FO608/29/1/11124.

537 Goldstein, 'Britain and Greater Greece', pp.348-9.

538 See for example Temperley minute, 28/4/1919, FO608/29/1/8333

539 H. Nicolson memo. 'Albania', 28/5/1919, FO608/29/1/11124

540 Mezes to H. Nicolson, 21/4/1919, FO608/46/8332.

541 Helmreich, *Paris to Sèvres*, pp.90-1; Albrecht-Carrié, *Italy*, pp.424-7; Woodall, 'Albanian Problem', pp.63-4.

542 P. Mantoux, 'Introduction' to P. Mantoux (ed.), (trans. A.S. Link), *The Deliberations of the Council of Four (March 24-June 28, 1919): Notes of the Delivery to the German Delegation of the Preliminaries of Peace: Supplementary Volume to the Papers of Woodrow Wilson*, 2 vols. (Princeton, 1955), esp. xxii-xxix; Albrecht-Carrié, *Italy*, pp.370-87.

543 *FRUS PPC*, V, p.483; Petsalis-Diomidis, *Greece*, p.150; Woodall, 'Albanian Problem', pp.66-7

544 Day to Wilson, 22/5/1919, 186.3411/18, pp.3-13 (M820, r.414), DOS, RG256; Woodall, 'Albanian Problem', pp.71-3.

545 Day to Wilson, 22/5/1919, 875.00/181 (M820, r.556), DOS, RG256; Woodall, 'Albanian Problem', pp.71-3, Helmreich, *Paris to Sèvres*, p.102; Nicolson, *Peacemaking*, pp.284-5; Albrecht-Carrié, *Italy*, pp.424-7.

546 Wilson to Lansing, 30/6/1919, 875.00/209 (M820, r.556), DOS, RG256; Woodall, 'Albanian Problem', p.73.

547 Woodall, 'Albanian Problem', pp.73-4.
548 H. Nicolson memo., 4/7/1919, FO608/120/3/12/17010; Helmreich, *Paris to Sèvres*, pp.164-5: By 1 August 1919 the other great power delegations appear to have known of the agreement and 'bandwagonned' in support.
549 *DBFP*, IV, no.10; Pastorelli, *L'Albania*, p.134; Woodall, 'Albanian Problem', pp.135-7, Petsalis-Diomidis, *Greece*, p.152.
550 *DDI*, Series 6, I, no.788; Helmreich, *Paris to Sèvres*, pp.42-3; Bianchiari and Sonnino cited in Woodall, 'Albanian Problem', pp.134-5.
551 Wallace to Lansing, 16/6/1919, 763.72119/5341 (M367, r.417), Records of the Department of State Relating to World War I and Its Termination, 1914-29, DOS, RG256; Crowe memo., 31/7/1919 FO608/54/120/3/12/17010; Helmreich, *Paris to Sèvres*, pp.164-5; Goldstein, 'Britain and Greater Greece', p.354; Grieve to Balfour, 1/7/1919, FO608/108/1/2/16920.
552 *FRUS PPC*, VIII, p.77; *DBFP*, IV, no.20; Miller, *Diary*, XX, pp.400-1.
553 H. Nicolson to Balfour, 4/7/1919, and Balfour to H. Nicolson, n.d., FO608/28/6/18300.
554 *FRUS PPC*, III, pp.852-55; *FRUS PPC*, IV, pp.44-57.
555 Committee for the Study of Territorial Questions Relating to Romania minutes, 3/3/1919, CAB29/9/WCP225; Nicolson, *Peacemaking*, p.264; Stickney, *Southern Albania*, pp.74-5.
556 Greek Committee minutes, 4/3/1919, CAB29/9/WCP263; Greek Committee minutes, 6/3/1919, CAB29/9/WCP244; Crowe minute, 6/3/1919, FO608/38/13/3967; Petsalis-Diomidis, *Greece*, pp.145-6.
557 Greek Committee minutes, 6/3/1919, CAB29/9/WCP244; *FRUS PPC*, IV, p.326.
558 Johnson memo., 8/5/1919, in Albrecht-Carrié, *Italy*, pp.162-4, 172-4, 510-4; Lederer, *Yugoslavia*, pp.208-10; Woodall, 'Albanian Problem', pp.66-8.
559 *FRUS PPC*, VI, pp.78-82; Albrecht-Carrié, *Italy*, pp.188-90.
560 Ibid.
561 Polk to Lansing, 14/5/1919, 763.72119/6176 (M367, r.425), DOS, RG256.
562 *DBFP*, IV, no.3.
563 Ed. Note, *DBFP*, IV, p.1 and no.2; Also at *FRUS PPC*, VI, pp.760-2.
564 *DBFP*, IV, nos.18, 20, 78; Albrecht-Carrié, *Italy*, pp.244-5, 248, no.49; *FRUS PPC*, VIII, pp.224-5; Miller, *Diary*, XX, pp.400-1.
565 On Albanian resistance to the Italians see for example *DBFP*, IV, no.10.
566 Polk to Lansing, 31/8/1919, 763.72119/6458 (M367, r.429), DOS, RG256; Council of Heads of Delegations minutes, 15/91919, *FRUS, PPC*, VIII, pp.224-5; Wilson to Polk, 21/9/1919, 763.72119/6865 (M367, r.436), DOS, RG256; Miller, *Diary*, XX, p.403; Woodall, 'Albanian Problem', pp.145-53; Albrecht-Carrié, *Italy*, p.147.
567 Phillips to Polk, 14/9/1919, 186.3411/808 (M820, r.436), American Commission, DOS, RG256; Wilson to Polk, 14/9/1919, 763.72119/6833a (M367, r.433), US Termination, DOS, RG256; Wilson to Polk, 21/9/1919, 763.72119/6865 (M367, r.436), US Termination, DOS, RG256; Council of Heads of Delegations minutes, *FRUS PPC*, VIII, pp.224-5; Polk cited in Woodall, 'Albanian Problem', pp.148, 151-3.

568 *DBFP*, IV, no.80; Polk to Lansing, 10/9/1919, 763.72119/6669 (M367, r.430), DOS, RG256; Polk to Lansing, 14/8/1919, 763.72119/6176 (M367, r.425), DOS, RG256; Lederer, *Yugoslavia*, p.238.

569 Polk to Lansing, 31/8/1919, 763.72119/6458 (M367, r.429), DOS, RG256; Miller *Diary*, XX, p.403; Polk cited in Woodall, 'Albanian Problem', p.145.

570 *DBFP*, IV, no.80

571 Ibid, no.78; Pastorelli, *L'Albania*, pp.169-70; Woodall, 'Albanian Problem', pp.154-5.

572 *DBFP*, IV, nos.119-21.

573 Ibid, no.122.

574 *DBFP*, IV, nos.129, 140, 147.

575 *DBFP*, IV, nos.141, 150-52, 154, 160-61, 165, 169.

576 *DBFP*, II, no.56.

577 *Correspondence relating to the Adriatic Question* (London, 1920), pp.11-14, 38-47; *DBFP*, II, no.63; Polk to Lansing, 13/12/1919, 763.72119/8251 (M367, r.452), DOS, RG256; Albrecht-Carrié, *Italy*, pp.267-70.

578 Franco-British memo., 9/1/1920, *Adriatic Question*, pp.11-14; Albrecht-Carrié, *Italy*, pp.268-70.

579 *Adriatic Question*, p.38; Albrecht-Carrié, *Italy*, pp.238, 270.

580 *DBFP*, II, nos.63-64.

581 Ibid, nos.66-67; Lederer, *Yugoslavia*, p.264.

582 Lederer, *Yugoslavia*, p.264.

583 *DBFP*, II, nos.64, 68, 70.

584 Ibid, no.70; Temperley, *History of Peace Conferences*, IV, p.343: Before presenting the proposals to the Yugoslav delegates, Venizelos had been invited to examine the document and had approved it.

585 Trumbić cited in Lederer, *Yugoslavia*, p.264.

586 *DBFP*, II, nos.70, 72; Lederer, *Yugoslavia*, pp.265-7; Albrecht-Carrié, *Italy*, p.272.

587 Wallace to Lansing, 16/1/1920, 763.72119/8703 (M367, r.457), DOS, RG256; Woodall, 'Albanian Problem', p.216.

588 Wallace to Lansing, 22/1/1920, 763.72119/8773 (M367, r.458), DOS, RG256; A. Leeper memo., 13/2/1920, *DBFP*, XII, no.101.

589 Lansing to Wilson, 22/1/1920, 763.72119/8681 (M367, r.456), DOS, RG256; Polk to Wilson, 24/1/1920, 763.72119/8703 (M367, r.457), DOS, RG256.

590 *DBFP*, II, no.80.

591 Bolling Wilson to Lansing, 27/1/1920, 763.72119/8833 (M367, r.463), DOS, RG256; E. Bolling Wilson to Lansing, 3/2/1920, 763.72119/9974 (M367, r.483), DOS, RG256.

592 Woodall, 'Albanian Problem', p.221.

593 Lansing to Wallace, 9/2/1920, *Adriatic Question*, pp.21-5; Also at Albrecht-Carrié, *Italy*, pp.276-9.

594 Kirk memo., 7/2/1920, 763.72119/9010½ (M367, r.468), DOS, RG256.

595 Woodall, 'Albanian Problem', p.221, n.23.

596 Lloyd George memo., 16/2/1920, Lloyd George MSS, House of Lords Record Office, London, LG/F/60/1/24 [hereafter cited as LG]; 17/2/1920,

186.3411/1070 (M820, r.437), DOS, RG256.
597 Wilson minutes, 17/2/1920, 186.3411/1070 (M820, r.437), DOS, RG256.
598 Memo., 25/2/1920, Lloyd George MSS, LG/F/60/1/25.
599 Memo., 25/2/1920, Lloyd George MSS, LG/F/60/1/25; Lansing to Wallace, 24/2/1920, *Adriatic Question*, pp.31-4; Albrecht-Carrié, *Italy*, pp.81-2.
600 Davis to Polk, 26/2/1920, *Adriatic Question*, pp.35-7; Albrecht-Carrié, *Italy*, pp.282-3.
601 Polk to Davis, 4/3/1920, *Adriatic Question*, pp.47-9.
602 *The Times*, 9/3/1920; For a fuller discussion of this Machiavellian 'open diplomacy' see Woodall, 'Albanian Problem', p.224, n.26.
603 Young to Curzon, 25/11/1920, FO371/4886/C13685.
604 *Hasan Prishtina*, nos.58-59, 66.
605 Pearson, *Albania*, I, pp.120-61 *passim*.
606 S. Bonsal, *Suitors and Supplicants: The Little Nations at Versailles* (New York, 1946), p.67; Woodall, 'Albanian Problem', pp.128-31.
607 Albanian Delegations to Clemenceau, 4/4/1919, 186.3411/138 (M820, r.415), DOS, RG256; Albanian Delegations to Clemenceau, 4/4/1919, 186.3411/139 (M820, r.415), DOS, RG256; M. Konitza to Admission in Paris, 14/4/919, 186.3411/144 (M820, r.415), DOS, RG256; Albanian Delegation in Paris to Clemenceau, 16/4/1919, 186.3411/148 (M820, r.415), DOS, RG256; M. Konitza to Balfour, 16/4/1919 and H. Nicolson minute, 16/4/1919, FO608/76/2/5/7451.
608 MacGinty, 'Small States', esp. pp.50-2; Page cited in Handel, *Weak States*, pp.5, 180.
609 Pano, 'Albanian-Americans Effort', p.6; Albrecht-Carrié, *Italy*, p.18.
610 Day to Built, 19/2/1919, 186.3411/62 (M820, r.415), DOS, RG256; Day to Mezes, 31/3/1919, 186.3411/133 (M820, r.415), DOS, RG256.
611 Herbert to 'Dear George' [Clerk], 21/8/1917, FO371/3059/164242; Drummond to Herbert, 3/8/1917, Hardinge MSS, FO800/197; Crowe minute, 17/5/1919, FO608/46/8/10041; Rothwell, *British War Aims*, p.134; Goldstein, 'Britain and Greater Greece', p.344.
612 O'Grady cited in Pano, 'Albanian-Americans Effort', p.11.
613 Sonnino cited in Woodall, 'Albanian Problem', p.124.
614 Tourtoulis, M. Konitza and M. Frasheri to Clemenceau, 17/6/1919 and Halil Pasha, Delegation of Albanian Colony in Turkey, Pandeli Evangjeli, Delegation of Albanian Colony in Romania and Delegation of National Albanian Party in the United States memo., 19/6/1919, FO608/28/2/ f207-215; Tourtoulis to Balfour, 11/9/1919, FO371/3593/128639.
615 Pearson, *Albania*, I, pp.132-42 *passim*; Stickney, *Southern Albania*, pp.116-23 *passim*; Swire, *Albania*, pp.303-11 *passim*.
616 MacMillan, *Peacemakers*, pp.5-6; Sharp, 'Minorities', p.178; A. Cobban, *The Nation State and National Self Determination* (London and Glasgow, 1969), pp.57-76.
617 R. Lansing, *The Peace Negotiations* (Boston, Massachusetts and London, 1921), pp.97-8.
618 Sharp, 'Minorities', p.178.

619 H. Wilson, 9/4/1920, FO371/4387/pid876/f876; Sharp, 'Minorities', p.184.
620 Toynbee quoted in Goldstein, 'British Peace Aims', p.422.
621 Ibid, pp.423, 428.
622 J. Headlam-Morley quoted in A. Headlam-Morley (ed.), *Sir James Headlam-Morley: A Memoir of the Paris Peace Conference 1919* (London, 1972), p.44 *emphasis added*; Also at Goldstein, 'New Diplomacy', p.399.

Chapter 7

623 Delvina to Herbert, 10/6/1920, Herbert MSS, DD/DRU/33/3
624 Phillips to DMI, 24/1/1919 FO371/3570/3815; Phillips to DMI, 26/6/1919, FO608/30/1/16235; Ed. note 1, *Hasan Prishtina*, p. 103.
625 'History of question of independence of Albania' memo., 2/3/1925, FO141/669/10; Woodall, 'Albanian Problem', pp.169-95 *passim*.
626 Phillips to DMI, 19/5/1919, and Eden minute, 11/5/1919, FO608/30/12/12241; Phillips memo., 31/12/1918, FO371/3570/13815.
627 Phillips to Clerk, 28/12/1918, FO371/3570/9031; d'Esperey cited in Woodall, 'Albanian Problem', pp.75-6.
628 Spears to Balfour, 6/1/1919, FO371/3570/4839.
629 Woodall, 'Albanian Problem', pp.79-80.
630 Derby to Curzon, 23/4/1919, FO608/76/8228; Balfour to French Ambassador, 5/1/1919, FO608/76/9148; H. Nicolson, 'Memo. on Troops in Scutari', 7/5/1919, FO608/76/9335; Phillips to Gribbon, 11/1/1919, FO371/3570/13815; *DDI*, Series 6, I, no.518.
631 Dodge to American Delegation in Paris, 19/6/1919, 186.3411/630 (M820, r.435), DOS, RG256.
632 DMI memo., 'Situation in Albania', 2/5/1919, FO371/3571/69428; Dodge to Lansing, 18/7/1919, 763.72119/6070 (M367, r.223), DOS, RG256; Lederer, *Yugoslavia*, p.279.
633 Durham to Herbert, 3/8/1919, Herbert MSS, DD/DRU/47; Phillips to DMI, 31/12/1918, FO371/3570/13815; DMI memo., 'Situation in Albania', 12/5/1918, FO371/3571/69428; Dodge to Lansing, 18 July 1919, 763.72119/6070 (M367, r.223), DOS, RG256; Swire, *Albania*, p. 290; *Albania*, Geographic Handbook, Naval Intelligence Division B.R.542 (London, 1945), pp.176,188; Pearson,*Albania*,I,p.119; Lederer,*Yugoslavia*, p.279; Fischer, *King Zog*, pp.18-9; Swire,*Albania*, pp.287, 289, 291.
634 Durham to Herbert, 17/5/1919, Herbert MSS, DD/DRU/47; Logoreci, *Albanians*, p.208; Swire,*Albania*, pp.289-90.
635 Brodie to Phillips, 9/1/1919, FO371/3570/13815; Various minutes, 24/2/1919, FO371/3570/31676; Phillips to DMI, 13/3/1919, FO608/76/2/7/4577.
636 *Hasan Prishtina*, no.60; Serbian Peace Conference Delegation to Curzon, 24/3/1919, FO371/3571/47222; Phillips to DMI, 3/4/1919, and Derby to Curzon, 5/4/1919, FO371/3571/53987; Phillips to DMI, 18/4/1919, FO371/3571/60719; Pichon to Day, 23/5/1919, FO371/3571/79180; Day to H. Nicolson, 17/6/1919, FO608/109/1/2/12816; Phillips to DMI,

21/6/1919, FO371/3571/92486; Sonnino cited in Woodall, 'Albanian Problem', pp.95-6.

637 *Hasan Prishtina*, no. 61.

638 See for example: Herbert to Harmsworth, 21/7/1919, FO371/3571/106271; Vatra, *An Appeal to the Great People of America* (Boston, 1919), in FO371/351/138342; Vatra memo., Aug. 1919, FO371/3571/146304.

639 See for example *Hasan Prishtina*, no. 58.

640 Durham to Herbert, 3/8/1919, Herbert MSS, DD/DRU/47.

641 Dodge to Lansing, 13/9/1919, 763.72119/7183 (M367, r.439), DOS, RG256; Swire, *Albania*, pp.286-8; Pearson, *Albania*, I, pp.130, 133.

642 Dodge to Lansing, 13/9/1919, 763.72119/7183 (M367, r.439), DOS, RG256; Pastorelli, *L'Albania*, pp.318-22.

643 Dodge to Lansing, 13/6/1919, 763.72119/5340 (M367, r.417), DOS, RG256; Dodge to Lansing, 19/6/1919, 763.72119/5411 (M367, r. 419), DOS, RG256; *DBFP*, IV, nos. 10, 15; Phillips to DMI, 27/7/1919, FO371/3571/106857; Imperiali to Balfour, 4/7/1919, FO371/3571/100530; Imperiali to Balfour, 11/7/1919, FO371/3571/101474; Balfour to des Graz, 26/7/1919, FO371/3571/106525; Balfour to des Graz, 29/7/1919, FO608/97/1/1/16637; Di Cellere to Lansing, 13/8/1919, 763.72119/6184, (M367, r.425), DOS, RG256; Lederer, *Yugoslavia*, p.234; Woodall, 'Albanian Problem', pp.170-4.

644 Colby to American Delegation in Paris, 9/11/1919, 186.3411/975 (M820, r.437), US Commission, Other Questions, DOS RG256.

645 Grieve to Balfour, 1/7/1919, FO608/108/1/2/16920; Albanian Delegation to FO, 5/9/1919, FO608/76/2/6/18644; *FRUS PPC*, VIII, pp.77,306; Pearson, *Albania*, I, p.132; Swire, *Albania*, p.288; Woodall, 'Albanian Problem', pp.190-4.

646 Phillips to DMI, 5/8/1919, FO371/3571/118658; Phillips to DMI, 12/8/1919, F 371/3571/121232.

647 Adams minute, 24/9/1919, FO371/3571/132899; Phillips to Buckler, 29/9/1919, 875.00/251 (M820, r.557), DOS, RG256; Phillips to DMI, 1/10/1919, FO371/3571/143125; Phillips to DMI, 24/10/1919, FO371/3571/133792; Phillips to DMI, 14/11/1919, FO371/3571/143125; Woodall, 'Albanian Problem', pp.174-6, 182-3.

648 *DBFP*, IV, p.155; Phillips to DMI, 24/10/1919, FO371/3571/153949; Phillips to DMI, 14/11/1919, FO371/3571/166766; Pastorelli, *L'Albania*, pp.303-7, Woodall, 'Albanian Problem', p.199.

649 Eden to DMI, 20/2/1920, FO371/3571/180772.

650 Eden to DMI, 14/11/1919, FO371/3571/166766; Phillips to DMI, 16/11/1919, FO371/3571/162839; Eden to DMI, 20/2/1919, FO371/3571/180772; *Hasan Prishtina*, no.60.

651 Eden to DMI, 14/11/1919, FO371/3571/166766; Phillips to DMI, 16/11/1919; FO371/3571/162839.

652 *Albania*, Geographical Handbook, p.208; Stickney, *Southern Albania*, p.123; Swire, *Albania*, p.311; Pearson, *Albania*, I, p.137.

653 Phillips to DMI, 31/1/920, and Phillips to DMI, 8/2/1920, FO371/3571/180096; Eden to DMI, 20/2/1920, FO371/3571/180772;

Phillips to DMI, 24/2/1920, FO371/3571/185677.

654 'The Assembly of Lusnia', n.d., Herbert MSS, DD/DRU; Pearson, *Albania*, I, p.137.

655 Pearson, *Albania*, I, pp.138-40; Pollo and Puto, *History of Albania*, p.177; A. Logoreci, *The Albanians: Europe's Forgotten Survivors* (London, 1977), pp.51-2; R. Marmullaku, *Albania and the Albanians* (London, 1975), p.33; *Albania*, Geographic Handbook, pp.208-9; P. Pipinelis, *Europe and the Albanian Question* (Chicago, 2nd ed.1963), p.39; Swire, *Albania*, pp.308-11; Stickney, *Southern Albania*, pp.120-3; Pastorelli, *L'Albania*, pp.322-4; Woodall, 'Albanian Problem', pp.203-4.

656 'The Assembly of Lusnia', n.d., Herbert MSS, DD/DRU; Pearson, *Albania*, I, p.139; Logoreci, *Albanians*, pp.51-2; Swire, *Albania*, pp 268, 311-3; Pollo and Puto, *History of Albania*, p.177; Marmullaku, *Albania*, p.33; *Albania*, Geographic Handbook, pp.208-9.

657 Woodall, 'Albanian Problem', p.205; Pastorelli, *L'Albania*, pp.326-8; Pearson, *Albania*, I, pp.140-1; Swire, *Albania*, pp.312-3.

658 'The Assembly of Lusnia', n.d., Herbert MSS, DD/DRU; Pearson, *Albania*, I, p.139.

659 Lamington to Crawford, 28/4/1920, FO371/3572/194951.

660 Pearson, *Albania*, I, p.142; B.J. Fischer, *King Zog and the Struggle for Stability in Albania* (Boulder, 1984), p.20; Swire, *Albania*, p.289; Phillips to War Office, 25/3/1920, FO371/3572/195649.

661 Phillips to War Office, 25/3/1920, FO371/3572/195649; Pearson, *Albania*, I, p.142; Fischer, *King Zog*, p.20; Swire, *Albania*, pp.289, 320-1; J. Swire, *King Zog's Albania* (London, 1937), p.59; 'Albanian Problem', pp.229-30.

662 Phillips to War Office, 25/3/1920, FO371/3572/195649; Stickney, *Southern Albania*, pp.126, 128.

663 Stickney, *Southern Albania*, pp.126, 128; Pearson, *Albania*, I, pp.144-5; Fischer, *King Zog*, p.20.

664 Woodall, 'Albanian Problem', p.237; Stickney, *Southern Albania*, p.126.

665 A. Leeper minute, 27/5/1920, FO371/3572/199719; Crowe minute, 27/5/1920, FO371/3571/20003.

666 Pearson, *Albania*, I, pp.143-4; Fischer, *King Zog*, pp.20-1; Pollo and Puto, *History of Albania*, p.173; 'Quick Revolution in Albania: Essad Pasha's New Fine Adventure', *The Evening Standard*, 26/4/1920, FO371/3572/194408: However, *The Evening Standard* in London reported that the Essadist forces had been successful in occupying Tirana and overthrowing the new Tirana government.

667 Pearson, *Albania*, I, pp.144, 147: When Rystemi returned to Albania he became a leading member of the *Bashkimi* (Union) Club in opposition to Zogu, but at the time of Essad's assassination they were believed to be in cahoots together.

668 Phillips to War Office, 25/3/1920, FO371/3572/195649.

669 Woodall, 'Albanian Problem', pp.230-1.

670 Annex 4 'Extract from Annual Report on Italy for 1920' in 'A History of the Question of the Independence of Albania' memo., 2/3/1925, FO141/669/10; Buchanan to Curzon, 24/5/1920, FO371/3572/201447.

671 Buchanan to Curzon, Rome, 24/5/1920, FO371/3572/201447.

672 Buchanan to Curzon, 13/3/1920, FO371/3572/187873; Pastorelli, *L'Albania*, pp.331-33; Woodall, 'Albanian Problem', pp.231-2.

673 Granville to Curzon, 29/4/1920, FO371/3572/195088; Pastorelli, *L'Albania*, pp.328-31.

674 Duncan to Buchanan, 28/5/1920, FO371/3572/201447; Buchanan to Curzon, 12/6/1920, FO371/3572/204247; Pastorelli, *L'Albania*, pp.342, 335-6.

675 Stickney, *Southern Albania*, p.124; Pastorelli, *L'Albania*, pp.335-6; Swire, *Albania*, pp.310, 317-8.

676 Ibid.

677 Delvina report, 10/6/1920, Herbert MSS, DD/DRU/33/3; Buchanan to Curzon, 12/6/1920, FO371/3572/204247; Duncan to Buchanan, 28/5/1920, FO371/3572/201447; Buchanan to Curzon, 24/5/1920, FO371/3572/201447.

678 Swire, *Albania*, p.321; Fischer, *King Zog*, p.22; Pipinelis, *Albanian Question*, p.42; Pearson, *Albania*, I, pp.147-8.

679 Duncan to Buchanan, 28/5/1920, FO371/3572/201454; Buchanan to Curzon, 12/6/1920, FO371/3572/204247; C. Sforza, *Makers of Modern Europe* (London, 1930), pp.161, 170.

680 Sforza, *Makers of Modern Europe*, pp.161, 170; Albrecht-Carrié, *Italy*, p.297; Swire, *Albania*, p.322; Also at Pearson, *Albania*, I, pp.149-50.

681 Skendi, *Albania*, pp.12-3; Fischer, *King Zog*, pp.22-3; Pearson, *Albania*, I, pp.150-1; Swire, *Albania*, pp.322-3.

682 See for example Handel, *Weak States*, pp.175-87.

683 Ibid, pp. 257-9; Baker Fox, *Power of Small States*, p.180; Vital, *Inequality of States*, pp.5, 187.

684 Rothstein, *Alliances and the Small States*, pp.194-5; Salmon, *Scandinavia*, p.14.

685 Holtsmark cited in Salmon, *Scandinavia*, pp.15-6.

686 Page cited in Handel, *Weak States*, pp.5, 180; See also Baker Fox, *Power of Small States*, p.187.

Chapter 8

687 Herbert to Grey, 10/11/1920, Herbert MSS, DD/DRU/33.

688 M. Konitza to Wilson, 5/5/1920, Herbert MSS, DD/DRU/35.

689 Roberts, 'History, theory and narrative turn', p.713.

690 J. Barros, *The Corfu Incident of 1923: Mussolini and the League of Nations* (Princeton, 1965), pp.xix, 14.

691 Albanian Delegation to unnamed, n.d./1920, Herbert MSS, DD/DRU/35; League of Nations, *Complaints of Macedonia*, p.179.

692 Memo. by British MPs, 26/6/1920, FO371/4885/C9; Herbert to Grey, 10/11/1920, Herbert MSS, DD/DRU/33/3; Herbert and Guinness to Lloyd George, 2/8/1920, FO421/4885/C2931; Myers to Harmsworth, 2/8/1920, FO371/4885/C2930; Herbert to Harmsworth, 2/11/1920, FO371/4885/C10317.

693 Eyres to Curzon, 15/3/1922, FO421/302, no.82; Barros, *Corfu Incident*, pp.16, 309: Barros argued that the Ambassadors' Conference consideration of the Albanian question was a 'usurpation of power' not directed to it by the Peace Conference, but based on its ability to 'overstep its allotted fields of endeavour'.

694 Curzon to Imperiali, 6/9/1920, FO421/299, no.57.

695 Curzon to Russell, 24/9/1920, FO421/299, no.72.

696 Secretary-General memo., 'Application by Albania for Admission to the League of Nations', 25/11/1920, FO 371/4886/C12126.

697 See for example League of Nations, *Complaints of Macedonia*, pp.13, 17

698 Secretary-General memo., 25/11/1920, FO371/4886/C12126.

699 *The Times*, London, 18/12/1920, FO 371/4886/C13685; Committee No.5 report, n.d., FO371/7048/775/W786; Pearson, *Albania*, I, p.157.

700 Pearson, *Albania*, I, p.157.

701 *The Times*, London, 18/12/1920, FO 371/4886/C13685.

702 League of Nations minutes cited in Stickney, *Southern Albania*, p.130; Pearson, *Albania*, I, pp.157-8.

703 Pearson, *Albania*, I, p.158.

704 *he Times*, 18/12/1920, FO 371/4886/C13685.

705 Committee No. 5 report, 6/12/1920, FO371/4886/C14095; Pearson, *Albania*, I, p.155; Stickney, *Southern Albania*, pp.129-30.

706 League of Nations, *Complaints of Macedonia*, p.31.

707 Herbert to Bob [Cecil] draft, 2/12/1920, Herbert MSS, DD/DRU/33/3; Cecil to Herbert, 7/12/1920, Herbert MSS, DD/DRU/33/3.

708 Cecil to Herbert, 7/12/1920, Herbert MSS, DD/DRU/33/3.

709 FO minute, 2/11/1920, FO371/5484/W928; Curzon to de Fleurian, 11/11/1920, FO371/5484/W1852.

710 Fisher minute, 16/12/1920, FO371/7048/W786.

711 Crowe minute, 20/12/1920, FO371/4886/C13685.

712 See for example Olliphant minute, 18/12/1920, FO371/4886/C13685.

713 *The Times*, London, 18/12/1920, FO371/4886/C13685; Schroeder, 'Historical Reality', pp.117-23.

714 Rumbold to Curzon, 27/12/1920 and Crowe to Rumbold, 31/12/1920, FO371/4886/C14978; Curzon to Eyres, 17/5/1921, FO421/300, no.84; Curzon to de Martino, 20/4/1921, FO421/300, no. 62: The irony of this view appears to have been missed: if Albanian frontiers were not fixed the southern Yugoslav frontier and the north-western Greek boundary were not either.

715 Temperley statement, 9/11/1920, FO371/4885/ C10317.

716 Curzon to de Martino, 20/4/1921, FO421/300, no.62; Curzon memo., 10/6/1921, FO371/300, no.107.

717 Eyres to Curzon, 6/4/1921, FO421/300, no.71; W. Bland and I. Price, *A Tangled Web: a history of Anglo-American relations with Albania (1912-1955)* (London, 1986), p.13.

718 Goldstein, 'Britain and Greece', pp.355-6.

719 Curzon memo., 10/6/1921, FO431/300, no.107.

720 For example Eyres to Curzon, 10/5/1921, FO421/300, no.88; Pearson,

Albania, I, p.160.
721 For example Herbert to Harmsworth, 2/11/1920, FO371/4885/C10317.
722 Granville to Curzon, 1/6/1921, FO421/300, no.99.
723 For example Evangjeli to US Government, 17/5/1921, Herbert MSS, DD/DRU/45; *Albania and Kosovo*, I, no.130: Pearson, *Albania*, I, p.160, Swire, *Albania*, p.343.
724 League of Nations minutes cited in Stickney, *Southern Albania*, p.131; Pearson, *Albania*, I, pp.163-5; Pollo and Puto, *History of Albania*, p.183.
725 M. Frasheri to Herbert, 6/6/1921, Herbert MSS, DD/DRU/33/1; Stickney, *Southern Albania*, pp.132-3; Pearson, *Albania*, I, pp.164-5.
726 For further details see Stickney, *Southern Albania*, pp.132-9.
727 League of Nations minutes cited in Stickney, *Southern Albania*, p.136; Pearson, *Albania*, I, p.166; Swire, *Albania*, p.292.
728 For example see Noli to Herbert, 18/7/1921, Herbert MSS, DD/DRU/45; United Committee of Kosovë and Çhamëria, 24/8/1920, quoted in Pearson, *Albania*, I, p.169; Stickney, *Southern Albania*, p.137; Swire, *Albania*, p.292.
729 H. Nicolson minute, 13/11/1920, FO371/4885,C10317; Pearson, *Albania*, I, pp.169-72; League of Nations minutes cited in Stickney, *Southern Albania*, pp.139, 141-4; Stavrianos, *Balkans since 1453*, pp.714-15.
730 Barros, *Corfu Incident*, p.10.
731 Young to Curzon, 25/11/1920, FO371/4886/C12253; A. Leeper minute, 26/11/1920, FO371/4886/C12253.
732 Curzon to de Martino, 20/4/1921, FO421/300, no.62; *Albania and Kosovo*, I, no.127; de Martino to Curzon, 20/6/1921, FO421/300, no.116; Pearson, *Albania*, I, p.164.
733 de Martino to Curzon, 20/6/1921, FO421/300, no.116,
734 Curzon to Hardinge, 30/6/1921, FO421/300, no.131.
735 Curzon to de. Martino, 17/9/1921, FO421/301, no.75.
736 Cheetham to Curzon, n.d./1921, FO421/301, no.19.
737 Crowe minute, 1/9/1921, FO421/301, no.61; Curzon to de Martino, 17/9/1921, FO421/301, no. 75; Conference of Ambassadors minutes, 28/9/1921, FO893/13/2.
738 Curzon to de Martino, 17/9/1921, FO421/301, no.75.
739 'Declaration relative to the Independence and Integrity of Albania' (British Empire, France, Italy and Japan), 9/11/921, FO93/117/2; 'History of question of independence of Albania' memo., 2/3/1925, FO141/669/10; Pearson, *Albania*, I, p.176.
740 Curzon to de Martino, 17/9/1921, FO421/301, no.75; Milo, 'Albania and the Balkan Entente', p.41; Pearson, *Albania*, I, pp.175-6; E. Manta, 'Reciprocal Relationship between Politics and Economics: The Renewal of the 1926 Treaty of Tirana', *Balkan Studies*, 37 (1996), pp.309-30, at p.311.
741 Chamberlain to Graham, n.d./12/1926, FO421/311, no.88; Graham to Chamberlain, 3/12/1926, FO421/311, no.90.
742 Barros, *Corfu Incident*, p.19; Pearson, *Albania*, I, pp.175-6,
743 On boundary commissions after World War One see S.B. Jones, *Boundary-Making: A Handbook for Statesmen, Treaty Editors and Boundary Commissioners* (Washington D. C., 1945) esp. pp.229-39.

744 Pearson, *Albania*, I, pp.175-6; Swire, *Albania*, p.364.
745 *DDI*, Series 7, II, no.205: Barros, *Corfu Incident*, pp.140-1.
746 Barros, *Corfu Incident*, pp.304, 307.
747 For further details of the 1922-26 boundary commissions see *Albania and Kosovo*, I, nos.136-60.
748 Rothstein, *Alliances and Small States*, pp.194-5; Salmon, *Scandinavia*, p.14; Vital, *Inequality of States*, p.189.
749 Sharp, 'Minorities', p.184.
750 Barros, *Corfu Incident*, pp.301-2, 304.
751 League of Nations, *Complaints of Macedonia*, pp.12, 22-3.

Conclusions

752 H. Nicolson quoted in League of Nations, *Complaints of Macedonia*, p.23.
753 Grey quoted in Durham, *Balkan Tangle*, p.258.
754 For further discussion of offensive and defensive realism see H.M. Scott, 'Paul W. Schroeder's International System: The View from Vienna', *International History Review*, 16 (1994), pp.663-80, esp. pp.666-8 and Rendell, 'Defensive Realism and the Concert of Europe', pp.523-40.
755 See for example R.W. Seton-Watson, *A History of Roumania from Roman Times to the Completion of Unity* (Cambridge, 1934), p.438; Also at Farrar, 'Aggression versus Apathy', p.269.
756 Curzon quoted in Petsalis-Diomidis, *Greece*, p.3.
757 Hylland Eriksen, *Ethnicity and Nationalism*, pp.161-2.
758 See for example C.E.J. Fryer, *The Destruction of Serbia in 1915* (New York, 1997), esp. pp.49-125.
759 For similar ideas see Verdery, 'Ethnicity', p.40 and Sharp, 'Genie', p.23.
760 *FRUS PPC*, III, p. 860; Nicolson, *Peacemaking*, pp.255-6.
761 Hylland Eriksen, *Ethnicity and Nationalism*, pp.1-4, 161-2; Gellner, *Nations and Nationalism*, pp.53-4.
762 O. Zimmer, 'Boundary mechanisms and symbolic resources: towards a process-orientated approach to national identity', *Nations and Nationalism*, 9 (2003), pp.173-93; R. Brubaker, *Ethnicity without Groups* (Cambridge, Mass., 2004).
763 Duijzings, *Religion and Politics*, pp.13-9.
764 R. Brubaker, *Nationalism Reframed: Nationhood and the National Question in the New Europe* (Cambridge, 1996), p.204; Verdery, 'Ethnicity', p.47.
765 Wilkinson, *Maps and Politics*, pp.316-7.
766 Doughty-Wylie, 2/10/1913, FO421/287/46121; Attachment in Doughty-Wylie, 5/10/1913, FO421/287/46428.
767 *DBFP*, II, no.141.

A Selective Who's Who

768 This is based on a variety of sources including: R. Elsie, *Historical Dictionary of Kosova* (Lanham Maryland, Toronto, Oxford, 2004); R. Elsie, *Historical Dictionary of Albania* (Lanham Maryland, Toronto, Oxford, 2004); R. Hutchings, *Historical Dictionary of Albania* (Lanham, Maryland, Toronto,

Oxford, 1966); and B.D. Destani and J. Tomes (eds.), *Albania's Greatest Friend: Aubrey Herbert and the Making of Modern Albania: Diaries and Papers 1904-1923* (London, 2011)

Appendices

769 http://en.wikipedia.org/wiki/Image; Albanian Vilayets of Ottoman Empire.jpg: [link no longer active] The newly independent state of Kosova (shown by dashed lines) is about one quarter the size of the former Ottoman *vilayet* (shaded and solid lines).
770 Based on Balkan Map 13, DOS, RG256.
771 'Annex to the Official Report of the Fifteenth Session' [trans. from French by D. Guy], SAC minutes, 17/12/1913, FO93/1/36.
772 Centre For Albanian Studies/collection of maps/1
773 Temperley, *History of the Peace Conference*, IV, p.338 [Kindly reproduced with permission of the Royal Institute of International Affairs].

Selected Bibliography

Primary Sources

Unpublished
The National Archives: Public Record Office (PRO), Kew, London
Admiralty Papers
ADM1   Admiralty and Secretariat Papers
ADM116   Admiralty and Secretariat Cases
ADM137   War of 1914-1918: War History Cases

Cabinet Papers
CAB21   Cabinet Registered Files
CAB23   Cabinet Office (Minutes and Conclusions)
CAB28   Cabinet Series Papers
CAB29   International Conferences
CAB37   Cabinet Papers 1880-1916

Foreign Office Correspondence
FO93   General Protocols
FO141   Consulate and Legation, Egypt: General Correspondence
FO286   Consulate and Legation, Greece (formerly Ottoman
            Empire): General Correspondence
FO294   Consulate Papers
FO320   Records of Commissions
FO371   General Correspondence: Political
FO372   Treaty Department
FO373   Peace Conference Handbooks
FO374   Peace Conference Acts
FO421   Confidential Print: South-East Europe
FO608   British Peace Conference Delegation
FO800   Private Collections: Ministers and Officers
FO881   Confidential Print (Numerical Series)

War Office
WO106   Directorate of Military Operations and Military
            Intelligence, and predecessors: Correspondence and Papers
WO107   Office of the Commander in Chief and War Office Quarter-
            master General's Department: Correspondence and Papers

Miscellaneous
GFM33   German Foreign Ministry Archives: Photostat copies

National Archives at College Park (NACP), College Park, Maryland
Department of State
M367   Records of the Department of State Relating to World War I and
           Its Termination, 1914-29
M820   General Records of the American Commission to Negotiate Peace,
           1918 to 1931
M1107   'Inquiry Documents' 1917-1919
M1211   Records of the Department of State relating to Internal Affairs of
           Albania, 1910-1944

Private papers
Aubrey Herbert MP (Somerset Record Office, Taunton)
David Lloyd George MP (House of Lords Record Office, London)

Published

Adoratsky, V.V., Maksakov, V.V., and Pokrovsky, M.N. (eds.),
    Красный Архив (*Krasnyi Arkhiv*), 106 vols. (Moscow, 1922-41), esp. vols. VI,
    VII, VIII, IX, XV, XVI, XXV, C

Bol'shemennikov, A.P., Erusalimskii, A.S., Mogilevich, A.A., and
    Rotschein, R.A. (eds.), *Международные отношения в эпоху империализма:*
    Документы из архив царского и временного правительств 1878-1917 гг
    (*International Affairs in the period of imperialism: Documents from the Archive of*
    the Tsar and Provisional Government 1878-1917), Series 2, 21 vols. and Series
    3, 10 vols. (Moscow, 1931-1940)
Bourne, K., and Watt, D.C. (gen. eds.), Dockrill, M. (series ed.),
    British Documents on Foreign Affairs: Reports and Papers from the Foreign Office
    Confidential Print, Part II, From the First to the Second World War, Series I, the
    Paris Peace Conference of 1919, 15 vols. (UPA, c.1989-91)
Bridge, F.R. (ed.), *Austro-Hungarian Documents Relating to the Macedonian*
    Struggle, 1896-1912 (Thessaloniki, 1976)

Carnegie Endowment for International Peace, *Report of the International*
    Commission to Inquire into the Causes and Conduct of the Balkan Wars (Wash-
    ington D.C., republ. 1993, of original of 1914) *Correspondence Relating to the*
    Adriatic Question (Misc. No.2, London, 1920)

Destani, B.D., and Tomes, J. (eds.), *Albania's Greatest Friend: Aubrey Herbert*
    and the Making of Modern Albania: Diaries and Papers 1904-1923 (London,
    2011)
Destani, B.D. (ed.), *Albania and Kosovo: Political and Ethnic Boundaries*
    1867-1946, 2 vols. (London, 1999)
Destani, B.D., (ed.), *Edith Durham-Albania and the Albanians: Selected*

Articles and Letters, 1903-1944 (London, 2001)

Destani, B.D. (ed.), *Ethnic Minorities in the Balkan States 1860-1971*, 6 vols. (London, 2003)

Destani, B.D. (ed.), *Faik Konitza: Selected Correspondence 1896-1942* (London, 2000)

Documents Diplomatiques Français, 1871-1914, Series 3, 1911-1914, 11 vols. (Paris, 1929)

Eisele, L.W., *A Digest of the Krasnyi Arkhiv*, vols. 31-106 (Ann Arbor, 1955)

Gooch, G.P., and Temperley, H. (eds.), *British Documents on the Origins of the War, 1898-1914*, 11 vols. (London, 1926-38), esp. vols. IX.i, IX.ii, X.i, X.ii, XI

League of Nations, *The Complaints of Macedonia: Memoranda, Petitions, Resolutions, Minutes, Letters and Documents, Addressed to the League of Nations, 1919-1939* (Geneva, 1979)

Mantoux, P., 'Introduction' to P. Mantoux (ed.), (trans. A.S. Link), *The Deliberations of the Council of Four (March 24-June 28, 1919): Notes of the Delivery to the German Delegation of the Preliminaries of Peace: Supplementary Volume to the Papers of Woodrow Wilson*, 2 vols. (Princeton, 1955)

Ministero Degli Affari Esteri (Commissione per la pubblicazione dei documenti diplomatici), *I Documenti Diplomatici Italiani*, Series 4: 1908-1914, 12 vols. (Roma, 1952-64), esp. vol.XII, Series 5: 1914-1918, 10 vols. (Roma, 1954-56), Series 6: 1918-1922, 2 vols. (Roma, 1956), esp. vol.I, and Series 7: 1922-1935, 10 vols. (Roma, 1953-1990), esp. vol.II.

Nuro, K., and Bato, N. (eds.), *Hasan Prishtina: Përmbledhje Dok mentesh 1908-1934* (*Hasan Prishtina: Published Documents 1908-1934*) (Tirana, 1982)

Pribram, A.F., (Myers D.P. and D'Arcy Paul, J.G. (trans.)), *The Secret Treaties of Austria-Hungary*, 2 vols. (Cambridge, Mass., 1920-21, repr. New York, 1967)

Rubinchek, L.S., (compiled, translated and annotated) *A Digest of the Krasnyi Arkhiv: A Historical Journal of the Central Archive Department of the U.S.S.R*, vols. 1-30 (Cleveland, 1947)

de Siebert, B. (ed.), *Entente Diplomacy and the World, 3 vols.* (New York and London, 1921)

U.S. Department of State (ed.), *Papers Relating to the Foreign Relations of the United States of America 1919: The Paris Peace Conference*, 13 vols. (Washington, D.C., 1942-47)

Woodward, E.L., and, Butler, R., *Documents on British Foreign Policy 1919-1939*, Series 1, 21 Vols. (London, 1947-78)

Secondary Sources

Books

Albania, Foreign Office Handbook, Historical Section No.17 (London, 1920).
Albania, Geographical Handbook, Naval Intelligence Division B.R.542 (London, 1945)
Albertini, L., *The Origins of the War of 1914* (Massey, I. (trans.)), 3 vols (London 1952-7)
Albrecht-Carrié, R., *Italy at the Paris Peace Conference* (New York, 1938)
Anderson, B., *Imagined Communities: Reflections on the Origin and the Spread of Nationalism* (London, 1983)

Baker Fox, A., *The Power of Small States: Diplomacy in World War II* (London, 1959)
Banac, I., *The National Question in Yugoslavia: Origins, History, Politics* (Ithaca, New York, 1992)
Banac, I. and Verdery, K. (eds.) *National Character and National Ideology in Interwar Eastern Europe* (New Haven, Connecticut, 1995)
Barros, J., *The Corfu Incident of 1923: Mussolini and the League of Nations* (Princeton, 1965)
Barth, R. (ed.), *Ethnic Groups and Boundaries: The Social Organisation of Cultural Difference* (Prospect Heights, Illinois, 1988 repr. of original 1969)
von Benda-Beckmann, K., and Verkuyten, M. (eds.), *Nationalism, Ethnicity and Cultural Identity in Europe: Comparative Studies in Migration and Ethnic Relations 1* (Utrecht, 1995)
Bland, W., and Price, I., *A Tangled Web: A History of Anglo-American Relations with Albania* (1912 -1955) (London, 1986)
Blumi, I., *Rethinking the Late Ottoman Empire: A Comparative Social and Political History of Albania and Yemen 1878-1918* (İstanbul, 2003)
Bonsal, S., *Suitors and Supplicants: The Little Nations at Versailles* (New York, 1946)
Bonsal, S., *Unfinished Business* (Garden City, New York, 1944)
Bosworth, R.J.B., *Italy, the Least of the Great Powers: Italian Foreign Policy before the First World War* (Cambridge, 1979)
Bourcart, J., *L'Albanie et les Albanais* (Paris, 1921)
Brailsford, H.N., *Macedonia, its Races and their Future* (London, 1906)
Bridge, F.R., *From Sadowa to Sarajevo: The Foreign Policy of Austria-Hungary, 1868-1914* (London, 1972)
Bridge, F.R., *Great Britain and Austria-Hungary, 1906-1914: A Diplomatic History* (London, 1972)
Brown, B., *The Past in Question: Modern Macedonia and the Uncertainties of Nation* (Princeton and Oxford, 2003)
Brubaker, R., *Ethnicity without Groups* (Cambridge, Mass., 2004)
Brubaker, R., *Nationalism Reframed: Nationhood and the National Question in the New Europe* (Cambridge, 1996)

Buchan, J., *Greenmantle* (London, 1916)

Buckley, W.J., *Kosovo: Contending Voices on Balkan Interventions*
(Grand Rapids, Michigan and Cambridge, 2000)

Burgwyn, H.J., *The Legend of the Mutilated Victory: Italy, the Great War, and the
Paris Peace Conference, 1915-1919* (London and Westport, Connecticut, 1993)

Carver, R., *The Accursed Mountains: Journeys in Albania* (London, 1998)

Chekrezi, C.A., *Albania Past and Present* (New York, 1919)

Clogg, R., *A Concise History of Greece* (Cambridge, 1992)

Clogg, R. (ed.), *Minorities in Greece: Aspects of a Plural Society* (London, 2002)

Cobban, A., *The Nation State and National Self-Determination*
(London and Glasgow, 1969)

Costa, N.J., *Albania: A European Enigma* (Boulder, 1995)

Costa, N.J., *Shattered Illusions: Albania, Greece and Yugoslavia* (Boulder, 1998)

Craig, G.A., and Gilbert, F. (ed.), *The Diplomats 1919-1939* (Princeton, 1953)

Crampton, R.J., *The Hollow Detente: Anglo-German Relations in the Balkans
1911-1914* (London, 1979)

Crampton, R.J., and Crampton, B., *Atlas of Eastern Europe in the Twentieth
Century* (London and New York, 1996)

Crowe, S. and Corp, E., *Our Ablest Public Servant: Sir Eyre Crowe 1864-1925*
(Brauton, 1993)

Curtright, L.H., *Muddle, Indecision and Setback: British Policy and the Balkan
States, August 1914 to the Inception of the Dardanelles Campaign* (Thessaloniki,
1986)

Cvijić, J., *La Peninsula Balkanique* (Paris, 1918)

Çami, M., *Fundamental Aspects of the Albanian National and Democratic Movement
in the Years 1913-1920: National Conference Dedicated to the 70th Anniversary of
the Proclamation of Independence November 19, 1982* (Tirana, 1983)

Dako, C.A., *Albania: The Master Key to the Near East* (Boston, Mass. 1919)

Dallin, A. *et al*, *Russian Diplomacy and Eastern Europe 1914-1917*
(New York, 1963)

Delanty, G., *Inventing Europe: Idea, Identity, Reality* (Basingstoke and
London, 1995)

Destani, B.D., *The Albanian Question* (London, 1996)

Destani, B.D., *Bibliography on Albania* (Belgrade, 1986)

Dieckhoff, A., *The Invention of a Nation: Zionist Thought and the Making of
Modern Israel* (London, 1993)

Djordjevic, D. (ed.), *The Creation of Yugoslavia* (Santa Barbara and Oxford, 1980)

Djordjević, V. (trans. A Karadjordjević), *Les Albanais et les Grandes
Puissances* (Paris, 1913)

Dockrill, M.L., and Fisher, J. (eds.), *The Paris Peace Conference, 1919 Peace
without Victory* (London, 2001)

Dockrill, M.L., and French, D. (eds.), *Strategy and Intelligence: British
Policy during the First World War* (London and Rio Grande, Ohio, 1996)

Dockrill, M.L., and Gould, J. D., *Peace Without Promise: Britain and the Peace*

Conferences, 1919-23 (London, 1981)

Dockrill, M.L., and McKercher, B. (eds.), *Diplomacy and World Power: Studies in British Foreign Policy 1890-195* (Cambridge, 1996)

Dogo, M., and Franzinetti, G. (eds.), *Disrupting and Reshaping: Early Stages of Nation-Building in the Balkans* (Ravenna, 2002)

Dragnich, A.N., *Serbia, Nicola Pašic and Yugoslavia* (New Brunswick New Jersey, 1974)

Dragnich, A.N., and Todorovich, S., *The Saga of Kosovo: Focus on Serbian-Albanian Relations* (Boulder and New York, 1984)

Duijzings, G., *Religion and the Politics of Identity in Kosovo* (London, 2000)

Duijzings, G. (gen. ed.), Janjić, D., and Maliqi, S. (eds.), *Kosovo-Kosova: Confrontation or Co-existence* (Nijmegen, 1996)

Dunn, S., and Fraser, G. (eds.), *Europe and Ethnicity: The First World War and Contemporary Ethnic Conflict* (London, 1996)

Durham, M.E., *High Albania* (London, 1909)

Durham, M.E., *The Struggle For Scutari (Turk, Slav and Albanian)* (London, 1914)

Durham, M.E., *Twenty Years of the Balkan Tangle* (London, 1920)

Dutton, D., *The Politics of Diplomacy: Britain and France in the Balkans in the First World War* (London and New York, 1998)

Elsie, R. (ed.), *Kosovo in the Heart of the Powder Keg* (Boulder, 1997)

Elsie, R., *A Dictionary of Albanian Religion, Mythology and Folk Culture* (London, 2001)

Elsie, R., *History of Albanian Literature*, 2 vols. (New York, 1995)

Elsie, R., *Historical Dictionary of Albania* (Lanham Maryland, Toronto, Oxford, 2004)

Elsie, R., *Historical Dictionary of Kosova* (Lanham Maryland, Toronto, Oxford, 2004)

Eubank, K.K., *Paul Cambon: Master Diplomatist* (Oklahoma, 1960)

Fay, S.B., *The Origins of the World War, Before Sarajevo: Underlying Causes of the War* (New York, 1929)

Fischer, B.J., *King Zog and the Struggle for Stability in Albania* (Boulder, 1984)

Fishta, G., (trans. R. Elsie and J. Mathie-Heck), *The Highland Lute (Lahuta e Malcis): The Albanian National Epic* (London, 2005)

Fitzherbert, M., *The Man who was Greenmantle: A Biography of Aubrey Herbert* (London, 1983)

Fleure, H.J., *The Treaty Settlement of Europe: Some Geographic and Ethnographic aspects* (London, 1921)

Fryer, C.E.J., *The Destruction of Serbia in 1915* (New York, 1997)

Gallagher, T., *Outcast Europe: The Balkans, 1789-1989* (London, 2001)

Gawrych, G.W., *The Crescent and the Eagle: Ottoman Rule, Islam and the Albanians, 1874-1913* (London and New York, 2006)

Geary, P.J., *The Myth of Nations: The Medieval Origins of Europe* (Princeton and Oxford, 2002)

Gedaktor, G., and Bromchei, U.V. (eds.), *Народы Мира: историко-этнорафический спрадочник* (*Countries of the World: History and Ethnographic Handbook*) (Moscow, 1988)

Gelfand, L.E., *The Inquiry: American Preparations for Peace, 1917-1919* (New Haven, 1963)

Gellner, E., *Encounters with Nationalism* (Oxford, 1994)

Gellner, E., *Nations and Nationalism: New Perspectives on the Past* (Oxford, 1983)

Geshkoff, T.I., *Balkan Union: A Road to Peace in South-Eastern Europe* (New York, 1940)

Gilbert, M., *The European Powers, 1900-1945* (London, 1965)

Glenny, M., *The Balkans: Nationalism, War and the Great Powers 1804-1999* (London, 2000, repr. of 1999 original)

Goldstein, E.D., *The First World War Peace Settlements, 1919-1925* (London, 2002)

Goldstein, E.D., *Winning the Peace* (Oxford, 1991)

Goslinga, G.T.A., *The Dutch in Albania* (Rome, 1972)

Gottlieb, W.W., *Studies in Secret Diplomacy during the First World War* (London, 1957)

Green, S.F., *Notes from the Balkans: Locating Marginality and Ambiguity on the Greek-Albanian Border* (Princeton and Oxford, 2005)

Grey of Fallodon, D.G., *Twenty-five Years 1892-1916*, 2 vols. (London, 1925)

Gueshov, I.E., *The Balkan League* (London, 1915)

Hall, D., *Albania and the Albanians* (London, 1994)

Hall, R.C., *The Balkan Wars 1912-1913: Prelude to the First World War* (London, 2000)

Handel, M., *Weak States in the International System* (London, 1981)

Hankey, M., *The Supreme Command 1914-1918*, 2 vols. (London, 1961)

Hankey, M., *The Supreme Control: At the Paris Peace Conference 1919, A Commentary* (London, 1963)

Hastings, A., *The Construction of Nationhood: Ethnicity, Religion and Nationalism* (Cambridge, 1997)

Headlam-Morley, A. (ed.), *Sir James Headlam-Morley: A Memoir of the Paris Peace Conference 1919* (London, 1972)

Headlam-Morley, J., *Studies in Diplomatic History* (London, 1930)

Heaton-Armstrong, D., *The Sixth Month Kingdom: Albania 1914* (London, 2005)

Helmreich, E.C., *The Diplomacy of the Balkan Wars 1912-1913* (Cambridge, Massachusetts, 1938)

Helmreich, P.C., *From Paris to Sèvres: The Partition of the Ottoman Empire at the Peace Conference of 1919-20* (Columbus, Ohio, 1974)

Henig, R.B., *The League of Nations* (New York, 1973)

Hetzer, A., and Viorel, S.R., *Albanien* (Munich, 1983)

Hinsley, F.H. (ed.), *British Foreign Policy under Sir Edward Grey* (Cambridge, 1977)

Hinsley, F.H., *Nationalism and the International System* (London, 1973)

Hinsley, F.H., *Power and the Pursuit of Peace: Theory and Practice in the History of*

Relations Between States (Cambridge, 1963)

Hobsbawn, E., *Nations and Nationalism since 1780: Programme, Myth, Reality* (Cambridge, 1990)

Hobsbawn, E., and Ranger, T., *The Invention of Tradition* (Cambridge, 1983)

Hodgkinson, H., *Scanderbeg* (London, 1999)

Hroch, M., *In the National Interest: Demands and Goals of European National Movements in the Nineteenth Century: A Comparative Perspective* (Prague, 1996)

Hroch, M., *The Social Interpretation of Linguistic Demands in European National Movements* (Florence, 1994)

Hroch, M., *Social Preconditions for National Revival in Europe: A Comparative Analysis of the Social Composition of Patriotic Groups among Smaller European Nations* (New York, 2000)

Hupchick, D.P., and Cox, H.E., *A Concise Historical Atlas of Eastern Europe* (London, 1996)

Hutchings, R., *Historical Dictionary of Albania* (London, 1966)

Hutchinson, J., and Smith, A.D., (eds.), *Nationalism* (Oxford, 1994)

Hylland Eriksen, T., *Ethnicity and Nationalism: Anthropological Perspectives* (London and Boulder, Colorado, 1993)

Jacques, E.E., *The Albanians: An Ethnic History from Prehistoric Times to the Present* (Jefferson, North Carolina, 1995)

Jakupi, A., *Two Albanian States and National Unification* (Prishtina, 1997)

Jelavich, B., *History of the Balkans Vol.II: Twentieth Century* (Cambridge, 1983)

Jelavich, B., *Russia's Balkan Entanglements 1806-1914* (Cambridge, 1991)

Jelavich, B., and Jelavich, C., *The Establishment of the Balkan National States 1804-1920* (Seattle and London, 1977)

Jones, S.B., *Boundary-Making: A Handbook for Statesmen, Treaty Editors and Boundary Commissioners* (Washington D.C., 1945)

Judah, T., *Kosovo: War and Revenge* (London, 2000)

Kaltenbach, F.W., *Self-Determination 1919* (London, 1938)

Kedourie, E., *Nationalism* (London, 1993)

Keiger, J.F.V., *France and the Origins of the First World War* (Basingstoke, 1983)

Kent, M., *The Great Powers and the End of the Ottoman Empire* (London, 1984)

Kola, P., *The Search for Greater Albania* (London, 2003)

Kolstø, P., *Myths and Boundaries in South Eastern Europe* (London, 2005)

Kondis, B., *Greece and Albania, 1908-1914* (Thessaloniki, 1976)

Kondis, B., *The Greeks of Northern Epirus and Greek-Albanian Relations: Historical Review from the Greek Edition* (Athens, 1996)

Konitza, F., *Albania: the Rock Garden of South-eastern Europe and Other Essays* (Boston, 1957)

Kyriakidis, S., *The Northern Ethnological Boundaries of Hellenism* (Thessaloniki, 1955)

Lampe, J., and Mazower, M., (eds.), *Ideologies and National Identities: the Case of Twentieth-Century Southeastern Europe* (New York, 2004)

Langer, W.L., *European Alliances and Alignments, 1871-1890* (2nd ed., New York, 1960)

Langhorne, R., *The Collapse of the Concert of Europe: International Politics 1890-1914* (London, 1981)

Lansing, R., *The Peace Negotiations* (Boston, Massachusetts, and London, 1921)

Lederer, I.J., *Yugoslavia at the Paris Peace Conference: A Study in Frontiermaking* (New Haven and London, 1963)

Leon, G.B., *Greece and the Great Powers 1914-1917* (Thessaloniki, 1974)

Leurdijk, D., and Zandee, D., *Kosovo: From Crisis to Crisis* (Aldershot, 2001)

Lichnowsky, C.M., *My Mission to London* (London, 1918)

Link, A.S., *Woodrow Wilson: Revolution, War and Peace during World War I* (Wilmington, Delaware, 1991)

Lloyd George, D., *Memoirs of the Peace Conference*, 2 vols. (New Haven, Connecticut, 1939)

Lloyd George, D., *The Truth about the Peace Treaties*, 2 vols. (London, 1938)

Lloyd George, D., *War Memoirs*, 6 vols. (London, 1933-1936)

Logoreci, A., *The Albanians: Europe's Forgotten Survivors* (London, 1977)

Lowe, C.J., and Mazari, F., *Italian Foreign Policy, 1870-1940* (London, 1975)

Lukacs, J.A., *The Great Powers and Eastern Europe* (New York, 1952)

Maccas, L., *La Question Gréco-Albanaise* (Paris, 1921)

MacDonald, S., (ed.), *Inside European Identities: Ethnography in Western Europe* (Providence, 1993)

MacFie, A.L., *The Eastern Question, 1774-1923* (New York, 2nd ed.1996)

MacMillan, M., *Peacemakers: The Paris Conference of 1919 and Its Attempt to End the War* (London, 2001)

Magocsi, P.R., *Historical Atlas of Central Europe: From the Early Fifth Century to the Present* (Seattle and London, 2002)

Malcolm, N., *Bosnia: A Short History* (London, 1994)

Malcolm, N., *Kosovo: A Short History* (London, 1998)

Mamatey, V., *The United States and East Central Europe 1914-1918: A Study in Wilsonian Diplomacy and Propaganda* (Princeton, 1957)

Marks, S., *The Illusion of Peace: International Relations in Europe 1918-1933* (Basingstoke, 2003)

Marmullaku, R., *Albania and the Albanians* (London, 1975)

Marston, F.S., *The Peace Conference of 1919, Organisation and Procedure* (London, 1944)

Mazower, M., *The Balkans* (London, 2001)

Medlicott, W.N., *The Congress of Berlin and After: A Diplomatic History of the Near East Settlement, 1878-1880* (London, 1938)

McCarthy, J., *Death and Exile: Ethnic Cleansing of the Ottoman Muslims, 1 821-1922* (Princeton, New Jersey, 1995)

McCarthy, J., *The Ottoman Peoples and the End of the Empire* (London, 2001)

Micgiel, J.S. (ed.), *State and Nation Building in East Central Europe: Contemporary Perspectives* (New York, 1996)

Mitrović, A., (ed.), *Срби и Албанци у XX веку* (*Serbs and Albanians in the 20th Century*) (Belgrade, 1991)

Medlicott, W. N., *The Congress of Berlin and After: A Diplomatic History of the Near Eastern Settlement 1878-1880* (London, 1938)
Mowat, R.B., *A History of European Diplomacy, 1914-1925* (London, 1927)

Neilson, K., *Britain and the Last Tsar: British Policy and Russia, 1894-1917* (Oxford, 1996)
Nicolson, H., *Curzon: The Last Phase 1919-1925 – A Study in the Old Diplomacy* (London 1930)
Nicolson, H., *Peacemaking 1919* (London, 1933)
Northedge, F.S., *The Troubled Giant: Britain among the Great Powers 1916-1939* (London, 1966)

Page, T.N., *Italy and the World War* (New York, 1920)
Pastorelli, P., *L'Albania nella Politica Estera Italiana 1914-1920* (Naples, 1970)
Pavlowitch, S.K., *A History of the Balkans 1804-1945* (London and New York, 1999)
Peacock, P., *One Candle for Albania* (Penzance, 1999)
Peacock, W., *Albania: The Foundling State of Albania* (London, 1914)
Pearson, O., *Albania in the Twentieth Century: A History*, 3 vols. (London, 2003), esp. vol. I, *Albania and King Zog: Independence, Republic and Monarchy 1908-1939*
Petrovich, M.B., *A History of Modern Serbia, 1804-1918*, 2 vols. (New York and London, 1976)
Petsalis-Diomidis, N., *Greece at the Paris Peace Conference 1919* (Thessaloniki, 1978)
Pettifer, J., *Albania and Kosovo* (London, 2001)
Pettifer, J., *Kosova Express: A Journey in Wartime* (London, 2005)
Pettifer, J., and Vickers, M., *The Albanian Question: Reshaping the Balkans* (London, 2007)
Pipinelis, P., *Europe and the Albanian Question* (Chicago, 2nd ed.1963)
Pollo, S., et al., *Histoire de l'Albania, des Origins à Nos Jours* (Roanne, 1974)
Pollo, S., and Puto, A., (Wiseman, C. and Hole, G. (trans.), *The History of Albania: From its Origins to the Present Day* (London, Boston and Henley, 1981)
Poulton, H., *The Balkans: Minorities and States in Conflict* (London, 2nd ed. 1993)
Pribram, A.F., *Austrian Foreign Policy, 1908-1918* (London, 1923)
Pribram, A.F., (Morrow, F.D. (trans.)), *Austria-Hungary and Great Britain 1908-1914* (London, 1951)
Pribram, A.F., *The Secret Treaties of Austria-Hungary*, 2 vols. (Cambridge, Mass., 1920-1)
Puto, A., *From the Annals of British Diplomacy (The anti-Albanian plans of Great Britain during the Second World War according to the Foreign Office Documents of 1939-1944)* (Tirana, 1981)
Puto, A., *L'Indépendence Albanaise et la Diplomatic des Grande Puissances, 1912-1914* (Tirana, 1982)
Rahimi, Sh., *Vilajeti i Kosovës më 1878-1912 (The Vilayet of Kosovo from 1878-1912)* (Prishtina, 1969)
Reed, J., *The War in Eastern Europe: Travels Through the Balkans in 1915*

(London, 1916, republ. 1994)

Rich, N., *Great Power Diplomacy 1814-1914* (New York, 1992)

Risaj, S., *Kosova, Albanians and Turks: Yesterday, Today and Tomorrow* (Prishtine, Istanbul and Tirana, 1993)

Robbins, K.G., *Sir Edward Grey: A Biography of Lord Grey of Fallodon* (London, 1971)

Robinson, V., *Albania's Road to Freedom* (London, 1941)

Robotycki, C. (ed.), *Cultural Identity and Ethnicity in Central Europe: Proceedings of the International Conference on Ethnic and National Minorities in Central and Eastern Europe* (Cracow, 2003)

Rodd, R., *Social and Diplomatic Memories, 1902-1919* (London, 1925)

Roshwald, A., *Ethnic Nationalism and the Fall of Empires: Central Europe, Russia and the Middle East, 1914-1923* (London and New York, 2001)

Rothstein, R.L., *Alliances and the Small States* (New York, 1968)

Rothwell, V.H., *British War Aims and Peace Diplomacy 1914-1918* (Oxford, 1971)

Roux, M., *Les Albanais en Yougoslavie: Minorité Nationale Territoire et Développement* (Paris, 1992)

Salandra, A., *Italy and the Great War, From Neutrality to Intervention* (London, 1932)

Salmon, P., *Scandinavia and the Great Powers 1890-1940* (Cambridge, 1997)

Sazonov, S., (N.A. Duddington (trans.), *Fateful Years, 1909-1916: Reminiscences of Sergei Sazonov, Russian Minister for Foreign Affairs* (New York, 1928)

Scales, L., and Zimmer, O., *Power and the Nation in European History* (Cambridge, 2005)

Schönfeld, R. (ed.), *Nationalitätenprobleme in Südosteuropa* (Munich, 1987)

Schöpflin, G., *Nations, Identity, Power: The New Politics of Europe* (London, 2000)

Schroeder, P.W., *The Transformation of European Politics 1763-1848* (Oxford, 1994)

Schwander-Sievers, S., and Fischer, B. J. (eds.), *Albanian Identities: Myth and History* (London, 2002)

Seton-Watson, H., *Nations and States: An Inquiry into the Origins of Nations and the Politics of Nationalism* (London, 1977)

Seton-Watson, H., and Seton-Watson, C., *The Making of the New Europe* (Seattle, 1991)

Seton-Watson, R.W., *The Balkans, Italy and the Adriatic* (London, 1915)

Seton-Watson, R.W., *A History of Roumania from Roman Times to the Completion of Unity* (Cambridge, 1934)

Seton-Watson, R.W., *The Rise of Nationality in the Balkans* (London, 1917)

Seton-Watson, R.W., *The Spirit of the Serb* (London, 1915)

Seymour, C., *Geography, Justice and Politics at the Paris Peace Conference of 1919* (New York, 1951)

Sforza, C., *Fifty Years of War and Diplomacy in the Balkans: Pasitch and the Union of the Yugoslavs* (New York, 1940)

Sforza, C., *Makers of Modern Europe* (London, 1930)

Sharp, A., *The Versailles Settlement: Peacemaking in Paris, 1919* (London, 1991)
Shotwell, J. T., *At the Paris Peace Conference* (New York, 1937)
Simonard, A., *Essai sur l'Indepéndence Albanaise* (Paris, 1942)
Skendi, S., (ed.), *Albania* (London, 1957)
Skendi, S., *The Albanian National Awakening, 1878-1912*
    (Princeton, New Jersey, 1967)
Smirnova, N. D., *История Албании в XX веке* (*History of Albania in*
    20th Century) (Moscow, 1983)
Smith, A. D., *The Ethnic Origins of Nations* (Oxford, 1991 repr. of original 1986)
Smith, A. D., *Myths and Memories of the Nation* (Oxford, 1999)
Smith, A. D., *The Nation in History: Historiographical Debates about Ethnicity*
    and Nationalism (Hanover, New Hampshire, 2000)
Smith, A. D., *Nationalism and Modernism: A Critical Survey of Recent Theories*
    of Nations and Nationalism (London, 1998)
Smith, A. D., *Nationalism: Theory, Ideology, History* (Cambridge, 2001)
State University of Tirana, *Historia e Shqipërisë II: 1909-1919* (*The History of*
    Albania II: 1909-1919) (Tirana, 1965)
Stavrianos, L. S., *The Balkans since 1453* (New York, 1958)
Steiner, Z., *The Lights that Failed: European International History, 1919-1933*
    (New York, 2005)
Stickney, E. P., *Southern Albania or Northern Epirus in European International*
    Affairs, 1912-1923 (Stanford, 1926)
Stieve, F., (E. W. Dickes, trans.) *Isvolsky and the World War: Based on Documents*
    Recently Published by German Foreign Office (New York, 1926)
Story, S., (ed.), *The Memoirs of Ismail Kemal Bey Vlora and his Work for the*
    Independence of Albania (London, 1920)
Sugar, P.F., (ed.), *Eastern European Nationalism in the Twentieth Century*
    (Washington D.C., 1995)
Sula, A.B., *Albania's Struggle for Independence* (New York, 1967)
Svolopoulis, C., *Greece and Great Britain During World War I* (Thessaloniki, 1985)
Swire, J., *Albania, the Rise of a Kingdom* (London, 1929)
Swire, J., *King Zog's Albania* (London, 1937)

Šufflay, M., *Srbi i Arbanasi: Njihova Simbioza u Srednjem Vjeku*
    (*Serbs and Albanians: Their Struggle in the Middle Ages*) (Zagreb, 1991, repbl.
    of 1925 original)

Tanenbaum, J.K., *General Maurice Sarrail, 1856-1929: The French*
    Army and Left Wing Politics (Chapel Hill, North Carolina, 1974)
Temperley, H.M.V., *A History of the Peace Conference of Paris*, 6 vols. (London, 1921)
Thaden, E.C., *Russia and the Balkan Alliance of 1912* (University Park,
    Pennsylvania, 1965)
Tillman, S.P., *Anglo-American Relations at the Paris Peace Conference of 1919*
    (Princeton, 1961)
Todorova, M., *Balkan Identities: Nation and Memory* (New York, 2004)
Todorova, M., *Imagining the Balkans* (Oxford, 1997)
Tomes, J., *King Zog: Self-made Monarch of Albania* (Stroud, 2003)

Trevelyan, G. M., *Grey of Fallodon: Being the Life of Sir Edward Grey, Afterwards Viscount Grey of Fallodon* (London 1937)

Trotsky, L., (Pearce, B., (trans.), Weissman, G., and Williams, D., (eds.)), *The Balkan Wars: The War Correspondence of Leon Trotsky* (New York, 1980)

Vasa, P., *La verite sur l'Albania et les Albanais* (Paris, 1879)

Venizelos, E.K., *La Grèce devant le Congrès de la Paix* (Paris, 1919)

Vermeulen, H., and Glovers, C., (eds.), *The Anthropology of Ethnicity: Beyond 'Ethnic groups and boundaries'* (Amsterdam, 1994)

Vickers, M., *The Albanians: A Modern History* (London, 1995)

Vickers, M., *Between Serb and Albanian: A History of Kosovo* (New York, 1998)

Vickers, M., and Pettifer, J., *Albania: From Anarchy to Balkan Identity* (London, 1997)

Vital, D., *The Inequality of States: A Study of the Small Power in International Relations* (Oxford, 1967)

Vital, D., *The Survival of Small States: Studies in Small Power/Great Power Conflict* (London, 1971)

Vopicka, C.J., *Secrets of the Balkans; Seven Years of a Diplomatist's Life in the Storm Centre of Europe* (Chicago, 1921)

Walters, F.P., *A History of the League of Nations*, 2 vols. (London, New York and Toronto, 1952)

Walworth, A., *Wilson and his Peacemakers: American Diplomacy at the Paris Peace Conference, 1919* (New York, 1986)

Wandycz, P.S., *France and her Eastern Allies 1919-1925: French-Czechoslovak-Polish Relations from the Paris Peace Conference to Locarno* (Minneapolis, 1962)

Weisband, E., *Turkish Foreign Policy 1943-45: Small State Diplomacy and Great Power Politics* (Princeton, 1973)

West, R., (ed.), *Black Lamb and Grey Falcon: The Record of a Journey through Yugoslavia in 1937*, 2 vols. (London, 1946)

Wilhelm Furst von Albanien, Prinzzu Wied, *Denkschrift uber Albanien* (Berlin, 1917)

Wilkinson, H.R., *Maps and Politics. A Review of the Ethnographic Cartography of Macedonia* (Liverpool, 1951)

Williamson, S.R., Jr., *Austria-Hungary and the Origins of the First World War* (London, 1991)

Wilson, K.M., (ed.), *Empire and Continent: Studies in British Foreign Policy from the 1880s to the First World War* (London, 1987)

Wilson, T.M., and Donnan, H., (eds.), *Border Identities: Nation and State at International Frontiers* (Cambridge, 1998)

Winnifrith, T.J., *Badlands-Borderlands: A History of Northern Epirus/ Southern Albania* (London, 2002)

Winnifrith, T.J. (ed.), *Perspectives on Albania* (Warwick, 1992)

Winnifrith, T.J., *Shattered Eagles: Balkan Fragments* (London, 1995)

Winnifrith, T.J., *The Vlachs: The History of a Balkan People* (London, 1987)

Young, A., *Albania* (Oxford, c.1997)
Young, G., *Nationalism and War in the Near East* (Oxford, 1915)

Zelenica, M., *Rat, Srbije i Crne Gore 1915 (War, Serbia and Montenegro in 1915)* (Belgrade, 1954)
Zeman, Z.A., *A Diplomatic History of the First World War* (London, 1971)
Zimmer, O., *A Confessed Nation: History, Memory and Nationalism in Switzerland, 1761-1891* (Cambridge, 2003)
Zimmer, O., *Nationalism in Europe, 1890-1940* (Basingstoke, 2003)
Zivojinovic, D.R., *America, Italy and the Birth of Yugoslavia, 1917-1919* (Boulder, 1972)

Articles and essays

Adamson, K., and Jovic, D., 'The Macedonian-Albanian political frontier: The re-articulation of post-Yugoslav political identities', *Nations and Nationalism*, 10 (2004), pp.293-312
Agelopoulos, G., 'Perceptions, constructions and definition of Greek national identity in late 19th and early 20[th]C Macedonia', *Balkan Studies*, 36 (1995), pp.247-63
Arnold, B., 'The contested past', *Anthropology Today*, 15 (1999), pp.1-4.

Babuna, A., 'The Bosnian Muslims and Albanians: Islam and Nationalism', *Nationalities Papers*, 32 (2004), pp.287-321
Babuna, A., 'Nationalism and the Bosnian Muslims', *East European Quarterly*, 33 (1999), pp.196-218
Barnes, J.S., 'The Future of the Albanian State', *Geographical Journal*, 52 (1918), pp.12-30
Blumi, I., 'A story of mitigated ambitions: Kosova's tortuous path to its postwar future', *Alternatives; Turkish Journal of International Relations*, 1 (2002), http://www.alternativesjournal.net/volume1/number4/blumi.htm
Blumi, I., 'Contesting the edges of the Ottoman Empire: Rethinking ethnic and sectarian boundaries in the Malësore, 1878-1912', *Middle East Studies*, 35 (2003), pp.237-56
Blumi, I., 'Teaching loyalty in the late Ottoman Balkans: Educational reform in the vilayets of Monastir and Yanya, 1878-1912', www.cssaeme.ilstu.edu/issues/v21/blumi.pdf
Blumi, I., 'Thwarting the Ottoman Empire: Smuggling through the Empire's new frontiers in Yemen and Albania, 1878-1910', *International Journal of Turkish Studies*, 9 (2003), pp.251-70
Bobroff, R., 'Devolution in wartime: Sergei D. Sazonov and the future of Poland, 1910-1916', *International History Review*, 22 (2000), pp.505-56
van den Bossche, G., 'Is there nationalism after Ernest Gellner? An exploration of methodological choices', *Nations and Nationalism*, 9 (2003), pp.491-509
Bryer, A., 'Skanderbeg: National Hero of Albania', *History Today*, 12 (1962), pp.426-34

Clayer, N., 'Bektachisme et nationalisme albanais', Revue des Études Islamiques, 60 (1992), pp.271-300

Connor, W., 'A nation is a nation, is a state, is an ethnic group, is a...', Ethnic and Racial Studies, 1 (1978), pp.377-400

Cvijić, J., 'The geographical distribution of the Balkan peoples', The Geographical Review, 5 (1918), pp.345-61

Crampton, R.J., 'The Balkans, 1909-1914', in F.H. Hinsley (ed.), British Foreign Policy under Sir Edward Grey (Cambridge, 1977), pp.256-70

Crampton, R.J., 'The Balkans as a Factor in German Foreign Policy, 1911-1914', The Slavonic and East European Review, 55 (1977), pp.370-90

Crampton, R.J., 'The decline of the Concert of Europe in the Balkans, 1913-1914', The Slavonic and East European Review, 52 (1974), pp.393-419

Dako, C.A., 'The independence of Albania a necessity for international peace', The Morning Star, 1 (1917), pp.161-68

Djorkić, D., 'Nationalism, history and identity in the Balkans: An overview of recent histories of Europe's south-east', Slavonic and East European Review, 81 (2003), pp. 512-24

Dockrill, M., and Steiner, Z., 'The Foreign Office at the Paris Peace Conference in 1919', International History Review, 2 (1980), pp.55-86

Dominian, L., 'Linguistic areas in Europe: Their boundaries and political significance', Bulletin of the American Geographical Society, 47 (1915), pp.401-39

Doya, A., 'Confraternal religion: From liberation theology to political reversal', History and Anthropology, 14 (2003), pp.349-81

Doya, A., 'The Politics of Religion in the Reconstruction of Identities: The Albanian situation', Critique of Anthropology, 20 (2000), pp. 421-38

Dunbalon, J. P., 'The League of Nations' place in the international system', History, 78 (1993), pp.421-42

Duţu, A., 'National identity and tensional factors in south eastern Europe', Eastern European Quarterly, 31 (1997), pp.195-205

Elsie, R., 'The Viennese scholar who almost became King of Albania: Baron Franz Nopsca and his contribution to Albanian studies', East European Quarterly, 33 (1999), pp.327-45

Evans, R.J.W., 'Essay and reflection: Frontiers and national identities in central Europe', International History Review, 14 (1992), pp.480-502

Farrar, Jr., L.L., 'Aggression versus Apathy: The limits of nationalism during Balkan Wars, 1912-1913', East European Quarterly, 37 (2003), pp.257-80

Farrar, Jr., L.L., 'Realpolitik versus nationalpolitik: Rethinking nationalism during the Eastern Crisis, 1875-1878', East European Quarterly, 30 (1996), pp.27-45

Fischer, B., 'Albanian highland tribal society and family structure in the process of twentieth-century transformation', East European Quarterly, 33 (1999), pp.281-301

Fischer, B., 'Italian policy in Albania', Balkan Studies, 26 (1985), pp.101-12

Goldstein, E.D., 'The British official mind and Europe', *Diplomacy and Statecraft*, 8 (1997), pp.165-78

Goldstein, E.D., 'British Peace Aims and the Eastern Question: The Political Intelligence Department and the Eastern Committee, 1918), *Middle Eastern Studies*, 23 (1987), pp.419-36

Goldstein, E.D., 'The Foreign Office and Political Intelligence, 1917-20', *Review of International Studies*, 14 (1988), pp.275-88

Goldstein, E.D., 'Great Britain and Greater Greece, 1917-1920', *The Historical Journal*, 32.2 (1989), pp.339-56

Goldstein, E.D., 'New Diplomacy and the New Europe at the Paris Peace Conference: The A. W. A. Leeper Papers', *East European Quarterly*, 21 (1988), pp.393-400

Gounaris, B.G., 'From peasants into urbanites: Ottoman Monastir', *European History Quarterly*, 31 (2001), pp.43-64

Gounaris, B.G., 'Social cleavages and national "awakening" in Ottoman Macedonia', *Eastern European Quarterly*, 29 (1996), pp.43-63

Grosby, S., 'Religion, ethnicity and nationalism: The uncertain perennialism of Adrian Hastings', *Nations and Nationalism*, 9 (2003), pp.7-13

Guy, N.C., 'The Albanian question in British policy and the Italian intervention, August 1914-April 1915', *Diplomacy and Statecraft*, 18 (2007), pp.109-31

Guy, N.C., 'Britain, Greece and the offer of Northern Epirus, August 1914 - December 1915' in G.T. Papanikos and N.C.J. Pappas (eds.), *European History: Lessons for the 21ˢᵗ Century. Essays from the 3rd International Conference on European History* (Athens, 2006), pp.335-44

Guy, N.C., 'Fixing the Frontiers: Ethnography and power-politics in the delimitation of Albania, 1912 to 1914', *Studies in Ethnicity and Nationalism*, 5 (2005), pp.27-49

Guy, N.C., 'Linguistic Boundaries and Geo-political Interests: the Albanian Boundary Commissions 1878 to 1926', *Journal of Historical Geography*, 34 (2008), pp.448-70

Hayne, M.B., 'Great Britain, the Albanian question and the Concert of Europe, 1911-1914', *Balkan Studies*, 38 (1987), pp.327-53

Helmreich, E.C., 'Montenegro and the foundations of the Balkan League', *Slavonic and Eastern European Review*, 15 (1937), pp.426-34

Hobsbawm, E.J., and Kertzer, D.J., 'Ethnicity and nationalism in Europe today', *Anthropology Today*, 8 (1992), pp.3-8

Hocevar, T., 'The Albanian economy, 1912-1944', *Journal of European Economic History*, 16 (1987), pp.561-68

Howard, C., 'The Treaty of London, 1915', *History*, 25 (1940-41), pp.347-55

Hroch, M., 'National self-determination from a historical perspective', *Canadian Slavonic Papers*, 37 (1995), pp.283-99

Jacobson, J., 'Strategies of French foreign policy after World War I', *Journal of Modern History*, 55 (1983), pp.78-95

Kaltsouris, T., 'Education and new nationalism in the Balkans: The case of Albania', *Balkan Studies*, 36 (1995), pp.137-50.

Kamusella, T., 'Upper Silesia: Between region, religion, nation and ethnicity', *East European Quarterly*, 38 (2005), pp.443-62

Karakostanoglou, V., 'The right to self-determination and the case of Yugoslavia', *Balkan Studies*, 32 (1991), pp.335-62

Kennedy, R., 'Woodrow Wilson, World War I and the American conception of national security', *Diplomatic History*, 25 (2001), pp.1-31

Kiss, E., 'A typology of nineteenth-century nationhood', *East European Quarterly*, 30 (1996), pp.47-62

Kitromilides, P., '"Imagined Communities" and the origins of the national question in the Balkans', *European History Quarterly*, 19 (1989), pp.149-94

Koenigsberger, H.G., 'Past and future history of nationalism', *European History Quarterly*, 26 (1996), pp.591-602

Kondis, B., 'The Greek minority in Albania', *Balkan Studies*, 36 (1995), pp. 83-102

Kondis, B., 'The Malissori uprising of 1911 and Greek-Albanian negotiations in the United States for a secret understanding', *Balkan Studies*, 18 (1977), pp.99-119

Kondis, B., 'The Northern Epirus question during the First World War', *Balkan Studies*, 30 (1989), pp.333-49

Kondis, B., 'The role of the Albanian factor upon the Greek-Bulgarian Understanding of 1912', *Balkan Studies*, 25 (1984), pp.377-87

Kostelancik, D.J., 'Minorities in inter-war Albania', *East European Quarterly*, 30 (1996), pp.75-97

Levene, M., 'Nationalism and its alternatives in the international arena: The Jewish question at Paris, 1919', *Journal of Contemporary History*, 28 (1993), pp.511-31

Levy, J., 'The theoretical foundations of Paul W. Schroeder's international system', *International History Review*, 16 (1994), pp.715-44

Leon, G., 'Greece and the Albanian question at the outbreak of the First World War', *Balkan Studies*, 11 (1970), pp.61-80

Liolin, A.E., 'Towards faith in Albania', *East European Quarterly*, 31 (1997), pp.181-94

Lowe, C.J., 'Britain and the Italian intervention 1914-1915', *Historical Journal*, 12 (1969), pp.533-48

Lowe, C.J., 'The failure of British diplomacy in the Balkans, 1914-1918', *Canadian Journal of History*, 4 (1969), pp.73-101

MacGinty, R., 'War cause and peace aim? Small states and the First World War', *European History Quarterly*, 21 (1997), pp.41-56

Magaš, B., 'On Bosnianness', *Nations and Nationalism*, 9 (2003), pp.19-23

Maksutovici, G., 'L'Albanie', in V. Moisuc and I. Calafeteanu, (eds.), *Assertion of Unitary, Independent National States in Central and Southeast Europe (1821-1923)* (Bucharest, 1980), pp.170-89

Mametey, V., 'The United States and the origins of the Adriatic question

(1918)', *Florida State University Studies*, 4 (1951), pp.45-60

Manta, E., 'Reciprocal relations between politics and economics: The renewal of the 1926 Treaty of Tirana', *Balkan Studies*, 37 (1996), pp.309-30

Mayer, A. J., 'Post-war nationalisms 1918-1919', *Past and Present*, 34 (1966), pp.114-26

Mikich, D., 'The Albanians and Serbia during the Balkan Wars' in B. Kiraly and D. Djurdjevich, (eds.), *East Central European Society and the Balkan Wars* (Boulder, 1987), pp.165-96

Milo, P., 'Albania and the Balkan entente', *Association International d'Études du Sud-Est Européen Bulletin*, 30 (2001), pp.39-66

Neilson, J.M., 'The scholar as diplomat: American historians at the Paris Peace Conference of 1919', *International History Review*, 14 (1992), pp.228-51

Newsome, W.B., '"Dead Lands" or new Europe? Eastern Europe after World War I', *East European Quarterly*, 36 (2002), pp.39-62

Okey, R., 'Serbian, Croatian, Bosnian? Language and nationality', *East European Quarterly*, 38 (2004), pp.419-41

Pano, G., 'The Albanian-American effort to influence Wilson's policy toward Albania, 1918-1920', *South East European Monitor*, 1 (1995), pp.1-11

Petrides, P., 'Les relations Bulgares et Austro-Hongroises durant les guerres Balkaniques', *Balkan Studies*, 25 (1984), pp.441-47

Philpott, W., 'Squaring the circle: The higher co-ordination of the Entente in the Winter of 1915-1916', *English Historical Review*, 114 (1999), pp.875-898

Pollo, S., '*La proclamation de l'independence Albanaise*', *Studia Albanica*, 2 (1965), pp.87-107

Prifti, P.R., 'Minority politics: The Albanians in Yugoslavia', *Balkanistica: Occasional Papers in Southeast European Studies*, 11 (1975), pp.7-18

du Quenoy, P., 'With allies like these, who needs enemies?: Russia and the problem of Italian entry into World War I', *Canadian Slavonic Papers*, 45 (2003), pp.409-40

Rady, M., 'Encounters with nationalism', *Slovo*, 8 (1995), pp.109-15

Rady, M., 'Historical sources of nationalism and the state in eastern Europe', *Slovo*, 6 (1993), pp.29-37

Raun, T.U., 'Nineteenth and early twentieth-century Estonian nationalism revisited', *Nations and Nationalism*, 9 (2003), pp.129-47

Remak, J., '1914 The third Balkan war. Origins reconsidered', *Journal of Modern History*, 43 (1971), pp.353-66

Rendell, M., 'Defensive realism and the Concert of Europe', *Review of International Studies*, 32 (2006), pp.523-40

Renzi, W.A., 'Great Britain, Russia and the Straits, 1914-1915', *Journal of Modern History*, 42 (1970), pp.1-20.

Renzi, W.A., 'Italy's neutrality and entrance into the Great War: A re-examination', *American Historical Review*, 73 (1968), pp.1414-32

Renzi, W.A., 'The Russian Foreign Office and Italy's entrance into the Great War, 1914-1915: A study in wartime diplomacy', *Historian*, 28 (1966), pp.648-68

Robbins, K.G., 'British diplomacy and Bulgaria, 1914-1915', *Slavonic and East European Review*, 49 (1971), pp.560-85

Roberts, G., 'History, theory and the narrative turn in IR', *Review of International Studies*, 32 (2006), pp.703-14

Schmidt-Neke, M., 'Nationalism and national myth: Skanderbeg and the twentieth-century Albanian regimes', *European Legacy*, 2 (1997), pp.1-7.

Schroeder, P.W., 'Balance of power and political equilibrium: A response', *International History Review*, 16 (1994), pp.745-54

Schroeder, P.W., 'Can diplomatic history guide foreign policy?' *International History Review*, 18 (1996), pp.358-70

Schroeder, P.W., 'Historical reality vs. neo-realist theory', *International Security*, 19 (1994), pp.108-48

Schroeder, P.W., 'Review article: System and systematic thinking in international history', *International History Review*, 15 (1993), pp.116-34

Scott, H.M., 'Paul W. Schroeder's international system: The view from Vienna', *International History Review*, 16 (1994), pp.663-80

Sencer, E., 'Balkan nationalism in the Ottoman Parliament, 1909', *East European Quarterly*, 38 (2004), pp.41-64

Seymour, C., 'The struggle for the Adriatic', *Yale Review*, 9 (1920), pp.462-81

Sfika-Theodosiou, A., 'The Italian presence on the Balkan front (1915-1918)', *Balkan Studies*, 36 (1995), pp.69-82

Sharp, A., 'Britain and the minorities at the Paris Peace Conference', in A.C. Hepburn (ed.), *Minorities in History* (London, 1978), pp.170-88

Sharp, A.J., 'The Foreign Office in Eclipse, 1919-22', *History*, 61 (1976), pp.198-218

Sharp, A., 'The genie that would not go back in the bottle: National self-determination and the legacy of the First World War and the Peace Settlement', in S. Dunn and G. Fraser (eds.), *Europe and Ethnicity: the First World War and Contemporary Ethnic Conflict* (London, 1996), pp.10-29

Sharp, A., 'Some relevant historians—the Political Intelligence Department of the Foreign Office, 1918-1920', *Australian Journal of Politics and History*, 34 (1988), pp.359-68

Skendi, S., 'Albanian political thought and revolutionary activity, 1881-1912' *Sdost-Forschungen*, 13 (1954), pp.159-99

Skendi, S., 'Beginnings of Albanian nationalist and autonomous trends: The Albanian League, 1878-1881', *American Slavic and East European Review*, 12 (1953), pp.219-32

Smith, A.D., 'Adrian Hastings on nations and nationalism', *Nations and Nationalism*, 9 (2003), pp.25-28

Smith, A.D., 'Memory and modernity: Reflections on Ernest Gellner's theory of nationalism', *Nations and Nationalism*, 2 (1996), pp.371-88

Stavrianos, L.S., 'The Balkan Committee', *Queen's Quarterly*, 31 (1941), pp.258-67.

Temperley, H.M.V., 'British secret diplomacy from Canning to Grey',
    Cambridge Historical Journal, 6 (1938), pp.1-32
Toptani, E.P., 'My Policy for Albania', *The Balkan Review*, 1 (1919), pp.329-38
Triadafilopoulos, T., 'Power politics and nationalist discourse in the struggle
    for "Northern Epirus": 1919-1921', *Journal of Southern Europe and the
    Balkans*, 2 (2000), pp.149-62
Tuathail, G.Ó, 'At the end of geopolitics? Reflections on a plural problematic
    at the century's end', *Alternatives*, 22 (1997), pp.35-55

Velebit, V., 'Kosovo: A case of ethnic change in population', *Eastern European
    Quarterly*, 33 (1999), pp.177-94
Voglis, P., 'Review article: In search of a convenient past: Nationalism, violence and
    historical writing in twentieth-century Europe', *Journal of Contemporary
    History*, 40 (2005), pp.381-88

Woods, H.C., 'Albania and the Albanians', *The Geographical Review*, 5 (1918),
    pp.257-73
Woods, H.C., 'The Situation in Albania', *Fortnightly Review*, 4 (1914), pp.460-72

Zimmer, O., 'Boundary mechanisms and symbolic resources: Towards a process-
    orientated approach to national identity', *Nations and Nationalism*, 9 (2003),
    pp.173-93
Zimmer, O., 'Competing memories of the nation: Liberal historians and their
    construction of the Swiss past 1870-1900', *Past and Present*, 168 (2000),
    pp.194-226

Unpublished

Goldstein, E.D., 'Britain prepares for peace: British peace preparations for the
    Paris Peace Conference, 1916-1919' (PhD Thesis, Cambridge University, 1984)

Kamouzis, D., 'The Temporary Success of the Joined Foreign Policies of Great
    Britain and Greece at the end of World War I: From the Paris Peace
    Conference to the Treaty of Sévres', (MPhil Thesis, University of Birmingham,
    2002)

Portolis, D., 'Greek Foreign Policy from September 1916 to October 1918'
    (PhD Thesis, University of London, 1974)

Woodall, R. L., 'The Albanian Problem during the Peacemaking 1919-1920'
    (PhD Thesis, Memphis State University, 1978)

Index

Terms such as Albania, independence, nationalism, great powers, British policy occur throughout the book and on almost every page. These terms are therefore not included or the page references indicated here give an idea of some of the main references, but should not be considered exhaustive.

9 781350 136670

www.ingramcontent.com/pod-product-compliance
Ingram Content Group UK Ltd.
Pitfield, Milton Keynes, MK11 3LW, UK
UKHW020731280225
455688UK00012B/598